EXPLOITATION, RESETTLEMENT, MASS MURDER

Studies on War and Genocide
General Editor: Omer Bartov, Brown University

Volume 1
The Massacre in History
    Edited by Mark Levene and Penny Roberts

Volume 2
National Socialist Extermination Policies: Contemporary German
    Perspectives and Controversies
    Edited by Ulrich Herbert

Volume 3
War of Extermination: The German Military in World War II, 1941/44
    Edited by Hannes Heer and Klaus Naumann

Volume 4
In God's Name: Genocide and Religion in the Twentieth Century
    Edited by Omer Bartov and Phyllis Mack

Volume 5
Hitler's War in the East, 1941–1945
    Rolf-Dieter Müller and Gerd R. Ueberschär

Volume 6
Genocide and Settler Society: Frontier Violence and Stolen Indigenous
    Children in Australian History
    Edited by A. Dirk Moses

Volume 7
Networks of Nazi Persecution: Bureaucracy, Business, and the
    Organization of the Holocaust
    Edited by Gerald D. Feldman and Wolfgang Seibel

Volume 8
Gray Zones: Ambiguity and Compromise in the Holocaust and Its
    Aftermath
    Edited by Jonathan Petropoulos and John K. Roth

Volume 9
Robbery and Restitution: The Conflict over Jewish Property in Europe
    Edited by M. Dean, C. Goschler and P. Ther

Volume 10
Exploitation, Resettlement, Mass Murder: Political and Economic
    Planning for German Occupation Policy in the Soviet Union,
    1940–1941
    Alex J. Kay

EXPLOITATION, RESETTLEMENT, MASS MURDER

Political and Economic Planning
for German Occupation Policy
in the Soviet Union, 1940–1941

ALEX J. KAY

Berghahn Books
New York • Oxford

First published in 2006 by
Berghahn Books
www.berghahnbooks.com

© 2006 Alex J. Kay

All rights reserved.
Except for the quotation of short passages for the purposes
of criticism and review, no part of this book may be reproduced in any form
or by any means, electronic or mechanical, including photocopying, recording,
or any information storage and retrieval system now known or to be invented,
without written permission of the publisher.

Library of Congress Cataloging-in-Publication Data

British Library Cataloguing in Publication Data

A catalogue record for this book is available
from the British Library.

ISBN 1–84545–186–4 hardback

Contents

Acknowledgements ix

List of Abbreviations xi

1. **Introduction** 1
   Organized Chaos: the German Occupation, 1941–1944 1
   The State of Existing Scholarship 3
   Aims of the Study 5
   The Importance of Economic Considerations 6
   Structure and Additional Parameters of the Study 8
   Source Material 10

2. **The Central Planning Organizations** 14
   The *Vierjahresplanbehörde*: Göring's Umbrella Organization 14
   The *Dienststelle Rosenberg*: the Eastern Experts of the NSDAP 18

3. **The Decision to Invade the Soviet Union: the Primacy of Economics by the End of 1940** 26
   Overview: a Combination of Long- and Short-term Factors 26
   July 1940: Military Proposals against Britain's Last Remaining Potential Ally on the Continent 27
   July–August: Long-term Strategic and Economic Gain for Germany in the East 32
   September–October: Alternatives and Objections to an Eastern Campaign 34
   November: Before and After Molotov's Visit to Berlin 35
   November–December: Food Supplies, the Public Mood in Germany and the Need to Fight a Longer War 38

4. Laying the Foundations for the *Hungerpolitik* — 47
   Backe's Presentations to the Supreme Leadership — 47
   Working around Potential Difficulties — 50
   Soviet Awareness of German Intentions — 54
   Thomas's Study of Mid-February 1941 — 56
   Setting Up an Economic Organization — 59

5. Planning a Civil Administration — 68
   Envisaging a Civil Administration — 68
   Selecting an Administrative Chief — 73
   Rosenberg as Administrative Chief: 'no better man' for the Job — 80
   Personnel and Tasks — 84

6. Population Policy — 96
   Germanic Resettlement — 97
   The Fate of the Soviet Jews: Pre-invasion Order for Genocide? — 104
   A Territorial Solution to the 'Jewish Question' — 108

7. Radicalizing Plans to Exploit Soviet Resources — 120
   Calculated Economic Considerations and Nazi Ideology — 120
   2 May 1941: the Meeting of the *Staatssekretäre* — 123
   Wide-ranging Agreement — 126
   The *Hungerpolitik* in Writing — 133
   Soviet Labour: Deployment in the Reich? — 139
   The Special Status of the Ukraine — 141

8. Expectations and Official Policy on the Eve of the Invasion — 158
   Counting on a Swift Victory — 159
   Economic and Agricultural Guidelines — 164
   The Standpoint of the Political Planners — 167

9. Post-invasion Decisions — 179
   16 July 1941: the Conference at FHQ — 180
   Ordering the Destruction of Leningrad and Moscow — 185
   The Concept of a Territorial Ministry in the East — 187

10. Conclusions	199
Appendices	211
Glossary	220
Bibliography	222
Index	235

Acknowledgements

This book constitutes the revised version of my doctoral thesis, which was submitted to the Philosophical Faculty I of the Humboldt-Universität zu Berlin under the title '*Neuordnung* and *Hungerpolitik*: The development and compatibility of political and economic planning within the Nazi hierarchy for the occupation of the Soviet Union, July 1940–July 1941' in January 2005.

I would like, first of all, to thank my doctoral supervisor, Professor Dr Ludolf Herbst, for taking on the original project and lending his support throughout. The second marker, Professor Dr Rolf-Dieter Müller, provided me with a series of helpful comments on the thesis following its submission, for which I am grateful.

For their assistance during my regular archival visits, I would like to thank Frau Grüner and her colleagues at the Bundesarchiv Berlin-Lichterfelde, where I carried out the bulk of my research, as well as the staffs at the Bundesarchiv-Militärarchiv (Freiburg im Breisgau), the Bundesarchiv Koblenz, the Institut für Zeitgeschichte (Munich), the Politisches Archiv des Auswärtigen Amts (Berlin), and the Militärgeschichtliches Forschungsamt (Potsdam).

For reading substantial parts of the draft thesis and even, in some cases, the draft in its entirety, and providing valuable suggestions, I would like to express my appreciation to Dr Bob Moore, David Stahel, Dr Christoph Jahr and Dr Pertti Ahonen. Pertti was also a constant source of encouragement and good ideas.

Without Dr Marion Berghahn, Professor Omer Bartov, in whose series 'Studies on War and Genocide' this book appears, and all at Berghahn Books, the current work would have remained a doctoral thesis. For their commitment and hard work I am very grateful.

On a more personal note, I would like to thank my parents, Annette and Edward, for their constant support and interest. My father has been unceasing in his encouragement of my academic aspirations. My biggest debt, however, I owe to my partner, Valentina Farle. She has been of incalculable support in so many ways, particularly in shaping the environment which made both the research and the writing possible. This book is dedicated to her.

LIST OF ABBREVIATIONS

AA	Auswärtiges Amt (German Foreign Office)
ADAP	*Akten zur deutschen auswärtigen Politik 1918–1945. (Serie C: 1933–1936; Serie D: 1937–1941; Serie E: 1941–1945)*
APA	Außenpolitisches Amt der NSDAP (Foreign Affairs Office of the NSDAP)
BA	Bundesarchiv (German Federal Archives, Berlin-Lichterfelde)
BAK	Bundesarchiv Koblenz (German Federal Archives, Koblenz)
BA-MA	Bundesarchiv-Militärarchiv (German Military Archives, Freiburg im Breisgau)
DAF	Deutsche Arbeitsfront (German Labour Front)
DAP	Deutsche Arbeiterpartei (German Workers' Party)
FHQ	Führerhauptquartier (Führer Headquarters)
Gestapo	Geheime Staatspolizei (Secret State Police)
Halder, *KTB*	Franz Halder, *Kriegstagebuch, Band I: Vom Polenfeldzug bis zum Ende der Westoffensive; Band II: Von der geplanten Landung in England bis zum Beginn des Ostfeldzuges; Band III: Der Rußlandfeldzug bis zum Marsch auf Stalingrad* (Stuttgart, 1962–64)
HSSPF	Höherer SS- und Polizeiführer (Higher SS and Police Leader)
Ia	first general staff officer (command section)
IfZ	Institut für Zeitgeschichte (Institute for Contemporary History, Munich)
IMG	*Der Prozess gegen die Hauptkriegsverbrecher vor dem Internationalen Militärgerichtshof, Nürnberg, 14. November 1945 – 1. Oktober 1946*, 42 vols, Nuremberg, 1947–49 (= IMT: *The Trial of the Major War Criminals before the International Military Tribunal, Nuremberg*)

KTB des OKW	*Kriegstagebuch des Oberkommandos der Wehrmacht (Wehrmachtsführungsstab) 1940–1945: Geführt von Helmuth Greiner und Percy Ernst Schramm*, ed. Percy Ernst Schramm (Frankfurt am Main, 1961–79)
La	Landwirtschaft (agriculture)
MGFA	Militärgeschichtliches Forschungsamt (Research Institute for Military History, Potsdam)
M.T.S.	Machine and Tractor Stations
Nbg. Dok.	Nürnberger Dokument (Nuremberg document)
n.d.	no date of publication given
n.pl.	no place of publication given
n.pub.	no publisher given
NSDAP	Nationalsozialistische Deutsche Arbeiterpartei (National Socialist German Workers' Party or Nazi Party)
Ob d H	Oberbefehlshaber des Heeres (Commander-in-Chief of the Army)
Ob.d.M.	Oberbefehlshaber der Marine (Commander-in-Chief of the Navy)
OKH	Oberkommando des Heeres (High Command of the Army)
OKM	Oberkommando der Marine (High Command of the Navy)
OKW	Oberkommando der Wehrmacht (High Command of the Armed Forces)
PAAA	Politisches Archiv des Auswärtigen Amts (Political Archives of the German Foreign Office, Berlin)
POW(s)	prisoner(s) of war
RAF	Royal Air Force
RAM	Reichsarbeitsministerium (Reich Ministry for Labour)
RFSS	Reichsführer-SS (Reich Leader SS), i.e., Heinrich Himmler
RGI	Reichsgruppe Industrie (Reich Group Industry)
RKFDV	Reichskommissar für die Festigung deutschen Volkstums (Reich Commissar for the Strengthening of German Nationhood), i.e., Heinrich Himmler
RM	Reichsmark
RMEL	Reichsministerium für Ernährung und Landwirtschaft (Reich Ministry for Food and Agriculture)
RMI	Reichsministerium des Innern (Reich Ministry of the Interior)
RMO	Reichsministerium für die besetzten Ostgebiete (Reich Ministry for the Occupied Eastern Territories)
RNSt	Reichsnährstand (Reich Food Estate)
RSHA	Reichssicherheitshauptamt (Reich Security Main Office)

RWM	Reichswirtschaftsministerium (Reich Ministry for Economics)
SA	Sturmabteilung (Storm Detachment)
SD	Sicherheitsdienst (Security Service)
SS	Schutzstaffel (Protection Echelon)
TBJG	Elke Fröhlich (ed.), *Die Tagebücher von Joseph Goebbels: Teil I, Aufzeichnungen 1923–1941*, 9 vols; *Teil II, Diktate 1941–1945*, 15 vols (Munich, 1987 and 1993–98)
USA	United States of America
USSR	Union of Soviet Socialist Republics
VB	*Völkischer Beobachter* (main newspaper of the NSDAP)
VJP	Vierjahresplan (Four-Year Plan)
VJPB	Vierjahresplanbehörde (Office of the Four-Year Plan)
Wi Fü Stab Ost	Wirtschaftsführungsstab Ost (Economic Command Staff East)
Wi Rü Amt	Wehrwirtschafts- und Rüstungsamt (War Economy and Armaments Office in the OKW)
Wi Stab Ost	Wirtschaftsstab Ost (Economic Staff East)

CHAPTER 1

INTRODUCTION

Organized Chaos: the German Occupation, 1941–1944

The power struggles and overlapping functions inherent in the National Socialist administrative and governmental 'system' can have no better example than that of 'the East' – an all-inclusive reference to the lands east of Germany, initially in particular Poland, but from 1941 onwards almost exclusively used to allude to the seemingly endless reaches of the Soviet Union, stretching from Germany's eastern border, beyond the Ural Mountains to the Orient. To judge from the administrative chaos, interagency competition and wide-ranging policy disputes which were an integral part of, and indeed characterized, the three-year German occupation of large swathes of the Soviet Union between 1941 and 1944, one could form the impression that what passed for policy in these largely lawless regions was improvised, a complex of ad hoc solutions to problems which had not been anticipated.

At least in part, this is indeed accurate, as it had certainly not been foreseen that a definitive military victory over the Red Army would elude the Wehrmacht, and furthermore that major hostilities would continue for the whole duration of the German presence in the Soviet territories. In fact, an occupation administration in the sense envisaged by the Nazi leadership prior to the commencement of military engagements – i.e., a civil/political administration – only came into being in a comparatively small area of the territory under German control for shorter or longer periods of the three-year time span. In the event, the occupied territories were always split into three layers: the areas still in the combat zone under the direct control of the military commander (this layer was rarely deeper than about twelve miles);[1] the areas immediately behind under military administration intended for transfer over to the civil administration (further divided into the Army Rear Area, which functioned for the most part as a communications zone, and the similarly named Army Group Rear Area);[2] and at the rear of those areas the territories under civil administration.[3] It is, therefore, necessary to make clear here that, for this as well as other reasons, such as the racial-ideological factors involved, German occupation policy in the Soviet Union cannot be assessed on the same basis as German occupation policy in France or in Denmark, for example, where major hostilities ceased and armistice terms were signed by the defeated nation. In the Soviet Union, the Nazi administrative apparatus was never in a position to administer a stabilized, complete territorial entity.

However, whilst many of the conditions facing Germany's would-be civil administrators in the Soviet Union were, as a result of the developments referred to above, not anticipated, this was in large part not due to an absence of advance planning for the occupation in the political and economic spheres. It can be argued that the 'organized chaos' experienced within the Nazi administrative apparatus in the Soviet Union belies the extensive preparations carried out during the course of the twelve months immediately prior to the commencement of 'Operation Barbarossa', the German invasion of the Soviet Union on 22 June 1941. The failure of the one prerequisite for the implementation of these terrible plans – decisive military victory – prevented the Nazi schemes from coming to fruition in anything like their entirety. Nevertheless, concrete plans, concepts and intentions on the part of Adolf Hitler, his lieutenants and their staffs did exist and are examined here. Although hostilities lasted for the duration of the German presence in the Soviet Union and the regions under civil administration never reached anything like the geographical extent envisaged, the German style of rule in those territories which were handed over by the military to the civil administration and the partial implementation of the Nazi regime's political and economic goals is enough to provide evidence of the realness of these plans.

If the disorder evident in German occupation policy in the Soviet Union cannot be clarified by pointing to a lack of planning prior to the military invasion, even if the preparations ultimately proved to be less than effective, perhaps the explanation lies in an inability on the part of the planners themselves and the German leadership as a whole to coordinate their various objectives and the exact methods by which they would be achieved. In this sense, perhaps the roots of the anarchy witnessed in German occupation policy can be found in the planning phase. Given that formal meetings of the Reich Cabinet ceased to take place after the end of 1937, and that Hitler thereafter practically forbade his ministers to assemble independently, no formal arena existed for the mutual exchange of ideas. An outlet was necessary for Hitler's henchmen and their subordinates in order to voice grievances on the one hand, but also to make proposals on the other hand. With no formal arena for mutual exchange, this outlet assumed the form of power struggles and interagency competition. All individuals and bodies, however, were ultimately dependent on Hitler's decisions and repeatedly sought him out to act as arbitrator in their disputes.

The State of Existing Scholarship

In the decades immediately following the end of the Second World War, it fell to non-German, in particular Anglo-Saxon, historians to analyse the German occupation of the Soviet Union. Despite its age and imperfections, Alexander Dallin's *German Rule in Russia, 1941–1945: A Study of Occupation Policies*, which first appeared in 1957, remains the best single-volume work encompassing both chronologically and geographically the entire German occupation in the Soviet Union.[4] For all its undeniable value, however, Dallin's book focuses primarily on the implementation of German occupation policy itself rather than the planning for it, which is the subject of the present study. Similar reservations must be applied – despite the somewhat misleading starting date featured in its title – to Gerald Reitlinger's *The House Built on Sand: The Conflicts of German Policy in Russia 1939–1945*, published in 1960.[5]

From the mid-1960s onwards, high-quality studies from German historians began to appear on a whole range of aspects of National Socialist Germany, including the atrocities committed in the occupied East. One of the finest and most influential of these was Andreas Hillgruber's *Hitlers Strategie: Politik und Kriegführung 1940–1941*, which focused, much like the current study, on the year-long period between the fall of France and the invasion of the Soviet Union.[6] As well written and convincingly argued as Hillgruber's work undeniably is, it is more an examination of Hitler's strategic thinking during this critical juncture in the war, and not an analysis of plans for German occupation policy. Although the next twenty years saw the increasing appearance of specialist studies focusing on specific aspects of the German invasion and occupation in the East, major works on the planning for this undertaking – in particular its economic aspects – had to wait until the early 1980s. Military histories of the German–Soviet conflict have been in abundance since the 1960s, but the purely military aspects of the war are not of primary concern for this study.

During the last two decades, several excellent publications have appeared which have dealt either exclusively or in large part with the National Socialist economic and/or political planning for the post-'Barbarossa' future of the Soviet territories, or directly related issues. The most important of these works have all been German-language publications and include Götz Aly and Susanne Heim's *Vordenker der Vernichtung: Auschwitz und die deutschen Pläne für eine neue europäische Ordnung*,[7] and several studies from Rolf-Dieter Müller, in particular 'Das "Unternehmen Barbarossa" als wirtschaftlicher Raubkrieg',[8] *Hitlers Ostkrieg und die deutsche Siedlungspolitik*,[9] and his contributions to *Der Angriff auf die Sowjetunion*, volume four of the monumental series *Das Deutsche Reich und der Zweite Weltkrieg* from the Militärgeschichtliches Forschungsamt in Potsdam.[10] More recently, the Berlin historian Christian Gerlach has produced his authoritative and exhaustively researched *Kalkulierte Morde: Die deutsche Wirtschafts- und Vernichtungspolitik in Weißrußland 1941 bis 1944*.[11]

One of the most significant contributions of these works to the state of existing scholarship has been to stress the importance of agricultural-economic considerations within National Socialist planning for both the war against the Soviet Union itself and the subsequent occupation, rather than racial-ideological motivations, which have so often been given the role of principal causal factor. Although the aim of improving Germany's raw materials and foodstuffs basis through a rapid victory over the Soviet Union and the colonial exploitation of the conquered territories had already on occasion been emphasized in the historiography as 'a decisive factor' in bringing about the decision to invade the Soviet Union,[12] very little had been produced on the economic planning itself. Rolf-Dieter Müller effectively led the way in pushing issues of an economic nature to the forefront of German scholarship on the subject, and he has been followed by the likes of Aly, Heim and Gerlach, amongst others. Their works have considered the motivations and aims which featured most prominently in the formulation of plans for the post-war occupation of the Soviet territories, though for the most part without providing a clear and structured picture of the gradual development of these plans themselves. Gerlach's *Kalkulierte Morde* has gone some way towards establishing a clear time sequence, but further work is required.

Moreover, an examination of the simultaneous development of plans by the economic planners on the one hand and by the political planners on the other hand, the extent of agreement between those involved and the compatibility of their respective plans with those of the other group of planners has not yet been systematically undertaken. As a result of this important issue being neglected by historians, very little exists in the historiography on the participation of planners from a specific policy area in the preparations of planners from another area, or the agreement of those from one field with the ideas of those from another. In other words, the extent of collaboration between different groups of planners has been barely touched upon. This omission could particularly be applied to the man charged with producing a blueprint for the future shape of the political administration in the East, Alfred Rosenberg. Unusually for one of the senior members of the Nazi leadership, Rosenberg has not been the subject of a comprehensive political biography in recent years. Robert Cecil's 1972 book, *The Myth of the Master Race: Alfred Rosenberg and Nazi Ideology*, as the title suggests, concentrates on Rosenberg's ideological influence on the Nazi movement.[13] In addition, being, as it is, over thirty years old, the book no longer reflects the state of existing scholarship. Fritz Nova's *Alfred Rosenberg: Nazi Theorist of the Holocaust* is more recent, but constitutes primarily an exploration of Rosenberg's ideological beliefs.[14] Valuable as it undeniably is, an awareness of Rosenberg's fundamental ideological approach towards the Soviet Union and its peoples must, however, be coupled with an examination of his concrete involvement in both the political and the economic planning for German occupation policy in the East.

Introduction 5

Aims of the Study

In light of these gaps in the secondary literature, the significance of this study is threefold. First, the development of both the political *and* the economic planning by senior bodies within the state and Nazi Party apparatuses for the German occupation policy in the Soviet Union is traced. Secondly, the extent to which these two aspects of planning and the approaches and objectives contained therein were compatible with each other is examined. Thirdly, the role of Alfred Rosenberg, not only in the political preparations for the occupation, but also with regard to his awareness of economic plans, his involvement in their formulation and the extent of his support for them, is thoroughly considered.

Examining the step-by-step development of both the political and the economic planning for the occupation of the Soviet Union, including how these two aspects intertwined and influenced both one another and the policy ultimately pursued by the regime itself, will demonstrate what the men involved had in store for Germany's supposed 'region of destiny',[15] aspects of which became reality for large parts of the Soviet Union and its population. Judging from the proposals of the political and economic planners, the notion expressed by the army leadership before the beginning of the campaign that in the East initial harshness would mean mildness for the future[16] would clearly not apply. As it was anticipated that major military engagements against the Soviet Union would last no longer than three months, the plans drawn up in both the political and the economic spheres prior to the attack were in large part intended for implementation during the period after the conclusion of hostilities. Thus, these plans provide above all an idea of how the Nazi leadership envisaged the expected future German hegemony in the occupied territories of the Soviet Union.

Ascertaining the extent to which the two strands of planning were compatible with one another involves scrutinizing the simultaneous development of the political and economic plans and establishing the priorities, aims and chosen methods of both groups of planners. In other words, were the respective sets of plans leading towards mutually shared aims in the East, or did the assumptions, methods and objectives contained therein fundamentally contradict one another? By extension, this should allow an assessment of the degree to which the discord amongst Nazi occupation agencies witnessed after the invasion of June 1941, and examined in several excellent works,[17] was present during the preparatory phase and how far this discord was based on unexpected events, miscalculations and misunderstandings, pure egotism or genuine policy disputes. Measuring the extent to which the political and economic plans were compatible with one another will involve considering how the respective policies were to be carried over in practice from the planners' desks in Berlin to the fields and forests of the European part of the Soviet Union. This in turn will assist in illustrating the degree to which the Nazi leadership and its planning staffs were in touch with reality – even a gruesome reality – and how feasible or otherwise their ideas were.

It is worth defining two concepts here which were of central importance for the formulation of occupation policy, namely the intended *Neuordnung* of the Soviet territories and the implementation of a *Hungerpolitik* in the regions under occupation. Particular emphasis will be attached throughout this study to the development of these concepts. The political Neuordnung in the East entailed the breaking up of the Soviet state into its constituent parts and the alteration of the existing political borders along ethnic and racial lines, as well as the displacement of large numbers of Soviet citizens from their homelands and the resettlement of Germanic peoples in their place. Neuordnung referred to both the process, thus 'reorganization' or 'reordering', and the desired end result of creating a political, racial and economic 'New Order' in Europe under German hegemony. The role of the occupied Soviet territories within this so-called 'New Order' would be to respond to the demands of a German-dominated continental Europe for agricultural produce and raw materials. The Soviet territories would not possess their own manufacturing capacity or heavy industry.

The Hungerpolitik, or 'starvation policy', was a strategy whereby substantial amounts of the agricultural produce of the European part of the Soviet Union, particularly its grain, would be forcefully removed to assist in the provisioning of German-occupied Europe and, above all, the entire invading army of over three million men. This would be achieved at the expense of the civilian population of the Soviet Union through the intentional sealing off of the so-called 'deficit territories' from those areas of the European part of the Soviet Union which were home to substantial amounts of agricultural produce, referred to as 'surplus territories'. The inevitable consequence of such a strategy would be the starvation of large sections of the Soviet population.

The Importance of Economic Considerations

That the German–Soviet war and the German occupation which ran parallel to it were of a uniquely barbarous nature has been widely acknowledged for a long time, despite the continued failure of a certain proportion of the German public to grasp the extent and pervasiveness of the inculpation of German agencies in the crimes committed in the East.[18] It is also the case that the German invasion of the Soviet Union in June 1941 has often been defined as essentially a racial-ideological war of annihilation, closely tied up with the subsequent genocide against the Jews and the large-scale resettlement plans envisaged by Adolf Hitler's elite cadre, the SS.[19] Whilst these characteristics were indeed fundamental to the nature of the war, the invasion of the Soviet Union was no purely ideological impulse on the part of Hitler, but had rather a more calculated agenda with agricultural-economic considerations at its core. This has been skilfully demonstrated in recent years by several historians, as mentioned above, and is increasingly becoming part of established scholarship, a trend which this study seeks to continue. Although calculated and grounded in economic validation, such considerations were only 'rational' in the Nazi sense of this word. For most people, there is no trace of rationalism in the ideas, words or actions of the Nazi movement. Whilst their plans may have been irrational, the basis on which these men sought to justify such concepts – when not on purely racial-ideological grounds – tells us something about their brand of 'rationalism' and their thinking in general.

With respect to Nazi motivations in invading the Soviet state, there is, of course, little doubt that Hitler had yearned for a war against the Soviet Union, and with it the destruction of Bolshevism, which acted as the ideological impetus for the military campaign, since the mid-1920s.[20] Likewise, the German–Soviet Non-Aggression Pact of 23 August 1939 was seen by Hitler and much of the Nazi leadership as a political necessity, a short-term 'tactical manoeuvre'.[21] The desire to destroy the enormous empire in the East, though at times intentionally muted, was never forgotten. Alongside the racial-ideological nature and aims of the war, however, there existed another, increasingly important aspect of the forthcoming campaign, a factor which was intrinsically linked to the acquisition of *Lebensraum* (living space) for the German nation. As Hitler himself put it in his so-called *Second Book*, written between May and July 1928, though not published during his lifetime: 'A healthy foreign policy will … always keep the winning of the basis of a people's sustenance immovably in sight as its ultimate goal ….'[22] The object of attaining Lebensraum was to provide more space and thus more natural resources in order to allow the German nation to exist on a self-sufficient, 'healthy' basis. Hence, a campaign designed to exploit resources in order to make the German sphere of influence – which by mid-1941 included much of continental Europe – self-sufficient, would have the desired 'side effect' of exterminating those elements of the Soviet population whom the Nazis considered to be racially inferior and politically antagonistic. The exterminatory aspect then, though welcome, was not in itself the principal aim of the undertaking.

In this context, the impact of the experiences of the First World War on both Germany's political and military leadership during the preparatory phase for 'Barbarossa' should not be underestimated. A collapse on the home front through privation or hardship – particularly in terms of food shortages – could under no circumstances be tolerated. By extension, an Anglo-Saxon naval blockade could not be allowed to wreak the same havoc which the British blockade of 1917–1918 had wrought.[23] In view of the combined Anglo-Saxon threat which it was likely Germany would have to face in the not-too-distant future, the German economy, on a precarious footing in large part as a result of the unabated pace of rearmament during the mid- to late 1930s, would have to be stabilized as soon as possible by a massive influx of heavy goods, raw materials and foodstuffs. This had to be achieved, however, without a corresponding drop in the German standard of living. In Hitler's eyes, and those of many of his political and economic subordinates, the only way this could be brought about was through a swift, decisive and massively rewarding victory over the Soviet Union. This would put Germany on a solid footing to wage the 'world war' – the war between continents – once it arrived.[24]

Structure and Additional Parameters of the Study

As contemporaries themselves recognized, the preparations for the eastern campaign and the subsequent occupation fell into four categories, though these categories inevitably overlapped: the tasks of the army; the SS and police; the economic organization; the political administration.[25] Given that the emphasis here is on the anticipated future structure, form and function of the territories in the East, the main focus of this study is logically on the political and economic preparations for the German occupation of the European part of the Soviet Union. The plans and goals of the SS, in other words the primarily racial and ideological aspects of the campaign and occupation, will also be taken into account, but to a more limited extent.[26] This is understandable, given that the intention of setting up an SS administration in the occupied Soviet territories for, say, settlement matters – one of the agency's primary concerns – did not as such exist, whereas both a civil/political and an economic administration, in the latter case for both the area under military jurisdiction and the area under civilian/Party control, were envisaged. Additionally, it is important to keep in mind that, whereas this study focuses primarily on the planning for the post-war occupation which took place during the pre-invasion period, much concrete SS planning for schemes which foresaw the wholesale reorganization of Eastern Europe along racial lines did not take place until after June 1941. The emphasis in this study, therefore, remains on the development and compatibility of political and economic planning. That is not to say that the different projects always took an entirely separate course of development,[27] but rather that the individuals and organizations involved, not to mention the specific motivations and, in some cases, the exact methods, were often different. As this study examines the political and economic preparations within the German leadership and directly subordinate state and Party bodies, the involvement of private enterprises in the economic planning is not explored here.[28]

The time frame selected for examination traces the preparations from the beginning of July 1940, when the first concrete proposals for a military campaign against the Soviet Union had begun to be made, to July 1941, when the campaign itself was under way and the administrative apparatus appointed. The decision to allow the study to overlap into the war itself rather than stopping on 22 June finds its justification in the fact that the personnel for the civil administration were not officially appointed to their posts until mid-July and that the form the administration would take was still in dispute right up to the signing of the relevant decrees by Hitler. The time frame selected allows the development over the course of twelve months of the preparations for 'Barbarossa' and the subsequent occupation to be illustrated in its entirety. This does not mean to say that the decision to invade the Soviet Union had been made as early as July 1940, almost a year before the commencement of the military campaign. Only towards the end of 1940 did Germany's political leadership commit itself to this course of action. Preparations had of course already begun, however, by the time the decision was unalterably made. Furthermore, the timing of the decision assists in determining the motivations for it and indeed conveys something about the aims of the Nazi leadership and the establishment of priorities for the forthcoming conflict.

In dealing with this period, the study takes an essentially chronological course, although certain key issues, such as the importance of the Ukraine in Nazi plans (see chapter 7, 'The Special Status of the Ukraine'), are dealt with thematically. The chronological approach is advantageous in that it allows a more effective monitoring of the planning process and the development of the plans themselves over the twelve-month period. In order to introduce institutions which feature repeatedly during the course of this study, and which made their entrance into the political and economic life of National Socialist Germany long before the planning phase for the German invasion of the Soviet Union commenced, the study begins with an overview of the most important of these institutions (see chapter 2). The principal planning organizations for the occupation of Soviet territories were, in the economic sphere, the Office of the Four-Year Plan (*Vierjahresplanbehörde*), and, in the political sphere, the Bureau Rosenberg (*Dienststelle Rosenberg*).[29] Although many different state and Party bodies took part in the planning process, the selection here has been limited to the two most important. In the case of the Office of the Four-Year Plan, most of the other key ministries and organizations involved in the economic planning either grew out of it (e.g., the Economic Staff East) or contributed key functionaries to its executive arm, the General Council for the Four-Year Plan (e.g., Herbert Backe from the Reich Ministry for Food and Agriculture; General Thomas from the War Economy and Armaments Office of the OKW). In this sense, the majority of bodies involved in the economic planning for the war were directly linked to the Office of the Four-Year Plan. Furthermore, the Four-Year Plan organization was under the control of the second most powerful man in the Reich, Hermann Göring, who was appointed to head the entire economic administration in the occupied Soviet territories.

The Bureau Rosenberg consisted of the Party functionaries around the Baltic-German Alfred Rosenberg, who planned the political restructuring, or Neuordnung, of the Soviet territories and would later make up the Berlin-based staff of the Reich Ministry for the Occupied Eastern Territories (*Reichsministerium für die besetzten Ostgebiete*), the administrative apparatus from mid-July 1941 onwards for those 'pacified' Soviet territories under German occupation. Many, though not all, of the senior posts in the

Bureau Rosenberg and then the East Ministry itself were filled by officials from the Foreign Affairs Office of the NSDAP (*Außenpolitisches Amt der NSDAP*), in particular its Eastern Office. The Foreign Affairs Office of the NSDAP was one of several agencies within the *Amt Rosenberg*, a collective term for the various offices of *Reichsleiter* Alfred Rosenberg. As a state and not a Party institution, the Reich Ministry for the Occupied Eastern Territories was not part of the *Amt Rosenberg*, but had of course recruited many of its employees from it.[30] An examination of the origins, make-up and function of the Four-Year Plan organization and the Bureau Rosenberg will thus provide an illustration of the foundations of the planning structure.

The third chapter of the study charts the initial phase – from July to December 1940 – of proposals and preparations for a military campaign, from the first purely military recommendations to the issuing of 'Directive No. 21: Case Barbarossa' at the end of the year and the growing awareness of the necessity to bolster the Reich's food supply in view of the increasing likelihood of having to fight a war of attrition against the Anglo-Saxon nations. Subsequent chapters follow a more thematic approach within a chronological framework. Hence, chapters 4 to 6 examine the foundations of the Hungerpolitik, which were laid in January and February 1941; the preparations for establishing a civil administration in the pacified Soviet territories, which began in March; and the preparatory work of the different SS offices for population policy in the East, respectively. Chapter 7 returns to the Hungerpolitik, and examines both its radicalization during the months of April and May and the wide-ranging support of key institutions for the proposals made. Chapters 8 and 9 analyse the attitudes and positions of the different planning groups in the final weeks before the invasion, and those issues relating to occupation policy settled during the immediate post-invasion period. In chapter 10, the main arguments contained in the study are summarized and evaluated, and conclusions are drawn which directly address the aims this study has set itself.

Source Material

It is more the aims of the study and its overall approach which justify a fresh examination of the topic, rather than the use of radically different or recently released sources. Nevertheless, the study is grounded in an extensive analysis of the relevant documentary material. Of particular importance are the files of the Reich Ministry for the Occupied Eastern Territories; the Plenipotentiary for the Four-Year Plan, especially the Task Force for Food; the Reich Chancellery; the Office of Alfred Rosenberg; and the Personal Staff of the *Reichsführer-SS* Heinrich Himmler. These files are located in the Bundesarchiv in Berlin-Lichterfelde. The files of the OKW Operations Staff and the War Economy and Armaments Office of the OKW, particularly the War Diary of the Staff Section, which are located in the Bundesarchiv-Militärarchiv in Freiburg im Breisgau, are likewise important.

Given the central role of Hermann Göring within the planning for the occupation of the Soviet Union, as designated head of the entire economic administration in the occupied Soviet territories, the Appointments Diary of Hermann Göring, located in the archives of the Institut für Zeitgeschichte in Munich, has also been consulted. The same applies to the Estate of Herbert Backe, which is to be found in the Bundesarchiv in Koblenz. Backe, as the *Staatssekretär* in the Reich Ministry for Food and Agriculture and head of the Task Force for Food in the Office of the Four-Year Plan, was of fundamental importance in the development of economic plans for the German occupation policy. Additional material from the Militärgeschichtliches Forschungsamt in Potsdam and the Politisches Archiv des Auswärtigen Amts in Berlin has also been consulted. These archival sources are used in conjunction with numerous published documents and diaries.

As will become clear to the reader during the course of this study, much of significance was passed between the planners by word of mouth and never put down on paper. This is explicitly stated by men as central to the planning process as Alfred Rosenberg and Herbert Backe. Secrecy was without doubt of the utmost importance, even if those in the know did not always succeed in avoiding information leaks. As a result of this approach, written documentary evidence is in some cases not on hand and this inevitably creates gaps in the available record. This state of affairs, with which all historians are confronted to varying degrees, necessitates piecing the material that is available together in an attempt to form a more detailed and clearer picture of the events in question. The reader will judge the extent to which this task has been successfully accomplished in this study.

Notes

1. Christian Hartmann, 'Verbrecherischer Krieg – verbrecherische Wehrmacht? Überlegungen zur Struktur des deutschen Ostheeres 1941–1944', *Vierteljahrshefte für Zeitgeschichte*, 52/1 (2004), pp. 1–75, here p. 7.
2. Ibid.
3. See Hans Umbreit, 'Auf dem Weg zur Kontinentalherrschaft', in Bernhard R. Kroener et al., *Das Deutsche Reich und der Zweite Weltkrieg, Band 5: Organisation und Mobilisierung des deutschen Machtbereichs* (Deutsche Verlags-Anstalt, Stuttgart, 1988), pp. 1–345, here pp. 80–81; Christian Gerlach, 'Militärische "Versorgungszwänge", Besatzungspolitik und Massenverbrechen: Die Rolle des Generalquartiermeisters des Heeres und seiner Dienststellen im Krieg gegen die Sowjetunion', in Norbert Frei et al. (eds), *Ausbeutung, Vernichtung, Öffentlichkeit: Neue Studien zur nationalsozialistischen Lagerpolitik* (K.G. Saur, Munich, 2000), pp. 175–208, here p. 179.
4. Alexander Dallin, *German Rule in Russia, 1941–1945: A Study of Occupation Policies* (Macmillan, London, 1957).
5. Gerald Reitlinger, *The House Built on Sand: The Conflicts of German Policy in Russia 1939–1945* (Weidenfeld & Nicolson, London, 1960).
6. Andreas Hillgruber, *Hitlers Strategie: Politik und Kriegführung 1940–1941* (Bernard & Graefe Verlag, Frankfurt am Main, 1965).
7. Götz Aly and Susanne Heim, *Vordenker der Vernichtung: Auschwitz und die deutschen Pläne für eine neue europäische Ordnung* (Hoffmann & Campe Verlag, Hamburg, 1991).

8. Rolf-Dieter Müller, 'Das "Unternehmen Barbarossa" als wirtschaftlicher Raubkrieg', in Gerd R. Ueberschär and Wolfram Wette (eds), *'Unternehmen Barbarossa': Der deutsche Überfall auf die Sowjetunion 1941: Berichte, Analysen, Dokumente* (Ferdinand Schöningh, Paderborn, 1984), pp. 173–196.
9. Rolf-Dieter Müller, *Hitlers Ostkrieg und die deutsche Siedlungspolitik: Die Zusammenarbeit von Wehrmacht, Wirtschaft und SS* (Fischer Taschenbuch Verlag, Frankfurt am Main, 1991).
10. See especially Rolf-Dieter Müller, 'Von der Wirtschaftsallianz zum kolonialen Ausbeutungskrieg', in Horst Boog et al., *Der Angriff auf die Sowjetunion* (Fischer Taschenbuch Verlag, Frankfurt am Main, 1991), pp. 141–245. This is the updated paperback edition of *Das Deutsche Reich und der Zweite Weltkrieg, Band 4: Der Angriff auf die Sowjetunion* (Deutsche Verlags-Anstalt, Stuttgart, 1983), and is used throughout this study.
11. Christian Gerlach, *Kalkulierte Morde: Die deutsche Wirtschafts- und Vernichtungspolitik in Weißrußland 1941 bis 1944* (Hamburger Edition, Hamburg, 1999).
12. Christian Streit, *Keine Kameraden: Die Wehrmacht und die sowjetischen Kriegsgefangenen 1941–1945*, 3rd edition (Dietz, Bonn, 1991) [1978], p. 26. In spite of it having first appeared almost thirty years ago, Streit's pioneering work on the treatment and fate of Soviet prisoners of war in German captivity remains the benchmark on the subject.
13. Robert Cecil, *The Myth of the Master Race: Alfred Rosenberg and Nazi Ideology* (B.T. Batsford, London, 1972).
14. Fritz Nova, *Alfred Rosenberg: Nazi Theorist of the Holocaust* (Hippocrene Books, New York, 1986). Dr Ernst Piper's biographical work *Alfred Rosenberg: Hitlers Chefideologe* (Blessing, Munich, 2005) unfortunately appeared too late for me to adequately take into account its findings.
15. Michael Burleigh, *Germany Turns Eastwards: A Study of Ostforschung in the Third Reich* (Pan Books, London, 2002) [1988], p. 261. The term was used by Alfred Rosenberg during a speech in Dresden in October 1943.
16. Franz Halder, *Kriegstagebuch, Band II: Von der geplanten Landung in England bis zum Beginn des Ostfeldzuges* (W. Kohlhammer Verlag, Stuttgart, 1963), p. 337, entry for 30 March 1941.
17. Gerlach, *Kalkulierte Morde*, and Dallin, *German Rule in Russia*, have already been mentioned. See also Timothy P. Mulligan, *The Politics of Illusion and Empire: German Occupation Policy in the Soviet Union, 1942–1943* (Praeger, New York, 1988).
18. This can be seen in the necessity for, and the numerous and varied objections to, the travelling exhibition *Vernichtungskrieg. Verbrechen der Wehrmacht 1941 bis 1944* from the Hamburger Institut für Sozialforschung. The exhibition was, however, very successful, with a total of approximately 860,000 visitors between March 1995 and July 1999. On this see Jan Philipp Reemtsma, 'Afterword: On the Reception of the Exhibition in Germany and Austria' in Hamburg Institute for Social Research (ed.), *The German Army and Genocide: Crimes Against War Prisoners, Jews and Other Civilians in the East, 1939–1944* (The New Press, New York, 1999), pp. 209–213. See also Theo J. Schulte, 'The German Soldier in Occupied Russia', in Paul Addison and Angus Calder (eds), *Time to Kill: The Soldier's Experience of War in the West* (Pimlico, London, 1997), pp. 274–283, here pp. 274–277.
19. See Heinrich Schwendemann, *Die wirtschaftliche Zusammenarbeit zwischen dem Deutschen Reich und der Sowjetunion von 1939 bis 1941: Alternative zu Hitlers Ostprogramm?* (Akademie Verlag, Berlin, 1993), pp. 205, 278–279, 281–282 and 295; Hillgruber, *Hitlers Strategie*, pp. 518–525.
20. Of fundamental importance here is Eberhard Jäckel, *Hitlers Weltanschauung: Entwurf einer Herrschaft*, ext. and rev. 4th edition (Deutsche Verlags-Anstalt, Stuttgart, 1991), esp. chap. 2, pp. 29–54.
21. Nicolaus von Below, *Als Hitlers Adjutant 1937–45* (von Hase & Koehler, Mainz, 1980), p. 184. See also Franz Halder, *Kriegstagebuch, Band I: Vom Polenfeldzug bis zum Ende*

der Westoffensive (W. Kohlhammer Verlag, Stuttgart, 1962), p. 86, entry for 27 September 1939.
22. Gerhard L. Weinberg (ed.), *Hitlers Zweites Buch: Ein Dokument aus dem Jahr 1928* (Deutsche Verlags-Anstalt, Stuttgart, 1961), p. 70: 'Eine gesunde Außenpolitik wird ... als letztes Ziel unverrückbar immer die Gewinnung der Ernährungsgrundlagen eines Volkes im Auge behalten ....'
23. See Robert Cecil, *Hitler's Decision to Invade Russia 1941* (David McKay Company, New York, 1975), p. 137. See also chapter 3, 'November-December: Food Supplies, the Public Mood in Germany and the Need to Fight a Longer War', in this study.
24. See Rolf-Dieter Müller (ed.), *Die deutsche Wirtschaftspolitik in den besetzten sowjetischen Gebieten 1941–1943: Der Abschlußbericht des Wirtschaftsstabes Ost und Aufzeichnungen eines Angehörigen des Wirtschaftskommandos Kiew* (Harald Boldt Verlag, Boppard am Rhein, 1991), p. 6.
25. See Halder, *KTB*, II, p. 485, Anlage 11, 'Punkte für die Besprechung mit den Chefs der Generalstäbe am 4. und 5.6.1941'; BA-MA, RH 19 III/722, fo. 83, 'Besprechung OKW/Abw. u. OKH am 5./6.6.41 in Berlin'.
26. The plans of Himmler and the SS for, and their activities in, the Soviet Union have been dealt with in several excellent studies. See in particular Isabel Heinemann, '*Rasse, Siedlung, deutsches Blut*': *Das Rasse- und Siedlungshauptamt der SS und die rassenpolitische Neuordnung Europas* (Wallstein, Göttingen, 2003); Götz Aly, '*Endlösung*': *Völkerverschiebung und der Mord an den europäischen Juden* (S. Fischer, Frankfurt am Main, 1995); Richard Breitman, *The Architect of Genocide: Himmler and the Final Solution* (The Bodley Head, London, 1991); Helmut Krausnick and Hans-Heinrich Wilhelm, *Die Truppe des Weltanschauungskrieges: Die Einsatzgruppen der Sicherheitspolizei und des SD 1938–1942* (Deutsche Verlags-Anstalt, Stuttgart, 1981).
27. On this see Götz Aly and Susanne Heim, 'Deutsche Herrschaft "im Osten": Bevölkerungspolitik und Völkermord', in Peter Jahn and Reinhard Rürup (eds), *Erobern und Vernichten: Der Krieg gegen die Sowjetunion 1941–1945*, *Essays* (Argon, Berlin, 1991), pp. 84–105, esp. pp. 98–100.
28. On the inclusion of private concerns in preparations for the economic exploitation of the East see Müller, 'Ausbeutungskrieg', pp. 177–184; idem, *Hitlers Ostkrieg*, pp. 49–81; Dietrich Eichholtz, *Geschichte der deutschen Kriegswirtschaft 1939–1945, Band I: 1939–1941*, 4th edition (K.G. Saur, Munich, 1999) [1969], chap. 5, pp. 197–246.
29. When referring for the first time to German institutions, titles or concepts peculiar to National Socialism or Germany in the 1930s and 1940s, the original German term will follow the English translation in parentheses, accompanied by the recognized abbreviation of the German original, should one exist. Thereafter, the English translation will be used unless a translation of the original German term is deemed to be problematic or usage of the term has become common in the English language (e.g., *Lebensraum*, *Luftwaffe*). The German abbreviation will also be used on occasion. Definitions of German institutions, titles and concepts referred to on more than one occasion are provided in the 'Glossary' at the end of the study.
30. Wolfgang Benz et al. (eds), *Enzyklopädie des Nationalsozialismus*, 4th edition (Deutscher Taschenbuch Verlag, Munich, 2001) [1997], p. 360.

CHAPTER 2

THE CENTRAL PLANNING ORGANIZATIONS

The *Vierjahresplanbehörde*: Göring's Umbrella Organization

Autarky – national economic self-sufficiency and independence – had been a fundamental aim within Nazi Germany long before 1941, and indeed long before the beginning of what ultimately became, and would subsequently become known as, the Second World War in 1939. As early as 1936, the drive to make Germany self-sufficient had been incorporated into government policy and a new and powerful body set up in order to achieve this. At this point in time, the man responsible for the rearming of Germany was President of the *Reichsbank* and Reich Minister for Economics, Dr Hjalmar Schacht. Between August 1935 and March 1936, Schacht was involved in a series of disputes with Richard Walther Darré, Reich Minister for Food and Agriculture, over the allocation of scarce foreign currency. Darré required the currency in order to import food products in short supply, such as oilseeds, whilst Schacht argued the necessity of obtaining raw materials needed by the armaments industry. Hermann Göring, at this point in time the second most powerful man in the Reich, was assigned by Hitler as arbitrator in the dispute, his official task being 'to secure the provisioning of the German people'. In actual fact, it was more a matter of reconciling rearmament with Germany's internal political stability. In order to bring this about, Göring – with Hitler's backing – granted the importing of foodstuffs priority over rearmament.[1] Despite the fundamental importance of rearmament to Nazi aims and the prosperity of the German economy, the immediate need was to maintain domestic stability and thus avoid the damaging psychological effects of the only alternative to cutting back on rearmament: food rationing.[2] This was the beginning of Göring's intervention in the economic sphere. Within a matter of months he would be in more or less complete control.

At the beginning of April 1936, acting on a proposal from Schacht and Reich War Minister Colonel-General Werner von Blomberg, Hitler gave Göring responsibility for improving the raw materials and foreign exchange position of the Reich.[3] Given that the involvement of numerous state and Party agencies was necessary in order to achieve this aim, as the decree appointing Göring made clear, Göring would be able to consult and indeed give instructions to all such bodies.[4] In this capacity, it was inevitable that the respective spheres of responsibility of Göring and Economics Minister Schacht would overlap and that the two men would clash – a state of affairs apparently not foreseen by the latter when proposing Göring's appointment. It was Schacht who, in the interests of a continuing upward trend in economic matters, now called for a temporary throttling back of the pace of rearmament. Göring, however, who saw his task as to secure the (re)arming of Germany, was unwilling to take Schacht's arguments on board.[5] Göring's role as Raw Materials and Foreign Exchange Commissar (*Rohstoff- und Devisenkommissar*) was, both chronologically and functionally, the stepping stone to his appointment as Plenipotentiary for the Four-Year Plan (*Beauftragter für den Vierjahresplan*).[6]

A lasting solution to Germany's economic problems, in particular the shortage of foreign currency, had by the summer of 1936 yet to be found.[7] During the last week of August, Hitler felt prompted by the prevailing state of affairs and his realization that Schacht's economic policies were no longer compatible with his own, emphasizing as the latter did rearmament without restrictions, to begin work himself on a lengthy memorandum on the future direction of German economic policy. 'The lack of judgement of the Reich Economics Ministry and the resistance of German industry to all large-scale plans' had induced him to draw up the memorandum, as Hitler told Professor Albert Speer, Reich Minister for Armaments and War Production, when handing him a copy of the document in 1944.[8] It was originally presented by Göring to government ministers on 4 September 1936 in a meeting lasting only one hour,[9] thus giving little time for discussion if one assumes that around half of the time would have been taken up with the handing out and reading of the document. The inevitability of war in order to obtain self-sufficiency was clearly stated in the memorandum:

> We are overpopulated and cannot feed ourselves on this basis. ... A final solution lies in an extension of living space or the raw material and nutritional basis of our people. It is the task of the political leadership to solve this question one day. ... I thus set [the] following task: I. The German army must be fit for action in 4 years. II. The German economy must be capable of waging war in 4 years.[10]

Although not explicitly stated in Hitler's memorandum, Göring announced to his audience that 'the clash with Russia is unavoidable'.[11] Five days later, a 'new Four-Year Programme' was announced at the annual Party Rally at Nuremberg.[12] The designation 'Four-Year Plan' (*Vierjahresplan*, VJP) became official with Hitler's 'Decree for the Implementation of the Four-Year Plan' of 18 October 1936.[13] Territorial expansion was now necessary, in the eyes of the leading Nazis, not only for ideological but also for economic reasons. Indeed, economic considerations had become predominant.

From now on, the Office of the Four-Year Plan (*Vierjahresplanbehörde*, VJPB), set up to achieve the objectives announced in Hitler's memorandum, would play a central role in the running of the German economy and would be the principal formulator of plans for the ruthless exploitation of Soviet resources in 1941. Colonel-General Hermann Göring, Reich Minister for Aviation and head of the Luftwaffe, was appointed as Plenipotentiary for the Four-Year Plan, a position which massively increased his already extensive powerbase. At this point in time, Göring also possessed de facto leadership of the so-called 'Jewish Question' (*Judenfrage*), as well as being President of the Reichstag since 1932 and Head of the Reich Forestry Office (*Chef des Reichsforstamtes*) since 1934. He was now the central figure in the Nazi state when it came to economic matters, despite being something of an amateur in the field. Dr Joseph Goebbels, Reich Minister for Public Enlightenment and Propaganda (*Reichsminister für Volksaufklärung und Propaganda*), referring to Göring's comprehension of the foreign exchange and raw materials issue, noted in his diary in May 1936: 'He doesn't understand too much about it ....'[14] However, as Goebbels also recognized, it was not necessary for Göring himself to be an economic expert: 'He brings the energy. Whether he also has the economic knowledge and experience? Who knows? Anyway, he'll make a lot of fuss.'[15] Göring provided the authority and the drive, whilst his advisers and planners within the leadership staff of the Four-Year Plan provided the know-how. Göring himself confessed to his own lack of expertise on several occasions. One of these occasions was whilst chairing the meeting of 12 November 1938 in the Aviation Ministry, which resulted in the expulsion of Jews from German economic life, following the destruction of the *Reichskristallnacht* pogrom against the country's Jewish population. Here Göring openly conceded that his experience in economic affairs was limited.[16]

The grip of the Four-Year Plan organization on the German economy in both the civil and military sectors was tightened – and that of the Reich Economics Ministry correspondingly loosened – in December 1939, three months after the German invasion of Poland had sparked off what ultimately developed into the Second World War. A decree issued by Göring on 7 December ordered an extension of the powers of the General Council for the Four-Year Plan (*Generalrat für den Vierjahresplan*) in order to safeguard the ongoing cooperation among those bodies involved in the formulation of economic policy. This was justified by the necessity to 'orientate all forces to a longer-lasting war'.[17] All those economic bodies represented within the Four-Year Plan organization were now subject to the authority of the General Council to issue directives.[18]

Alongside Göring, eleven other men sat on the General Council: eight *Staatssekretäre*,[19] Reich Commissar for Price Setting (*Reichskommissar für die Preisbildung*) Josef Wagner,[20] who was simultaneously Gauleiter of Westphalia-South and of Silesia, Chief of the War Economy and Armaments Office General Georg Thomas, and a representative of the NSDAP. In one of those many peculiarities inherent in the Nazi state, the Staatssekretäre, as members of the General Council, were superior to their own ministers in their respective ministries. These Staatssekretäre were: Herbert Backe (Food and Agriculture), Dr Friedrich Landfried (Economics), Dr Friedrich Syrup (Labour), Wilhelm Kleinmann (Transport) and Dr Wilhelm Stuckart (Interior). In addition to these five, the two Staatssekretäre in the Office of the Four-Year Plan, Paul Körner and Erich Neumann, and the Staatssekretär in the Reich Forestry Office, Friedrich Alpers, also sat on the council.[21] In practical terms, the council was chaired by Körner, Göring's 'closest and most intimate colleague'[22] and, according to Göring's second wife Emmy, his 'only real friend'.[23]

The congregation of Staatssekretäre became an important aspect of governance within National Socialist Germany following the abandonment of formal cabinet meetings at the end of 1937. The final session of the Reich Cabinet took place on 9 December 1937[24] and Hitler thereafter practically forbade his ministers to assemble independently. The Secret Cabinet Council (*Geheimer Kabinettsrat*), set up by 'Führer decree' on 4 February 1938, proved to be a non-starter. Its nominal purpose was to advise Hitler in matters of foreign policy and was chaired by former Reich Foreign Minister Konstantin Freiherr von Neurath. Head of the Reich Chancellery Dr Hans-Heinrich Lammers, new Foreign Minister (as of 4 February 1938) Joachim von Ribbentrop, Deputy of the Führer Rudolf Heß and Chief of the OKW Field Marshal Wilhelm Keitel also sat on the council.[25] The council could only be summoned by Hitler, however, and had no right to convene a meeting itself. As Hitler never summoned it, the council never met.[26]

Recently, attention has turned to the importance of the regular and often several-days-long conferences of the Reichs- and Gauleiter as a means of disseminating information and coordinating policy, and as an opportunity for exchanging viewpoints with Hitler and other senior figures in the Nazi regime.[27] Despite the obvious value of these conferences, not least in terms of the 'continuous' issuing of directives which evidently took place, it appears that the exchange of ideas was limited to discussions in pairs or in small groups,[28] thereby failing to offer a wider forum for debate. In view of this, the Staatssekretäre – as the fundamental medium of policy coordination – increased in importance. Bodies like the Office of the Four-Year Plan borrowed the Staatssekretäre from their respective ministries for purposes of interagency coordination. Meetings of the Staatssekretäre became in effect a substitute for cabinet government.[29] The most well-known example of such a meeting is the so-called Wannsee Conference of 20 January 1942.

At the top of the apparatus tasked with the later economic exploitation of the Soviet Union, and indeed containing many of those men who made up the General Council for the Four-Year Plan, would be the Economic Command Staff East (*Wirtschaftsführungsstab Ost*, Wi Fü Stab Ost). This organization was directly subordinate to Göring in his capacity as Plenipotentiary for the Four-Year Plan and directed on his behalf, as in the case of that body's General Council, by Körner. The Wi Fü Stab Ost, as it was known, would be responsible for the 'unified leadership of the economic administration' not only in the operations area but also in the political administrative areas which were later to be set up.[30] Thus, this dual control in the occupied Soviet territories would lie in the same hands as the leadership of the entire German war economy – those of Göring and his Four-Year Plan organization. How the Wi Fü Stab Ost came into being and what role it played during the planning phase for the invasion are examined later in the study.

Could any other government or NSDAP agency have realistically occupied the function of the Office of the Four-Year Plan during the preparatory phase for the war in the East and taken on its leading role in the realm of economic planning? The body which immediately springs to mind is the Economics Ministry under Walther Funk, Schacht's successor since the latter's resignation on 27 November 1937.[31] However, by the end of 1939, as mentioned above, the VJPB had secured almost complete executive control over the apparatus of the German economy. The Economics Ministry was indeed represented within the General Council for the Four-Year Plan, by Staatssekretär Friedrich Landfried, but he was one among several officials, and by no means the most influential. In addition, there was no other institution which, as early as the spring and summer of 1939, was busying itself so openly with the planning of economic expansion, conquest and occupation, as the Office of the Four-Year Plan.[32] The decisive factor, however, which explains the dominance of the VJPB in the economic planning for 'Barbarossa' and the subsequent occupation of Soviet territories, was the fact that Göring and his Four-Year Plan organization were already in charge of the economic exploitation of the other European territories under German occupation. Responsibility for this task was awarded to Göring for the reason that 'the German war economy ... requires a uniform planning for those territories occupied by German troops'. This commission allowed Göring to issue directives to the head of each civil administration within the framework of those tasks incumbent on him as Plenipotentiary for the Four-Year Plan.[33] Thus, it was to be expected that the same would apply in the occupied Soviet territories and that, in accordance with this, the VJPB would dominate the economic planning for the occupation policy to be pursued there.

The *Dienststelle Rosenberg*: the Eastern Experts of the NSDAP

The Bureau Rosenberg (*Dienststelle Rosenberg*), also known as the Staff Rosenberg (*Stab Rosenberg*), consisted of a group of functionaries under the leadership of Reichsleiter Alfred Rosenberg who were responsible for planning the future administrative system and structure – in other words the political configuration – of the territories to be conquered from the Soviet Union. The men who were to make up the Bureau Rosenberg during the planning phase for Operation Barbarossa, and later the Reich Ministry for the Occupied Eastern Territories (*Reichsministerium für die besetzten Ostgebiete*, RMO) when it was set up in the wake of the invasion,[34] came largely from the Foreign Affairs Office (*Außenpolitisches Amt*, APA) of the NSDAP, in particular its Eastern Office, headed by Dr Georg Leibbrandt.[35]

The APA, led by Rosenberg himself, had been instituted on 1 April 1933. The organization had essentially two tasks: to convey the foreign policy goals of the Nazi leadership to all formations and subdivisions within the Party, and to enlighten foreign nations and their representatives in Germany as to the nature, in particular the supposedly peaceful character, of National Socialist politics.[36] All of those employed by the APA were Party members, most of them between the ages of thirty and forty.[37] In view of the Nazi Party's foreign political aims and Rosenberg's status as the Party's 'eastern expert', it is natural that the APA took a particular interest in issues relating to the territories of the Soviet Union.[38]

Among the senior members of the APA or those who were recruited for the Bureau Rosenberg, several possessed personal experience of Russia and 'the East' in general. Rosenberg had been born in 1893 in Revel (now Tallinn), the capital city of Estonia, had studied in Moscow and only emigrated to Germany after the end of the First World War, when already in his mid-20s, after having experienced the revolutions of 1917 and the Russian military surrender at first hand. Leibbrandt, Arno Schickedanz, staff leader in the APA, and Professor Gerhard von Mende, later head of the regional department Caucasus in the 'Main Department I: Policy' in the RMO,[39] were also so-called *Volksdeutsche*, or ethnic Germans. Leibbrandt came from Hoffnungsthal near Odessa in the Ukraine and Schickedanz from Riga, the capital city of Latvia.[40] Mende was also a Baltic-German.[41] Dr Otto Bräutigam, who became Leibbrandt's deputy in the Policy Department of the East Ministry, had formerly been resident in Russia, the Ukraine and the Caucasus for a total of eight years.[42] These men were thus the nearest thing that the Nazi movement had to 'eastern experts', who would advise on what could be expected of the vast and largely unknown lands to the east and their diverse peoples and how German eastern policy should be formulated.

The Eastern Office of the APA had originally been only a 'department' within that agency, before being upgraded to an 'office' in consequence of a recommendation made in November 1937 by Leibbrandt, the department's head since 1934, citing its 'large field of work as well as its importance'.[43] This sub-body dealt with all questions which in any way related to the Soviet Union or Eastern Europe, in particular those concerning the national movements of Russian and other Eastern European peoples.[44] In doing this, its employees had 'collected and examined reports from and about Russia in depth, compiled a detailed population-political list of the different trends in Russia and naturally also made contact with anti-Soviet circles, but only for the purpose of observation'.[45] By 1935 at the latest, the making of certain preparations for the division of the USSR into several nation states had also become part of the Eastern Office's brief. The apparent danger posed by the Soviet Union, so it was believed, could only be removed in the long term if the enormous empire was one day to be dismantled into its component parts.[46] Adolf Hitler himself told the Japanese Military Attaché in Berlin, General Hiroshi Oshima, in July 1935 that the 'massive bloc of Soviet Russia' must be cut up into its original, historical pieces, and declared himself determined to do everything he could to promote and accelerate this development.[47] The policy pursued by Germany in the Soviet Union after the invasion of June 1941 would indeed remain true to this intention.

During the first months of 1939, by which time the APA counted approximately sixty 'experts',[48] Rosenberg and Leibbrandt attempted to place the uniform organization of the treatment of the so-called 'eastern problems' in their own hands within the framework of the APA.[49] Seeking to lay the foundations for what were at this point in time only theoretical preparations for war in the East, they declared:

> Solely the interests of the German people are decisive. The guiding principles must follow from the views of the Führer, as set down in '*Mein Kampf*', and from the various statements of Reichsleiter Rosenberg. ... The interests of foreign peoples and groups are to be considered exclusively *after* the German interests and only in so far as they are of use to German critical interests.[50]

In writing this, Rosenberg was reinforcing his status as the Nazi Party's expert on the East and perhaps also staking a claim to be at the forefront when plans to carve up the Soviet Union actually became reality. Indeed, on 14 June 1939 the APA produced a memorandum recommending the securing of west Ukraine and Belarus during the forthcoming *Polish* campaign![51] Though forwarded to Head of the Reich Chancellery Lammers the following day, this proposal was not taken up at the time. The German–Soviet Non-Aggression Pact of 23 August then established the form that the impending territorial partition would in fact take. Nevertheless, the 14 June 1939 memorandum provides an idea of the nature and extent of the schemes being formulated by Rosenberg and his staff and gives one indication as to why Rosenberg would later be given responsibility for the civil administration in the occupied territories of the USSR.

Rosenberg was not averse to repeated attempts at self-advancement, even if most of them inevitably ended in disappointment for the APA chief. From mid-1937, at the latest, onwards he occupied himself with the idea of setting up a central authority which would be responsible for repulsing 'world Bolshevism'.[52] Rosenberg's campaign culminated in a draft of a decree from March 1938 to be signed by Hitler appointing Rosenberg as 'General Plenipotentiary of the German Reich for the Defence against World Bolshevism and for the Safeguarding of the National Socialist World View'. According to Rosenberg's draft, as General Plenipotentiary he would have the status of a minister, thus entitling him to attend sessions of the Reich

Cabinet,[53] although what would in fact turn out to be the final cabinet meeting of the Nazi period had already taken place the previous December. Regardless of this, it was never likely that Hitler would authorize either Rosenberg's overall control over 'all ministries and authorities' in questions relating to 'the struggle against world Bolshevism' or the transfer to the Bureau of the General Plenipotentiary of all organizations dealing directly with Bolshevism, Jewry 'and their possible combating'.[54] This extensive encroachment on the prerogatives of other Nazi grandees reached its apotheosis in the stipulation that statements concerning 'fundamental questions of the National Socialist ideological outlook' could only be issued following explicit consultation with Rosenberg.[55]

The reaction of the dyed-in-the-wool anti-Bolshevist Rosenberg seventeen months later to the German–Soviet Pact was not surprising. Whilst recognizing the advantages of such a treaty for Germany, Rosenberg believed that Foreign Minister Joachim von Ribbentrop's trip to Moscow constituted 'a moral loss of respect in view of our now 20-year struggle' against Bolshevism. For Rosenberg, it seemed as though the struggle against Moscow had been a 'misunderstanding'.[56] In his diary, he posed the rhetorical question: 'How can we still speak of the salvation and organization of Europe, when we must request help from the destroyer of Europe?'[57] In all likelihood, however, Rosenberg was aware that the pact with the Soviet Union could only be a temporary state of affairs. Accordingly, he did not withdraw the books he had published on the Soviet Union and its peoples,[58] and the work of his Foreign Affairs Office by no means ceased.

In September 1940 the APA intensified its political instruction and study work with the publication of fortnightly newsletters reporting on events in the Soviet Union.[59] Topics included foreign policy and economics; the new western regions of the Soviet Union (which included the Baltic States and eastern Poland); labour and social policy; and art, literature and science, with source material taken from leading Soviet daily newspapers such as *Izvestiya* and *Pravda*. In the same month, Rosenberg sent Hitler a report on the results of research so far on the political organization of the Soviet Union. According to Rosenberg, the report provided for the first time 'a factually impeccable picture of the structure in the East'. Interest in the Soviet Union within the Nazi Party and its affiliated formations was at this point in time particularly high, and Rosenberg's paper was intended to provide instruction on this matter.[60] Hermann Göring, to whom Rosenberg sent a copy of the report the following month, confirmed his interest in the research and praised the report as having given him a good overview of the topic.[61]

Up to this point in time, the work carried out by Rosenberg and his staff in the APA had been largely confined to gathering data on the Soviet Union and putting together political reports and historical studies on its politics, peoples and activities. By autumn 1940, however, military preparations were well under way for an actual invasion and the spring of the following year would see the start of the transformation of theoretical sketches for the political future of the Soviet territories into detailed plans. With Rosenberg's appointment on 20 April 1941 as Hitler's Plenipotentiary for the Central Treatment of Questions of the Eastern European Space (*Beauftragter für die zentrale Bearbeitung der Fragen des osteuropäischen Raumes*), the setting up of the Bureau Rosenberg would become official.[62]

Given its nature and field of work, the APA, in particular its Eastern Office, seems to have been the ideal precursor to a bureau charged with planning the political reorganization of the occupied territories of the Soviet Union – that which became the Bureau Rosenberg. Was there, however, ever a realistic alternative to this set-up? Could any other government or Party agency have occupied the role assumed by the APA and the Bureau Rosenberg during the preparatory phase for the war in the East? The Foreign Office (*Auswärtiges Amt*, AA) was perhaps an option. Foreign Minister von Ribbentrop was by this point in time, however, already largely out of favour. He had never been much more than a foreign policy secretary to Hitler, who was himself particularly dominant in the realm of foreign affairs. Hitler's firm belief that Great Britain would not go to war over Poland in 1939 was backed all the way by the vain Ribbentrop, who still harboured resentment over his treatment by the British during his spell as German Ambassador in London from 1936 to 1938, and yet, based on this unsuccessful two-year experience, believed he understood the British. It is little wonder that upon receiving the British ultimatum on the morning of 3 September 1939 Hitler is said to have turned angrily to Ribbentrop and asked: 'What now?'[63] Even Ribbentrop's most notable achievement, the negotiation of the Non-Aggression Pact with the Soviet Union in August 1939 was no longer of any value given the Nazi regime's intention to attack the Soviets. As architect of this treaty, the subsequent course of events had undermined Ribbentrop and to a large extent sidelined him. In any case, the civil servants of the German Foreign Office were certainly not the kind of men Hitler wanted running, or for that matter planning, the administration of the occupied Soviet territories. According to one of their own, the career diplomat Otto Bräutigam – who was himself seconded to the East[64] – the politicians and diplomats of the Foreign Office were, in Hitler's eyes, 'reactionaries and degenerates who crawled on their stomachs before foreign countries and were incapable of adopting a truly German stance'.[65] The important tasks in the occupied Soviet territories would essentially be awarded instead to 'men of the Party' – men who had joined the NSDAP well before and not after Hitler and the Nazis had come to power. The appointment of Rosenberg himself as head of the future civil administration in the East is dealt with later in the study.

Notes

1. Dieter Petzina, *Autarkiepolitik im Dritten Reich: Der nationalsozialistische Vierjahresplan* (Deutsche Verlags-Anstalt, Stuttgart, 1968), pp. 32–33. See also Ian Kershaw, *Hitler 1936–1945: Nemesis* (Penguin, London, 2001), p. 10.
2. Ian Kershaw, *Hitler 1889–1936: Hubris* (Penguin, Harmondsworth, 1999), pp. 579–580.

3. BA, R 26 I/35, fo. 4, 4 April 1936. See also *Der Prozess gegen die Hauptkriegsverbrecher vor dem Internationalen Militärgerichtshof, Nürnberg, 14. November 1945 – 1. Oktober 1946*, vol. 9 (Sekretariat des Gerichtshofs, Nuremberg, 1947), pp. 318–319; Georg Thomas, *Geschichte der deutschen Wehr- und Rüstungswirtschaft (1918–1943/45)* (Harald Boldt Verlag, Boppard am Rhein, 1966), p. 111; Alfred Kube, *Pour le mérite und Hakenkreuz: Hermann Göring im Dritten Reich* (R. Oldenbourg Verlag, Munich, 1986), pp. 141 and 147; Petzina, *Autarkiepolitik*, p. 40.
4. BA, R 26 I/35, fo. 4.
5. Petzina, *Autarkiepolitik*, pp. 42–43.
6. Ibid., p. 40.
7. See ibid., pp. 45–48.
8. *Akten zur deutschen auswärtigen Politik 1918–1945, Serie C: 1933–1936*, vol. 5/2 (Vandenhoeck & Ruprecht, Göttingen, 1977), pp. 793–801, doc. 490, here p. 793, fn. 1: 'Der Unverstand des Reichswirtschaftsministeriums und der Widerstand der deutschen Wirtschaft gegen alle großzügigen Pläne haben ihn veranlaßt, diese Denkschrift auf dem Obersalzberg auszuarbeiten.'
9. *IMG*, vol. 36 (1949), pp. 488–491, doc. 416–EC.
10. *ADAP, Serie C: 1933–1936*, vol. 5/2: 'Wir sind überbevölkert und können uns auf der eigenen Grundlage nicht ernähren' (p. 796); 'Die endgültige Lösung liegt in einer Erweiterung des Lebensraumes bzw. der Rohstoff- und Ernährungsbasis unseres Volkes. Es ist die Aufgabe der politischen Führung, diese Frage dereinst zu lösen' (p. 797); 'Ich stelle damit folgende Aufgabe: I. Die deutsche Armee muß in 4 Jahren einsatzfähig sein. II. Die deutsche Wirtschaft muß in 4 Jahren kriegsfähig sein' (p. 801).
11. *IMG*, vol. 36, p. 490: '[Die Denkschrift] geht von dem Grundgedanken aus, daß die Auseinandersetzung mit Rußland unvermeidbar ist.'
12. Max Domarus (ed.), *Hitler: Reden und Proklamationen 1932–1945*, I/2 (Süddeutscher Verlag, Munich, 1965), p. 637. This was, strictly speaking, the second 'Four-Year Plan'. The first had been announced by Hitler on 10 February 1933; see Domarus (ed.), *Reden und Proklamationen*, I/1, p. 207: '... deutsches Volk, gib uns vier Jahre Zeit ....'
13. Kube, *Pour le mérite und Hakenkreuz*, pp. 157–158. For the text of the decree see BA, NS 8/167, fo. 144, 'Verordnung zur Durchführung des Vierjahresplanes'. On the purpose, activities and composition of the Office of the Four-Year Plan see, above all, Aly and Heim, *Vordenker der Vernichtung*, pp. 49–68; Petzina, *Autarkiepolitik*.
14. Elke Fröhlich (ed.), *Die Tagebücher von Joseph Goebbels*, I/2 (K.G. Saur, Munich, 1987), p. 607, entry for 3 May 1936: 'Aber auch Göring wird sich schwer tuen, mit der Devisen- und Rohstofffrage fertig zu werden. Er versteht nicht allzuviel davon und ist auf Ratschläge angewiesen.'
15. Ibid., p. 701, entry for 20 October 1936: 'Die Energie bringt er mit, ob auch die wirtschaftl. Kenntnis und Erfahrung? Wer weiß! Immerhin wird er viel Wind machen.'
16. *IMG*, vol. 28 (1948), pp. 499–540, doc. 1818-PS, here pp. 506–507.
17. Aly and Heim, *Vordenker der Vernichtung*, p. 58.
18. Petzina, *Autarkiepolitik*, pp. 134–136.
19. The term *Staatssekretär* (plural: *Staatssekretäre*) remains throughout in its German form, as the literal translation – 'state secretary' or 'secretary of state' – denotes a position in the British civil service a rank higher (the equivalent of the German *Minister*). These men were not, however, *Minister*, but rather their deputies, i.e., permanent secretaries. The term *Unterstaatssekretär*, denoting the deputy of the *Staatssekretär*, also remains in German throughout. The same applies to other government, NSDAP or SS ranks, though not to military ranks or positions in the occupied territories.
20. Richard Overy, *The Dictators: Hitler's Germany and Stalin's Russia* (BCA, n.pl., 2004), p. 416. Overy describes the position of Reich Commissar for Price Setting, set up on 29 October 1936, as the 'most important office ..., since price inflation might well have undermined the whole strategy'.
21. Aly and Heim, *Vordenker der Vernichtung*, pp. 58–59.
22. Ibid., p. 61, quoting from the *Deutsche Allgemeine Zeitung* of 11/12 March 1934.

23. BA, 99 US 7/1106, fo. 105, post-war comments of Emmy Göring, 2 September 1948.
24. For the minutes see BA, R 43 I/1476, fos. 90–97, 'Niederschrift über die Sitzung des Reichsministeriums am Donnerstag, dem 9. Dezember 1937 vormittags 10.30 Uhr in der Reichskanzlei'.
25. BA, 99 US 7/1108, fo. 92, post-war comments of Hans-Heinrich Lammers, 7 September 1948. Lammers lists Hermann Göring and Martin Bormann as also being on the council, whereas this is contradicted by Wolfgang Benz, who gives Joseph Goebbels as the remaining member; Benz et al. (eds), *Enzyklopädie des Nationalsozialismus*, p. 481.
26. BA, 99 US 7/1108, fo. 92.
27. Martin Moll, 'Steuerungsinstrument im "Ämterchaos"? Die Tagungen der Reichs- und Gauleiter der NSDAP', *Vierteljahrshefte für Zeitgeschichte*, 49 (2001), pp. 215–273.
28. Ibid., pp. 270 and 272.
29. Mark Roseman, *The Villa, the Lake, the Meeting: Wannsee and the Final Solution* (Penguin, London, 2002), p. 57.
30. BA, R 26 IV/33a, 'Richtlinien für die Führung der Wirtschaft in den neubesetzten Ostgebieten (Grüne Mappe)', Teil I (2. Auflage), July 1941, p. 5.
31. Kershaw, *Hitler 1936–1945*, p. 42.
32. Dietrich Eichholtz, 'Institutionen und Praxis der deutschen Wirtschaftspolitik im NS-besetzten Europa', in Richard J. Overy et al. (eds), *Die "Neuordnung" Europas: NS-Wirtschaftspolitik in den besetzten Gebieten* (Metropol, Berlin, 1997), pp. 29–62, here p. 34.
33. See Martin Moll (ed.), *"Führer-Erlasse" 1939–1945* (Franz Steiner Verlag, Stuttgart, 1997), p. 120, doc. 28, 'Weisungsrecht des Beauftragten für den Vierjahresplan gegenüber dem Reichskommissar für die besetzten niederländischen Gebiete', 19 May 1940 and p. 125, doc. 34, 'Weisungsrecht des Beauftragten für den Vierjahresplan gegenüber dem Reichskommissar für die besetzten norwegischen Gebiete', 5 June 1940: 'Da die deutsche Kriegswirtschaft eine einheitliche Planung auch für die von den deutschen Truppen besetzten Gebiete erfordert, ordne ich an, daß auch Generalfeldmarschall Göring im Rahmen der ihm als Beauftragter für den Vierjahresplan obliegenden Aufgaben dem Reichskommissar Weisungen erhalten kann.' See also *IMG*, vol. 30 (1948), pp. 595–597, doc. 2537-PS, 'Erlass des Führers und Reichskanzlers über die Verwaltung der besetzten polnischen Gebiete', 12 October 1939.
34. See Otto Bräutigam, *So hat es sich zugetragen ... Ein Leben als Soldat und Diplomat* (Holzner-Verlag, Würzburg, 1968), p. 301.
35. On Leibbrandt see Kurt Pätzold and Erika Schwarz, *Tagesordnung: Judenmord. Die Wannsee-Konferenz am 20. Januar 1942* (Metropol, Berlin, 1992), pp. 225–227.
36. Thomas Marschner (ed.), *Findbücher zu Beständen des Bundesarchivs, Band 73: Außenpolitisches Amt der NSDAP, Bestand NS43* (Bundesarchiv, Koblenz, 1999), p. vii.
37. Hans-Adolf Jacobsen, *Nationalsozialistische Außenpolitik 1933–1938* (Alfred Metzner Verlag, Frankfurt am Main/Berlin, 1968), p. 600.
38. Seppo Myllyniemi, *Die Neuordnung der baltischen Länder 1941–1944: Zum nationalsozialistischen Inhalt der deutschen Besatzungspolitik* (n.pub., Helsinki, 1973), p. 41.
39. Ibid., p. 58.
40. Jacobsen, *Nationalsozialistische Außenpolitik*, pp. 56 and 60; Pätzold and Schwarz, *Tagesordnung*, p. 225.
41. Myllyniemi, *Die Neuordnung der baltischen Länder*, p. 58.
42. Bräutigam, *So hat es sich zugetragen*, p. 322.
43. BA, NS 43/3, fo. 178, letter from Leibbrandt to Rosenberg, 4 November 1937.
44. Ibid.
45. BA, NS 43/49, fos. 24–40, 'Kurzer Tätigkeitsbericht des Aussenpolitischen Amtes der NSDAP', October 1935, here fo. 34: '... Berichte aus und über Russland eingehend gesammelt und geprüft, eine genaue Bevölkerungspolitische Aufstellung der verschiedenen Tendenzen in Russland selbst gemacht und naturgemäss auch mit Antisowjet-Kreisen, aber nur zwecks Beobachtung, Fühlung genommen.'

46. See Jacobsen, *Nationalsozialistische Außenpolitik*, p. 85; correspondence between Leibbrandt and Professor Dr Jacobsen from 4 April 1968.
47. Theo Sommer, *Deutschland und Japan zwischen den Mächten 1935–1940* (Mohr, Tübingen, 1962), p. 34.
48. Reinhard Bollmus, 'Alfred Rosenberg – "Chefideologe" des Nationalsozialismus?' in Ronald Smelser and Rainer Zitelmann (eds), *Die braune Elite: 22 biographische Skizzen* (Wissenschaftliche Buchgesellschaft, Darmstadt, 1989), pp. 223–235, here p. 230. Up to 1938, the APA had approximately eighty employees; Jacobsen, *Nationalsozialistische Außenpolitik*, p. 600.
49. BA, NS 43/3, fos. 12 and 83, letters from Leibbrandt to Rosenberg and from Rosenberg to *SS-Obergruppenführer* Werner Lorenz, head of the *Volksdeutsche Mittelstelle*, 18 February and 2 March 1939.
50. Ibid., fo. 123, 'Grundsätzliches', 27 January 1939: 'Ausschlaggebend ist einzig und allein das Interesse des deutschen Volkes. Die Gesichtspunkte haben aus der Einstellung des Führers, wie sie in *"Mein Kampf"* niedergelegt sind, und aus den verschiedenen Ausführungen des Reichsleiters Rosenberg zu erfolgen. ... Interessen fremder Völker und Gruppen sind ausschließlich *nach* den deutschen Interessen zu berücksichtigen und nur insofern als sie den deutschen Lebensinteressen dienlich sind.'
51. For the full text see Hans-Günther Seraphim (ed.), *Das politische Tagebuch Alfred Rosenbergs aus den Jahren 1934/35 und 1939/40* (Musterschmidt-Verlag, Göttingen, 1956), pp. 142–147, here p. 145.
52. BA, NS 8/175, fos. 38–44, 'Denkschrift über Einrichtung und Ausbau einer Zentralstelle zur Abwehr des Weltbolschewismus', 30 June 1937.
53. Ibid., fos. 22–23 and 28, 'Akten-Notiz für den Führer' and 'Entwurf einer Anordnung des Führers', March 1938.
54. Ibid., fos. 24–27, 'Geheime Anordnung des Führers und Reichskanzlers an die Reichsministerien', March 1938, here fos. 24 and 25–26.
55. Ibid., fos. 29–31, 'Erste Ausführungsbestimmungen des Führers', March 1938, here fo. 31.
56. Seraphim (ed.), *Das politische Tagebuch Alfred Rosenbergs*, pp. 72–73, entry for 22 August 1939.
57. Ibid., p. 75, entry for 25 August 1939: 'Wie können wir noch von der Rettung und Gestaltung Europas sprechen, wenn wir den Zerstörer Europas um Hilfe bitten müssen?'
58. See Rosenberg's diary entry for 1 June 1941, published in the *Frankfurter Rundschau*, no. 140, 22 June 1971.
59. BA, NS 22/1042, 'Mitteilungen über die Sowjet-Union', fortnightly reports from the *Hauptstelle Ostland, Gauschulungsamt der NSDAP, Danzig-Westpreußen*, November 1940 – May 1941.
60. BA, NS 43/3, fo. 104, letter from Rosenberg to Ribbentrop, 23 October 1940.
61. BA, NS 8/167, fos. 59–60, exchange of letters between Rosenberg and Göring, 5 and 28 October 1940.
62. For the text of the decree see BA, R 6/4, fo. 3; reproduced in *IMG*, vol. 26 (1947), pp. 383–384, doc. 865-PS.
63. Paul Schmidt, *Statist auf diplomatischer Bühne 1923–45* (Athenäum-Verlag, Bonn, 1953), p. 473: 'Was nun?'
64. See Bräutigam, *So hat es sich zugetragen*, p. 300.
65. Ibid., p. 333.

CHAPTER 3

THE DECISION TO INVADE THE SOVIET UNION: THE PRIMACY OF ECONOMICS BY THE END OF 1940

Overview: a Combination of Long- and Short-term Factors

The desire on the part of Germany's political and military leadership to invade the Soviet Union was based on a series of motives which combined during the second half of 1940 to bring about a concrete decision to that effect. Hitler's long-held racial and ideological prejudices against both the Soviet state and its people, to the effect that Bolshevism was the enemy of Europe and had to be removed and Slavs were worthless 'subhumans' who were destined to work as slaves for their German masters, were shared by a substantial proportion of Nazi Party members and meant that any proposals to launch an attack on the Soviet Union would always fall on fertile ground. These prejudices made war between Nazi Germany and the Soviet Union at some time in the future a likely occurrence. They did not provide sufficient motivation, however, to wage war against the Soviets in mid-1941, when Great Britain remained undefeated, thus bringing about the dreaded situation of a two-front war. Hence, the invasion of the Soviet Union was no purely ideological impulse.

In addition to the racial-ideological motivations which doubtless existed, there were also military and economic considerations which played a major role in the decision to invade. The military reasoning had both long- and short-term aspects to it. Germany was concerned that the Soviet Union, once in a state of military readiness, would turn westwards against the Reich. This was largely speculation, however, fuelled by an ever-present fear of the 'Bolshevik Asiatic hordes' overrunning 'civilized' Europe. Although a Soviet attack on Germany could perhaps have become a reality at a later date, the anxiety caused by this potential turn of events was not decisive in bringing about the German decision to launch an invasion. Far more influential, particularly in army circles, was the frustration arising out of Germany's apparent inability either to bring Great Britain to the peace table or to defeat the island nation militarily by launching an amphibious landing, and the belief that Britain's surrender could be brought about through a successful military strike against its only other potential European ally: the Soviet Union.

Only with the appearance of agricultural-economic and wider strategic arguments for a more extensive occupation of the European part of the Soviet Union did the proposal for a limited military strike against the Soviets become a 'war of annihilation' and campaign for Lebensraum, grain and raw materials. It is true that the acquisition of Lebensraum in the East had long been a central aim of Hitler's, but this was very much an integral part of his ideological thinking regarding the Soviet state and played only a small role in the primarily military proposals of July 1940. The perceived necessity of obtaining Lebensraum increased in importance, though, when placed in the broader context of crucial economic considerations, which were brought to the fore during the final months of 1940. Economic factors had indeed already been present in propositions made within military circles in the summer of 1940, but their significance had been limited. By the end of 1940, however, economic arguments had assumed the key role in plans being developed for the invasion and occupation of the Soviet Union.

July 1940: Military Proposals against Britain's Last Potential Ally on the Continent

It was in the wake of the overwhelming military defeat of France at the end of June 1940, and with France and the Low Countries under occupation, that the Soviet Union once more became an issue at the forefront of German political and military thinking. The immediate target for Germany, however, was Great Britain, which remained undefeated. Hitler had hoped that the surrender of France would persuade her ally, Britain, to give up the fight and come to the peace table. This had not happened, however. Hitler's long-held belief that an alliance between Germany and Britain was possible and, even for the latter, desirable had been proved to be erroneous. Britain had not remained passive during Germany's conflict with the 'mortal enemy',[1] France, even if that nation had been unable to hinder Germany's rapid victory, and it was looking less and less likely that an alliance with Britain against the Soviet Union – for Hitler, the ideal strategic state of affairs – could be formed.[2] Thus, there seemed to be nothing for it but to attempt an amphibious landing against the island nation and to bring Britain down by the use of direct force.

The prerequisite for a successful invasion of Great Britain was German control of the skies, which would then make it possible to carry out a naval landing. In accordance with this intention, Hitler had instructed in the middle of June that the German army be reduced to 120 divisions, as this branch of the armed forces would have a less significant role to play in the expected invasion of Great Britain than the Luftwaffe and the navy.[3] The Chief of the General Staff of the Army, Colonel-General Franz Halder, nevertheless noted in his war diary the necessity of retaining some 'strike power in the East', in view of the recent Soviet march into the Baltic States and the Soviet Union's desire for the Romanian territories of Bessarabia (in present-day Moldova) and North Bukovina.[4] For almost two months the Luftwaffe attacked Royal Air Force bases in south-east England. Just as the RAF was beginning to buckle under the onslaught, it was Commander-in-Chief of the Luftwaffe Göring, not head of state Hitler, who made the fatal tactical error of switching the focus of the attack to London, the systematic nightly bombing of which began on 7 September 1940. Although the Battle of Britain would continue until the end of October, this shift to so-called 'terror bombing' of the British capital effectively marked a move away from the idea of an amphibious landing and towards the increasingly remote hope that this tactic would force the British government to the peace table. As it turned out, however, the Luftwaffe was simply not powerful enough to bomb Britain into submission.[5] The Battle of Britain ultimately resulted in heavy German losses (1,733 German aircraft as against 915 British)[6] and in the postponement and eventually the abandonment of 'Operation Sea Lion', the proposed German invasion.

A naval landing against Britain had in any case always been viewed as particularly risky by the German leadership and it was felt that making peace with Britain was far more desirable than an invasion. Hitler had for many years believed that Britain would agree to an alliance with Germany on the basis that the latter would not attempt to challenge Britain's naval hegemony or the integrity of its Empire, whilst Britain would give Germany a free hand in Europe, allowing her to extend her territory eastwards at the expense of the Soviet Union in the quest for Lebensraum. In effect, Britain would remain Europe's (and the world's) pre-eminent naval power, whilst Germany would be Europe's foremost land power. His false assessment of where Britain's interests in Europe and the wider world lay and the likelihood of that nation forming an alliance with Nazi Germany had led Hitler to base his entire alliance policy and foreign political decisions on little other than his own narrow view of international relations. This corresponded in no way to the attitude of Britain, although Hitler's repeated expressions of hope that Britain would 'see sense', right down to the end of the war, indicate his firm belief in the compatibility of the interests of the two nations, particularly in opposing the spread of Soviet power and, with it, Bolshevism.[7]

Simultaneously to the prosecution of the Battle of Britain, ideas began to be exchanged in German leadership circles as to the possibility of an invasion of Europe's other major power, the Soviet Union, thus indicating the general lack of conviction about the feasibility of a landing against

Britain. Even if Germany had succeeded in gaining control of the skies and formulating a workable plan for launching an amphibious assault against southern England, it is quite possible that seeds of doubt regarding the presence of the USSR to Germany's rear would have given the Nazi leadership pause for thought before embarking on a potentially problematic naval landing in the west. The ever-present fear of a two-front war, which was a constant factor in German strategic thinking (though abandoned in June 1941), worked both ways – there was clearly a tangible mistrust of Soviet machinations during an amphibious landing against Britain.

In a discussion between Halder and the Staatssekretär in the Foreign Office, Ernst von Weizsäcker, on 30 June 1940, the latter expressed Hitler's view vis-à-vis the Soviet Union. Halder took down Weizsäcker's comments in his war diary in his usual style: 'c) Eyes very much directed towards the East. d) England will probably require another demonstration of our military power before it yields and leaves our rear free for the East.'[8] Given that Halder's diary entry is at least a second- and possibly a third-hand version of Hitler's alleged comments (it is not clear whether Weizsäcker had heard Hitler's sentiments from Hitler himself or whether Weizsäcker had been informed of what had been said by someone else),[9] an analysis of Hitler's words and his thinking in general at the end of June 1940 based on this source is problematic. If this was a true representation of Hitler's sentiments, however, it unmistakably expressed the desire, both in the long term and now indeed in the short term, to take on the Soviet Union: a demonstration of Germany's military power against the Soviets would persuade Britain to surrender in order that Germany could turn eastwards once again, presumably to finish the USSR off.

On 3 July 1940, three days after his discussion with Weizsäcker, Halder started down the road of turning Hitler's apparent desire into military reality by assigning Colonel Hans von Greiffenberg, Chief of the Operations Department in the General Staff, to examine how to carry out a military strike against the Soviet Union in order to force recognition of Germany's dominant role in Europe.[10] It appears that Halder was indeed the first senior figure in the German leadership to voice the real possibility of a German invasion of the USSR and to make preparations to that effect. Despite his likely knowledge of Halder's 'precautions', the Commander-in-Chief of the Army, Field Marshal Walther von Brauchitsch, considered it necessary in mid-July 1940 to quash rumours of German–Soviet tensions. One of the arguments he used was that the Soviets were faithfully fulfilling the economic agreements, whereby, in accordance with the trade treaty of 11 February 1940, both countries would deliver goods to the value of between 640 and 660 million Reichsmark over the next two years.[11] The circulation of rumours to the effect that the German–Soviet relationship was in a state of deterioration could only have been disadvantageous for Germany and perhaps even have threatened the vital deliveries arriving from the east.

In a discussion on 13 July 1940 between Hitler and Halder at the Berghof, the former's mountain retreat on the Obersalzberg above Berchtesgaden in southern Germany, the intention to launch an amphibious landing against Britain clearly remained. Hitler was puzzled, however, as to why Britain refused to make peace. Like the army leadership, Hitler saw the explanation in Britain's continued hope in the Soviet Union, and deemed it necessary, therefore, to compel her with the use of force to agree to peace. This, however, according to Halder, was not particularly to Hitler's liking. The reason for this was Hitler's belief that military defeat for Britain would bring about the disintegration of her empire, something which could in no way benefit Germany – German blood would thus be shed to achieve something whose beneficiaries would only be Japan, the United States and 'others' (by which the Soviet Union was presumably meant).[12] Three days later, Halder discussed the preparations for the invasion of Britain with Field Marshal von Brauchitsch.[13] On the same day, Hitler signed 'Directive No. 16 regarding the Preparations for a Landing Operation against England'. The preamble ran:

> Since England, despite its militarily hopeless situation, still shows no signs of readiness to come to an agreement, I have decided to prepare a landing operation against England and, if necessary, to implement it.
>
> The purpose of this operation is to eliminate the English motherland as [the] basis for the continuation of the war against Germany and, if it should be required, to occupy it fully.[14]

Although the operational plans began thereafter to be carried out, the qualifications in the preamble to the directive ('if necessary', 'if it should be required') illustrate Hitler's half-heartedness.

Only at the end of a meeting with the commanders-in-chief of the three branches of the armed forces, Chief of the OKW Field Marshal Wilhelm Keitel and Chief of the OKW Operations Staff General Alfred Jodl on 21 July 1940, having discontinued the planned reduction in the size of the army, did Hitler speak for the first time about the possibility of an invasion of the USSR. He instructed Field Marshal von Brauchitsch to tackle the 'Russian problem'. As a matter of fact, Brauchitsch was able to present Hitler that same day with studies which the Army High Command (*Oberkommando des Heeres*, OKH) had been working on since the end of June 1940, a fact which supports the assertion that the proposal to invade the Soviet Union was first made by the army leadership. Hitler announced the 'political aim' to be accomplished, in the event of an invasion and the future partition of the Soviet state, following the defeat of the Soviet army: a Ukrainian kingdom, a Baltic federation and, depending on one's reading of Halder's brief notes, either the occupation of the territory between Belarus and Finland or the handing over of the Russian territory between Belarus and Finland to the latter.[15]

This appears to have been the first concrete statement to come from the Nazi leadership, and certainly from Hitler, referring to the post-invasion occupation of Soviet territories. Moreover, it was now already evident that, in the event of an invasion of the Soviet Union, it would not be a conventional military conflict, but would also possess clear political aims. Interestingly, despite Hitler's emphasis on the need to protect Berlin and the Silesian industrial region from air attacks – thus suggesting the 'defensive' nature of a German attack on the Soviet Union – Halder admitted that the Soviets 'do not want a war' and that no signs existed which indicated Soviet activities against Germany. Indeed, the idea of forming a political coalition made up of Germany, Spain, Italy and the Soviet Union, in order to bring Great Britain down, remained during the second half of July 1940 one of the options being considered.[16] Hitler arguably still viewed the task of forcing Britain to the peace table as his top priority.

Following Hitler's instruction to the army leadership on 21 July 1940 to make theoretical preparations for a strike against the Soviet Union, Halder directed Major-General Erich Marcks, Chief of Staff of the 18th Army, to carry out a comprehensive operational study.[17] The resulting 'Operational Draft East' of 5 August 1940 saw the purpose of the campaign as being purely to defeat the enemy armed forces and to remove any possibility of 'Russia', as the author insisted on referring to the Soviet Union, being a threat to Germany in the foreseeable future. In order to protect Germany against enemy bombers – no other reason was given – 'Russia' should be occupied up to the line of the upper Dvina, Volga and lower Don rivers. The 'final objective' (*Endziel*) was referred to later in the study as being the line Archangel–Gorky–Rostov.[18] This line was effectively what would become known as the 'AA' (Archangel–Astrakhan) line, the designated minimum limit for the German military advance, and far beyond the eastern boundaries of Belarus and the Ukraine.[19] Reaching this line would involve occupying Moscow, considered by Marcks to be the economic, political and spiritual centre point of Russia. Conquering the capital would result in the collapse of the 'Russian Empire'. Marcks believed that between nine and seventeen weeks would be required in order for the aims of the military campaign to be accomplished.

The major areas of 'Russia's' war economy were also provided by Marcks – the food and raw materials area of the Ukraine and of the Donets Basin, and the armaments centres around Moscow and Leningrad (St Petersburg) – but these were mentioned more in terms of what Germany should occupy in order to weaken the Soviet Union and speed up victory rather than in terms of what Germany could win for itself. Marcks recommended that a military administration be prepared for the occupied territories and that the Ukraine, Belarus and the Baltic States be earmarked for the transition to independence under native, non-Bolshevik, governments.[20] Although political invasion aims – particularly the intention to break up the Soviet state into its component parts – were thus already evident at this stage, the proposed campaign had not yet assumed the form of a 'war of annihilation' of which the extensive exploitation of both the Soviet Union's natural resources and its people would be integral parts.

July–August: Long-term Strategic and Economic Gain for Germany in the East

It was not only the army leadership which instructed at the end of July 1940 that an operational study be prepared. Following the meeting of 21 July, Grand Admiral Erich Raeder, Commander-in-Chief of the Navy, had commissioned a memorandum dealing with the USSR to be drawn up. A week later, Rear Admiral Kurt Fricke, the Chief of the Operations Department in the Naval War Staff, presented his 'Reflections on Russia' to Raeder. According to Fricke, Great Britain remained, and would continue to be, Germany's principal opponent.[21] Nevertheless, Germany's economic and demographic requirements, it was suggested, coincided with what the Soviet Union possessed:

> The securing of our homeland requires for the future ... the consolidation of the spatial impregnability, i.e., an extension which prevents an unhindered surprise entry of vital areas of German soil, a deep piece of interspersed open country, so to speak ..., which simultaneously obtains for the German people the necessary Lebensraum for the future. ... It further demands the most autarkic economy possible, especially with regard to those goods which are vital in wartime (e.g., oil, foodstuffs).[22]

Thus, the lands of the Soviet Union were now being thought of by some as the source of vital goods, in particular oil and foodstuffs, which would, if not make Germany wholly autarkic, at least cover its supplies during periods of war. Although the USSR was very suitable as both a provider of raw materials and a sales market – conditions which, according to Fricke, would 'under normal circumstances' have been used to the advantage of both nations – the obtaining of Lebensraum to the detriment of the Soviet Union would secure Germany for the future. In addition, Fricke's study – almost two-thirds of which was taken up with military considerations – described the Soviet Union as a military and ideological threat to Germany. These claims were justified on the basis of Soviet expansionism and 'the spirit of Bolshevism', respectively. The latter was seen as a danger for those nations adjoining the USSR and, in the interest of Europe, had to be removed.[23] Without explicitly recommending immediate German offensive action against the Soviet Union, a possible war in the East was depicted in the study in a promising light.

Although the German navy would not have a central role to play in the forthcoming campaign against the Soviet Union, it is perhaps not surprising that it was the naval leadership, and not the army leadership, which widened the invasion proposals in order to include strategic and economic considerations. Given the necessity for the navy to deploy its ships in several arenas around the globe, a requirement exacerbated by the particularly extensive naval presence of Great Britain, the High Command of the Navy (*Oberkommando der Marine*, OKM) was accustomed to looking at the wider strategic picture. The High Command of the Army, on the other hand, aware of Hitler's emphasis on the importance of land warfare and on Germany establishing itself as Europe's foremost land power, would have been more inclined to concentrate on the immediate military-tactical picture.

On 29 July 1940, General Jodl informed his closest colleagues of Hitler's decision, at the earliest possible opportunity, to remove the danger of Bolshevism from the world 'once and for all' through a surprise attack on the Soviet Union. Those present were the senior officers of the National Defence Section (Section L) within the OKW Operations Staff and included the department's head, Colonel, later Major-General, Walter Warlimont.[24] Both Fricke's reference in his paper of 28 July to 'the spirit of Bolshevism' and Jodl's comment a day later on the danger of Bolshevism demonstrate the continued significance of anti-Bolshevism for the German leadership's willingness to launch an invasion against the Soviet Union. Although not decisive in bringing about the decision in 1940 to wage war against the Soviets, the strength of anti-Bolshevik feeling within both the political and the military leadership would help to dictate the type of war it would become.

On 31 July 1940, on the Obersalzberg, Hitler addressed the heads of the OKW, army and navy on the entire war situation. Here, Hitler announced his 'definite decision to deal with Russia' in the spring of 1941, the war aims now being the 'destruction of the life force of Russia' and the obtaining of the Ukraine, the Baltic States and Belarus. As a reward for her participation in a future war against the Soviet Union, Finland would be extended to the White Sea at the expense of Russia. The fate of the areas to be occupied by German forces was clear enough – they would go 'to us'.[25] The increasing importance, though not yet predominance, of economic objectives at this stage was once again evident in Hitler's inclusion in his operational proposals of a move to secure the oil-rich region of Baku on the western shore of the Caspian Sea.[26]

Ten days after Hitler's 31 July 'decision', a comprehensive military-geographical study of the European part of the USSR produced by the General Staff of the Army appeared which argued for the occupation of the most important industrial and geographical areas of the Soviet Union not only with a view to weakening the Soviet capacity to fight, but also on the basis of how Germany could profit in the long term from the occupation of these areas.[27] According to the study, an occupation of the Ukraine, Moscow and Leningrad would be particularly advantageous. The Ukraine was judged to be 'both agriculturally and industrially the most valuable part of the Soviet Union'. Baku, at the eastern end of the Caucasus, as the supplier of 73 per cent of Soviet mineral oil production, and the industrial area of the Ural Mountains were also regarded as 'very important', though located at some distance from Germany.[28] Even in the event of an occupation of all these territories, however, the war would not necessarily be at an end because of the 'enormously extensive Asian Russia' lying beyond the Urals and the Caspian Sea. With a population of around forty million and its own agricultural and industrial resources, this was no longer an 'absolutely empty wilderness'. The section entitled 'Military Judgement' ended with a prophetic note of caution: 'Main opponent[s] in the case of any attack are space and climate. In this case, the enormous extent of the area assumes the utmost importance.'[29] This analysis from the Army General Staff followed the lead given by the report of the Naval War Staff from 28 July in emphasizing the vital importance of economic considerations for Germany's long-term interests. The Ukraine, as 'both agriculturally and industrially the most valuable part of the Soviet Union', was of particular significance and would indeed remain so for the German planners.

September–October: Alternatives and Objections to an Eastern Campaign

Despite Rear Admiral Fricke's positive paper of 28 July 1940, Grand Admiral Raeder himself, though of the opinion that a landing against Britain should only be undertaken as a last resort,[30] was at the same time very much against an invasion of the Soviet Union. He was also able to propose an alternative course of action. Instead of a campaign against the USSR, Raeder advised the pursuance of a strategy focused on the Mediterranean Sea. He presented his ideas to Hitler on several occasions, the best example probably being his one-to-one discussion with Hitler on 26 September 1940. The fact that the discussion took place with only Hitler and Raeder present, the suggestion having come from the latter, indicates the importance Raeder attached to the points he raised.[31] Raeder urged that all German forces be concentrated against Britain and argued that the Mediterranean was of central importance to the island nation. By focusing on the Mediterranean he hoped to break British supply lines whilst at the same time securing German control of the region and in the long run protecting Germany's continental position from an attack from the south.[32] Raeder advised securing the Canary Islands as the prerequisite for taking Gibraltar, the western gateway to the Mediterranean. Capturing the Suez Canal would provide a position from which to advance through Palestine and Syria as far as Turkey. This would secure East Africa. Raeder then turned to north-western Africa, which was coveted by the British, with the assistance of Charles De Gaulle's Free French and perhaps also the USA, as a resistance base and – more worryingly for Germany – a jumping-off point for an Allied invasion of Italy. To prevent this happening, Raeder proposed taking action against Dakar, the coastal capital city of Senegal, and pointed to the importance of working together with the French. Despite Hitler's agreement 'in principle' with Raeder's line of thought,[33] one cannot help but think that the approach recommended by the Commander-in-Chief of the Navy was simply too indirect and not dynamic enough for Hitler. More importantly, it did not offer the same potential economic rewards which an occupation of the Soviet Union's European territories did. Nevertheless, the course of action recommended by Raeder was immeasurably less risky.

By the beginning of October 1940, concern was being voiced in other circles regarding a German attack on the Soviet Union. One of these circles was the German Foreign Office, where Staatssekretär von Weizsäcker was an active member of the opposition to Hitler. Weizsäcker had appointed Hasso von Etzdorf as the representative of the Foreign Office with the OKH and, in this capacity, to make contact with Halder and work for the aims of the opposition to Hitler. It was indeed Halder who informed Etzdorf of the decision to invade the Soviet Union, after which Etzdorf went about collecting as much useful information on the USSR as he could. During this period, he met an official in the German embassy in Moscow, Gebhardt von Walther, to whom he posed the question as to the effects a German attack on the Soviet Union would have.[34] As the conversation had to be broken off, Walther shortly afterwards sent a memorandum to Etzdorf, in which he gave his answer to the question posed.[35] In the memorandum Walther argued that the Soviet leader, Joseph Stalin, was no threat to Germany, not least because 'he actually does not have any aims' with regard to the latter, and that an occupation of the Ukraine, the Baltic and Belarus – contrary to the findings of the Army General Staff's study of the European USSR from 10 August – would be more of a burden for Germany's economic position than a help. His judgement of the Ukraine, given the high esteem in which this region was held by the German leadership, cast a big question mark over the feasibility of plans which would soon be in the pipeline for the agricultural exploitation of the Soviet Union:

> In the heavily overpopulated Ukraine, the agricultural production, also in the long term, would sink to nil even quicker than in the last war, as an advantageous exploitation, as a result of the peculiar agricultural structure (*sovkhozy* and *kolkhozy* combined with motor and tractor stations, based on central administration under 100% mechanization, in which machines for cultivation and harvesting do not belong to the agricultural firm, but are rather assigned by the central control to the individual firms; very high fuel requirement), is only possible for the Soviet Union itself.[36]

Staatssekretär Weizsäcker was also of the opinion that an occupation of Soviet territories would not even result in an increase in Germany's grain supply.[37] Walther's report was passed on by Etzdorf to Halder, who, despite meeting with Hitler on 4 November, two days after receiving the document, does not appear to have brought it up with the latter.[38] Instead, on this day Hitler informed Halder, Keitel, Jodl and Brauchitsch, among others, that 'everything must be done in order to be ready for the great settling of accounts' with 'Russia', which remained 'the entire problem of Europe'.[39]

November: Before and After Molotov's Visit to Berlin

Two days after Hitler's 4 November 1940 meeting with the military leadership, Göring, since 19 July Reich Marshal (*Reichsmarschall*), a title created especially for him following the fall of France and affording him the status of the highest-ranking officer in the Wehrmacht, informed the top functionaries of the Four-Year Plan – Staatssekretäre Körner, Neumann and Backe, Unterstaatssekretär in the Reich Economics Ministry General Hermann von Hanneken, and Chief of the War Economy and Armaments Office General Thomas – of the intentions of the political leadership towards the Soviet Union.[40] For the first time, Göring also instructed Thomas to make preparations for a longer war,[41] a direction he repeated a week later, on 11 November.[42] Thomas had in fact already been informed by Keitel of recent developments as early as 2 August, just two days after Hitler's announcement of his 'definite decision to deal with Russia'.[43] Lieutenant-General Erich Stud, head of the section Industrial Armaments of the Army in the Army Weaponry Office (*Heereswaffenamt*), had already met with officers from various departments within the Wi Rü Amt on 1 November 1940 to discuss the setting up of an organization to take care of the seizure of 'the most important military-economic industrial plants and raw material deposits' in the European part of the Soviet Union.[44] The circle of the initiated was growing ominously wider. Göring's commission to Thomas could be read not only as an indication of Germany's long-term military intentions, but also of what it expected to obtain from the Soviet Union following a successful campaign – the resources of the East would equip Germany to wage war against the Anglo-Saxon powers, if necessary.

Thus, it appears that the German leadership had already determined on war with the Soviet Union *prior* to the visit to Berlin on 12 November 1940 of Soviet Foreign Minister Vyacheslav Molotov.[45] A month earlier, German Foreign Minister von Ribbentrop had written to Joseph Stalin and invited Molotov to visit Berlin in order to discuss questions 'so decisive for the future of our peoples'.[46] The concept of forming a continental block with the Soviet Union against Great Britain was still at that point in time a possible option, but a discussion between Hitler and Benito Mussolini on 28 October 1940 contained the last relatively clear indication that this idea was still being entertained. A certain degree of scepticism was in fact already evident in Hitler's comments regarding the likelihood of the two nations reaching an agreement which would balance the two sets of interests.[47]

The discussions which took place on 12 and 13 November between Molotov, Ribbentrop and Hitler contained many protestations of good intentions from both sides, but it was clear that the two parties entertained a fundamental lack of trust of the other's aims with respect to those lands over which there remained some uncertainty as to their allocation to either the German or Soviet sphere of influence.[48] These territories comprised Bulgaria, Romania, Turkey and, above all, Finland. Although Hitler stated his recognition that Finland belonged to the Soviet sphere of influence, as had been agreed in August 1939 at the time of the German–Soviet Non-Aggression Pact, he insisted that this country was of the utmost economic importance to Germany for the duration of the war.[49] With this statement, Hitler probably had in mind the nickel-mining area adjacent to Petsamo (present-day Pechenga, in Russia) and the Norwegian territory around

Kirkenes, which bordered Finland and was home to iron ore deposits with a content of 85 to 90 per cent iron. These iron ore deposits were required by Germany for mixing with Swedish iron ore for the purpose of manufacturing high-quality types of steel.[50] Although Molotov declared at the end of the two days that the discussions had undoubtedly been 'very useful', he was clearly rather dissatisfied with the responses he had received from Hitler and Ribbentrop to his questions regarding German intentions.[51] One historian has talked about these meetings as possessing 'an air of unreality',[52] whilst another has been content to describe Molotov's visit more simply as 'a disaster'.[53]

Two pieces of evidence provide particularly strong support for the argument that Hitler had decided on war against the Soviet Union before Molotov's visit and not afterwards, by which time it had once more been illustrated that the aims and interests of the two states stood directly opposed to each other and could not be accommodated. The first is Hitler's 'Directive No. 18', which was issued on 12 November 1940 – the day Molotov arrived in Berlin – and was concerned largely with the securing of France and the Iberian Peninsula. A short section on 'Russia', located towards the end of the directive, read: 'Political discussions with the aim of clarifying Russia's attitude in the immediate future have commenced. Regardless of the outcome of these discussions, all preparations for the East which have already been ordered verbally are to be continued. Directives on this will follow as soon as an outline of the army's operational plan has been presented to and approved by me.'[54] The second piece of evidence is a comment from Grand Admiral Raeder made in the wake of Molotov's visit. Raeder found Hitler to be 'still inclined to pursue the conflict with Russia', the key word here being 'still'.[55] From these two pieces of evidence one can draw the conclusion that Hitler had already made his decision before Molotov's visit, which he probably viewed as an opportunity to confirm to himself that the decision he had taken was the correct one, as was customary with him.

The unwillingness of Great Britain to come to the negotiating table had clearly resulted in the awareness among the political and military leadership in Germany that the Reich would have to fight a longer war against the Anglo-Saxon powers, as it was becoming increasingly apparent that the USA would not see out the war sitting on the sidelines. With the prevailing state of its resources and industrial capacity, Germany was not equal to this task, and saw the Soviet Union and its natural wealth in raw materials and foodstuffs as the answer to this dilemma.[56] A 'peripheral' campaign in the Mediterranean did not offer the same potential gains.[57] Moreover, the only realistic alternative in Hitler's conception to a successful Blitzkrieg against the Soviet Union was Germany's total military defeat and complete downfall. Only the seizure of the USSR's raw materials and foodstuffs could equip Germany to wage war against its remaining opponents and bring about ultimate victory. Furthermore, victory against the Soviet Union would allow Hitler to implement his long-term ideological aims in the East. Failure of the Blitzkrieg, however, meant for Hitler not only the loss of the eastern campaign, but indeed of the entire war.[58]

In actual fact, there was a good deal to be said for the Mediterranean alternative, aimed squarely against Great Britain and championed by Grand Admiral Raeder. Between September and November 1940, Hitler had indeed given this option considerable attention, as his meetings with Vichy Foreign Minister Pierre Laval, Spain's General Francisco Franco and Vichy's head of state Marshal Henri Pétain demonstrate. Seizing Gibraltar and the Suez Canal, the western and eastern gateways to the Mediterranean, with the assistance of Spain and Vichy France, would have opened up both the possibility of the Axis powers exerting greater control over West Africa (thus preventing a potential Anglo-American landing) and of forcing Great Britain out of the Near East, with this region's extensive supplies of mineral oil providing a significant additional motivation. These actions would have been combined with an attempt to draw the Soviet Union closer to the Axis, thereby consolidating the trade agreement between the Soviet and German governments. Hitler's inability to reach agreements with either Spain or, more importantly, Vichy France on their entry into the war meant that by the time Molotov visited Berlin on 12 November the Mediterranean option had all but been abandoned.[59] The destruction of British strength in the Mediterranean and the Near East would simultaneously have bolstered Germany's own strategic and economic position and made an Anglo-American landing in West Africa highly unlikely. Whether such a strategy would have sufficed to bring about a British surrender, however, is impossible to say.

November–December: Food Supplies, the Public Mood in Germany and the Need to Fight a Longer War

As 1940 progressed, the supplying of the German people and those in the occupied and annexed territories with foodstuffs was becoming increasingly problematic, in large part due to the ongoing British naval blockade. In May 1940, the Staatssekretär in the Reich Ministry for Food and Agriculture, Herbert Backe, who also sat on the General Council for the Four-Year Plan, had written a report on the provisioning of Europe's population with foodstuffs. In the report, Backe had pointed out that around sixty-three million of Europe's 515 million people (approximately 12 per cent) were completely dependent for their food supply on overseas imports. Although exactly half of the sixty-three million were in the United Kingdom and Ireland, 17.2 million of them were inhabitants of Greater Germany (including what had been Czechoslovakia). Backe pointed out that a 'very considerable increase in the agricultural production' of the Balkan States and the Soviet Union was possible, to the extent that 'at least' Greater Germany's deficit could be covered. To achieve this aim, however, would require at least a decade of systematic work.[60]

In another report on Europe's grain economy, probably written around the same time, Backe argued that only the Soviet Union could cover those losses which would occur if the naval blockade continued. However, although the Soviets had exported considerable amounts of grain prior to the First World War, Backe considered it doubtful whether they were still in a position to do so, or indeed to master the transport difficulties involved. Such amounts could only be made available with a corresponding 'reduction in consumption', the possibilities for which would have to be looked into.[61] Whether Backe was referring at this point in time to a controlled reduction in the consumption of all involved – i.e., also the German people – or merely of the Soviet population is not entirely clear. However, to avoid the fulfilment of his prophecy of 19 May 1940 to the effect that 'If [the] war lasts more than two years, it is lost,'[62] Germany's economic planners would have to find a radical solution to the problems facing the Reich. By the beginning of 1941, there would be no lack of clarity with regard to where Backe stood on this matter or what solution he proposed.

As is discussed in the next chapter, the difficulties involved in supplying the people of German-occupied Europe aroused fears within Germany's political elite of a consequential negative effect on the public mood within the Reich. This realization increased the necessity, as the Nazi leadership saw it, of obtaining as much as possible from the fertile lands of the East – a policy of exploitation which would have the most devastating consequences for the Soviet population. That the German leadership was willing to contemplate the loss of vital Soviet deliveries of raw materials and foodstuffs – 'killing the goose that lays the golden eggs',[63] so to speak – can be explained as follows: despite the increase in the flow of deliveries between the two countries in accordance with the trade agreements of February 1940 and, later, January 1941, the agricultural deliveries from the Soviet Union did not entirely cover German shortages; the USSR demanded industrial and military goods – crucial for a country in Germany's position – in return; and, a fundamental factor from Hitler's point of view, the growing German dependence on deliveries from the Soviet Union, which could theoretically be stopped at any moment, was highly undesirable.[64]

During Molotov's visit to Berlin in November 1940, he had, in addition to his discussions with Hitler and Ribbentrop, also met with Göring. The latter lamented that, as Germany was at war, difficulties were arising due to Soviet demands for German deliveries of arms. Göring hoped that a 'broad platform' could be found for the delivery of German goods.[65] At the beginning of December 1940, Halder recorded the Soviet willingness to deliver one million tons of grain, but also their expectation of 'larger deliveries in return'.[66] Indeed, not only increasing Soviet demands, but doubt as to the reliability of the Soviets' own future deliveries had undeniably given certain figures within the German political and military leadership cause for concern since mid-September 1940 at the latest.[67] The longer the war in the West lasted and with it the British blockade, and the more serious Germany's strategic situation became through the increased support of the

USA for Britain, the greater Germany's precarious economic (and political) dependence on the Soviet Union would inevitably become.[68]

Memories of the First World War, more specifically what the Nazis saw as the decisive effect of the British naval blockade on the supply of food to the German home front and consequently on the population's morale, strength of resistance and belief in ultimate victory, were particularly influential in shaping the mentality, and subsequently in formulating the policies, of the Nazi leadership in this matter.[69] As early as 11 August 1939, Hitler himself had announced to the then League of Nations High Commissioner in the Free City of Danzig, Carl J. Burckhardt: 'I need the Ukraine, in order that no one is able to starve us again, like in the last war.'[70] With this comment, Hitler was referring to the Ukraine's foodstuffs, above all its grain. A series of related comments from leading figures in Germany's political and military elites during the years 1940 and 1941 indicates the effect that the blockade during the 'Great War' and its consequences had had in moulding National Socialist political thought. The Reich Minister for Food and Agriculture, Richard Walther Darré, noted in his diary entry of 19 July 1940 that it had been the limitations in the area of food and agriculture which 'initiated the catastrophe' during the 1914–1918 war.[71] Staatssekretär Erich Neumann commented in a speech in April 1941: 'It is well-known how much the scarcity of foodstuffs and raw materials, caused by the [British] blockade, contributed to wearing down the home front [during the First World War].'[72] A report dating from June 1941 and produced by the War Economy and Armaments Office in the OKW stated: 'In spite of the incomparable performance of its army, when all is said and done Germany lost the world war of 1914–18 for economic reasons, owing to insufficient supplies of raw materials and foodstuffs.'[73] Given that such a point of view was clearly widespread in the Nazi hierarchy, it is little wonder that the leadership sought to avoid at all costs a repeat of the situation the next time around, in which Germany would find itself with inadequate access to a broad base of foodstuffs and raw materials.

In accordance with these multifaceted considerations, 'Directive No. 21: Case Barbarossa', issued on 18 December 1940, instructed the German armed forces to be prepared, even before the end of the war against 'England', as Adolf Hitler was in the habit of referring to the United Kingdom, to crush the Soviet Union in a rapid campaign. Echoing Major-General Marcks's operational draft of 5 August 1940, the line to be reached would be that between the River Volga in the south and Archangel in the north, thus providing 'protection against Asiatic Russia' and preventing the Soviet air force from attacking territory within the German Reich. The directive also stressed the importance of an early occupation of the Donets Basin, a major source of coal, and of swiftly reaching Moscow, the capture of which would be 'politically and economically a decisive success'.[74]

Hitler's directive also resembled in several respects the operational study of Lieutenant-Colonel Bernhard Loßberg of the National Defence Section within the OKW Operations Staff, produced three months earlier.[75] Both set the principal aim of the military campaign as being to 'annihilate' the mass of Soviet forces positioned immediately east of the border and to prevent the withdrawal of fighting troops 'into the expanses of the Russian space'. Hitler, corresponding to the recommendation made by Loßberg, ordered the Soviet armaments industry in the Ural region not to be attacked by the Luftwaffe until after the conclusion of major hostilities. This was necessary in order to concentrate all forces against the Soviet air force and in support of the advancing German army. Both documents also divided the theatre of operations into two halves and gave the northern half priority, although Hitler attached less importance than Loßberg to the capture of Moscow and would gradually amend his strategy over the coming months to concentrate increasingly on the Ukraine.[76]

In terms of justification, however, Hitler's Directive No. 21 conceded that these measures would be taken only in the event that the Soviet Union should alter its attitude towards Germany.[77] This was purely a case of Hitler covering himself – the decision to launch an offensive against the Soviet Union in 1941 had been made. Indeed, 1941, according to Germany's Supreme Commander-in-Chief (i.e., Hitler), was the year in which 'all continental European problems' must be solved, as from 1942 onwards the USA would be in a position to intervene.[78] The fundamentally covert nature of the preparations to be made in accordance with Directive No. 21 was also stressed in the order. The number of officers to be called in for the preliminary work was to be kept to a minimum. Additional employees were to be initiated as late as possible and then only as many as were absolutely necessary for each individual task.[79]

On the very day that Directive No. 21 was issued, Alfred Rosenberg gave Georg Leibbrandt, head of the Eastern Office in the APA, the task of drafting a plan for the possible future administration of the Soviet Union.[80] Rosenberg's blueprints of April and May 1941, no doubt in part drawn from Leibbrandt's own work and the work of the APA in general, would provide the basis for the setting up of a civil administration in those territories of the Soviet Union occupied by German forces in the weeks and months following the invasion of June.

During the Christmas holidays, just a few days after the issuing of Directive No. 21, Staatssekretär Backe sat himself down to redraft the annual report of the Reich Ministry for Food and Agriculture on the food situation in Germany. This would be the third draft of the memorandum. Backe felt that neither the first nor the second version, produced in November and December 1940, respectively, had portrayed the food situation dramatically enough. Upon completion of the revised report at the beginning of January, Backe passed it on to his superior, Reich Minister Darré, for the latter's signature.[81] On 9 January 1941, the same day he had received it, Darré forwarded the report, just like every year, to Hitler via the Head of the Reich Chancellery, Lammers.[82]

Already before the beginning of the war, Germany had not been autarkic; 17 per cent of its annual food requirements had to be imported from overseas.[83] Continental Europe as a whole required imports of twelve to thirteen million tons of grain a year.[84] This was bound to increase in wartime due to loss of efficiency and Germany's inability to import from the western hemisphere as a result of the British sea blockade. Indeed, by the end of 1940, the grain deficit for continental Europe – much of which was under German occupation – had already risen significantly.[85] Thus, the need, in the eyes of the Nazis, to take decisive action to combat Germany's and German-occupied Europe's lack of self-sufficiency was becoming ever more pressing. In addition to the report on the food situation for the economic year 1940/41, Backe, without the assistance of other members of the ministry, had also produced a description of the likely food situation in the coming third war year, which would begin on 1 August 1941, corresponding to the start of the new economic year. Backe then presented his findings to a combined session of the Reich Ministry for Food and Agriculture and the Reich Food Estate (*Reichsnährstand*, RNSt), the latter being responsible for the supervision of all aspects of rural life, from production to distribution.[86] According to Backe, all those present voiced their full agreement with the findings of his account.[87]

It was not only Backe and his colleagues in the Reich Ministry for Food and Agriculture who were drawing alarming conclusions from Germany's food situation. The army leadership, in a discussion on 23 December 1940, noted that they did not regard Germany's position in the following year as necessarily secure and merely hoped to 'muddle through' 1941.[88] A month earlier, the well-informed former German Ambassador to Italy, Ulrich von Hassell, had noted in his diary that Prussian Finance Minister Johannes Popitz and the former Lord Mayor of Leipzig, Carl Friedrich Goerdeler, who had also served as Reich Price Commissioner (*Reichskommissar für die Preisüberwachung*), had informed themselves about the food situation. Their findings showed that, if all available supplies were to be exhausted, Germany could perhaps manage until 1 August 1941, but that certain parts of German-occupied territory would soon suffer deprivation.[89] Presentations during January 1941 not only to Göring but also to Hitler would provide Backe with the opportunity to expound his assessment of the food situation in Germany, suggest potential solutions and illustrate the possibilities offered by the forthcoming invasion of the Soviet Union.

Notes

1. Adolf Hitler, *Mein Kampf* (Mariner Books, New York, 1999) [1925/1926], pp. 665–666.
2. See Jäckel, *Hitlers Weltanschauung*, pp. 35–38 and 46–47.
3. Ernst Klink (and Horst Boog), 'Die Militärische Konzeption des Krieges gegen die Sowjetunion', in Boog et al., *Der Angriff auf die Sowjetunion*, pp. 246–395, here pp. 311–312.
4. Halder, *KTB*, I, p. 372, entry for 25 June 1940.
5. Kershaw, *Hitler 1936–1945*, pp. 309–310. In mid-September, Professor Dr Franz Alfred Six, the head of those mobile SS commandos foreseen for activities in Great Britain, was

informed that the landing would not in fact take place; Andrej Angrick, *Besatzungspolitik und Massenmord: Die Einsatzgruppe D in der südlichen Sowjetunion 1941–1943* (Hamburger Edition, Hamburg, 2003), p. 75.
6. Richard J. Overy, *The Air War 1939–1945* (Europa Publications, London, 1980), p. 34.
7. See, for example, Kershaw, *Hitler 1936–1945*, pp. 771–772.
8. Halder, *KTB*, I, p. 375, entry for 30 June 1940: 'c) Augen stark auf den Osten gerichtet. d) England wird voraussichtlich noch einer Demonstration unserer militärischen Gewalt bedürfen, ehe es nachgibt und uns den Rücken frei läßt für den Osten.'
9. In Weizsäcker's private papers there is unfortunately no mention of either his discussion with Halder or the comments apparently made by Hitler at some point prior to this discussion. In fact, there is no diary entry at all for 30 June 1940 or any notes from this date; Leonidas E. Hill (ed.), *Die Weizsäcker-Papiere 1933–1950* (Propyläen Verlag, Frankfurt am Main/Berlin/Vienna, 1974), pp. 207–211. Notes made by Weizsäcker on 23 May 1940 indicate, however, that the idea for a military campaign against the Soviet Union had already then begun to germinate; pp. 204–205: '… im Osten wird es wohl noch eine weitere Abrechnung geben.'
10. Halder, *KTB*, II, p. 6, entry for 3 July 1940.
11. Müller, 'Ausbeutungskrieg', pp. 31–32. For the text of the German–Soviet trade treaty of 11 February 1940, see *ADAP, Serie D: 1937–1941*, vol. 8 (P. Keppler, Baden-Baden/Frankfurt am Main, 1961), pp. 599–605, doc. 607.
12. Halder, *KTB*, II, p. 21, entry for 13 July 1940. See similar comments from Hitler, reproduced in Georg Meyer (ed.), *Generalfeldmarschall Wilhelm Ritter von Leeb: Tagebuchaufzeichnungen und Lagebeurteilungen aus zwei Weltkriegen* (Deutsche Verlags-Anstalt, Stuttgart, 1976), p. 252, entry for 14 August 1940.
13. Halder, *KTB*, II, p. 23, entry for 16 July 1940.
14. Walter Hubatsch (ed.), *Hitlers Weisungen für die Kriegsführung 1939–1945*, 2nd edition (Bernard & Graefe Verlag, Koblenz, 1983) [1962], pp. 61–65, doc. 16, 'Weisung Nr. 16 über die Vorbereitungen einer Landungsoperation gegen England', here pp. 61–62: 'Da England, trotz seiner militärisch aussichtslosen Lage, noch keine Anzeichen einer Verständigungsbereitschaft zu erkennen gibt, habe ich mich entschlossen, eine Landungsoperation gegen England vorzubereiten und wenn nötig, durchzuführen. Zweck dieser Operation ist es, das englische Mutterland als Basis für die Fortführung des Krieges gegen Deutschland auszuschalten, und wenn es erforderlich werden sollte, in vollem Umfang zu besetzen.'
15. Halder, *KTB*, II, pp. 32–33, entry for 22 July 1940: 'Politisches Ziel: Ukrainisches Reich. Baltischer Staatenbund. Weiß-Rußland – Finnland. Baltikum "Pfahl im Fleisch"' (p. 33).
16. Ibid., pp. 31–33, entry for 22 July 1940.
17. Ibid., p. 41, fn. 2.
18. Gerd R. Ueberschär and Lev A. Bezymenskij (eds), *Der deutsche Angriff auf die Sowjetunion 1941: Kontroverse um die Präventivkriegsthese* (Primus Verlag, Darmstadt, 1998), pp. 223–238, 'Der "Operationsentwurf Ost" des Chefs des Generalstabes der 18. Armee, Generalmajor Erich Marcks, vom 5. August 1940', here pp. 223 and 227.
19. See Bräutigam, *So hat es sich zugetragen*, pp. 301–302.
20. Ueberschär and Bezymenskij (eds), *Der deutsche Angriff auf die Sowjetunion*, pp. 223 and 231–232.
21. Michael Salewski, *Die deutsche Seekriegsleitung 1935–1945, Band III: Denkschriften und Lagebetrachtungen 1938–1944* (Bernard & Graefe Verlag, Frankfurt am Main, 1973), pp. 137–144, doc. 6, 'Betrachtungen über Rußland', 28 July 1940, here p. 138.
22. Ibid., p. 139: 'Die Sicherung unseres Heimatlandes bedarf aber für die Zukunft … des Ausbaus der räumlichen Unangreifbarkeit, d.h. einer Erweiterung, die ein ungehindertes, überraschendes Betreten lebenswichtiger Teile deutschen Bodens verhindert, sozusagen ein tiefes Vorgelände …, das gleichzeitig den notwendigen Lebensraum dem deutschen Volke für die Zukunft schafft. … Sie verlangt weiter nach möglichst autarkischer Wirtschaft, zumal der im Kriege lebenswichtigen Güter (z.B. Öl, Nahrungsmittel).'
23. Ibid., pp. 139–140.

24. Walter Warlimont, *Inside Hitler's Headquarters 1939–1945* (Weidenfeld & Nicolson, London, 1964), p. 111.
25. Halder, *KTB*, II, pp. 49–50, entry for 31 July 1940.
26. Ibid., p. 50.
27. MGFA, unreferenced, 'Erster Entwurf zu einer militärgeographischen Studie über das europäische Rußland', Generalstab des Heeres, Abteilung für Kriegskarten und Vermessungswesen (IV. Mil.-Geo.), completed on 10 August 1940, p. 19.
28. Ibid., pp. 18–19.
29. Ibid., p. 19: 'Hauptgegner bei jedem Angriff sind Raum und Klima. Dabei kommt der ungeheuren Größe des Raumes die allergrößte Bedeutung zu.'
30. Gerhard Wagner (ed.), *Lagevorträge des Oberbefehlshabers der Kriegsmarine vor Hitler 1939–1945* (J.F. Lehmanns Verlag, Munich, 1972), p. 109, 'Vortrag des Ob.d.M. beim Führer am 11 Juli 1940 (Obersalzberg)'.
31. Ibid., p. 145.
32. Ibid., pp. 75–76.
33. Ibid., p. 143, 'Vortrag des Ob.d.M. beim Führer am 26.9.40. 17 Uhr (ohne Zeugen)'.
34. Robert J. Gibbons, 'Opposition gegen "Barbarossa" im Herbst 1940', *Vierteljahrshefte für Zeitgeschichte*, 23 (1975), pp. 332–340, here pp. 332–333.
35. PAAA, Handakten Etzdorf, Vertrauliche Aufzeichnungen des Vertreters des Auswärtigen Amts beim OKH, Nr. 1, R 27334, fos. 337490–337495, 10 October 1940, here fo. 337490; reproduced in Gibbons, 'Opposition gegen "Barbarossa"', pp. 335–340.
36. PAAA, Handakten Etzdorf, Vertrauliche Aufzeichnungen des Vertreters des Auswärtigen Amts beim OKH, Nr. 1, R 27334, fos. 337494–337495: 'Stalin muß eine kriegerische Verwicklung mit Deutschland umsomehr vermeiden, als er eigentlich Ziele gegen Deutschland nicht hat' (fo. 337494); 'In der stark überbevölkerten Ukraine würde die landwirtschaftliche Produktion noch stärker als im letzten Kriege auch auf längere Sicht auf Null sinken, denn eine vorteilhafte Ausnützung ist infolge der eigenartigen Struktur der Landwirtschaft (Sowchose und Kolchose verbunden mit Motor- und Traktor-Stationen, basierend auf zentralistischer Verwaltung unter 100%iger Motorisierung, wobei Bestellungs- und Erntemaschinen nicht zum landwirtschaftlichen Betrieb gehören, sondern von der Zentrale den einzelnen Betrieben zugeteilt werden; sehr starker Treibstoffbedarf), nur der Sowjet-Union möglich' (fo. 337495).
37. Hill (ed.), *Die Weizsäcker-Papiere*, p. 226, notes from 17 November 1940.
38. Sigrid Wegner-Korfes, 'Botschafter Friedrich Werner Graf von der Schulenburg und die Vorbereitung von "Barbarossa"', in Bernd Wegner (ed.), *Zwei Wege nach Moskau: Vom Hitler-Stalin-Pakt bis zum 'Unternehmen Barbarossa'* (Piper, Munich, 1991), pp. 185–202, here pp. 195–196.
39. Halder, *KTB*, II, p. 165, entry for 4 November 1940: 'Rußland. Bleibt das ganze Problem Europas. Alles muß getan werden, um bereit zu sein zur großen Abrechnung.' Jürgen Förster incorrectly quotes this passage as 'das große Problem Europas', thus affording a more straightforward interpretation of Halder's remark; Jürgen Förster, 'Hitlers Wendung nach Osten: Die deutsche Kriegspolitik 1940–1941', in Wegner (ed.), *Zwei Wege nach Moskau*, pp. 113–132, here p. 122.
40. Thomas, *Geschichte*, p. 261.
41. *IMG*, vol. 30, p. 273, doc. 2353–PS.
42. Percy Ernst Schramm (ed.), *Kriegstagebuch des Oberkommandos der Wehrmacht (Wehrmachtführungsstab) 1940–1945: Geführt von Helmuth Greiner und Percy Ernst Schramm*, vol. I: 1 August 1940–31 December 1941 (Bernard & Graefe Verlag, Frankfurt am Main, 1965), p. 168, entry for 11 November 1940.
43. Ibid., p. 969, doc. 23, 'Aktennotiz über die Entwicklung der Rüstungslage im Sommer 1940', 20 August 1940, Chef Wi Rü Amt. See also Thomas, *Geschichte*, p. 234.
44. Erhard Moritz (ed.), *Fall Barbarossa: Dokumente zur Vorbereitung der faschistischen Wehrmacht auf die Aggression gegen die Sowjetunion (1940/41)* (Deutscher Militärverlag, Berlin, 1970), pp. 337–338, doc. 107, 'Aktenvermerk über eine Besprechung Generalleutnants Stud mit Offizieren aus den Abteilungen des Wehrwirtschafts- und

Rüstungsamtes zur Schaffung einer Organisation für die wirtschaftliche Ausplünderung des zu erobernden sowjetischen Gebiets', 1 November 1940.
45. Hitler's Luftwaffe adjutant, Captain Nicolaus von Below, later argued that the decision was made after Molotov's visit; Below, *Als Hitlers Adjutant*, p. 251.
46. *ADAP, Serie D: 1937–1941*, vol. 11/1 (Gebr. Hermes KG, Bonn, 1964), pp. 248–253, doc. 176, 13 October 1940, here p. 253. For Stalin's reply, see pp. 300–301, doc. 211, 'Der Botschafter in Moskau an das Auswärtige Amt', 22 October 1940 (Stalin's letter dated 21 October).
47. Hillgruber, *Hitlers Strategie*, p. 352. See *ADAP, Serie D: 1937–1941*, vol. 11/1, pp. 348–357, doc. 246, 'Aufzeichnung über die Unterredung zwischen dem Führer und dem Duce in Anwesenheit des Reichsaussenministers und des italienischen Aussenministers in Florenz in Palazzo Vecchio am 28. Oktober 1940', 28 October 1940, here pp. 353–354 and 357.
48. See *ADAP, Serie D: 1937–1941*, vol. 11/1, pp. 448–461 and 462–478, docs. 325, 326, 328 and 329.
49. Ibid., pp. 463–464, doc. 328.
50. Ibid., pp. 353–354, doc. 246.
51. Ibid., p. 478, doc. 329.
52. Overy, *The Dictators*, p. 489.
53. Edward E. Ericson, *Feeding the German Eagle: Soviet Economic Aid to Nazi Germany, 1933–1941* (Praeger, Westport, CT, 1999), p. 145.
54. Hubatsch (ed.), *Hitlers Weisungen für die Kriegsführung*, pp. 67–71, doc. 18, 'Weisung Nr. 18', 12 November 1940, here p. 71: 'Politische Besprechungen mit dem Ziel, die Haltung Russlands für die nächste Zeit zu klären, sind eingeleitet. Gleichgültig, welches Ergebnis diese Besprechungen haben werden, sind alle schon mündlich befohlenen Vorbereitungen für den Osten fortzuführen. Weisungen darüber werden folgen, sobald die Grundzüge des Operationsplanes des Heeres mir vorgetragen und von mir gebilligt sind.'
55. Wagner (ed.), *Lagevorträge des Oberbefehlshabers der Kriegsmarine*, p. 154, 'Besprechung des Ob.d.M. beim Führer am 14.11.40. 13 Uhr': 'Führer ist immer noch geneigt, die Auseinandersetzung mit Rußland zu betreiben.'
56. See Christian Gerlach, 'Die Ausweitung der deutschen Massenmorde in den besetzten sowjetischen Gebieten im Herbst 1941: Überlegungen zur Vernichtungspolitik gegen Juden und sowjetische Kriegsgefangene' in Christian Gerlach, *Krieg, Ernährung, Völkermord: Forschungen zur deutschen Vernichtungspolitik im Zweiten Weltkrieg* (Hamburger Edition, Hamburg, 1998), pp. 10–84, here p. 13.
57. Ludolf Herbst, *Das nationalsozialistische Deutschland 1933–1945. Die Entfesselung der Gewalt: Rassismus und Krieg* (Suhrkamp, Frankfurt am Main, 1996), p. 336.
58. See Hillgruber, *Hitlers Strategie*, pp. 391–392.
59. On this see Kershaw, *Hitler 1936–1945*, pp. 325–332.
60. BA, NS 10/107, fos. 2–7, 'Europas Nahrungsmittelversorgung', 19 May 1940, here fo. 2.
61. Ibid., fos. 8–11, 'Europas Getreidewirtschaft', n.d., here fo. 9.
62. BAK, N 1075/5, 'Für Montag den 20.5.40': 'Wenn Krieg über zwei Jahre dauert, ist er doch verloren.'
63. Norman Rich, *Hitler's War Aims: Ideology, the Nazi State, and the Course of Expansion* (Norton, New York, 1992) [1973], p. 207.
64. Gerlach, 'Die Ausweitung der deutschen Massenmorde', p. 14. For the view that Soviet grain deliveries of 2.5 million tons, determined by the trade agreement of 10 January 1941, would in fact have been sufficient to cover the German shortfall up to and including 1943 see Herbst, *Das nationalsozialistische Deutschland*, p. 350.
65. *ADAP, Serie D: 1937–1941*, vol. 11/2 (Gebr. Hermes KG, Bonn, 1964), pp. 498–499, doc. 348.
66. Halder, *KTB*, II, p. 207, entry for 3 December 1940.
67. See BAK, N 1094/I 65a, fo. 116, entries in Richard Walther Darré's diary for 18 and 19 September 1940; Hill (ed.), *Die Weizsäcker-Papiere*, p. 219, notes from 27 September 1940; Halder, *KTB*, II, p. 311, entry for 13 March 1941.

68. Hillgruber, *Hitlers Strategie*, p. 257.
69. See Ludolf Herbst, *Der Totale Krieg und die Ordnung der Wirtschaft: Die Kriegswirtschaft im Spannungsfeld von Politik, Ideologie und Propaganda 1939–1945* (Deutsche Verlags-Anstalt, Stuttgart, 1982), pp. 70–73; Streit, *Keine Kameraden*, p. 191.
70. Carl J. Burckhardt, *Meine Danziger Mission, 1937–1939* (Georg D.W. Callwey, Munich, 1960), p. 348: 'Ich brauche die Ukraine, damit man uns nicht wieder wie im letzten Krieg aushungern kann.'
71. BAK, N 1094/I 65a, fo. 115.
72. BA, R 26 I/6, fos. 1–25, 'Der Vierjahresplan', 29 April 1941, here fo. 3: 'Es ist bekannt, wie sehr die durch die Blockade verursachte Nahrungsmittel- und Rohstoffnot zur Zermürbung der Heimatfront beitrug.' See also Göring's comments at the discussion on 16 September 1941; BA, R 26 IV/51, fo. 114.
73. BA-MA, RW 19/473, fols. 167–176, 'Gedanken zu dem Thema: "Wirtschaftlicher Durchhaltekrieg statt Krieg der schnellen militärischen Entscheidung"', June 1941, here fo. 167: 'Den Weltkrieg 1914–18 hat Deutschland trotz der unvergleichlichen Leistungen seiner Armee letzten Endes aus wirtschaftlichen Gründen, auf Grund der ungenügenden Rohstoff- und Nahrungsmittel-Versorgung verloren.'
74. Hubatsch (ed.), *Hitlers Weisungen für die Kriegsführung*, pp. 84–88, doc. 21, 'Weisung Nr. 21: Fall Barbarossa', 18 December 1940, here pp. 84–85 and 87.
75. Ibid., pp. 85–87. For the full text of Loßberg's study see Moritz (ed.), *Fall Barbarossa*, pp. 126–134, doc. 32, 'Operationsstudie des Gruppenleiters Heer in der Abteilung Landesverteidigung im OKW für die Aggression gegen die Sowjetunion (Loßberg Studie)', 15 September 1940.
76. On this see Kershaw, *Hitler 1936–1945*, pp. 408–415.
77. Hubatsch (ed.), *Hitlers Weisungen für die Kriegsführung*, pp. 87–88.
78. Schramm (ed.), *KTB des OKW*, I, p. 996, doc. 45, 21 December 1940.
79. Hubatsch (ed.), *Hitlers Weisungen für die Kriegsführung*, p. 88.
80. Jacobsen, *Nationalsozialistische Außenpolitik*, p. 86; correspondence between Leibbrandt and Professor Dr Jacobsen from 4 April 1968.
81. BA, R 3601/3371, fos. 16–20, letter from Backe to Darré, 9 February 1941.
82. Ibid., fos. 28–31, letter from Darré to Lammers, 'Betr.: Bericht über die Versorgungslage Getreide, Fleisch und Fett im Wirtschaftsjahr 1940/41', 9 January 1941.
83. Herbert Backe, *Um die Nahrungsfreiheit Europas: Weltwirtschaft oder Großraum*, 2nd edition (Goldmann, Leipzig, 1943) [1942], Darstellung 1, inside front cover.
84. Aly and Heim, *Vordenker der Vernichtung*, p. 366.
85. Ibid., p. 366, fn. 2. An RMEL report from 14 December 1940 entitled 'Die erste Kriegsernte in Europa' put continental Europe's grain deficit at 21.7 million tons, the equivalent of the food requirements for almost fifty million people.
86. William Carr, *Arms, Autarky and Aggression: A Study in German Foreign Policy 1933–1939* (W.W. Norton & Company, New York, 1973), pp. 53–54.
87. BA, R 3601/3371, fo. 19.
88. Halder, *KTB*, II, p. 240, entry for 23 December 1940.
89. Ulrich von Hassell, *Die Hassell-Tagebücher 1938–1944: Aufzeichnungen vom Andern Deutschland* (Goldmann, Berlin, 1994), p. 218, entry for 23 November 1940.

Chapter 4

Laying the Foundations for the *Hungerpolitik*

Staatssekretär Backe's turn-of-the-year reflections on the precarious footing of Germany's and German-occupied Europe's food supply would put economic considerations at the forefront of high-level preparations for the forthcoming eastern campaign and occupation during the first two months of 1941. Backe's presentations to the supreme leadership, the dissemination of his proposals and the response of other leading figures and agencies constituted a process which would culminate in the commissioning of plans for an all-encompassing economic organization tasked with plundering Soviet resources. This process would also establish the acquisition of foodstuffs as the prime objective of the occupation, a position it would retain throughout the preparatory phase for the campaign and occupation and indeed during the war in the East itself.

Backe's Presentations to the Supreme Leadership

The gradual realization within the Nazi leadership during the second half of 1940 of the necessity to increase Germany's access to foodstuffs and raw materials at the expense of the Soviet Union in expectation of a drawn-out war against Great Britain and the USA had brought with it very little in the way of concrete ideas as to how this might be effected. That Hitler was responsive to proposals along these lines, however, is clear. On 9 January 1941, he explained to the military leadership that the destruction of the Soviet Union, the land of which offered 'immense riches', would leave Germany 'unassailable'. The former territories of the Soviet Union would then be economically and politically dominated by Germany but, significantly, not incorporated into the Reich. This vague idea was probably the first indication of what developed into the conception of Reich Commissariats (*Reichskommissariate*), territorial units under German civil administration.[1] According to Hitler, complete control over these regions would allow Germany in the future to wage war against continents and ensure that it could not be defeated by anyone. During the Soviet campaign, Europe would 'hold its breath'.[2] Hitler was at this stage almost certainly unaware of the contents of Staatssekretär Backe's end-of-year report on the food situation, as Reich Minister Darré had only forwarded it to Head of the Reich Chancellery Lammers on the day of Hitler's speech. What Hitler's speech indicates, then, is that he was already thinking along the same lines as Backe. It was unlikely that the implications of the latter's report would be lost on Hitler when the time came for him to read it or be briefed on it, as the case may be.

On 13 January 1941, in the presence of Staatssekretäre Körner and Neumann, Backe gave Reichsmarschall Göring, in the latter's capacity as Plenipotentiary for the Four-Year Plan, a presentation regarding the food situation.[3] As well as holding the position of Staatssekretär in the RMEL, Backe had also headed the agricultural group within the Four-Year Plan organization since 1936, occupying alongside this a place on that body's General Council. Göring was clearly a fan.[4] On the same day, evidently as a result of what he had heard from Backe,[5] Göring sent a circular to all Reich ministers, Deputy of the Führer Rudolf Heß, the OKW and all NSDAP Gauleiter, among others, announcing that, due to the anticipated failure of the harvest in the second 'war year' (August 1940–July 1941, corresponding to the economic year) to meet expectations and uncertainty as to how long the war would last, it was necessary to take certain measures in the area of food rationing. The most significant of these would be the reduction in the summer of meat rations.[6] Staatssekretär Neumann for one recognized the inevitability of such a measure and had indeed prepared the circular prior to Backe's presentation in the expectation that Göring would declare himself in agreement with the proposed reduction of meat rations.[7]

Remarkably, Reich Minister for Food and Agriculture Darré, Backe's immediate superior, did not receive a copy of the circular. He was not even informed of it by anyone in his ministry and had to instead find out about it second-hand almost a month later.[8] Even then, he had difficulty in obtaining answers from his own members of staff to his questions regarding the circular.[9] The fact that it was simply not necessary even to notify Darré of the issuing of such an important circular in his own area of responsibility illustrates the extent to which Backe had by this time usurped the power of his minister. This had much to do with Backe's presence on the General Council for the Four-Year Plan and his consequent proximity to the deciding voice in German economic policy, Reichsmarschall Göring, but also with Backe's own drive, dependability and ideological commitment.

The Berlin-based Institute for Research into War Economy was of the opinion that meat was both an important foodstuff and also very much in demand as a luxury item.[10] With the planned reduction of meat rations, the

German people themselves were now about to feel the pinch. This revelation can only have made the economic experts more determined to obtain as much as possible from the Soviet Union during the forthcoming campaign. The gravity with which the looming meat reduction was viewed by the Nazi leadership can be seen from an entry in Joseph Goebbels's diary:

> Yesterday: ... Backe presented me with the state of our provisioning. Meat must be reduced by 100 g per week from 2 June. The Wehrmacht is too well-provided for and consumes too much. Three times as much per head compared with the civilian population. ... I must now pose the question as to how I shall tell this to my child. I will await the most favourable moment possible and then come out with the announcement. The arguments I have to offer are convincing. Backe presides over his department, by the way, in masterly fashion. With him, everything which is at all possible will be done.[11]

Goebbels's reference to the German people as 'my child' indicates the importance of propaganda and the state of the public mood for the Nazi regime. Food shortages could lead to dissatisfaction among the German people, a dip in support for the war or perhaps even for the regime itself. Such a turn of events, even in a dictatorship, could not be contemplated.

Responsibility for reporting public opinion – with unusual candour – to the Nazi leadership fell upon the Security Service (*Sicherheitsdienst*, SD) of the SS.[12] The number of pages dedicated by the SD to instances of major public discontent over the food situation in the weeks and months prior to the RMEL's annual report illustrate both the effect of food shortages on the population and the resultant concern of the Nazi leadership. Between the beginning of July and the end of December 1940, when Backe redrafted the RMEL's report, complaints from the population and the correspondingly negative effect on their mood were described in the reports – which appeared roughly every four days – of 29 July (shortages of, and high prices for, fruit and vegetables), 1 August (reduction of bread rations), 30 September (shortages of fruit and vegetables), 10 October (shortages of rye and wheat), 28 October (shortages, once again, of fruit and vegetables), 7 November (meat shortages), 21 November (shortages of bread, pork, fruit and vegetables; reduction of fat rations), 5 December (fruit shortages) and 16 December (reduction of butter rations).[13] The report of 21 November represented something of a low point in the public mood with regard to the food situation. It is worth quoting this report at some length:

> In recent reports, it has been unanimously stressed that the population occupies itself very much at present with the question of food supply and observes the changes in the allocation of food which have occurred in the last weeks and months with, in part, a certain anxiety. The point of departure for these anxieties are the difficulties which have come to light recently in the *allocation of meat and fat*, the *reduction of bread rations*, the inadequate supply of the markets with *vegetables and fruit*, along with the almost complete cancellation of *game, poultry and fish deliveries*. As the reports

further say, the discernible price trend in the areas of these articles is observed with growing unrest. Complaints have not only arisen as a result of the direct price increases of different foodstuffs which have occurred, but above all because the already long-established tendency of deterioration in quality alongside steady prices continues.[14]

The spate of reports and the increasing anxiety evident within them could only have encouraged Staatssekretär Backe to make a grave assessment of Germany's food situation in his revised end-of-year report. The resources of the Soviet Union would have to provide a solution to the deficiency of provisioning for the civilian population and the threat to German morale.

Before the month of January 1941 was out, Backe had also presented his ideas to Hitler. How this meeting came about is difficult to determine due to the absence of conclusive documentation. A likely explanation is that Hitler had read or been briefed on Backe's report, which had been forwarded to Head of the Reich Chancellery Lammers on 9 January, and had subsequently called Backe in to provide him with a verbal assessment of the prevailing supply situation. During his presentation Backe assured Hitler that 'the occupation of the Ukraine would liberate us from every economic worry'. Such an unequivocal statement was exactly what Hitler wanted to hear. It is not difficult to imagine the conclusions he would have drawn from this sweeping comment. Backe went on to point out, though, that the Ukraine was indeed the only 'surplus territory' (*Überschußgebiet*) in the Soviet Union; the whole of European Russia, on the other hand, was not.[15] This remark begs the question as to what kind of policy was to be pursued in those areas which did not produce agricultural surpluses, in order that Germany was nevertheless able to obtain the envisaged quantities of grain. In all likelihood, though the documentary evidence again does not allow for absolute certainty, Backe proposed to Hitler a method which was aimed at artificially creating the grain surpluses which did not occur naturally. Exactly what this strategy entailed will become clear over the following pages.

Working around Potential Difficulties

Despite Backe's strength of conviction, there were still some doubts being raised both among his fellow economic planners and within senior circles of the German military about the potential effects of a military campaign in the East. At some point in January, most likely on 29 of that month,[16] Reichsmarschall Göring presided over a meeting of his economic advisers during which those present gave their view as to the economic repercussions of waging war with the Soviet Union. All those present, with the notable exception of Backe, responded negatively, pointing to the loss of large quantities of supplies arriving punctually from the Soviet Union on the basis of the treaties concluded between the two states and the uncertainty of what could be obtained to replace these losses. In addition, the substantial transit shipments which came from the Far East via the Soviet Union would also be lost. On the whole, it was generally felt that the 'tremendous consumption of economic goods of all types that would be entailed by such a war was in no ratio whatsoever to the difficulties arising'. Backe, on the other hand, held the view that large amounts of grain could be extracted from the Soviet territories.[17]

The outcome of this meeting indicates that, at least up to and including January 1941, at a time when the decision to invade the Soviet Union had already been made, most of the Reich's senior economic planners were sceptical about the potential economic and agricultural gains to be made from an invasion and did not, therefore, have mass starvation in mind as a 'solution' to the lack of grain surpluses available in the Soviet territories. Already at this stage, however, Backe's proposals very probably had the support of Hitler and quite possibly Göring. Hitler's mindset was such, particularly in the case of the Soviet Union, where ideological motives combined with strategic and economic motivations (indeed perceived necessities), that objections or potential difficulties were expected to be worked around. It was up to the economic planners to find a solution, whatever that might be, to the supposed problem.

In the middle of January, misgivings arose from the calculations of the War Economy and Armaments Office in the OKW regarding the consequences for the German supply situation of even a short interruption in the delivery of raw materials from the USSR, which would inevitably occur in the event of a German invasion. In the case of certain metals, such as tungsten, manganese, chrome and platinum, considerable disruption of the German war economy would undoubtedly result.[18] At the end of the month, Colonel-General Halder also began to have second thoughts about whether there was any sense at all in conducting military operations against the Soviet Union. More specifically, he believed that Germany's economic base would not be significantly enhanced.[19] Halder's general doubts about the logic of a German invasion probably arose less from a reassessment of Soviet military strength – the German military's appraisal of which remained largely unchanged – than from an awareness of the growing capacity of the Anglo-Saxon powers and the dangers posed by a two-front war.[20] In view of the doubts which had arisen in the War Economy and Armaments Office during the preceding days, General Thomas informed Field Marshal Keitel during a presentation on 22 January 1941 that he intended to prepare a paper detailing his misgivings.[21] Keitel's reaction is not known, but it can be assumed that the Chief of the OKW, echoing Hitler's standpoint that an occupation of key Soviet territories would solve Germany's economic problems, rejected Thomas's doubts.

It was less this probable rebuff from Keitel than the outcome of meetings with members of the military and political leadership over the following days which appears to have encouraged Thomas to approach the whole conception of a war in the East very differently, and to stimulate him to produce a report which would unite him with Staatssekretär Backe in advocating a ruthless exploitation of the Soviet Union. Discussions during the last days of January with Keitel, Göring and Reich Minister for Armaments and Munitions Dr Fritz Todt, among others, gave Thomas the opportunity to explore expectations within leadership circles.[22] The discussion with Göring and Todt, which lasted two and a half hours, took place on 29 January, and was also attended by Körner, Neumann, Unterstaatssekretär Hanneken, Staatssekretär Syrup of the Reich Labour Ministry and head of the department Research and Development in the VJPB Carl Krauch, as well as Backe, who would no doubt have used the occasion to enunciate his assessment of the measures necessary to be taken in the Soviet Union.[23]

On 8 February, in a presentation on the fuel and rubber situation, Thomas nevertheless warned Keitel and General Jodl that, in the event of an eastern campaign, supplies of aviation fuel would only last until autumn 1941, whilst those of vehicle fuel would only last until mid-August. Thomas illustrated, 'with utmost gravity', the threatening dangers of the prevailing supply situation, only to receive a response from Keitel to the effect that 'the Führer would not let himself be influenced in his plans by such economic difficulties'.[24] This comment by Keitel did not mean that economic factors were irrelevant to Hitler. As has been shown, economic considerations were of the utmost importance both in the motivations for launching an invasion and in the early preparations for German occupation policy in the Soviet Union. What Keitel's comment meant was that Hitler expected such 'difficulties' to be overcome, much as Backe and his colleagues were in the process of overcoming the problem of an absence of naturally occurring grain surpluses in the Soviet territories. Thomas was expected to 'work towards the Führer'.[25]

In accordance with this expectation, Thomas, by 12 February at the latest, had informed himself fully of the plans, already at an advanced stage, being formulated by the civil servants in the RMEL and the Reich Food Estate. On this day, Thomas discussed with members of his staff the paper being produced by the Wi Rü Amt on the military-economic effects of the anticipated operations against the Soviet Union, a paper intended for Hitler himself and that which had been mentioned to Keitel the previous month. It was remarked by someone present that the Reich Food Estate estimated the grain deficit of Germany and those lands it occupied to be five million tons. A 10 per cent reduction of Soviet consumption, according to the Reich Food Estate, would make four million tons available for German use. This compared very favourably with the normal Soviet surplus of one million tons and even with the amount of 2.5 million tons promised by the Soviets in accordance with the trade agreement of 10 January 1941. The figure of 2.5 million tons was, according to the Soviets, only possible 'by falling back on the national grain reserves'.[26] The method recommended by the Reich Food Estate for the production of four million tons must have been the solution which Backe had had in mind to the problem of limited grain surpluses – if the surpluses did not occur naturally, they would be created by the application of force. One might wonder if at any point in time it occurred to the officials working in the Reich Ministry for Food and Agriculture and the

Reich Food Estate how ironic it was that their offices – institutions responsible for securing the nourishment of the German people – were initiating a murderous policy of starvation against the Soviet population.

As can be seen, the war against the Soviet Union had already assumed its uniquely criminal character in the intentions and indeed the plans of the Nazi leadership by early February 1941. This development is typically judged to have taken place a month later with the concrete preparations for the deployment of the mobile 'task forces' (*Einsatzgruppen*) of the Security Police and SD and with the formulation of the so-called 'criminal orders'.[27] The ideas for the 'starvation policy', however, had already begun to be formed within the staffs of the Reich Ministry for Food and Agriculture and the Reich Food Estate during the final weeks of 1940, with Staatssekretär Backe taking the lead role, although Richard Walther Darré, head of both agencies as Reich Minister for Food and Agriculture and Reich Farming Leader (*Reichsbauernführer*), was almost undoubtedly ignorant of these preparations. This can be established from a series of letters written by Backe and Darré himself during the days directly after the beginning of Operation Barbarossa and over subsequent weeks.[28] In one of these letters, dated 26 June 1941, Backe informed Darré that, at the time of his initiation into the preparations for 'Barbarossa', he was informed that Hitler did not want these preparations to be carried out in the various ministerial departments and that, on the contrary, the undertaking should be transferred – as a 'Four-Year Plan task' – to Göring in his capacity as Plenipotentiary for the Four-Year Plan. No other person was to be notified of the preparations without express permission from above to that effect. In the event that Darré questioned Backe regarding the latter's duties, Darré was to be referred to Staatssekretär Körner. The 'particular secrecy' of the matter, continued Backe, thus made it impossible for him to inform Darré of what was taking place.[29] The consequence of this approach was that Darré was officially informed of these preparations only after the military campaign was already under way. Hitler's reasons for keeping Darré in the dark when it came to the preparations taking place will have included the necessity of maintaining secrecy, but must also have had something to do with his lack of faith in the Reich Minister for Food and Agriculture when it came to matters of a particularly far-reaching or radical nature.

The Reich's highest authorities, Adolf Hitler and, next to him, Hermann Göring, appear to have reacted positively to what they heard from Backe during January 1941, and the conversion of General Thomas by the beginning of February brought one of the key Wehrmacht sections – the War Economy and Armaments Office – on board. Both the importance of these economic-agricultural considerations and the willingness of Germany's political and military leadership to formulate a criminal strategy on the basis of such considerations were thus established well before the other criminal preparations against the Soviet state and various sections of its population were made. The foundations for the 'war of annihilation' (*Vernichtungskrieg*) against the Soviet Union had been laid.

Soviet Awareness of German Intentions

A discussion of the extent to which the Soviet government was aware of German intentions to wage a war of conquest and annihilation and the nature of its reaction to that which it was privy to is admittedly in no way indispensable to a study which, like this one, endeavours to trace and analyse the planning for German occupation policy in the USSR. Nevertheless, such a discussion does provide an opportunity to demonstrate that neither the German decision to invade the Soviet Union nor the form and character of its proposed occupation policy were seriously influenced by the actions or attitude of the Soviet government.

Whilst certain circles in Germany were planning the invasion, dismemberment and exploitation of the Soviet Union, Joseph Stalin was avoiding doing anything that could in any way give Hitler a reason to attack. Not surprisingly, given this approach from the Soviet leader, British attempts to improve relations between the two governments and encourage a rapprochement were in vain. Stalin did not want to be viewed by Hitler as being in the enemy's camp. The principal aim of the British was, for the moment, to induce Moscow into decreasing its deliveries of raw materials to Germany in order to enhance the effectiveness of the British naval blockade. It was hoped to bring this about by arranging a rival trade agreement with the Soviets which would result in a reduction in the large quantities flowing into Germany.[30] In addition to refusing to deal with the British, Stalin also appointed an ambassador to the French government in Vichy and expelled from Moscow the diplomatic representatives of Norway, Belgium, Yugoslavia and Greece, all of them countries occupied by Germany.[31]

It was not only Moscow's unwillingness to negotiate with Germany's enemies but also its strict adherence to the conditions of the trade agreement and its open-handedness in dealings with Germany herself which demonstrated Stalin's compliance and determination not to alienate Hitler. In a telegram to the German Foreign Ministry, Karl Schnurre, the head of the German delegation to the economic negotiations which resulted in the German–Soviet trade agreement of 10 January 1941, described what Germany had obtained through the negotiations as 'the maximum' which could have been furnished by the Soviet economy, when making allowances for the Soviets' own requirements.[32] Stalin was convinced that it could not be in Germany's interests to attack the Soviet Union if the latter faithfully complied with the agreement to deliver such large and valuable quantities of foodstuffs and raw materials. This refusal to believe that Germany could contemplate attacking its trading partner would become an obsession with Stalin and have fatal consequences for the Soviet Union and its people.[33]

Even when news started to filter through to the Soviet leadership that plans were indeed under way for a German invasion, it was initially ignored. As early as February 1941, the Soviet Ambassador in Berlin, Vladimir Dekanozov, reported to Foreign Minister Molotov on what appeared to be German preparations for war. Molotov, who had negotiated the Non-

Aggression Pact with Germany in August 1939, played down the threat. Consequently, Dekanozov's fears were not expressed directly to Stalin, a fact which, given the intensely paranoid and suspicious atmosphere within the Soviet establishment, should not come as a great surprise. The Russophile German Ambassador in Moscow, Friedrich Werner Graf von der Schulenburg, informed Dekanozov in May of Hitler's concrete plans to invade the Soviet Union. This time the information was passed via Molotov to Stalin, who merely commented: 'We shall consider that disinformation has now reached the level of ambassadors.'[34]

In response to the advanced German military build-up for an attack, General Georgi Zhukov, the Chief of the Soviet General Staff, and Marshal Semyon Timoshenko, the then People's Commissar for Defence, drew up their own offensive plan in mid-May 1941, in which they proposed a preemptive strike against the Wehrmacht. When it was presented to Stalin, however, the Soviet dictator, seeking to avoid any provocation of Hitler, strictly prohibited the implementation of the plan.[35] In mid-June, the new People's Commissar for State Defence of the USSR, V.N. Merkulov, sent a report to Stalin in which a source at the German Aviation Headquarters verified that the final preparations for an attack had been made. Across the front of the report Stalin scribbled: 'Comrade Merkulov, you can send your "source" from the staff of the German air force to his fucking mother. This is not a "source", but disinformation.'[36] Two days before the invasion, the Commissar for Foreign Trade, Anastas Mikoyan, received information from the chief of the port of Riga that all twenty-five German merchant ships in the harbour were preparing to sail on 21 June, regardless of whether they had loaded or unloaded their cargoes. He told Stalin that this highly unusual action could only be preparation for war. Stalin replied that, since Hitler would regard detaining the ships as an act of provocation, they should be allowed to put to sea.

Massive troop concentrations and ominously regular overhead flights by the Luftwaffe were dismissed as attempts by Hitler to induce Stalin to make further concessions to his German 'allies'. On 21 June, Ambassador Dekanozov sought out Lavrenti Beria, the Head of the NKVD (People's Commissariat for Internal Affairs), the Soviet security police, to inform him that an attack would commence the next day. Beria assured Stalin that the ambassador would be called to account for 'bombarding' them with disinformation! On the same day, Beria dismissed a report from the head of military intelligence on the force Germany had massed on the frontier with the comment: 'My people and I, Iosif Vissarionovich, firmly remember your wise prediction: Hitler will not attack us in 1941.'[37] Such responses from the Soviet Union's most senior political leaders to the mounting and imminent threat from the west were negligent in the extreme.

As General Thomas later remarked, the Soviets continued making their deliveries to Germany as scheduled right up until the moment of attack.[38] The last Soviet grain trains crossed the western border of the USSR during the night of 21/22 June 1941, passing as they went German troops in the process of launching their surprise attack in the other direction.[39] As can be seen, not only was there no intention whatsoever on the part of Stalin to attack Germany, but the Soviet leader indeed did everything he possibly could to maintain good relations and curry favour with the USSR's most powerful western neighbour – although it should be kept in mind that Germany had only become one of its western neighbours as a result of Poland being carved up between that nation and the Soviet Union in September 1939. Nevertheless, even Colonel-General Halder, along with other senior officers, acknowledged that the Soviets would do anything to avoid a war with Germany, even to the point of making territorial concessions, and that an offensive on the part of the Red Army was highly unlikely.[40] Any talk of a 'preventive war', now or then, thus ignores the facts completely.[41]

Thomas's Study of Mid-February 1941

On 20 February 1941, Field Marshal Keitel presented Hitler with a memorandum (dated 13 February) from General Thomas entitled: 'The Military-Economic Consequences of an Operation in the East'.[42] A second copy was sent to Reichsmarschall Göring.[43] Additional copies were also intended for Keitel, the chiefs of the army, Luftwaffe and navy general staffs, Thomas himself and his colleague Colonel Jansen.[44] The tone of the paper was very different from the memorandum produced four months earlier by Gebhardt von Walther, and indeed from the stance hitherto held by Thomas himself. Beginning with an examination of agricultural productivity in the European part of the Soviet Union, the report identified the Ukraine and the Volga region as the two areas disposing of large grain surpluses. Indeed, 90 per cent of the deliveries made to Germany in 1940 had come from central Ukraine. Northern and north-western Russia were unmistakably 'shortage territories' (*Mangelgebiete*), whilst an average harvest in central Russia, despite the large yields, barely sufficed for the provisioning of what was, by comparison, a dense population.[45] Retaining the collective farms, argued Thomas, would make it easier to exploit the land. Hasty alterations to the agricultural system, on the other hand, would lead to serious disruption.[46] Some credence must be lent to this claim, given that, of 49.3 million Soviets who worked in agriculture in 1940, a massive forty-seven million (over 95 per cent) were working in collective farms.[47]

In perhaps the most important section of the paper, Thomas then suggested that the German grain deficit could be offset at the expense of the Soviet population.

> If it appears uncertain as to whether M.T.S. [Machine and Tractor Stations] and supplies can be protected from destruction in large amounts, if, moreover, as a result of the effects of war, a harvest of 70% at the most can be expected, it must be considered that the Russian is accustomed to adapting his needs to poor harvests and that with a population of 160 million, even a *small*

reduction of the consumption per head would free up considerable quantities of grain.

Under these circumstances, it could be possible to meet the German *shortfall* for 1941 and 1942.[48]

Here, Thomas was following the lead of Backe and his colleagues in the RMEL and the Reich Food Estate in transforming a negative state of affairs into (an opportunity for) something 'positive' – at least in their eyes – by manipulating the parameters. Thomas then went on to point out, though without commenting on the obvious implications of his statement, that, as those products most important to Germany were in the main to be found in regions bordering the Baltic or Black Seas or the Arctic Ocean, transporting them back to Germany would probably prove to be easier than provisioning the newly occupied territories themselves.[49]

There were, however, also words of caution. A 'significant improvement' of the provisioning of Germany and German-occupied Europe with grain could probably only be achieved following a rebuilding of Soviet agriculture and the securing of fuel requirements, so vital to Soviet agriculture. An improvement of Germany's meat supply – of particular relevance at the time, given the forthcoming reduction in meat rations – was, 'with certainty', not to be expected.[50] Thomas concluded that the first months could witness a relief for Germany on both the food front and the raw materials front, provided that the destruction of supplies could be avoided, the transport issue solved and the mineral oil region of the Caucasus – provider of 89 per cent of the USSR's mineral oil – obtained intact. Although lying at the furthest extreme of the territory which the German leadership expected to conquer, the importance of occupying the oil-rich region around Baku had been stressed by Hitler on 31 July 1940, by the Army General Staff on 10 August and now by General Thomas in mid-February 1941. Indeed, Thomas deemed the Caucasus to be 'indispensable' for the exploitation of the occupied Soviet territories. In the event of a longer-lasting war, the winning over of the Soviet population 'in all territories' to cooperation with the invaders would be a necessary prerequisite to providing 'effective relief' for Germany.[51] This solitary recommendation of humane treatment of the native population, albeit for selfish purposes and only in the event of a longer-lasting campaign, was lost among the calculations and proposals for the ruthless exploitation of Soviet resources. The notion of winning over the Soviet population would find no place in Nazi Germany's Hungerpolitik.

Whether Thomas's report actually gave 'a new direction' to the preparations for the attack on the USSR, as has been argued,[52] is, for two reasons, questionable. First, whilst corresponding to Hitler's expectations and, in part, validating the Hitlerian view that the confiscation of the Soviet Union's extensive resources would be a massive boost for Germany, the contents of the memorandum did not go significantly further. Secondly, and perhaps more importantly, the ideas expressed by Thomas had already been aired the previous month by Staatssekretär Backe, and indeed in presentations to both Göring and Hitler. Given that Thomas met with Backe just two weeks before producing his study, on which occasion Backe, having recently presented his ideas to Hitler on the reduction of food supplies for the Soviet population, would undoubtedly have expounded these ideas, it seems particularly likely that significant aspects of Thomas's study can be traced back to Backe.[53] Indeed, Thomas recommended at the end of January that his staff collaborate with Backe, his colleague on the General Council for the Four-Year Plan.[54]

Nevertheless, the Nazi leadership obviously felt that Thomas had proved his commitment to the forthcoming war and its goals, and rewarded him accordingly. A discussion between General Thomas and Reichsmarschall Göring took place on 26 February, at the outset of which Thomas now presented his paper personally to Göring, who praised it. Göring himself had already received Hitler's 'approval' for his assumption of control over the entire economic administration in the Soviet territories. During the course of their discussion, Göring transferred 'the preparation for the entire administration' of the economic organization in the East to Thomas, emphasizing that the latter would have a 'completely free hand'. The 'exploitation of the food sector', intended at this point in time to be separate to the economic organization, would, hardly surprisingly, be taken over by Staatssekretär Backe.[55]

Both Thomas and Göring were of the opinion that the mineral oil territory of Baku on the Caspian Sea must at all costs be occupied – an occupation of the Ukraine on its own would be of 'no value'. It appears that Göring, unlike Hitler, was willing to listen to those concerns voiced by Thomas, among them the observation that the operation could only be supplied with vehicle fuel for two months following the invasion. Göring responded by saying that he would ask the Romanian head of government, General Ion Antonescu, to expand Romanian oil capacity more rapidly.[56] A meeting between Göring and Antonescu took place in Vienna on 5 March 1941 and Göring indeed opened the discussion by requesting Antonescu to assist in raising Romanian oil production as far as possible. Antonescu declared himself ready to do everything in his powers to increase the production of Romanian oil.[57] Göring, voicing his own concerns, remarked to Thomas on 26 February on 'the dangers of the whole operation', which as he saw it threatened in the form of a failure of the necessary supply organization. He added that he was always urging Hitler of the importance of increasing the size of the supply organization whilst at the same time reducing the number of divisions to be employed. Only a portion of these divisions would in any case see real action, argued the Reichsmarschall.[58]

Setting Up an Economic Organization

Two days after his meeting with Göring on 26 February 1941, Thomas informed members of his staff that Göring had instructed him, in order to facilitate the implementation of the anticipated economic tasks, to produce 'an extended organizational draft' for an organization which would 'support and expand the measures of the Four-Year Plan'. The main tasks of this military-economic body, which would operate independently of both military and civil administrations in the occupied Soviet territories, were the 'seizure of raw materials' and the 'takeover of all important concerns'. Its units were to accompany the military advance directly behind the front line in order to avoid the destruction of supplies and to secure the 'evacuation' of important goods. They would also be required to administer the occupied industrial districts and evaluate the 'economic districts' contained therein. The organization would deal with everything which concerned the war economy.[59] For the time being, it would carry the codename 'Oldenburg'.

On 19 March 1941, three weeks after their 26 February meeting, Thomas presented the Wi Rü Amt's proposals for a military-economic organization to Göring, who declared himself 'fully in agreement'.[60] The establishment of this organization, which became the Economic Staff East (*Wirtschaftsstab Ost*, Wi Stab Ost) and first met as such on 9 June 1941,[61] was the most concrete consequence of Thomas's February 1941 appointment. In actual fact, despite the relatively tame description of its tasks in the notes to Thomas's discussion of 28 February with members of his staff (i.e., the 'seizure of raw materials' and the 'takeover of all important concerns'), the twofold purpose of the Wi Stab Ost consisted of ensuring the immediate provisioning of the German army from the land and the supplying of the German war economy with as many resources as possible out of the occupied Soviet territories. In his 1944/45 contribution to the unfinished 'History of the Economic Staff East', Major-General Hans Nagel listed the five main priorities of this organization. At the top of the list was: 'Easing of the German food situation through comprehensive provisioning of the troops from the land and evacuation of all surpluses to the Reich for the sustenance of the German population (grain, meat, oil crops).'[62] Thus, the Economic Staff East was nothing other than a gigantic organization for plundering the Soviet Union.[63]

Although the Wi Stab Ost would be responsible for the 'takeover of all important concerns', the aim in the occupied Soviet territories would not be to resurrect the economic infrastructure there as soon as possible. Instead, the economic organization would set itself priorities, with the emphasis being laid on those products which were of crucial importance to the German war economy: grain, oil crops, mineral oil and light metals.[64] The most important single area would be food production and anything related to it, such as equipment or installations required for the manufacture of agricultural tractors. The selection of which plants were to be restored depended to a large extent on the conditions found by the Germans in the

Soviet territories, particularly following the devastation which would inevitably be brought about by the military advance. Hence, the plants were to be investigated first and the decision as to whether or not to restore them made afterwards.[65] This general outlook was no doubt influenced by Hitler's fundamental aversion to the reconstruction or even the maintenance of Soviet manufacturing and processing capacity. Following the expected decisive German victory in the East, it was intended that Soviet industry would be neglected and that the occupied eastern territories would function merely as a vast pool of material, in particular agricultural, and human resources, as is discussed in more detail later in the study. Herein lay something of a contradiction, as the existing Soviet industrial infrastructure could clearly not be completely neglected if raw materials and foodstuffs were to be transported to Germany on a long-term basis.[66]

The first head of the future Wi Stab Ost, whose immediate superior was General Thomas, was the Luftwaffe general Dr Wilhelm Schubert, who assumed the leadership of the Planning Staff Oldenburg (*Arbeitsstab Oldenburg*) on 25 March 1941.[67] This selection presumably had much to do with his knowledge of Russia, where he had spent many years, several of them indeed in the capacity of military attaché to the German embassy in Moscow after the First World War.[68] The decision also, no doubt, was influenced by his direct link, as a senior Luftwaffe officer, to Reichsmarschall Göring. The Wi Stab Ost was directly subordinated to the Economic Command Staff East (*Wirtschaftsführungsstab Ost*, Wi Fü Stab Ost). This small management committee, in an effort to coordinate the entire German economy in the same hands, was headed by Göring in his capacity as Plenipotentiary for the Four-Year Plan and directed on his behalf by Staatssekretär Körner. The committee was under the overall operational control of General Thomas, through whom Göring's instructions and orders for Lieutenant-General Schubert were issued.[69] The Wi Fü Stab Ost would be responsible for the 'unified leadership of the economic administration' not only in the operations area but also in the areas of political administration which were later to be set up.[70] Although several members of the military were at the summit of the economic organization, the specialists and decision-makers within the organization itself were experts from the various economics-driven ministries and other central offices.[71] For example, the men who made up the Wi Fü Stab Ost alongside Göring, Körner and Thomas were Herbert Backe (Reich Ministry for Food and Agriculture), Hermann von Hanneken (Reich Economics Ministry) and Friedrich Alpers (Reich Forestry Office).[72] With the exception of Hanneken, all the men named also sat on the General Council for the Four-Year Plan.

The proposed structure of the economic organization in the East had been determined by 8 May 1941, when General Thomas, on behalf of the Chief of the OKW, issued an order detailing its organization, deployment and tasks.[73] Below Göring, the Economic Command Staff East and the Economic Staff East were the five Economic Inspections (*Wirtschaftsinspektionen*, Wi

In), which would be directly responsible for the entire economic operation in all territories, and below them the twenty-three Economic Commands (*Wirtschaftskommandos*, Wi Ko), which would deal with the on-the-spot, practical execution of all economic tasks. In the area of the Economic Commands, twelve branch offices were to be distributed among important locations.[74] From the Economic Staff East down to the Economic Commands, each of these bodies was divided into three large groups. Responsibility for the entire commercial economy, including raw materials, forestry, finance, property and trade, lay in the hands of Group W, which was headed by Ministerialdirektor Dr Gustav Schlotterer from the Reich Ministry for Economics. Group M was responsible for armaments, the requirements of the troops and the transport of economic goods, whilst Group La, led by Ministerialdirektor Dr Hans-Joachim Riecke from the RMEL, dealt with all questions of food and agriculture.[75] The number of people comprising the entire economic organization of the Wehrmacht for the Soviet area would initially stand at 6,845, excluding several thousand agricultural, industrial and commercial specialists. Of this number, 428 made up the Economic Staff East, 1,750 the five Economic Inspections and 2,530 the twenty-three Economic Commands.[76]

Although it had initially been intended that the agricultural sector would be separate from the economic organization under Thomas's control, Thomas had managed in mid-March 1941 to obtain Backe's agreement to its incorporation.[77] This is unlikely to have limited Backe's own room for manoeuvre, given his standing with Hitler and Göring, and especially in light of Thomas being more or less ousted from his leading role on the Economic Command Staff East by mid-May 1941. This can be seen in the discrepancy between a draft of a letter from Göring to the Army Commander-in-Chief, Field Marshal von Brauchitsch, dated 29 April and the final version of the letter, sent out sometime during the first two weeks in May. The draft has Thomas in charge of the staff, whilst according to the final version he is merely one, 'among others', of those belonging to the staff.[78]

Thomas's positive assessment of the potential gains to be made from a military campaign against the Soviet Union was, like his original misgivings, based on economic factors. By the time he came to write his study of 13 February 1941, the options available to him had been increased by the radical nature of the proposals being made by Backe and his colleagues in the Reich Ministry for Food and Agriculture and the Reich Food Estate. At the time of the First World War, Russia had regularly produced considerable surpluses of foodstuffs, sometimes as much as eleven million tons of grain per year, which it then exported.[79] In the intervening twenty-five years, however, industrialization had led to increased urbanization and the Soviet population, indeed exclusively the urban population, had grown by over thirty million. As a result, expected grain surpluses were limited to one or two million tons.[80] Thus, the conditions facing the Wehrmacht in 1941 were very different to those which had confronted Kaiser Wilhelm II's occupation army in 1918, at a time when duty dictated the securing of the requirements of the native population before provisioning oneself beyond the immediate needs of the occupying forces.

Despite the altered agricultural situation in the East, the Nazi economic planners were not only giving the proposed invasion the rubber stamp, but indeed with an entirely different order of priorities for the allocation of resources to that followed by the German army in 1918 (1. occupying army, 2. civilian population, 3. Germany). The Soviet population would no longer feature on the list of priorities.[81] Three months into the military campaign, at a meeting to discuss how the territories occupied by Germany could be exploited more effectively, the order of priorities was stated explicitly. In first place were the fighting troops, followed by those troops stationed in enemy territory and then those based in the Reich. After that came the German civilian population and 'only then' the inhabitants of the occupied territories.[82]

With significant grain surpluses no longer to be expected, however, any proposals advocating the economic exploitation of the Soviet Union should have been dismissed on the grounds of common sense.[83] Nevertheless, the approach of the economic specialists to this problem was not to conclude that available Soviet resources were not sufficient to sustain Germany and its troops, and therefore to argue on this basis against an invasion, but rather to crank the demands up a notch by declaring food supplies actually required for the nourishment of the Soviet population fair game and advocating the reduction of Soviet consumption. This had the inevitable consequence of effectively condemning large portions of the Soviet population to starvation. By incorporating these designs into his own view of the situation, General Thomas thus assented to Backe's 'starvation strategy'.

Almost two years after the war against the Soviet Union began, the Consultant for Eastern Questions in the Four-Year Plan organization, Lieutenant Dr Friedrich Richter, sent a letter from the front in which he began by commenting on some of the reasons for launching the campaign in June 1941, before moving on to German occupation policy during the subsequent two years:

> Economic interests and the predicament, as a result of the isolation of Europe, of having to obtain yet more grain, oil crops and oil from our own sphere of influence also brought about for many an affirmation of the campaign on economic grounds, although experts at the time pointed out that Russia already in peacetime could only fulfil German treaty demands at the greatest cost to itself, much less so after disruption of the transport routes and economic life there. [Oberregierungsrat Dr Otto] Donner and my house [i.e., the VJPB] also pointed at the time to this expected deterioration. The Backesian thesis [*Backesche These*] developed out of this situation[:] one must separate the western and southern Russian territories, as main producers, from their consumer territories in central Russia and incorporate them once more into the European supply zone; a real possibility if one is militarily in a position to keep the central Russians from their fields for a long period of time and if one wins over the inhabitants of the occupied territory.[84]

By the time Lieutenant Richter wrote this, in May 1943, there had been attempts, albeit comparatively limited ones, to win over parts of the Soviet population, particularly Ukrainian nationalists, in response to the altered war situation. In mid-1941, however, few were giving any thought as to how they might win over the inhabitants of the occupied territory. Thus, this prerequisite for the successful implementation of the proposals of the economic planners did not exist. More important for the purposes of this study, however, is the fact that Lieutenant Richter's letter confirms that German officials were by no means in unison as to the advisability of an eastern campaign, that there was indeed a fair amount of opposition to such an undertaking from economic experts on economic grounds, and that Backe's proposals provided at least a potential 'solution' to the misgivings of those around him. With Backe and Thomas working in tandem, the 'Backesian thesis' described by Lieutenant Richter would be taken to its extreme.

Notes

1. Hillgruber, *Hitlers Strategie*, p. 365, fn. 65.
2. Schramm (ed.), *KTB des OKW*, I, pp. 253–258, entry for 9 January 1941, here p. 258: 'Wenn diese Operation durchgeführt würde, werde Europa den Atem anhalten.' Foreign Minister Joachim von Ribbentrop was also present.
3. BA, R 3601/3371, fo. 16; IfZ, ED 180/5, Terminkalender Hermann Göring, fo. 7, entry for 13 January 1941.
4. On Backe's appointment to the Office of the Four-Year Plan see Anna Bramwell, *Blood and Soil: Richard Walther Darré and Hitler's 'Green Party'* (The Kensal Press, Abbotsbrook, Bucks., 1985), pp. 110–113.
5. See BA, R3601/3371, fo. 8, letter from Darré to *Ministerialdirektor* Dr Alfons Moritz, 12 February 1941.
6. Ibid., fos. 10–11, 'Rundschreiben', 13 January 1941, here fo. 10.
7. Ibid., fos. 6–7, letter from Moritz to Darré, 13 February 1941.
8. Ibid., fo. 12, letter from Darré to the administrative head of the Reich Food Estate, Ministerialdirektor Rudolf Harmening, 11 February 1941.
9. See ibid., fo. 5, letter from Darré to Moritz, 13 February 1941.
10. BA, R 16/1299, fo. 81, Institut für Wehrwirtschaftliche Forschung, Beiträge zur Wehrwirtschaft: V, 'Der deutsche Ernährungshaushalt und seine wehrwirtschaftliche Unabhängigmachung', 118 pages, edited on behalf of the institute by Dr Hans Weiss, Berlin, 1937.
11. *TBJG*, I/9 (1998), pp. 283–284, entry for 1 May 1941: 'Gestern: ... Backe trägt mir den Stand unserer Ernährung vor. Fleisch muß ab 2. Juni um 100 gr pro Woche gekürzt werden. Die Wehrmacht ist zu gut gestellt und verzehrt zu viel. Das Dreifache pro Kopf gegenüber der Zivilbevölkerung. ... Ich stehe nun vor der Frage, wie ich es meinem Kinde sagen soll. Ich werde einen möglichst günstigen Moment abpassen, und dann heraus mit der Meldung. Die Argumente, die ich dafür anführen kann, sind überzeugend. Backe beherrscht übrigens sein Ressort meisterhaft. Bei ihm wird getan, was überhaupt nur möglich ist.' See also Halder, *KTB*, II, p. 408, entry for 12 May 1941.
12. The SD reports are compiled in Heinz Boberach (ed.), *Meldungen aus dem Reich 1938–1945: Die geheimen Lageberichte des Sicherheitsdienstes der SS*, 17 vols (Pawlak Verlag, Herrsching, 1984). See also Cecil, *Hitler's Decision to Invade Russia*, p. 141.

13. Boberach (ed.), *Meldungen*, vol. 5, nos. 110, 111, 128, 131, 136 and 139, pp. 1429–1431, 1439–1440, 1630, 1664, 1717 and 1745; vol. 6, nos. 143, 147 and 150, pp. 1796–1798, 1846 and 1873–1874. For the poor state of the domestic mood less than four weeks prior to 'Barbarossa', see Halder, *KTB*, II, p. 432, entry for 28 May 1941.
14. Boberach (ed.), *Meldungen*, vol. 6, no. 143, pp. 1796–1798, here p. 1796: 'In den Meldungen der letzten Zeit ist übereinstimmend hervorgehoben worden, daß die Bevölkerung gegenwärtig sich sehr stark mit der Frage der Lebensmittelversorgung beschäftigt und die in den letzten Wochen und Monaten eingetretenen Veränderungen in den Lebensmittelzuteilungen zum Teil mit einer gewissen Besorgnis verfolgt. Ausgangspunkt für diese Besorgnisse seien die in der letzten Zeit zutage getretenen Schwierigkeiten in der *Fleisch- und Fettzuteilung*, die *Kürzung der Brotrationen*, die unzulängliche Belieferung der Märkte mit *Gemüse und Obst*, wie auch der nahezu völlige Ausfall von *Wild, Geflügel und Fischanlieferungen*. Wie es in den Berichten weiter heißt, werde auch die auf diesen Warengebieten zu beobachtende Preisentwicklung mit wachsender Unruhe verfolgt. Es werde nicht nur darüber geklagt, daß bei verschiedenen Lebensmitteln direkte Preiserhöhungen eingetreten seien, sondern vornehmlich darüber, daß die bereits seit längerer Zeit festzustellende Tendenz der Qualitätsverschlechterung bei gleich bleibenden Preisen anhalte.'
15. See BA-MA, RW 19/164, fo. 126, 'Vortrag Hauptmann Emmerich beim Amtschef', 30 January 1941.
16. See IfZ, ED 180/5, Terminkalender Hermann Göring, fo. 15, entry for 29 January 1941. According to Göring's appointments diary, this was the only occasion in January on which Göring presided over a meeting of all his senior economic advisers including Backe.
17. BA, 99 US 7/1074, fo. 69, post-war comments of Paul Körner, 30 July 1948.
18. BA-MA, RW 19/164, fo. 106, war diary of the Wi Rü Amt, entry for 21 January 1941.
19. Halder, *KTB*, II, p. 261, entry for 28 January 1941.
20. Hillgruber, *Hitlers Strategie*, p. 370.
21. BA-MA, RW 19/164, fo. 111, 'Vortrag Amtschef bei GFM Keitel', 22 January 1941.
22. Müller, 'Ausbeutungskrieg', p. 169.
23. IfZ, ED 180/5, Terminkalender Hermann Göring, fo. 15, entry for 29 January 1941. Two days earlier, Thomas had met for two hours with Göring, Körner, Neumann, Hanneken and Chief of the Ministerial Office in the Reich Aviation Ministry Karl Bodenschatz to discuss raw materials; IfZ, ED 180/5, Terminkalender Hermann Göring, fo. 14, entry for 27 January 1941.
24. BA-MA, RW 19/185, fos. 175–176, 'Aktennotiz', 8 February 1941. See also Schramm (ed.), *KTB des OKW*, I, pp. 312–313 and 316–317, entries for 8 and 11 February 1941.
25. For this concept see Kershaw, *Hitler 1889–1936*, chap. 13, pp. 527–591, esp. pp. 529–531.
26. BA-MA, RW 19/164, fo. 150, 'Vortrag Obstlt. Matzky, Major Knapp, Hptm. Emmerich beim Amtschef', 12 February 1941; also in BA-MA, WF-01/15885, fo. 15.
27. On this, with examples from the historiography, see Gerlach, *Kalkulierte Morde*, pp. 68–71.
28. BAK, N 1094/II 20, Mappe III, 25 and 26 June 1941, letters from Backe to Darré; BAK, N 1094/II 20, Mappe II, 27 June 1941, letter from Darré to Göring; BAK, N 1094/II 20, Mappe II, 22 July 1941, letter from Darré to Ministerialdirektor Dr Gritzbach. See also BAK, N 1094/I 65a, fo. 123, entry in Darré's diary for 5 March 1941.
29. BAK, N 1094/II 20, Mappe III, 26 June 1941, letter from Backe to Darré.
30. Lothar Kettenacker, 'Großbritannien und der deutsche Angriff auf die Sowjetunion', in Wegner (ed.), *Zwei Wege nach Moskau*, pp. 605–619, here p. 611.
31. Jürgen Förster, 'Hitlers Entscheidung für den Krieg gegen die Sowjetunion', in Boog et al., *Der Angriff auf die Sowjetunion*, pp. 27–68, here p. 61. See also PAAA, Handakten Etzdorf, Vertrauliche Aufzeichnungen des Vertreters des Auswärtigen Amts beim OKH, Nr. 1, R 27334, fo. 337439, 'Aussenpolitische Nachrichten, mitgeteilt durch Rittmeister v. Etzdorf', 16 July 1940.
32. *ADAP*, Serie D: *1937–1941*, vol. 11/2, pp. 788–789, doc. 560, here p. 788.

33. See Kettenacker, 'Großbritannien', p. 611.
34. Michael Burleigh, '"See you again in Siberia": the German–Soviet war and other tragedies', in Michael Burleigh (ed.), *Ethics and Extermination: Reflections on Nazi Genocide* (Cambridge University Press, Cambridge, 1997), pp. 37–110, here pp. 37–38.
35. Gerd R. Ueberschär, 'Hitlers Überfall auf die Sowjetunion 1941 und Stalins Absichten: Die Bewertung in der deutschen Geschichtsschreibung und die neuere "Präventivkriegsthese"', in Ueberschär and Bezymenskij (eds), *Der deutsche Angriff auf die Sowjetunion 1941*, pp. 48–69, here p. 57.
36. Michael Burleigh, *The Third Reich: A New History* (Pan Books, London, 2001), p. 486.
37. Ibid., pp. 486–487. Stalin was born Iosif Vissarionovich Dzhugashvili. By 1912 he had adopted the name Stalin ('of steel').
38. *IMG*, vol. 30, p. 272, doc. 2353-PS.
39. Herbst, *Das nationalsozialistische Deutschland*, p. 351.
40. Halder, *KTB*, II, p. 396, entry for 5 May 1941; Klaus Gerbet (ed.), *Generalfeldmarschall Fedor von Bock: The War Diary 1939–1945* (Schiffer, Atglen, PA, 1996), p. 205, entry for 27 March 1941; Moritz (ed.), *Fall Barbarossa*, doc. 32, p. 128. See also Hill (ed.), *Die Weizsäcker-Papiere*, p. 232, notes from 16 January 1941.
41. For an excellent evaluation and refutation of the 'preventive war' theory and its principal proponents – Viktor Suvorov (real name: Vladimir Rezun), Joachim Hoffmann and Ernst Topitsch – see Ueberschär, 'Hitlers Überfall auf die Sowjetunion 1941 und Stalins Absichten'. See also Wolfram Wette, 'Die NS-Propagandathese vom angeblichen Präventivkriegscharakter des Überfalls' in the same volume, pp. 38–47. It is remarkable that Hoffmann was in fact one of the contributors to volume four of *Das Deutsche Reich und der Zweite Weltkrieg*, produced by the Militärgeschichtliches Forschungsamt.
42. For the full text of the memorandum, see Thomas, *Geschichte*, pp. 515–532, 'Die Wehrwirtschaftlichen Auswirkungen einer Operation im Osten'. For the date of the handover see BA-MA, RW 19/164, fo. 171, 'Vortrag Hpt. Emmerich beim Amtschef', 19 February 1941.
43. BA-MA, RW 19/164, fo. 171.
44. Ibid., fos. 150–151.
45. Thomas, *Geschichte*, pp. 515–516.
46. Ibid., p. 517.
47. Mark Harrison, *Accounting for War: Soviet Production, Employment, and the Defence Burden, 1940–1945* (Cambridge University Press, Cambridge, 1996), pp. 98 and 100.
48. Thomas, *Geschichte*, p. 517: 'Wenn es auch ungewiß erscheint, ob es gelingt, M.T.S. und Vorräte in großem Umfange vor der Vernichtung zu bewahren, wenn außerdem infolge der Einwirkungen eines Krieges im Höchstfalle eine 70%ige Ernte erwartet werden kann, so muß man doch berücksichtigen, daß der Russe gewöhnt ist, seinen Verbrauch schlechten Ernten anzupassen, und daß bei einer Bevölkerung von 160 Mill. auch eine *kleine Senkung* des je Kopf-Verbrauchs erhebliche Getreidemengen freimacht. Unter diesen Voraussetzungen könnte es möglich sein, den deutschen *Zuschußbedarf* für 1941 und 1942 zu decken.'
49. Ibid., p. 524.
50. Ibid., pp. 517–518.
51. Ibid., pp. 531–532.
52. By Rolf-Dieter Müller in Müller, 'Ausbeutungskrieg', p. 169. For a contrasting view see Roland Peter, 'General der Infanterie Georg Thomas', in Gerd R. Ueberschär (ed.), *Hitlers militärische Elite, Bd. 1: Von den Anfängen des Regimes bis Kriegsbeginn* (Primus Verlag, Darmstadt, 1998), pp. 248–257, here p. 253. Peter attaches too much importance, however, to Thomas's call for collaboration with the Soviet population.
53. Müller himself points out the likelihood that Backe influenced aspects of Thomas's study; Müller, 'Ausbeutungskrieg', p. 170.
54. See BA-MA, RW 19/164, fo. 126.
55. Ibid., fo. 180, 'Vortrag Amtschef beim Reichsmarschall', 26 February 1941; also in BA-MA, WF-01/15885, fo. 28.

56. BA-MA, RW 19/185, fos. 170–171, 'Aktennotiz über Vortrag beim Reichsmarschall am 26.2.1941', 27 February 1941.
57. *ADAP, Serie D: 1937–1941*, vol. 12/1 (Vandenhoeck & Ruprecht, Göttingen, 1969), pp. 182–187, doc. 126, here pp. 182–183 and 185.
58. BA-MA, RW 19/185, fo. 170. See also Nbg. Dok. NI 7291, 'Aktennotiz über Vortrag beim Reichsmarschall am 26.2.1941', Thomas, 27 February 1941; this complete version of Thomas's set of notes on the meeting contains an additional five points (three to seven), of which point six on page three is of particular relevance here.
59. *IMG*, vol. 27 (1948), pp. 169–171, doc. 1317–PS, 'Aktennotiz. Besprechung beim Herrn Amtschef, General der Inf. Thomas am 28.2.41', 1 March 1941; BA-MA, RW 19/164, fo. 187, 'Besprechung Amtschef mit Chef Ro, Oberstlt. Witte, Oberstlt. Matzky, Oberstlt. Lutter, Major v. Gusovius, Major v. Payr, Major Huch, Hptm. Hamann über W Wi-Organisation bei den Ostoperationen', 28 February 1941; also in BA-MA, WF-01/15885, fo. 30.
60. BA-MA, RW 19/164, fo. 228, 'Vortrag bei Reichsmarschall Göring am 19.3.41', 20 March 1941; also in BA-MA, RW 19/185, fo. 19.
61. Thomas, *Geschichte*, p. 258. On the *Wirtschaftsstab Ost*, see above all Müller (ed.), *Abschlußbericht des Wirtschaftsstabes Ost*, pp. 1–18, and Gerlach, *Kalkulierte Morde*, pp. 142–150.
62. Müller (ed.), *Abschlußbericht des Wirtschaftsstabes Ost*, pp. 24–25: 'Entlastung der deutschen Ernährungsbilanz durch umfassende Truppenverpflegung aus dem Lande und Abtransport aller Überschüsse ins Reich zur Versorgung der deutschen Bevölkerung (Getreide, Fleisch, Ölsaaten).'
63. Armin Nolzen, '"Verbrannte Erde": Der Rückzug der Wehrmacht aus den eroberten Gebieten, 1941/42–1944/45', p. 16; paper presented at the *Jahrestagung 2002 des Arbeitskreises Militärgeschichte e.V.* in Augsburg, 1–3 November 2002. I am grateful to Armin Nolzen for providing me with a copy of this unpublished paper. It is soon to appear in Günther Kronenbitter, Markus Pöhlmann and Dierk Walter (eds), *Besatzung: Funktion und Gestalt militärischer Fremdherrschaft von der Antike bis zum 20. Jahrhundert* (Ferdinand Schöningh, Paderborn, 2006) under the title '"Verbrannte Erde": Die Rückzüge der Wehrmacht in den besetzten sowjetischen Gebieten, 1941/42–1944/45'.
64. BA, R 26 I/13, fo. 1, order from Göring to various ministers, 27 July 1941. See also *IMG*, vol. 31 (1948), p. 84, doc. 2718–PS, 'Aktennotiz über Ergebnis der heutigen Besprechung mit den Staatssekretären über Barbarossa', 2 May 1941.
65. BA, 99 US 7/1110, fols. 175–176, post-war comments of Hans Nagel, 8 September 1948. Nagel's comments are supported by the contents of the official handbook for the economic administration of the occupied eastern territories; BA, R 26 IV/33a, 'Richtlinien für die Führung der Wirtschaft in den neubesetzten Ostgebieten (Grüne Mappe)', Teil I (2. Auflage), July 1941, pp. 3–5.
66. See Müller, 'Raubkrieg', p. 183.
67. Müller (ed.), *Abschlußbericht des Wirtschaftsstabes Ost*, p. 43.
68. Ibid., pp. 10–11.
69. Ibid., p. 412. See also BA, 99 US 7/1112, fo. 17, post-war comments of Hans Nagel, 9 September 1948.
70. BA, R 26 IV/33a, p. 5.
71. Müller (ed.), *Abschlußbericht des Wirtschaftsstabes Ost*, p. 30. See also Gerlach, *Kalkulierte Morde*, p. 145.
72. BA-MA, RW 19/164, fo. 228. Both Dietrich Eichholtz and Norbert Müller add the name of Friedrich Syrup (Reich Labour Ministry) to this short list; Eichholtz, *Geschichte der deutschen Kriegswirtschaft*, I, p. 234, fn. 127; *Europa unterm Hakenkreuz. Die Okkupationspolitik des deutschen Faschismus (1938–1945), Band 5: Die faschistische Okkupationspolitik in den zeitweilig besetzten Gebieten der Sowjetunion (1941–1944)* (Deutscher Verlag der Wissenschaften, Berlin, 1991), document selection and introduction by Norbert Müller, p. 35, fn. 23. See also BA, R 3901/20136, fo. 12, 24 November 1941, where Erich Neumann (Office of the Four-Year Plan) and Friedrich Landfried (Reich

Economics Ministry) are listed as members of the Wi Fü Stab Ost, whereas both Alpers and Syrup are absent.
73. For the text of the order, see Müller (ed.), *Abschlußbericht des Wirtschaftsstabes Ost*, pp. 412–417, 'OKW/Wi Rü Amt, Befehl über Gliederung, Einsatz und Aufgaben der Wi Org Ost vom 8.5.1941'.
74. Müller (ed.), *Abschlußbericht des Wirtschaftsstabes Ost*, pp. 33–34. See also *IMG*, vol. 27, pp. 32–38, doc. 1157–PS, 'Besprechung mit den Wehrmachtteilen am Dienstag, den 29 April 1941, 10 Uhr', here p. 33.
75. *IMG*, vol. 27, pp. 33–34. See also BA, R 26 IV/33a, 'Richtlinien für die Führung der Wirtschaft in den neubesetzten Ostgebieten (Grüne Mappe)', Teil I (2. Auflage), July 1941, p. 7; BA, R 43 II/686a, fos. 55–56; Gerlach, *Kalkulierte Morde*, pp. 147–148.
76. Karl Brandt, *Management of Agriculture and Food in the German-Occupied and Other Areas of Fortress Europe: A Study in Military Government* (Stanford University Press, Stanford, CA, 1953), p. 73.
77. BA-MA, RW 19/164, fo. 213, 'Besprechung Amtschef bei Staatssekretär Backe', 12 March 1941.
78. BA-MA, RW 19/739, fo. 68, draft of a letter from Göring to Brauchitsch, 29 April 1941; BA-MA, RW 19/739, fo. 267, 'Aktenvermerk. Betr.: Wirtschaftsorganisation Barbarossa', 14 May 1941.
79. Gerlach, *Kalkulierte Morde*, p. 48.
80. Backe, *Um die Nahrungsfreiheit Europas*, p. 162.
81. Herbst, *Das nationalsozialistische Deutschland*, pp. 355–356; Theo J. Schulte, *The German Army and Nazi Policies in Occupied Russia* (Berg, Oxford, 1989), pp. 87–88; Müller, 'Raubkrieg', p. 189.
82. *IMG*, vol. 36, pp. 105–109, doc. 003–EC, 'Wirtschaftsaufzeichnungen für die Berichtszeit vom 15.8. bis 16.9.1941', 16 September 1941, Major-General Hans Nagel, here p. 107.
83. See Herbst, *Das nationalsozialistische Deutschland*, pp. 355–356.
84. BA, R 6/60a, fos. 1–4, 'Auszug aus einem Feldpostbrief von Leutnant Dr. Friedrich Richter, Referent für Ostfragen vom Vierjahresplan, vom 26.5.1943', here fo. 1: 'Wirtschaftliche Interessen und die Zwangslage, infolge der Isolierung Europas noch mehr Getreide und Ölsaaten und Öl aus dem eigenen Machtbereich zu schaffen, haben bei vielen eine auch wirtschaftliche Bejahung des Feldzuges bewirkt, obwohl Fachleute damals darauf hinwiesen, daß Rußland schon friedensmäßig nur unter schwersten eigenen Opfern die deutschen Vertragsforderungen erfüllen könne, wieviel weniger erst nach Störung der Verkehrswege und des wirtschaftlichen Kreislaufes. Auch Donner und mein Haus haben damals auf diese zu erwartende Verschlechterung hingewiesen. Aus dieser Lage hat sich die Backesche These entwickelt, man müsse die west- und südrussischen Gebiete als Haupterzeuger von ihren Abnehmergebieten im zentralen Rußland trennen und wieder in die europäische Versorgung einbauen; eine reale Möglichkeit, wenn man auf lange Zeit militärisch in der Lage ist, die zentralen Russen von ihren Äckern fernzuhalten, und wenn man die Bewohner des besetzten Gebietes für sich gewinnt.'

CHAPTER 5

PLANNING A CIVIL ADMINISTRATION

The first two months of 1941 were characterized by the development of preparations for the ruthless economic exploitation of the Soviet territories. Concerning the establishment of a civil administration to deal with political affairs in the occupied East, on the other hand, little had been undertaken. The men to whom responsibility for carrying out the political planning for the occupation would be given were, therefore, already playing catch-up in the struggle for power in the soon-to-be occupied eastern territories. They were faced with having to promote their own proposals against economic objectives which had effectively already been approved by the Reich leadership and incorporated into policy. This set of circumstances in itself indicates that the economic aims of the forthcoming campaign and occupation were given a higher priority by Germany's supreme leadership than the political aims. Only in March 1941 would concrete preparations begin to be made as to the future political shape of the occupied Soviet territories and then, towards the end of that month, as to who would be charged with the responsibility for running those territories. The man selected as the future head of the civil administration, Alfred Rosenberg, only started to play a central role in the political planning for the occupation at the beginning of April. The blueprints drawn up by Rosenberg and his staff between April and June, addressing the administrative division of the occupied regions, the selection of personnel and their function and tasks, would only be finalized after the military campaign had commenced, awaiting as they did the approval, or otherwise, of Hitler.

Envisaging a Civil Administration

Exactly when the idea was lit upon, as opposed to when concrete preparations began, for the establishment of a civil/political administration in the occupied Soviet territories is difficult to determine. On at least two occasions during the first half of February 1941, Army Quartermaster-General Eduard Wagner, the man responsible for matters of military administration in the occupied territories, discussed the establishment of a military administration in the Soviet Union with Colonel-General Halder.[1] It is clear that those at the forefront of planning for the future economic organization were already aware by the end of February, however, that a civil and not a military administration was to be set up, as shown by the minutes of a discussion between senior members of General Thomas's War Economy and Armaments Office.[2] As mentioned earlier,[3] Hitler's reference in his speech of 9 January 1941 to Germany politically dominating the former territories of the Soviet Union but not incorporating them into the Reich could constitute the first indication of what developed into the conception of Reich Commissariats, territorial units under civil administration. This remark, however, was almost certainly too vague to have been the effective starting point of proposals for a civil administration. The likeliest scenario is that the decision was gradually settled upon to entrust the occupied eastern territories to a civil and not a military administration. Supposed discussions between Hitler, Göring, Rosenberg and *Reichsführer-SS* Heinrich Himmler in Munich on 24 February[4] were probably not significant, even in the unlikely event that they in fact took place. According to his appointments diary, Göring was in any case in Berlin and not in Munich on the day in question.[5] On 3 March, Thomas – who had met with Deputy Chief of the OKW Operations Staff Major-General Walter Warlimont two days earlier[6] – and the Chief of the Raw Materials Section in the Wi Rü Amt discussed the preparations under way for the East. They recorded that there were no plans to establish a military administration. Instead, a civil administration under the control of Party men would be set up.[7]

Also on 3 March 1941, Warlimont's immediate superior, General Jodl, gave instructions as to how the 'Guidelines for Special Fields to Directive No. 21 (Case Barbarossa)' were to be altered in accordance with the wishes of Hitler, who had rejected a draft of the guidelines that same day.[8] The whole of the territory to be occupied by German forces would be dissolved into separate states with their own governments, with whom the German leadership would be able to make peace. The task of the occupying forces would be to establish 'socialist' state structures dependent on Germany. Given the difficulty of such administrative tasks, they would not – indeed, could not – be entrusted to the army, the depth of whose operations area would be restricted as far as possible. No military administration, it was foreseen, was to be set up to the rear of the operations area; the 'quick, political construction of new state structures' would instead be incumbent on civil administrators, so-called Reich Commissars (*Reichskommissare*). These Reich Commissars would be responsible for large areas, to be demarcated in accordance with national traditions. For the time being, discussions with the Staatssekretäre Dr Wilhelm Stuckart of the Interior Ministry and Backe of the Food Ministry, both of whom sat on the General

Council for the Four-Year Plan, were deemed to be 'unnecessary'. If later events are anything to go by, Stuckart was already at this point expected to be involved in subsequent consultations on the relevant decree(s) appointing the civil administrators in the occupied Soviet territories and in the allocation of officials for the civil administration. The appearance of Backe's name in the draft guidelines requires little explanation as he had already been assigned to deal with the food sector in the Soviet territories. It was probably concluded by those drafting the guidelines that discussions with Stuckart and Backe were not yet necessary for the reason that preparations for the future civil administration were not sufficiently advanced to warrant such discussions. It is likely that Hitler's desire to transfer the administration of the occupied Soviet territories as soon as possible – indeed, prior to the cessation of hostilities – over to political officials, rather than leaving it in the hands of the military, is to be accounted for by the belief that it would not be sensible to delay the implementation of the Nazi leadership's racial-ideological plans and its radical policy of economic exploitation until after the conclusion of the military campaign, but rather to implement them from day one alongside military activities.[9] Indeed, this is confirmed by the entry for 6 March 1941 in the war diary of the OKW Operations Staff, which recorded that Hitler wanted to install the political administration in the occupied eastern territories as soon as possible in order to wage simultaneously the 'battle of weapons' and the 'battle of ideologies'.[10] The use of the term 'Reich Commissar' could be interpreted as an indication of Hitler's intention to develop a close relationship between the occupied eastern territories and the Reich.[11]

The drafting of the 'Guidelines for Special Fields' was the first occasion on which either the shape of the future political administration in the Soviet Union, once in the hands of German forces, or its tasks had been so explicitly stated or indeed mentioned at all at such a senior level, and as such constituted the starting point for the formulation of the political aims of German occupation policy. In comparison with the economic preparations, which had begun several months earlier, contemplation of the future political administration of the East came relatively late in the day. Even once the planning for the political administration of the Soviet territories was finally under way, its progress was fairly slow. Although talk of Reich Commissars already took place at the beginning of March, it would be almost another two months before the post of Reich Minister for the Occupied Eastern Territories, which would eventually be bestowed on Rosenberg, was envisaged.

Now conforming to Hitler's wishes, the OKW's 'Guidelines for Special Fields' was issued on 13 March 1941.[12] In the final document it was foreseen that the newly occupied area, in accordance with the foundations set by national traditions and following the boundaries of the three army groups, would 'first of all' – suggesting either a measure of limited duration or Hitler's own uncertainty – be divided into 'North (Baltic), Centre (Belarus) and South (Ukraine)'. It was confirmed that the political administration in these areas would pass over to Reich Commissars, who would receive their instructions directly 'from the Führer'. No mention at this stage was made of any intermediate or coordinating authority. In addition to supporting the Reich Commissars in the implementation of their political tasks, the military commanders, as the supreme representatives of the Wehrmacht in these areas of civil administration, would be responsible for the 'exploitation of the land and the securing of its economic value' for the purposes of the German economy and for the provisioning of the troops. The 'unified leadership of the economic administration' in both the operations area and the areas of political administration, however, fell to Reichsmarschall Göring, who in turn had already transferred these tasks to General Thomas. In the operations area of the army, Reichsführer-SS Himmler, 'by order of the Führer', had responsibility for carrying out 'special tasks' in preparation for the transfer of this territory to the political administration.[13] As can be seen, the proposed hierarchical structure[14] in the occupied Soviet territories and, in particular, the allocation of tasks to the different delegates lacked all clarity. This clearly did not bode well for either the setting of priorities, both prior to and during the campaign and occupation, or the implementation of these tasks in practice.

The 'Guidelines for Special Fields' were particularly significant, as they listed together the most important non-military undertakings of the coming campaign and occupation: the setting up of a political administration in territory transferred from the military to the Reich Commissars, directly answerable to Hitler; the economic exploitation of the Soviet Union under the leadership of Göring and for the benefit not only of the invading troops, but of Germany itself; and the sinister 'special tasks' of Himmler and his racial warriors, the SS. These various undertakings were to commence either immediately, as in the case of the economic exploitation and the actions of the SS and police, or as soon as possible, as in the transfer of occupied territory to the political administrators. For none of the tasks, however, was a time frame specified; they were both short- and at the same time long-term activities.

Only three days after the OKW's 'Guidelines for Special Fields' were issued, however, Field Marshal von Brauchitsch and Army Quartermaster-General Wagner – who would be responsible during March and April 1941 for negotiating the regulations allowing the deployment of the Security Police and the SD in army formations – presented the draft of a set of administrative instructions for 'Barbarossa' in an attempt to persuade Hitler to appoint a military administration in the style of France or Belgium. Hitler, however, fiercely rejected this proposal, saying that he would place the administration in each case in political hands, as the army did not understand much about politics.[15] On 17 March, a day after this heated exchange, a five-and-a-half-hour discussion took place between Hitler, Colonel-General Halder and Colonel Adolf Heusinger, Chief of the Army's Operations Department. Hitler vaguely sketched the future shape of the East, though the fate of both the Ukraine and the Don Cossack people at this point in time were deemed to be 'in question'. The Caucasus, however, should later be handed over to Turkey, though 'exploited' by Germany beforehand.[16] This suggests that the civil administrations referred to four days earlier, on 13 March, would be a temporary measure before the final fate of the respective territories – in the case of the Caucasus, to be handed over to Turkey – was to be decided and fulfilled.

At the end of March 1941, Hitler delineated his thoughts on the coming campaign and the future of the eastern territories to a much wider audience. On 30 March, he addressed over 200 senior officers in the Reich Chancellery. Among those present was Halder, who recorded the key points of the speech, which lasted almost two and a half hours.[17] Hitler once again claimed that Great Britain was placing its hope in the USA and the Soviet Union. The tasks of the forthcoming campaign against the latter would be to 'smash' the Soviet armed forces and 'dissolve' the state, as had already been declared at the beginning of March. The speech reached its climax when Hitler moved on to 'colonial tasks' – the ideological aims of the campaign. It would be a struggle between two opposing ideologies; Bolshevism was criminal and an 'enormous danger for the future'. Hitler stipulated the 'annihilation of the Bolshevik commissars and the Communist intelligentsia', thus laying the foundations for the infamous Commissar Order (*Kommissarbefehl*),[18] dismissed the idea of courts martial for felonies committed by German troops,[19] and emphasized the different nature of the war in the East as compared with the war in the West.[20] This was clearly an attempt on the part of Hitler to make the military not only passive collaborators of the SS and its murderous Einsatzgruppen, as had been the case in Poland in 1939, but active participants in their gruesome activities; it would not be difficult to achieve this. The military leadership set the example and their subordinates, on the whole, followed. By this time, other senior military officers, namely those involved in the economic planning for the East, had already been completely enveloped in the nefarious preparations for the 'war of annihilation'. Hitler's address of 30 March significantly increased the likelihood of 'Barbarossa' being a 'war of annihilation' not only in terms of agricultural exploitation but also in the very nature of the military engagements. With regard to the future appearance of the occupied Soviet territories, Hitler announced that northern Russia would be handed over to Finland, a likely military ally in the forthcoming campaign, and that protectorates would be established over the Baltic States, the Ukraine and Belarus. The 'new states' would have to be 'socialist [*sic*] states', though without their own intelligentsia. Either Hitler did not deem it necessary to explain the fate of the Soviet Union's educated classes, or Halder did not deem it necessary to record it. The formation of a new intelligentsia would also have to be prevented – 'a primitive socialist intelligentsia' would suffice.

Selecting an Administrative Chief

It has been argued that during February and March 1941 Reichsmarschall Göring had cherished the desire, and indeed the expectation, that he would become head of any civil (i.e., political) administration to be formed in the occupied Soviet territories.[21] This assumption, however, appears to be based on a questionable interpretation of the sources. Göring was already aware by the second half of February at the latest that he would be in charge of the entire economic administration of the occupied Soviet territories. On 26 February, as mentioned earlier, he met with Thomas and handed over to him the responsibility for making the relevant preparations. The war diary of the Staff Section of the War Economy and Armaments Office in the OKW recorded part of the meeting as follows:

> [The] R.M. [i.e., Reichsmarschall] has received permission from the Führer that he assumes the entire administration of the territory 'Barbarossa' which is to be occupied. [The] R.M. transfers the preparation for the entire administration to the Chief of the [War Economy and Armaments] Office. ... [The] R.M. views the operation as a support for the economic provisioning, in particular also for the VJP.[22]

It is true that there is no qualification of the parameters of Göring's forthcoming function; the reference is simply to 'the entire administration'. In the context of their meeting, however, Thomas and Göring would have been perfectly well aware of exactly what they were discussing. Additionally, two days later, when Thomas met with the Chief of the Raw Materials Section in the Wi Rü Amt and other members of his staff, part of the relevant entry in the war diary read: 'Clear stipulation that the organization is not dependent on the military or the civil administration, but will probably cooperate with these.'[23] This could only have been a reference to the economic organization and the remark makes it clear that the economic, military and civil administrations were separate entities and indeed seen as such by Thomas, who had discussed the forthcoming eastern operations at length with Göring only two days previously. Even in the unlikely event that Göring was in fact in the running for the position of head of the civil administration in the East, it came to nothing. It was only at the end of March, though, that Reichsleiter Alfred Rosenberg entered the picture as the most likely candidate for the role of civil administrative chief in the occupied territories of the Soviet Union. Exactly what form his appointment would take, however, did not become entirely clear until shortly before the campaign began. Whether Rosenberg had been in Hitler's mind for a longer period of time is impossible to determine.

On 28 March 1941, Rosenberg was in Berlin, having been called back from Frankfurt am Main on 'official business'.[24] Rosenberg had intended to remain in Frankfurt at least until Friday 28 March and, according to his adjutant, would therefore have been available in Berlin from 10 a.m. on the

Saturday, but 'perhaps also Sunday', for a meeting he had been seeking with Göring.[25] This suggests that he was called back to Berlin at short notice and indeed, given that he was due to give a speech on 28 March on the occasion of the opening of the Institute for Research into the Jewish Question (*Institut zur Erforschung der Judenfrage*), that the matter was of some importance. It was not until 2 April, however, five days after his return to the capital, that Rosenberg actually met with Hitler, as it turned out, to discuss the political administration of the soon-to-be-conquered territories of the Soviet Union. Indeed, there is no evidence to suggest that Rosenberg knew until the meeting itself of his appointment by Hitler two days earlier as head of a Political Central Office for Eastern Questions (*Politisches Zentralbüro für Ostfragen*).[26] This is borne out by the entry in his diary for 2 April, from which it appears that although Rosenberg knew beforehand that the discussion would relate to the future of the East – he had already prepared a memorandum that day – this was the extent of his knowledge of its purpose.[27] Given his role as head of the Foreign Affairs Office of the NSDAP and that organization's interest in the Soviet Union, it was not unusual for him to produce such papers.

Although Rosenberg himself was not immediately informed of his appointment, certain other people had already been made aware of his intended jurisdiction with regard to the political administration of the territories in question several days before, Chief of the Reich Security Main Office (*Reichssicherheitshauptamt*, RSHA) SS-Gruppenführer Reinhard Heydrich and Reichsmarschall Göring among them. This can be seen from notes made by Heydrich pertaining to Rosenberg's powers directly after a meeting with Göring on 26 March.[28] Both men were clearly aware of Rosenberg's likely role in the political administration of the Soviet territories by the day of their meeting at the latest, and quite possibly beforehand. This did not bode well for Rosenberg, however, who was almost certainly not involved in discussions relating to future jurisdiction in the East prior to the beginning of April 1941. It foreshadowed his three-year stint as a poorly informed and relatively powerless Reich Minister for the Occupied Eastern Territories.

The two-hour meeting on 2 April between Hitler and Rosenberg gave both men the opportunity to expound their views on, and their plans for, the Soviet Union. Hitler, for his part, marked out 'in detail' the anticipated development in the East. Rosenberg described what he heard as something 'which I do not want to write down today. I will, however, never forget it.'[29] Exactly what it was that Rosenberg would never forget can only be conjectured, but there was no lack of horrifying plans in the pipeline capable of provoking such a reaction, whether it was the 'starvation strategy', Reichsführer-SS Himmler's 'special tasks' or the extermination of the 'Bolshevik leaders' now being expected of the regular armed forces.[30] What is not convincing, however, is the assumption that the true meaning of Rosenberg's reaction lies in the context of a 'concrete decision' taken by Hitler during the active preparation for the Soviet campaign for the comprehensive murder of the Jews of Europe.[31] Although Rosenberg also stated in the same diary entry that Hitler had asked him 'about the current Jewish proportion [of the population] in the Soviet Union',[32] this occurred later in their discussion and cannot be assumed to have related to what Rosenberg did not 'want to write down' but would 'never forget'. In any case, not only is this interpretation of Rosenberg's words reading rather a lot into a statement which could feasibly have referred to a whole host of different issues, but it has, moreover, been demonstrated that even an order to liquidate all *Soviet* Jews was not issued before the attack on the Soviet Union.[33] Whatever the exact nature of the discussion between the two men, Rosenberg certainly left the meeting in good spirits, convinced that the fate of millions of people had been laid in his hands. He had no doubt been led on by Hitler, who had ended the discussion with the words: 'Rosenberg, now your great hour has come!'[34]

The so-called 'Memorandum No. 1' which Rosenberg gave to Hitler towards the end of their meeting on 2 April was, as the title suggests, the first memorandum on the aims and methods of the future German occupation to be found in the files of the Foreign Affairs Office of the NSDAP.[35] It had in part been drafted following consultation with Arno Schickedanz, staff leader in the APA and childhood friend of Rosenberg.[36] Rosenberg expected a military conflict between Germany and the USSR to lead to 'an exceptionally rapid' occupation of a substantial part of the latter and accepted as a matter of course that the Soviet Union, upon being conquered, would be dissolved into smaller administrative units. This concept corresponded to the preparatory work which had been carried out by the Eastern Office of the APA since the mid-1930s.[37]

In his paper from 2 April, Rosenberg divided the area in which Germany was interested into seven regions: Greater Russia, Belarus, the Baltic States, the Ukraine, the Don region, the Caucasus and Soviet Turkistan. He then made it clear that the treatment meted out to the occupied lands would vary from region to region and depend on the political aim to be achieved in that particular territory. A lasting weakening of Greater Russia was foreseen in order to give the other territories the possibility to develop independently of the Soviet 'heartland'. This intended 'weakening' could, suggested Rosenberg, be brought about in three ways: first, through 'a complete annihilation of the Bolshevik-Jewish state administration', without encouraging the establishment of a new state apparatus to replace it; secondly, through 'a very extensive economic exploitation'; and, thirdly, through the allocation of large swathes of Russian territory to the new administrative units, particularly Belarus, the Ukraine and the Don region. In addition, these measures, continued Rosenberg, would open up the possibility of using Greater Russia as a dumping-ground for 'undesirable' elements from the other Soviet territories.

Not all regions would be subjected to quite this level of destructive treatment, however. The Baltic States – Estonia, Latvia and Lithuania – would be attached to Germany in the course of one or two generations. In order for this to take place, though, the memorandum predictably foresaw the necessity of carrying out extensive expulsions of the Baltic intelligentsia, particularly the Latvian. Those expelled would be replaced by German settlers, possibly from amongst the Volga Germans. Danes, Norwegians, Dutch and, after a 'successful end to the war', English would also come into consideration for such a settlement. Both the elimination of the intelligentsia of the Soviet states and the use of the East as colonial territory for German settlers had already been touched upon by Hitler on 30 March when he addressed senior members of the military in the Reich Chancellery. Hitler had referred to 'colonial tasks',[38] a phrase which suggests that he viewed the Soviet territories as land to be settled by Germans. This appears to be the first time this intention had been mentioned at a senior level during the opening months of 1941. Given that Rosenberg had already written his 'Memorandum No. 1' when he met with Hitler on 2 April, it is unlikely that Hitler communicated this desire to Rosenberg, but rather that the two of them were thinking along the same lines. This was to be expected, however, as the obtaining of Lebensraum in the East for German settlement had long been one of Hitler's cherished goals and Rosenberg would have been well aware of this.[39]

In his paper of 2 April, Rosenberg did not have much that was positive to say about Belarus, which he considered to be 'culturally much more backward' than Lithuania and 'more exploited by Jewry than Poland' had been. In view of the perceived necessity of weakening the heart of Greater Russia, however, Rosenberg advocated that an attempt be made to arouse in Belarus 'a life of its own' as well as to establish a viable state structure. He claimed that the actual capital city of the territory was Smolensk – in fact part of Russia – and that, in accordance with this, half of the province of Smolensk and part of the province of Kalinin (prior to 1931 and since 1990, Tver) should be attached to Belarus. This would result in the eastern border of Belarus being pushed almost 150 miles (approximately 240 km) in the direction of Moscow at the expense of Russia. Rosenberg also argued that, in the event that the establishment of a certain degree of political independence for Belarus was viewed as being desirable, dismemberment of that territory – perhaps to the advantage of the Polish General Government (*Generalgouvernement*) – was not to be recommended.[40] Following the German invasion in June 1941, however, the district of Bialystok, which had been part of Belarus since the Soviet invasion of eastern Poland in 1939, was attached to the *Gau* of East Prussia.[41]

As reflected in his paper of 2 April, Rosenberg saw the long-term task for the Ukraine as being the possible establishment of sovereignty, in order to achieve which the promotion of its independent existence would be both necessary and desirable. The aim of this tactic was to keep Greater Russia permanently in check and to secure the 'Greater German Lebensraum' in the East. Importantly, Rosenberg separated the political and economic tasks in the Ukraine, the latter being to build a massive basis for the supply of raw materials and food to the Greater German Reich.[42] This idea was very much in line with the plans being developed simultaneously by the experts in the Reich Ministry for Food and Agriculture and, by this time, the Four-Year Plan organization. For Rosenberg, however, the economic treatment of the Ukraine was to be geared towards attaining the political aim of keeping Greater Russia in check.[43] In his conception for the Ukraine, the political aim was thus given priority over the economic aim.

In terms of the make-up of a civil administration for the Soviet territories, Rosenberg recommended that a single body be set up, but limited 'more or less' to the duration of the war. It is not entirely clear whether Rosenberg was referring here only to the war against the Soviet Union or also to the expected confrontation with Britain and the USA. If he was referring merely to the former, as seems likely, the administrative body recommended by him would have a very short existence, as the military campaign against the Soviet Union was expected to be over within three months at the most. According to Rosenberg, the role of this central office would be threefold: to issue political instructions to the individual administrative territories; to secure the delivery to Germany of essentials for the war effort; and to prepare and oversee the implementation in the occupied territories of policies issued from above, in questions of currency, transport and the production of oil, coal and food. In the event that an administrative body was to be set up, however, with only economic – and not political – considerations in mind, this would no doubt, argued Rosenberg, 'soon prove its inadequacy'.[44] For Rosenberg, of course, considerations of a purely political nature were highly important and he would probably in any case have urged that a great deal of weight be attached to them, but he may also have already been aware of the leading role earmarked for Göring and the economic organization in the occupied East and was attempting here to provide a counterbalance.

In the final paragraph of his paper, Rosenberg stressed the expediency of taking into consideration at an early stage the points he had raised. His final sentence attempted to justify the application of a completely different – in other words, more savage and criminal – approach on the part of the occupying forces, to that employed in Western Europe: 'In view of the enormous spaces and the difficulties of administration resulting from that alone, as well as in view of the living conditions created by Bolshevism, which are completely different from those in Western Europe, the entire question of the USSR requires a different treatment to what has been applied in the individual countries of Western Europe.'[45]

Five days after his meeting with Hitler, Rosenberg was a little more specific about exactly how the difference in the treatment of the USSR and Western Europe he had mentioned in his 'Memorandum No. 1' would be reflected in the organization of the civil administration in the East. In order to deal with the unique problems there, argued Rosenberg, 'a central leadership of the work of the different Reich Commissariats is urgently necessary'. This would, first, relieve the strain on Hitler, who would not constantly have to deal with four or five eastern administrations and, secondly, enable the whole area to be supervised from one position, thus making sure that the assigned tasks would be correctly carried out. As 'Protector-General for the occupied eastern territories', with his seat in Berlin, Rosenberg proposed himself. All official business between the authorities in the 'old Reich' and the Reich Commissariats would go through the Protector-General. Rosenberg did not foresee the establishment of a new, large Reich authority as being necessary.[46] His suggestion for his own promotion was not immediately acted upon by Hitler – there were as yet, of course, no occupied eastern territories beyond Poland to be presided over – but Rosenberg's leadership of a Political Central Office for Eastern Questions was upgraded less than two weeks later to the position of Hitler's Plenipotentiary for the Central Treatment of Questions of the Eastern European Space (*Beauftragter für die zentrale Bearbeitung der Fragen des osteuropäischen Raumes*).[47]

In addition to putting himself forward for the central leadership position for the occupied Soviet territories, Rosenberg also made suggestions in his memorandum of 7 April for who should be appointed as Reich Commissars in the East. The seven regions into which Rosenberg, in his earlier memorandum of 2 April, had divided the Soviet territory in which Germany was interested had now been reduced to potentially six administrative entities, but perhaps only four, depending on the fate of 'Moscow' and Soviet Turkistan. The regions of 'the Baltic Sea provinces' and Belarus – now being referred to as 'Weißruthenien'[48] – would be combined and placed under the leadership of the Gauleiter of Schleswig-Holstein, Hinrich Lohse. The Reich Commissariats of the Caucasus and of the Ukraine would be placed in the hands of, interestingly, Staatssekretär Herbert Backe and Arno Schickedanz.[49] In January, Backe had assured Hitler that the occupation of the Ukraine would liberate Germany from every economic worry. As the Soviet Union's only 'surplus territory', the proposed agricultural exploitation of the occupied East would be particularly extensive in the Ukraine. The Ukraine was also of special significance for Rosenberg, but for different reasons. Rosenberg added in his memorandum that, if he had the choice, he would nominate Backe for the Caucasus and Schickedanz for the Ukraine.[50] Backe had been born in the coastal city of Batumi in Georgia in the Caucasus,[51] spoke fluent Russian and, according to Rosenberg, had never entirely abandoned his attachment to his birthplace.[52]

The Ministerpräsident of Braunschweig, Dietrich Klagges, was proposed by Rosenberg for the Don-Volga region and the Gauleiter of East Prussia, Erich Koch, for the area now referred to simply as 'Moscow'. As an indication of the unlikelihood of a civil administration being set up in Soviet Turkistan (comprising present-day Turkmenistan, Kazakhstan, Uzbekistan, Tajikistan and Kyrgyzstan), or even perhaps of the Germans occupying the area, no one was selected for this post.[53] This was to be expected, however, given that Turkistan lay beyond the Caspian Sea in the Asian part of the Soviet Union and Rosenberg's task, in accordance with the military aims of the forthcoming campaign, was to politically reshape the *European* 'East'.[54]

Rosenberg also recommended that Göring, as Plenipotentiary for the Four-Year Plan, appoint the head of an 'oil commission' to work alongside the Reich Commissar in the Caucasus.[55] This is to be explained by the importance of the Caucasus as 'the oil centre of Russia', as Rosenberg had pointed out in his memorandum of 2 April.[56]

It is worth drawing attention to the reasons Rosenberg gave for his selection of the brutal, even by Nazi standards, Erich Koch for the position of Reich Commissar in Moscow.

> This occupation will indeed have a completely different character to that in the Baltic Sea provinces, in the Ukraine and in the Caucasus. It will be geared towards the oppression of any Russian or Bolshevist resistance and requires an absolutely *ruthless* personality, not only on the part of the military representation but also the potential political leadership. The resulting tasks need not be recorded. In case a permanent military administration is not foreseen, the undersigned recommends as Reich Commissar in Moscow the Gauleiter of East Prussia, Eric Koch.[57]

This recognition of the necessity of a brutal approach evinced the same spirit and severity as that being seen among the economic planners. When Hitler and Rosenberg next met, on 10 April, Hitler declared himself 'in agreement' with Rosenberg's memorandum.[58]

Rosenberg's preference once again, as in his diary entry for 2 April 1941, not to record the 'resulting tasks', in this case for the area around Moscow, indicates that many of the details of the plans being developed at the time were only passed on orally and, as a result of this understandable secrecy, have not been passed down to us in written documentation. In a similar vein to Rosenberg, Staatssekretär Backe noted on one occasion, probably sometime during 1941: '[One should] be aware that the enemy is always listening in. He must not be allowed to quote [us]. The spoken word, on the other hand, is harmless.'[59]

Although with regard to the treatment of the area around Moscow no significant discord within the Nazi leadership seemed likely, the position of the Ukraine within these schemes was looking increasingly uncertain. Admittedly, Rosenberg had emphasized the existence of separate political and economic aims to be pursued in the Ukraine in his 'Memorandum No. 1' of 2 April, but how could such disparate intentions be simultaneously and faithfully implemented? Rosenberg himself attempted to provide something of a solution to this looming dilemma in a paper dated 29 April 1941.[60] In this paper he acknowledged that securing the supply of the German Reich with raw materials and foodstuffs stood at the top of German demands in the East, but argued: 'In the long run, this aim can also be achieved in certain territories with less force precisely by means of a sympathetic special treatment of the peoples concerned, than if the solutions to this task are enforced with the methods of the military or political power with neglect for the national and political situation.'[61] This is an early example of the tendency for Rosenberg to be at odds with the economic planners over the methods used to implement an aim, rather than the aim itself. This trend would continue to be evident over subsequent months. The regions referred to by Rosenberg as 'certain territories' were clearly those marked out by him for more favourable treatment, above all the Ukraine. He was perhaps attempting to reconcile his position with that of the economic planners, whose plans he very likely had some knowledge of, whilst continuing to promote as the central aim his cherished wish of Ukrainian autonomy. Whatever Rosenberg's motivations, he was attempting a very precarious balancing act and the Ukraine would inevitably become the principal bone of contention within the Nazi hierarchy not only in the run-up to the invasion, but also during the occupation itself.

Rosenberg as Administrative Chief: 'no better man' for the Job

In light of this apparent incompatibility in the respective approaches of the economic planners and Rosenberg, it is worth considering more fully the reasons for Rosenberg's selection as the head of a future civil administration in the occupied territories of the Soviet Union. Since his position as head of a Political Central Office for Eastern Questions had been upgraded by Hitler on 20 April 1941 to become the latter's Plenipotentiary for the Central Treatment of Questions of the Eastern European Space, Rosenberg had been slated as the head of a future civil administration in the occupied territories of the Soviet Union. Admittedly, his own recommendation of 7 April that he be appointed Protector-General for the Occupied Eastern Territories had not been acted upon, but it would not be long before it became clear that his future title would be even more prestigious – Reich Minister for the Occupied Eastern Territories.

The post of Reich Minister for the Occupied Eastern Territories appeared indeed – at least at first glance – to be all-powerful. It should already have become clear over the course of this study how the Nazi leadership viewed the territories of the Soviet Union, the mythical 'East', where the allegedly overcrowded Germany would find Lebensraum and security for its people. 'What India was for England, the territories of Russia will be for us. If only I could make the German people understand what this space means for our future!', declared Hitler in August 1941.[62] This was not an isolated expression of Hitler's feelings on the issue. A month later he commented: 'The Russian space is our India and, just like the English, we will rule this, our colonial expanse, with a handful of men.'[63] On 16 September 1941, Hitler told the German Ambassador in Paris, Otto Abetz, that the 'new Russia as far as the Urals' would be Germany's India, but more favourably situated for Germany than India was for Britain.[64] British rule in India apparently represented for Hitler 'the desirable aim' of the German administration in the East,[65] although this patently ignored the vast difference between the Raj and the brutal Nazi subjugation and occupation of the Soviet Union and the rest of Eastern Europe.[66] In fact, Hitler was attempting to compare two sets of nations which were simply not comparable. This was just one more example of his reduction of everything to simplistic formulas. In July 1941, three and a half weeks after the beginning of Operation Barbarossa, Hitler announced that Germany would create a 'Garden of Eden' in the newly acquired eastern territories.[67]

Why was it, though, that Alfred Rosenberg was chosen to head the future civil administration in what were for the Nazis the most important lands in Europe, for which they had far-reaching and, in many cases, almost unimaginable plans? Though he was a long-term member of the NSDAP and Reichsleiter for ideology and foreign policy, and had deputized for Hitler as head of the Party during the latter's spell in Landsberg Prison in the wake of the so-called Beer-Hall Putsch of November 1923, Rosenberg had never held a major position in the state hierarchy. Expectant of being appointed Foreign Minister after the Nazi seizure of power, he had been bitterly disappointed when Joachim von Ribbentrop, whom he regarded as a 'small man',[68] was instead given the post in February 1938.[69] Conversely, it has been suggested that it was the very fact that Rosenberg was 'owed' a job that led Hitler to appoint his one-time deputy as Reich Minister for the Occupied Eastern Territories.[70] Although it would be attaching too much importance to this factor to see the whole explanation for Rosenberg's selection therein, there may indeed be some truth in it. If there had ever been a senior post which Rosenberg, at least in theory, had in effect been waiting for, it was this one. In mid-June 1941, Propaganda Minister Joseph Goebbels wrote that Rosenberg's 'life's work' was 'justified' in the campaign against the Soviet Union.[71]

Hitler had in March 1941 already made it clear to the military leadership how difficult the forthcoming administrative tasks in the East would be. These tasks would thus be incumbent on the civil administrators, the Reich Commissars. Rosenberg, however, was not known as a man of action, but rather as a theorist and ideologue. Commenting in early May 1941 on Hitler's commissioning of Rosenberg for tasks 'in the Eastern question', Goebbels claimed that Rosenberg 'can only theorize, but not organize'.[72] Reichsführer-SS Himmler, anticipating future disputes between the two men over jurisdiction, simply wrote: 'To work with or even under Rosenberg is definitely the most difficult thing that there is in the NSDAP.'[73] Himmler had made this remark in a letter to the Head of the Party Chancellery, Reichsleiter Martin Bormann, who also had little time for Rosenberg. Reich Treasurer Franz Xaver Schwarz was disappointed with Rosenberg's appointment in the East because he did not consider him to be the man to get to grips with the difficult task at hand.[74] Even Gauleiter Hinrich Lohse, a long-term acquaintance and the man appointed on Rosenberg's suggestion in July 1941 as Reich Commissar in the Baltic, wrote less than flatteringly in January 1943 in celebration of Rosenberg's fiftieth birthday: 'If the Führer appointed Alfred Rosenberg after the beginning of the eastern campaign as Reich Minister for the Occupied Eastern Territories, he will have had his particular and own reasons, which lie beyond the scope of our reflections here.'[75]

Hitler had not chosen Rosenberg for his organizational or man-management skills, however, and certainly not for his popularity. Although Hitler could fix the overall political and economic aims to be achieved in the East – and the methods to be used, for that matter – he was, as always, rather less forthcoming when it came to administrative tasks and detailed planning.[76] Hitler needed a blueprint for the future shape of the territories in the East and, whatever his shortcomings in the eyes of the Führer and the rest of the Nazi leadership, Rosenberg was considered to be the best man for the job. A matter of days before the commencement of 'Barbarossa', Goebbels wrote in his diary that Rosenberg 'knows the problems' in the East 'very well'.[77] The extent to which Rosenberg actually did know the East and its supposed 'problems' can be debated, but his preoccupation with such matters was certainly more extensive than that of his colleagues. Rosenberg was the only man in the upper echelons of the Nazi leadership to possess first-hand knowledge of Soviet Bolshevism and the USSR.[78] His Baltic origin and experiences in Russia sufficed for Hitler to class him as an 'expert'.

At Nuremberg after the war, former Head of the Reich Chancellery Hans-Heinrich Lammers stated that he had been called to Hitler during the second half of April 1941 to discuss 'preparatory measures' in anticipation of a surprise *Soviet* attack on Germany. He went on:

> [Hitler] continued saying that he needed a man who was acquainted with the political and economic conditions in the eastern area and who, in case of war, could make preparations for setting up a civilian administration in the Russian areas which might be occupied. The Fuehrer then added that he had chosen Reichsleiter Rosenberg for this post. He was to have an undefined and as far reaching as possible power of attorney which would give him the authority to establish contact with all the relevant Reich Ministries and to negotiate with them.[79]

Lammers then claimed to have expressed misgivings about Rosenberg occupying the post, misgivings which Hitler apparently brushed aside with the remark that he had 'no better man than Rosenberg'.[80] At this moment in time, i.e., April 1941, it was not under discussion whether Rosenberg would be appointed Reich Minister for the Occupied Eastern Territories. As Lammers also commented, there was no mention at the time of his discussion with Hitler 'of the setting up of any Eastern Ministry'.[81] The establishment of a separate ministry in the East is discussed more fully in chapter 9 of this study, but it is worth pointing out here that the first reference to the post of Reich Minister for the Occupied Eastern Territories, as far as can be determined, came from Rosenberg himself in a paper dated 25 April and entitled 'Memorandum No. 3. Re.: USSR'.[82] Given that he referred here to the 'Reich Minister and Protector-General for the occupied eastern territories' and that he had recommended himself for the post of Protector-General for the Occupied Eastern Territories two and a half weeks earlier, it is highly likely that Rosenberg now saw himself as the future Reich Minister.

In addition to his experiences in the Soviet Union, Rosenberg was also a loyal and pliable disciple of Hitler's. As the occupation period in the East would amply demonstrate, he lacked the ruthlessness and political skill necessary to succeed in promoting his own interests. Unlike Göring or Himmler, for example, Rosenberg was not already in possession of a large power base from which to stake his claim to even greater power. Were there any other realistic alternatives to the selection of Rosenberg as East Minister Elect? The possibility of Göring having staked his claim to executive powers over the eastern administration has already been discussed.[83] In hindsight, any such claim was not likely to have become reality. By early 1941 it was already clear that Göring was to be economic overlord in the East, just as he was in the rest of occupied Europe, but it was never likely that his power would be extended yet further to incorporate the civil administration. Hitler was not in the habit of placing too much power in the hands of any one man. As mentioned above, Hitler explained his choice to Lammers by claiming that he had 'no better man than Rosenberg', which indicated the deficiencies of any other potential candidate rather than the aptness of Rosenberg for the position. The statement also suggests that no one else had been realistically considered for the job. From this one can draw the additional conclusion that there were only a limited number of men in the Nazi hierarchy who were both sufficiently trusted by Hitler and available for the post.

A fortnight after the official appointment of the first members of the civil administration in the East, Hitler, talking about the necessity of controlling 'immense regions with a handful of men', exclaimed: 'What a chance for men from the Party!'[84] If nothing else, Rosenberg was certainly a Party man. He was already in the NSDAP – at that time still the German Workers' Party (*Deutsche Arbeiterpartei*, DAP) – by February 1919 at the latest.[85] Hitler did not become a member until the second half of September 1919.[86] Hence, Rosenberg had already been in the Party for at least seven months before Hitler joined. Of those who had been prominent in the NSDAP in its infant years, he was the only one other than Hitler who was still prominent twenty or more years later.[87]

At least with Rosenberg at its head it was likely that the administration in the East would be kept in the hands of the Party. In this case at least, the reality matched the expectation. Rosenberg himself bore the title of Reichsleiter, the highest rank in the NSDAP. Each Reichsleiter was appointed by Hitler to a specific area of expertise, Rosenberg being responsible since 1933 for ideology and foreign policy.[88] When it came to the occupied Soviet territories, Hitler appointed all Reich and General Commissars. Both Reich Commissars, Lohse in the 'Ostland' and Koch in the Ukraine, were Gauleiter. With regard to the ten men (twenty-four in total had been foreseen by Rosenberg)[89] occupying the position of General Commissar (*Generalkommissar*), four in the 'Ostland' and six in the Ukraine, it is worth mentioning that Wilhelm Kube (General Commissar in *Weißruthenien*) had formerly been Gauleiter in the Kurmark,[90] and Alfred Frauenfeld (Crimea)[91] was also a former Gauleiter, whilst Ernst Leyser (Zhytomyr)[92] was a deputy

Gauleiter. Both Karl-Siegmund Litzmann (Estonia) and Heinrich Schöne (Volhynia-Podolia) held the rank of Obergruppenführer in the SA,[93] whilst Claus Selzner (Dnipropetrovs'k) was Oberbefehlsleiter[94] in the NSDAP and Dr Adrian von Renteln (Lithuania) Reichsamtsleiter.[95]

Of the nineteen men appointed – by Rosenberg himself – to the position of District Commissar (*Gebietskommissar*) in the 'Ostland', fifteen were 'old fighters' (*Alte Kämpfer*), the term used to refer to those members of the NSDAP who were active during the early rise of the movement,[96] whilst the others were already members of the Party at the time of the seizure of power in 1933.[97] The administration of the post-invasion occupation in the East would thus be in the hands, not of the army, the ministerial bureaucrats or the career diplomats, but rather of those men whom Hitler trusted the most and on whose loyalty he could rely: men of the Party. As can be seen, the selection of Rosenberg to draft the future political shape of the East and then to function as the administrative head of the occupied Soviet territories was by no means an illogical one.

Personnel and Tasks

In his first two memoranda since being brought in by Hitler to sketch out the administrative structure of the occupied East, Rosenberg had proposed how the area under occupation would be divided up for administration, which objectives – both political and economic – were to be pursued and what kind of treatment each of these regions would accordingly face. In the second of these two memoranda, Rosenberg also recommended potential Reich Commissars.[98] The Reich Commissars were, however, only the most senior of a mass of administrative officials appointed in the East. By mid-April 1941, Rosenberg had already gathered together in his staff '3,000 experts on Russia'! Even Rosenberg, however, was not entirely convinced of their quality, recognizing as he did the lack of suitable people, despite using all the card indexes at his disposal. He posed himself the question as to how many of them were really fit to be employed.[99] Indeed, as far as structural problems in themselves are to be made responsible, the 'failure' of the civil administration in the occupied eastern territories has to a large extent been put down to the 'misguided manpower policy'.[100] Officials were recruited from a whole host of institutions, including the APA, which had in the meantime become largely functionless, the Foreign Ministry, the Interior Ministry, the German Labour Front (*Deutsche Arbeitsfront*, DAF) and the SA.[101]

Although Rosenberg was responsible for appointing all civil administrators in the occupied eastern territories under the rank of General Commissar, he was assisted in this not only by members of his own staff, but also by state authorities such as the Foreign Ministry, the Interior Ministry and the Reich Chancellery. On 9 May 1941, for example, Privy Councillor (*Geheimrat*) Georg Großkopf in the Foreign Office reported to Foreign Minister von Ribbentrop on a meeting he had had that day with Rosenberg and Alfred Meyer, Rosenberg's deputy.[102] Großkopf was the Foreign Minister's permanent liaison officer to the Bureau Rosenberg[103] and, as such, the first port of call for Rosenberg or anyone on or connected with his staff seeking to make contact with the Foreign Office. One of several wishes expressed by Rosenberg during the meeting was that Großkopf personally compile a list of people known to him who appeared to be suitable for use in the East when the time came. There is no reason to believe that Rosenberg's desire was left unfulfilled.

Wilhelm Stuckart, the Staatssekretär in the Ministry of the Interior, attached a list of potential candidates for the posts of General and Main Commissar (*Hauptkommissar*), of which Rosenberg had foreseen twenty-four and approximately eighty, respectively,[104] to a letter he sent to Head of the Reich Chancellery Lammers on 4 July 1941.[105] This list had been compiled by Stuckart's ministry and would also receive attention from Lammers and his colleagues in the Reich Chancellery. In certain instances, Rosenberg made requests for particular officials to be seconded to his staff. Days before the commencement of the eastern campaign, for example, Rosenberg asked Ribbentrop to place the German envoys Dr Hermann Neubacher and Siegfried Kasche at his disposal. He also requested that the same be done with all those officials working in the Russian department of the German Foreign Office, the embassy in Moscow and the consulates in the USSR – in other words, those who would be freed up as a result of the invasion.[106] These examples of the recruitment procedure provide a valuable illustration of not only inter-ministerial cooperation, but also cooperation between Party and state agencies.

Beyond the question of personnel, it also had to be determined exactly what all these men would do. What was their function? What tasks would be incumbent on them? Erich Koch, for example, was regarded by those around Hitler at the FHQ as the right man for the tasks to be carried out in the Ukraine and as a 'second Stalin'.[107] Given Hitler's admiration for the Soviet leader – in spite of his loathing of Bolshevism – this translated as a real compliment.[108] If this was the type of man selected by Hitler and his lieutenants as their representative in the Ukraine, what does that say about the expected role of the Reich Commissars as heads of the civil administration in the East and, by the same token, their subordinates? Were these civil administrators envisaged as instruments of reconstruction or as instruments of terror? To a certain extent, as in related questions, this would differ from region to region. In one of his first memoranda, Rosenberg stated that the occupation of Moscow would possess 'a completely different character' to the occupations of the Baltic States, the Ukraine or the Caucasus. The occupation of Moscow would be 'oriented to the oppression of any Russian and Bolshevik resistance and require an absolutely ruthless personality'. The tasks to be carried out were evidently of such a destructive nature that Rosenberg judged it preferable not to record them, as he himself wrote.[109]

In contrast, the function of the Reich Commissar for the combined territories of Estonia, Latvia, Lithuania and Belarus would be 'for the most part an exceptionally positive one'. The aim in this Reich Commissariat would be to strive for the form of a German protectorate and then to convert the area into a part of the Greater German Reich through the 'Germanization of those elements with whom it is racially possible, through colonization of Germanic peoples and through the resettlement of undesirable elements'.[110] The aim of the work to be carried out in the Reich Commissariat Ukraine would again be somewhat different. The priority in the Ukraine would be the securing of foodstuffs and raw materials for Germany and with it the strengthening of the German prosecution of the war. Following this, the task of the Reich Commissar would be to establish a free Ukrainian state in closest alliance with the Greater German Reich.[111]

The first task of the entire civil administration was, of course, to represent the interests of Germany in the occupied Soviet territories.[112] In terms of more concrete, day-to-day tasks for which the civil administrators in the East would be responsible, Rosenberg envisaged certain 'urgent administrative assignments' in the official handbook he issued for the civil administration of the occupied eastern territories. These instructions were known as the 'Brown Folder' (*Braune Mappe*) because of the colour of their binding. The most important of these 'urgent administrative assignments' were:

a) policing measures,
b) utilization of the economic forces of the territory for the provisioning of the occupying troops and for [the] purposes of the German war economy,
c) seizure of supplies and equipment of all kinds essential to the war effort and vital for [our] existence,
d) provisioning of the population,
e) participation in the maintaining or setting up of inland navigation, [and] the rail and postal services,
f) supervision of the civilian population, participation in counter-espionage, mobilization of the population for work,
g) removal of potentially extant enemy organizations.[113]

The first point on the list demonstrates a fundamental lack of awareness on Rosenberg's part of the limits of his own jurisdiction. As the 'Decree of the Führer regarding the Securing of the Newly Occupied Eastern Territories by the Police' of 17 July had already made perfectly clear, any and all 'policing measures' were 'a matter for the Reichsführer-SS and Chief of the German Police' Himmler.[114]

How the fourth task listed by Rosenberg, 'provisioning of the population', would correspond in practice with the policy of reducing the food supply of the Soviet population to the point of starvation was obviously something to which the future East Minister had not given a great deal of thought. The Commander of Army Group Centre in the Soviet Union, Field Marshal Fedor von Bock, also seemed to believe that this would be the principal task of Rosenberg and his staff and came to the conclusion: 'His mission will be a difficult one. The region is barren in places. Its yields will scarcely suffice to feed the civilian population.'[115]

However willing Rosenberg was to give support to the priorities set by the economic planners, as is further demonstrated by the second and third tasks listed above, he had clearly not thought the two sets of proposals through to the point of seriously considering how they would combine in practice.

In view of limitations in personnel, Rosenberg recognized the necessity that the German civil administrators be assisted in the implementation of their tasks by indigenous officials. He thus declared himself against 'a *general* annihilation of all state, local and village functionaries. ... A *general* eradication during the initial military engagements and also later with the deployment of civilian power would be, politically and socially, a measure which would have dire consequences.'[116] The projected murder of Soviet officials of 'higher and senior' rank, however, found no opposition from Rosenberg.[117] His reference to the eradication of functionaries following 'the deployment of civilian power' indicates that the killing programme would continue to be implemented even after the military engagements had ceased.

The various duties listed above also necessitated a close working relationship between the civil administration and the other major agencies in the occupied East, namely the economic organization, the SS and the military. According to the 'Decree of the Führer regarding the Appointment of Wehrmacht Commanders in the Newly Occupied Eastern Territories' of 25 June 1941, one of the jobs of the Reich Commissars was to carry through the demands of the Wehrmacht in the area under civil administration.[118] For the purpose of securing the newly occupied eastern territories through the police, for which a decree, mentioned above, appeared on the same day as Rosenberg was officially appointed as Reich Minister for the Occupied Eastern Territories, a Higher SS and Police Leader (*Höherer SS- und Polizeiführer*, HSSPF) was attached to each Reich Commissar. According to the decree, the HSSPF were to be subordinate to their respective Reich Commissar.[119] However, given that they were directly answerable to Himmler, this official position of the HSSPF in the occupied territories existed to a large extent only on paper. As was the case with Himmler himself, whose official title was Reichsführer-SS and Chief of the German Police, the HSSPF combined Party (SS) and state (police) functions, thus making them all the more powerful and facilitating the successful implementation of their tasks. The relationship between the Reich Minister for the Occupied Eastern Territories and the – at least officially – directly subordinated Reich Commissars operated on a similar basis, as the dual role of the Reich Commissars as Gauleiter gave them direct access to Hitler. Both Hinrich Lohse and, especially, Erich Koch did indeed make use of this right to direct access to Hitler. Even in the Ukraine, Koch requested that associates address him as Gauleiter rather than Reich Commissar. As such, Koch was accountable to Reichsleiter Martin Bormann, Head of the Party Chancellery. Whilst Bormann was certainly no particular friend of Rosenberg's, he *was* close friends with Koch, the two of them communicating per *Du* rather than using the more formal *Sie*. Thus, Koch was able to go over Rosenberg's head by appealing directly to Hitler through Bormann.[120]

That a cooperative working relationship between the Reich Commissar and the HSSPF attached to him was expected is shown by the example of Erich Koch, who would ultimately be appointed to run the Reich Commissariat Ukraine. Koch, the man recommended by Rosenberg in his memorandum of 7 April 1941 as the 'absolutely ruthless personality' required to administer the Reich Commissariat 'Moscow', was still being considered for this position as the military campaign got under way. With reference to their meeting of 24 June 1941, Reichsführer-SS Himmler sent Rosenberg a letter informing the latter of the four men he intended to appoint to the post of Higher SS and Police Leader in the Soviet Union. If Koch was to be appointed Reich Commissar in Moscow, remarked Himmler, a swap would 'naturally' have to take place in the occupation of the position of HSSPF for Moscow, the candidate at this point in time being SS-Gruppenführer Erich von dem Bach-Zelewski.[121] This would be necessary, as Reich Treasurer Schwarz pointed out in a discussion with Chief of the SS Main Office SS-Gruppenführer Gottlob Berger, because 'a successful collaboration' between Koch and Bach-Zelewski was not deemed to be possible.[122] This can be explained by the serious quarrel which took place between the two men in 1935 when Bach-Zelewski was chief of police in Königsberg, the administrative seat of Koch's Gau, East Prussia. Koch refused to work with Bach-Zelewski again and the conflict eventually had to be settled in January of the following year by Hitler, who decided in favour of the Gauleiter.[123]

In the event, Koch – particularly brutal even by Nazi standards – in fact rejected the post of Reich Commissar in Moscow in June on the basis that the task concerned was 'entirely negative'![124] This gives an impression of just how terrible the nature of German occupation policy in this region was intended to be. The selection of SS-Gruppenführer von dem Bach-Zelewski as Higher SS and Police Leader for Russia-Centre, which incorporated Moscow and the surrounding area, corresponds to the image of him as a man who, in the words of Hitler, could 'wade through a sea of blood' and was 'even more severe and brutal' than Himmler's right-hand man, Reinhard Heydrich.[125] The notorious SS and Police Leader (*SS- und Polizeiführer*) in Lublin, former Gauleiter of Vienna Odilo Globocnik, was slated by Rosenberg to take charge beyond the Ural Mountains in the most easterly of the Russian General Commissariats, Sverdlovsk (Yekaterinburg).[126] Globocnik would later be appointed to run 'Aktion Reinhardt', the murder of the General Government's Jews in the extermination camps of Belzec, Sobibór and Treblinka.[127] Koch was clearly in the picture when it came to the horrors which had been planned for central Russia and its inhabitants. His preferred destination would have been the Baltic,[128] an area which was ultimately placed under the jurisdiction of Hinrich Lohse. Instead, Koch had to settle for the Ukraine, which, according to Hitler, would be without doubt the most important territory for the first three years of the eastern occupation.[129] This, however, at least initially, did not appear to satisfy Koch either. According to Otto Bräutigam, the deputy leader of the Policy

Department in the East Ministry, Koch expressed himself 'very listlessly' regarding his new commission. He would only fulfil it for as long as it was required by the Office of the Four-Year Plan, which was responsible, as shown earlier, for the economic exploitation of the occupied eastern territories. Koch was only interested, or so he claimed, in his Gau of East Prussia.[130]

At the beginning of April 1941, when Alfred Rosenberg had begun to contemplate who might be appointed to the most senior positions in the future civil administration in the East, his friend and colleague Arno Schickedanz had been his preferred choice for the position eventually awarded to Erich Koch – that of Reich Commissar in the Ukraine. As an alternative, Rosenberg had proposed Herbert Backe. For obvious reasons, however, Backe was considered 'indispensable' in Germany.[131] By mid-May, with Koch's most likely destination still Moscow, the Gauleiter of Thuringia, Fritz Sauckel, was being spoken of as a possible candidate for the Ukraine.[132] By the time it came to confirming the selections in mid-July, however, Sauckel's name came up only briefly. It is not immediately apparent why Sauckel appears to have been considered for the post of Reich Commissar in the Ukraine only fleetingly. At the same time, however, it is highly unlikely that Hitler, who ultimately had the last say in appointing all Reich and General Commissars, i.e., the positions of significance in the civil administration, already had Sauckel in mind at this stage for the post of Plenipotentiary for Labour Procurement (*Generalbevollmächtigter für den Arbeitseinsatz*). Sauckel was appointed to this position on 21 March 1942 and, in this capacity, was responsible for providing the German Reich with a massive army of forced labour, the bulk of which, often by employing methods of extreme brutality, was obtained from the occupied eastern territories. With Rosenberg voluntarily proposing men like Backe and Sauckel for the post of Reich Commissar in the Ukraine – a territory he himself had marked out for favourable treatment – one wonders what exactly Rosenberg's notion of such concepts as 'autonomy' and 'independence' in fact was, words he regularly bandied about when discussing the Ukraine.

Notes

1. Halder, *KTB*, II, pp. 278 and 281, entries for 11 and 14 February 1941.
2. See BA-MA, RW 19/164, fo. 187.
3. See chapter 4, 'Backe's Presentations to the Supreme Leadership'.
4. Müller, 'Ausbeutungskrieg', p. 171, who cites as his source Below, *Als Hitlers Adjutant*, pp. 262–263. However, Below merely mentions that Hitler held a speech in Munich on 24 February on the occasion of the anniversary of the founding of the Party (in actual fact, the anniversary of the renaming of the 'DAP' the 'NSDAP') and nothing about any such discussion(s).
5. IfZ, ED 180/5, Terminkalender Hermann Göring, fo. 28, entry for 24 February 1941.
6. Schramm (ed.), *KTB des OKW*, I, p. 340, entry for 1 March 1941.
7. BA-MA, RW 19/164, fos. 197–198, 'Vortrag Chef Ro beim Amtschef', 3 March 1941, here fo. 198.

8. Schramm (ed.), *KTB des OKW*, I, pp. 341–342, entry for 3 March 1941.
9. See Müller, 'Raubkrieg', p. 180.
10. Schramm (ed.), *KTB des OKW*, I, p. 346.
11. Myllyniemi, *Die Neuordnung der baltischen Länder*, p. 55, fn. 25.
12. Hans-Adolf Jacobsen, 'Kommissarbefehl und Massenexekutionen sowjetischer Kriegsgefangener', in Hans Buchheim et al., *Anatomie des SS-Staates, Band II* (Walter-Verlag, Olten, 1965), pp. 198–201, doc. 1, 'Richtlinien auf Sondergebieten zur Weisung Nr. 21 (Fall Barbarossa)'.
13. Ibid., pp. 199–200.
14. See Appendix 2.
15. Hildegard von Kotze (ed.), *Heeresadjutant bei Hitler 1938–1943: Aufzeichnungen des Majors Engel* (Deutsche Verlags-Anstalt, Stuttgart, 1974), pp. 96–97. For similar comments see *TBJG*, II/1 (K.G. Saur, Munich, 1996), p. 118, entry for 24 July 1941.
16. Halder, *KTB*, II, pp. 318–321, entry for 17 March 1941, here p. 320.
17. Ibid., pp. 335–337, entry for 30 March 1941.
18. For the text of the decree see BA-MA, RW 4/v. 578, fos. 41–44, 'Richtlinien für die Behandlung politischer Kommissare', 6 June 1941; reproduced in Ueberschär and Wette (eds), *"Unternehmen Barbarossa"*, pp. 313–314, doc. 8. On the genesis of the Commissar Order and the other 'criminal orders' see Ralf Ogorreck, *Die Einsatzgruppen und die "Genesis der Endlösung"* (Metropol, Berlin, 1996), pp. 19–41; Jürgen Förster, 'Das Unternehmen "Barbarossa" als Eroberungs- und Vernichtungskrieg' in Boog et al., *Der Angriff auf die Sowjetunion*, pp. 498–538; Helmut Krausnick, 'Kommissarbefehl und "Gerichtsbarkeitserlaß Barbarossa" in neuer Sicht', *Vierteljahrshefte für Zeitgeschichte*, 25/4 (1977), pp. 682–738.
19. This measure would be incorporated into the so-called 'Jurisdiction Decree Barbarossa' (*Gerichtsbarkeitserlaß Barbarossa*) of 13 May 1941. For the text of the decree, see *IMG*, vol. 34 (1949), pp. 252–255, doc. 050–C, 'Erlass über die Ausübung der Kriegsgerichtsbarkeit im Gebiet "Barbarossa" und über besondere Massnahmen der Truppe'.
20. Halder, *KTB*, II, pp. 335–337, entry for 30 March 1941.
21. Gerlach, *Kalkulierte Morde*, p. 143, fn. 90 and p. 156.
22. BA-MA, RW 19/164, fo. 180: 'R.M. hat vom Führer Genehmigung erhalten, daß er die gesamte Verwaltung des zu besetzenden Gebietes "Barbarossa" übernimmt. R.M. übergibt die Vorbereitung für die gesamte Verwaltung dem Amtschef. ... R.M. betrachtet die Aktion als eine Stützung der wirtschaftlichen Versorgung, insbesondere auch des VJP.'
23. Ibid., fo. 187: 'Klare Festlegung, dass die Organisation nicht abhängig ist von der Militär- oder Zivilverwaltung, wohl aber Zusammenarbeit mit dieser.'
24. BA, NS 8/63, fo. 260, 'Aktennotiz für die Presse', 28 March 1941.
25. BA, NS 8/167, fo .35, letter from SA-Standartenführer Dr Werner Koeppen to SA-Brigadeführer Görnert, 22 March 1941; fo. 40, 'Betrifft: Errichtung einer Reichsstiftung für deutsche Ostforschung', letter from Rosenberg to Göring, 7 March 1941.
26. Reitlinger, *The House Built on Sand*, p. 134. See also Yitzhak Arad, 'Alfred Rosenberg and the "Final Solution" in the Occupied Soviet Territories', *Yad Vashem Studies on the European Jewish Catastrophe and Resistance*, 13 (1979), pp. 263–286, here p. 265; Cecil, *The Myth of the Master Race*, p. 195.
27. Rosenberg's diary entry for 2 April 1941, published in the *Frankfurter Rundschau*, no. 140, 22 June 1971.
28. See Aly, *"Endlösung"*, p. 270, 'Vermerk Heydrichs vom 26.3.1941'. See also IfZ, ED 180/5, Terminkalender Hermann Göring, fo. 44, entry for 26 March 1941.
29. Rosenberg's diary entry for 2 April 1941: 'Der Führer entwickelte dann ausführlich die voraussichtliche Entwicklung im Osten, was ich heute nicht niederschreiben will. Ich werde das aber nie vergessen.'
30. See Streit, *Keine Kameraden*, p. 28; BA-MA, RW 19/185, fo. 170; BA-MA, RW 19/164, fo. 180.

31. This is Joachim C. Fest's interpretation of Rosenberg's diary entry; Fest, *Hitler: Eine Biographie* (Ullstein, Frankfurt am Main, 1973), p. 930. The same interpretation is to be found in Hermann Graml, *Reichskristallnacht: Antisemitismus und Judenverfolgung im Dritten Reich* (Deutscher Taschenbuch Verlag, Munich, 1988), p. 222.
32. Rosenberg's diary entry for 2 April 1941: 'Der Führer fragte mich ... über den jetzigen jüdischen Anteil in der Sowjetunion ....'
33. See Christian Streit, '*Wehrmacht, Einsatzgruppen*, Soviet POWs and anti-Bolshevism in the emergence of the Final Solution', in David Cesarani (ed.), *The Final Solution: Origins and Implementation* (Routledge, London, 1996), pp. 103–118, here pp. 104–108. See also Peter Longerich, *Politik der Vernichtung: Eine Gesamtdarstellung der nationalsozialistischen Judenverfolgung* (Piper, Munich, 1998), pp. 310–320; Gerlach, 'Die Ausweitung der deutschen Massenmorde', pp. 25–26; Philippe Burrin, *Hitler und die Juden: Die Entscheidung für den Völkermord* (S. Fischer, Frankfurt am Main, 1993) [1989], pp. 116–132. For a contrasting view, see Helmut Krausnick, 'Die Einsatzgruppen vom Anschluß Österreichs bis zum Feldzug gegen die Sowjetunion: Entwicklung und Verhältnis zur Wehrmacht', in Krausnick and Wilhelm, *Die Truppe des Weltanschauungskrieges*, pp. 11–278, here pp. 162–165. See chapter 6, 'The Fate of the Soviet Jews: Pre-invasion Order for Genocide?', in this study.
34. Rosenberg's diary entry for 2 April 1941: 'Rosenberg, jetzt ist Ihre große Stunde gekommen!'
35. Myllyniemi, *Die Neuordnung der baltischen Länder*, p. 56. For the full text of the memorandum see *IMG*, vol. 26, pp. 547–554, doc. 1017–PS, 'Denkschrift Nr. 1. Betrifft: UdSSR', 2 April 1941.
36. See Rosenberg's diary entry for 2 April 1941.
37. See chapter 2, 'The *Dienststelle Rosenberg*: the Eastern Experts of the NSDAP'.
38. Halder, *KTB*, II, p. 336, entry for 30 March 1941.
39. See Hitler, *Mein Kampf*, pp. 654–655 and 664.
40. *IMG*, vol. 26, pp. 549–550. See Appendix 3 in this study.
41. Moll (ed.), *"Führer-Erlasse"*, pp. 189–190, doc. 101, 'Erster Erlaß des Führers über die Einführung der Zivilverwaltung in den neu besetzten Ostgebieten', 17 July 1941, and pp. 191–192, doc. 103, decree from Hitler, 22 July 1941; BA-MA, RW 4/v. 578, fos. 121–122, decree from Hitler, 22 July 1941.
42. *IMG*, vol. 26, p. 551.
43. Ibid.
44. Ibid., pp. 553–554.
45. Ibid., p. 554: 'In Anbetracht der ungeheuren Räume und der allein daraus erwachsenden Schwierigkeiten der Verwaltung sowie in Anbetracht der von den westeuropäischen völlig abweichenden Lebensverhältnisse, wie sie durch den Bolschewismus hervorgerufen worden sind, bedürfte die Gesamtfrage der UdSSR einer anderen Behandlung als sie bei den einzelnen Ländern Westeuropas zur Anwendung gebracht worden ist.'
46. Ibid., pp. 555–560, doc. 1019–PS, 'Anhang zur Denkschrift Nr. 2. Personelle Vorschläge für die Reichskommissariate im Osten und die politische Zentralstelle in Berlin', 7 April 1941, here pp. 557 and 559.
47. BA, R 6/4, fo. 3, 20 April 1941; reproduced in *IMG*, vol. 26, pp. 383–384, doc. 865–PS.
48. On the term 'Weißruthenien', see Wolfgang Benz et al. (eds.), *Einsatz im "Reichskommissariat Ostland": Dokumente zum Völkermord im Baltikum und in Weißrußland 1941–1944* (Metropol, Berlin, 1998), p. 17.
49. *IMG*, vol. 26, pp. 555–556 and 559.
50. Ibid., p. 556.
51. 'Herbert Backe', *Das Reich*, No. 23, Berlin, 7 June 1942, p. 1.
52. *IMG*, vol. 26, p. 556.
53. Ibid., pp. 556–557 and 559.
54. See Bräutigam, *So hat es sich zugetragen*, p. 302.
55. *IMG*, vol. 26, p. 556.
56. Ibid., p. 552.

57. Ibid., p. 557: 'Diese Besetzung wird wohl einen gänzlich anderen Charakter tragen als in den Ostseeprovinzen, in der Ukraine und im Kaukasus. Sie wird auf die Niederhaltung jeglichen russischen und bolschewistischen Widerstandes ausgerichtet sein und eine durchaus *rücksichtslose* Persönlichkeit bedürfen, sowohl seitens der militärische Vertretung als auch der eventuellen politischen Führung. Die Aufgaben, die sich hieraus ergeben, brauchen jetzt nicht aufgezeichnet zu werden. Falls nicht eine dauernde Militärverwaltung vorgesehen ist, empfiehlt der Unterzeichnete als Reichskommissar in Moskau den Gauleiter von Ostpreußen, Erich Koch.'
58. Rosenberg's diary entry for 11 April 1941, published in the *Frankfurter Rundschau*, no. 140, 22 June 1971.
59. BAK, N 1075/5, 'Kleine Notizblockzettel mit Texten und Zahlen', undated (1941?): 'Klar sein, dass stets der Feind mithört. Er darf nicht zitieren können. Gesprochenes Wort dagegen ist unschädlich.'
60. *IMG*, vol. 26, pp. 560–566, doc. 1024–PS, 'Allgemeiner Aufbau und Aufgaben einer Dienststelle für die zentrale Bearbeitung der Fragen des osteuropäischen Raumes'.
61. Ibid., p. 562: 'Dieses Ziel kann in bestimmten Gebieten auch gerade durch eine verständnisvolle Sonderbehandlung der betreffenden Volkstümer auf die Dauer gesehen mit weniger Kraftmitteln erreicht werden, als wenn unter Außerachtlassung dieser völkischen und politischen Situation nur mit den Mitteln der militärischen oder Polizeimacht die Lösungen dieser Aufgabe erzwungen werden.'
62. Hugh R. Trevor-Roper (ed.), *Hitler's Table Talk, 1941–1944: His Private Conversations*, 3rd edition (Enigma Books, New York, 2000) [1953], p. 24, entry for 8–11 August 1941. See Army Quartermaster-General Eduard Wagner's letter home to his wife, dated 20 September 1941; Elisabeth Wagner (ed.), *Der Generalquartiermaster: Briefe und Tagebuchaufzeichnungen des Generalquartiermeisters des Heeres, General der Artillerie Eduard Wagner* (Günter Olzog Verlag, Munich, 1963), p. 202.
63. Werner Jochmann (ed.), *Adolf Hitler: Monologe im Führerhauptquartier 1941–1944. Die Aufzeichnungen Heinrich Heims* (Albrecht Knaus Verlag, Hamburg, 1980), pp. 62–63, entry for 17/18 September 1941: 'Der russische Raum ist unser Indien, und wie die Engländer es mit einer Handvoll Menschen beherrschen, so werden wir diesen unseren Kolonialraum regieren.'
64. PAAA, Handakten Etzdorf, Vertrauliche Aufzeichnungen des Vertreters des Auswärtigen Amts beim OKH, Nr. 3, R 27336a, fo. 337768.
65. BA, R 6/34a, fo. 12, 19 September 1941. This comment comes from notes made by Dr Werner Koeppen, Alfred Rosenberg's liaison at FHQ, on Hitler's 'table talk' of 1941.
66. On the British legacy in India see Niall Ferguson, *Empire: How Britain Made the Modern World* (Penguin, London, 2004), pp. 216–218 and 366.
67. *IMG*, vol. 38 (1949), p. 88, doc. 221–L, 'Aktenvermerk'.
68. See Rosenberg's diary entry for 1 June 1941.
69. On Rosenberg's feelings towards Ribbentrop, see Seraphim (ed.), *Das politische Tagebuch Alfred Rosenbergs*, pp. 70–71, 72–73 and 75–76, entries for 21 May, 22 and 25 August 1939. See also Joachim C. Fest, 'Alfred Rosenberg – The Forgotten Disciple', in Joachim C. Fest, *The Face of the Third Reich: Portraits of the Nazi Leadership* (Da Capo Press, New York, 1999) [1963], pp. 163–174, here p. 171.
70. Reitlinger, *The House Built on Sand*, pp. 128–129.
71. *TBJG*, I/9, p. 379, entry for 16 June 1941.
72. Ibid., p. 301, entry for 9 May 1941: 'Er kann nur theoretisieren, aber nicht organisieren.'
73. BA, NS 19/3874, fo. 13, letter from Himmler to newly appointed Head of the Party Chancellery Martin Bormann, 25 May 1941: 'Mit ganz ohne Rosenberg zu arbeiten ist bestimmt das Schwierigste, was es in der NSDAP. gibt.' Reproduced in Helmut Heiber (ed.), *Reichsführer!... Briefe an und von Himmler* (Deutsche Verlags-Anstalt, Stuttgart, 1968), pp. 87–88, doc. 77, here p. 88.
74. BA, NS 19/2696, fo. 2, letter from SS-Gruppenführer Gottlob Berger to Himmler, 'Betr.: Besprechung mit Reichsschatzmeister Schwarz am 1.7.1941', 2 July 1941.

75. BA, R 90/16, fo. 348, 'Alfred Rosenberg zu seinem 50. Geburtstag', n.d.: 'Wenn der Führer nach Beginn des Ostfeldzuges Alfred Rosenberg zum Reichsminister für die besetzten Ostgebiete ernannt hat, so wird er hierfür seine besonderen und eigenen Gründe gehabt haben, die hier außerhalb des Rahmens unserer Betrachtungen liegen.'
76. On Hitler's 'unmethodical' approach to matters of government see Kershaw, *Hitler 1889–1936*, p. 535; Overy, *The Dictators*, p. 87.
77. *TBJG*, I/9, pp. 385–386, entry for 18 June 1941: 'Er kennt die dortigen Probleme sehr genau.'
78. See Arad, 'Alfred Rosenberg and the "Final Solution"', p. 263.
79. *Trials of War Criminals before the Nuernberg Military Tribunals under Control Council Law No. 10, Nuernberg, October 1946–April 1949*, vol. XII (United States Government Printing Office, Washington, 1951), pp. 1322–1323.
80. Ibid., p. 1323.
81. Ibid.
82. Nbg. Dok. PS 1020, fos. 1–15, 'Denkschrift Nr. 3. Betrifft: UdSSR', 25 April 1941, here fos. 2, 4 and 15.
83. See 'Selecting an Administrative Chief' in this chapter.
84. Trevor-Roper (ed.), *Hitler's Table Talk*, p. 19, entry for 1–2 August 1941.
85. *IMG*, vol. 32 (1948), p. 388, doc. 3557-PS.
86. Kershaw, *Hitler 1889–1936*, p. 127.
87. Cecil, *The Myth of the Master Race*, p. 3.
88. See Ernst Klee, *Das Personenlexikon zum Dritten Reich: wer war was vor und nach 1945*, 2nd edition (S. Fischer, Frankfurt am Main, 2003), p. 508; Joachim Lilla, *Statisten in Uniform: Die Mitglieder des Reichstags 1933–1945* (Droste Verlag, Düsseldorf, 2004), p. 525. According to Fritz Nova, Rosenberg was not promoted to the position of Reichsleiter – 'for the Office for Supervision of the Total Intellectual Schooling of the Party' – until 24 January 1934; Nova, *Alfred Rosenberg*, p. 246.
89. *IMG*, vol. 26, pp. 584–592, doc. 1039-PS, 'Bericht über die vorbereitende Arbeit in Fragen des osteuropäischen Raumes', 28 June 1941, here p. 587.
90. See Helmut Heiber, 'Aus den Akten des Gauleiters Kube', *Vierteljahrshefte für Zeitgeschichte*, 4 (1956), pp. 67–92, here p. 77.
91. *IMG*, vol. 38, pp. 91–92. Frauenfeld had originally been foreseen by Rosenberg as Main Commissar in Vitebsk; Nbg. Dok. PS 1036, fos. 1–40, 'Besetzte Ostgebiete', 25 June 1941, here fo. 2. For the post of General Commissar in the Crimea, Rosenberg had proposed former Gauleiter Josef Leopold; Nbg. Dok. PS 1036, fo. 6.
92. Gerlach, *Kalkulierte Morde*, p. 165, fn. 242. Leyser had originally been foreseen by Rosenberg as Main Commissar in Mogilev; Nbg. Dok. PS 1036, fo. 2. For the post of Main Commissar in Zhytomyr, in the General Commissariat Kiev, Rosenberg had proposed deputy Gauleiter Karl Linder; Nbg. Dok. PS 1036, fo. 3.
93. BA, R 43 II/690a, fo. 7, attachment to letter from Dr Lammers to Reich Minister Rosenberg, 18 July 1941; BA, R 6/30, fo. 34, 'Die Generalkommissariate und Aufbaustäbe des Reichskommissariats Ukraine', 6 February 1942.
94. BA, R 6/30, fo. 34.
95. BA, R 43 II/690a, fo. 9, attachment to letter from Dr Lammers to Reich Minister Rosenberg, 18 July 1941. See also Benz et al., *Enzyklopädie*, pp. 601–606.
96. More specifically, the 'old fighters' or 'old guard' were those Party members who possessed a membership number under 100,000. The granting of the membership number 100,000 took place in 1928; Benz et al., *Enzyklopädie*, p. 358.
97. See Dieter Rebentisch, *Führerstaat und Verwaltung im Zweiten Weltkrieg: Verfassungsentwicklung und Verwaltungspolitik 1939–1945* (Franz Steiner Verlag, Stuttgart, 1989), p. 326.
98. See 'Selecting an Administrative Chief' in this chapter.
99. Rosenberg's diary entry for 11 April 1941, published in Robert Kempner, 'Der Führer hat mir einen Kontinent anvertraut: Aus geheimen Aufzeichnungen zum Überfall auf Rußland', *Vorwärts*, no. 28, 2 July 1981, p. 20.

100. Rebentisch, *Führerstaat und Verwaltung*, p. 325. See also Myllyniemi, *Die Neuordnung der Baltischen Länder*, p. 64.
101. For the Interior Ministry: *IMG*, vol. 26, pp. 584–592, doc. 1039-PS, 'Bericht über die vorbereitende Arbeit in Fragen des osteuropäischen Raumes', here p. 590; for the DAF, the SA and the Interior Ministry: Helmut Heiber, 'Der Generalplan Ost', *Vierteljahrshefte für Zeitgeschichte*, 6 (1958), pp. 281–325, here p. 283, fn. 4. The SA, with 4.5 million members in June 1934, was (or at least had been) one of the largest of the Nazi organizations; Hartmann, 'Verbrecherischer Krieg – verbrecherische Wehrmacht?', p. 73, fn. 412.
102. PAAA, Pol. Abt. XIII, Nr. 25, R 105192, fo. 198867, letter from Großkopf to Ribbentrop, 9 May 1941.
103. *IMG*, vol. 26, p. 586.
104. Ibid., p. 587. On the Main Commissars see Gerlach, *Kalkulierte Morde*, p. 166.
105. BA, R 43 II/688, fos. 12–16, attachment to letter from Stuckart to Lammers, 4 July 1941; BA, R 6/21, fo. 100, letter from Rosenberg to Lammers, 5 July 1941.
106. PAAA, Pol. Abt. XIII, Nr. 25, R 105192, fos. 198835–198836, 'Betr.: Unterredung mit Reichsleiter Rosenberg am 19.6.1941', Georg Großkopf, 19 June 1941.
107. BA, R 6/34a, fo. 13, 19 September 1941.
108. See ibid., fo. 28.
109. See *IMG*, vol. 26, p. 557.
110. Ibid., p. 574: 'Ziel eines Reichskommissars für Estland, Lettland, Litauen und Weissruthenien, muß es sein, die Form eines deutschen Protektorats zu erstreben und dann durch Eindeutschung rassisch möglicher Elemente, durch Kolonisierung germanischer Völker und durch Aussiedlung nicht erwünschter Elemente dieses Gebiet zu einem Teil des Großdeutschen Reiches umzuwandeln.' Similar comments are to be found in Rosenberg's 'Anweisung an den Reichskommissar des Reichskommissariats Ostland', sent to Lohse on 21 July 1941; BA, R 92/2, fos. 16–22, here fos. 17–19.
111. See *IMG*, vol. 26, p. 567.
112. BA, R 90/256a, 'Die Zivilverwaltung in den besetzten Ostgebieten (Braune Mappe)', Teil I: Reichskommissariat Ostland, 3 September 1941, p. 25.
113. Ibid., p. 12: 'a) polizeiliche Maßnahmen, b) Nutzbarmachung der wirtschaftlichen Kräfte des Gebietes für die Versorgung der Besatzungstruppe und für Zwecke der deutschen Kriegswirtschaft, c) Sicherstellung von kriegs- und lebenswichtigen Vorräten und Einrichtungen aller Art, d) Versorgung der Bevölkerung, e) Mitwirkung bei Inganghaltung bzw. Wiederingangsetzung der Binnenschiffahrt, des Eisenbahn- und des Postverkehrs, f) Überwachung der Zivilbevölkerung, Mitwirkung bei der Abwehr, Heranziehung der Bevölkerung zu Dienstleistungen, g) Auflösung etwa noch bestehender gegnerischer Organisationen.'
114. For the full text of the decree see Moll (ed.), *"Führer-Erlasse"*, pp. 188–189, doc. 100, 'Erlaß des Führers über die polizeiliche Sicherung der neu besetzten Ostgebiete vom 17. Juli 1941', here p. 188.
115. Gerbet (ed.), *Generalfeldmarschall Fedor von Bock: The War Diary*, pp. 240–241, entry for 6 July 1941.
116. Nbg. Dok. PS 1020, fos. 7–8: 'Jedoch muss durchaus abgesehen von einer *generellen* Vernichtung aller staatlichen, kommunalen und dörflichen Funktionäre. ... Eine *generelle* Austilgung in den ersten Kampfhandlungen und auch später bei Einsatz der Zivilgewalt wäre politisch und sozial eine Massnahme, die sich später furchtbar rächen müsste.' See also Warlimont, *Inside Hitler's Headquarters*, pp. 163–168.
117. Nbg. Dok. PS 1020, fos. 6–7.
118. For the full text of the decree see Moll (ed.), *"Führer-Erlasse"*, pp. 178–179, doc. 92, 'Erlaß des Führers über die Ernennung von Wehrmachtbefehlshabern in den neu besetzten Ostgebieten', 25 June 1941, here p. 179.
119. Ibid., p. 189.
120. Dallin, *German Rule in Russia*, p. 126.
121. BA, NS 19/2803, fo. 2, letter from Himmler to Rosenberg, 24 June 1941.

122. BA, NS 19/2696, fo. 2, letter from SS-Gruppenführer Gottlob Berger to Himmler, 'Betr.: Besprechung mit Reichsschatzmeister Schwarz am 1.7.1941', 2 July 1941.
123. BA, NS 19/2822, fo. 4, letter from Koch to Minister of the Interior Dr Wilhelm Frick, 'Betrifft: Wiedereinsetzung des SS-Gruppenführers von dem Bach-Zelewski als Leiter der Staatspolizei in Königsberg', 7 September 1935; BA, R 20/45b, fos. 1–2, Bach-Zelewski's diary, entry for 27 June 1941.
124. BA, R 6/21, fo. 101, letter from Reichsleiter Rosenberg to Dr Lammers, 5 July 1941.
125. See Miroslav Kárný et al. (eds), *Deutsche Politik im "Protektorat Böhmen und Mähren" unter Reinhard Heydrich 1941–1942: Eine Dokumentation* (Metropol, Berlin, 1997), p. 283, doc. 106.
126. Nbg. Dok. PS 1036, fo. 14. The official who compiled the list, quite possibly Rosenberg himself, spelt Globocnik variously as 'Globotschmig' and 'Globotschnig'.
127. Gerlach, *Kalkulierte Morde*, p. 712.
128. Bräutigam, *So hat es sich zugetragen*, p. 341.
129. *IMG*, vol. 38, p. 91.
130. PAAA, Handakten Etzdorf, Vertrauliche Aufzeichnungen des Vertreters des Auswärtigen Amts beim OKH, Nr. 2, R 27335, fo. 337727, communication from Consul General Bräutigam, 12 August 1941.
131. BA, R 6/21, fo. 101.
132. BA-MA, RW 4/v. 759, fo. 29, attachment to letter from Dr Lammers to Field Marshal Keitel, 20 May 1941; *ADAP, Serie D: 1937–1941*, vol. 12/2 (Vandenhoeck & Ruprecht, Göttingen, 1969), doc. 573, p. 772, 'Aufzeichnung des Vortragenden Legationsrats Großkopf (Abt. Deutschland)', 30 May 1941.

CHAPTER 6

POPULATION POLICY

In addition to economic exploitation and the redrawing of borders with a view to exerting political and administrative control over the occupied regions and their peoples, occupation policy in the Soviet territories would contain a third central feature, which can essentially be summed up as 'population policy'. This was a key aspect of the Nazi programme to reorder occupied Europe along racial lines to create a Neuordnung under German hegemony. The racial Neuordnung was inextricably linked with the political and economic aspects of this wide-reaching, though not clearly delineated, process. Intended population policy in the occupied Soviet territories would essentially encompass the following three tasks: the murder of racial and political 'undesirables'; the expulsion – often further eastwards – of substantial sections of the indigenous population from their homes; and the resettlement of peoples of 'Germanic' racial stock in the occupied East. Hence, a 'Germanization' (*Germanisierung*) of the land was to take place; due to their alleged racial inferiority, a Germanization of the people themselves was out of the question. From the point of view of the Nazi leadership, a Germanization of the land would have the dual purpose of remedying the supposed problem of a lack of Lebensraum for the German people, whilst at the same time securing the conquered territories on a biological level in the long term.[1]

These tasks were largely incumbent on the ideological and racial elite in the various offices of the *Schutzstaffel*, commonly known as the SS, under the command of the Reichsführer-SS and Chief of the German Police, Heinrich Himmler. Like the Economic Staff East, the SS would be required to implement their tasks during both the initial period of military hostilities itself and its aftermath, i.e., during the envisaged post-victory occupation. Though much SS planning for the future shape of the occupied eastern territories took place only after the beginning of the military campaign against the Soviet Union, knowledge of SS activities during the first six months of 1941 can be pieced together to form an idea of what this increasingly powerful organization had in mind for the East.

Germanic Resettlement

In addition to preparing the proposed structure of the German administration for the occupied Soviet territories, Alfred Rosenberg's memoranda of April and May 1941 had laid the (potential) foundations for the future territorial set-up in the East and the envisaged expulsions and resettlements which were to take place there. Settlement plans, though, were the acknowledged field of expertise of the SS, in particular its newest branch, the Office of the RKFDV. It was around the same time that Rosenberg's proposals appeared that Reichsführer-SS Himmler's ruminations on resettling the occupied Soviet territories after the war with people of Germanic stock began to take a more concrete form. In this context, Himmler was acting in his capacity as Reich Commissar for the Strengthening of German Nationhood (*Reichskommissar für die Festigung deutschen Volkstums*, RKFDV), a position to which Hitler had appointed him as early as 7 October 1939, in the wake of the Polish campaign.[2] Himmler had chosen the title himself.[3] His principal task as RKFDV was the resettlement within the Greater German Reich of ethnic Germans living outside its boundaries, though in territory under German arms. It also worked in the other direction: Himmler was charged with the expulsion beyond the Reich's borders of any groups which he considered to be a 'damaging influence'.[4] Although the Office of the Reich Commissar for the Strengthening of German Nationhood had initially been set up with those Polish territories under German occupation in mind, the decision to invade the Soviet Union opened up massive new vistas for Himmler and his staff. In an article from 1941, SS-Brigadeführer Ulrich Greifelt, Chief of the Staff Main Office of the RKFDV, described the strengthening of German nationhood as the 'central task in the East'.[5]

It was not only Germans themselves, however, who were proposed for resettlement in the occupied Soviet territories. Other Nordic or Germanic peoples were also to be shifted eastwards with the aim of, from the National Socialist point of view, improving the quality of the racial stock there. In a letter dated 4 April 1941 and addressed to the Higher SS and Police Leader[6] North-West in the Netherlands, SS-Brigadeführer Hanns Rauter, the main topic of which was the settlement of Reich Germans in the Netherlands, Himmler also mentioned his intention to move 'capable' Dutch people to the East 'after the conclusion of the war'. With this in mind, he continued, it seemed appropriate not to satisfy 'too quickly' the desire of the Dutch to find employment possibilities in their native land.[7] In the National Socialist racial pecking order, the Dutch, like the Flemish, the Danish, the Swedish and the Norwegian peoples,[8] as a 'Germanic race', occupied a relatively lofty position. As a means of consolidating Germanic settlements in the occupied eastern territories, but also because it was believed that the Netherlands were not able to feed their population in the long run,[9] Himmler wanted to encourage the Dutch to try their luck in the East.

Six days after writing to SS-Brigadeführer Rauter, Himmler wrote to a Dr Reese, who was attached to the military commander in Belgium and northern France and in the process of putting together a 'major work about "The Dutch and the Reich"'. Himmler, who remarked that he also came into contact with 'the Dutch and Flemish question', requested information from Reese as to the exact formulation of the latter's topic and whether or not important sections of the work were already completed.[10] Sometime between then and 9 May 1941, Himmler issued an order to his staff in the Office of the Reich Commissar for the Strengthening of German Nationhood to prepare for the recruitment of Dutch and Flemish people for settlement in the East after the war.[11]

The eight-page draft 'Report on the Preparatory Work for the Obtaining of Dutch and Flemish Settlers for the New Eastern Territories' claimed that, as a result of the overpopulation in the Netherlands and Belgium, there was interest 'in principle' in a rural settlement. In support of this assertion, the author(s) of the report pointed to the pre-war search of Dutch farmers for new settlement land in Normandy. An exact figure for those willing to resettle in the occupied Soviet territories could not be given, as this would to a large extent be dependent on the economic situation after the war. Echoing Himmler's letter to SS-Brigadeführer Rauter five weeks earlier, the report then suggested that the prerequisite for a large-scale resettlement of Dutch and Flemish people in the East was for employment possibilities in the Netherlands, Belgium and the adjoining French territory to remain restricted. It was not, therefore, in the interests of a 'purposeful eastern policy' to pursue the removal of the difficulties experienced by the 'north-western economic territory', i.e., the Low Countries and northern France. These difficulties were those involved in the conversion of the economies of the Netherlands and Belgium from 'intercontinental economy' to 'European *Grossraum* economy'. The smaller number of employment possibilities in the two countries were 'inevitably' related to this economic conversion. The report further argued that the limited job prospects should not be balanced out by 'artificial industrial concentration' but rather by 'generous population transfers'.[12]

In the future *Großraum* economy (*Großraumwirtschaft*), these territories would not be autonomous economic entities, but rather parts of a greater whole, a German-dominated economy encompassing the entire breadth of continental Europe. If a certain group of workers would be more effective two or three thousand miles away, then that is where they would be sent. It was up to the RKFDV to see to it that this was done. Such an action would represent the practical side of a programme which the Reich Ministry for Economics had been working on since the previous summer. In a speech to the Grand Advisory Committee of the Reich Group Industry (*Reichsgruppe Industrie*, RGI) on 3 October 1940, Ministerialdirektor Gustav Schlotterer, head of the eastern section in the RWM, had explained that it was desirable to construct a Großraumwirtschaft in order 'to produce a sensible division of labour between the agrarian and industrial areas of Europe' and 'because we want to produce as cheaply as possible in the European Großraum'. For these reasons, centres of production 'which are useless' and 'have only shot up under the protection of foreign exchange, customs, or quota arrangements' would be closed.[13]

The author(s) of the RKFDV report from 9 May 1941 recognized, however, that the willingness of those circles which 'set the tone' in the Netherlands to cooperate with Germany was 'decidedly slight'. In Flanders, where nationalist circles comprised a larger proportion of the population than in the Netherlands and also possessed a greater resonance amongst the other sections of the population, willingness to work with Germany was more substantial. The fear already evident in national socialist and nationalist circles in the Netherlands, according to the report, that an intensive recruitment for the East would deprive these circles of exactly those people who – at least from a point of view sympathetic to the Nazis – were needed in the Netherlands, indicates the serious nature of preparations already under way for the resettlement of western Europeans in the occupied East. In accordance with an order from Himmler, the actual recruitment and the subsequent settlement itself would be left until after the war. In order to ensure later success, however, general preparations would have to take place beforehand. Moreover, the author(s) deemed it advisable to already send to the East some employers and those amongst the urban population who were willing. This would serve as a preparatory foundation for the later large-scale resettlement.[14]

On 13 May, four days after the draft RKFDV report had been produced, SS-Hauptsturmführer Dr Günther Stier from the Office of the RKFDV discussed with the Higher SS and Police Leader North-West in The Hague the readiness of members of the Dutch population to resettle in the eastern territories.[15] Though economic considerations cannot be said to have been driving the planned resettlement of the occupied Soviet territories, they did have a significant role to play when it came to resettling workers in a particular branch of employment, as can be inferred from Gustav Schlotterer's October 1940 speech, quoted above. Whether or not Hitler was aware at this point in time of the preparations of the Office of the RKFDV to settle Dutch and Flemish people in the Soviet territories cannot with certainty be determined. On one occasion in October 1941 he claimed that four million Germans would be resettled in the East in ten years' time, with at least ten million there in twenty years. The settlers would not just come from the Reich, however, but 'rather above all [sic] from America, but also from Scandinavia, Holland and Flanders'.[16]

With regard to pre-'Barbarossa' plans for the wider Nazi programme of a comprehensive reordering and resettling of 'the East' along racial lines, the available evidence is fairly meagre. Long-term Nazi plans for the resettlement of Germanic peoples in the occupied Soviet territories, and the expulsion of substantial sections of the native population, are often summarized under the catch-all heading General Plan East (*Generalplan Ost*).[17] The infamous Generalplan Ost – at least as it is known today – was essentially a product of post- and not pre-invasion planning. Reports from the front received by the political and military leaderships back in Germany during the first days of the Soviet campaign appeared to fully justify their high pre-invasion expectations. Reichsführer-SS Himmler felt relaxed enough to play tennis on two consecutive days.[18] Although planning for post-victory resettlement within the territories to be conquered from the Soviet Union appears to have been neglected somewhat prior to the invasion itself, Himmler evidently believed that the time had now come to attend to this, for him most stimulating, issue. On 24 June, two days after 'Barbarossa' began, the Reichsführer-SS met for forty-five minutes in his office on the Prinz Albrechtstrasse in Berlin with SS-Standartenführer Professor Dr Konrad Meyer, who combined his functions as Director of the Institute for Agrarian Studies at the University of Berlin with his role as Chief of the RKFDV Planning Office. Himmler requested Meyer to draw up a sketch for resettlement possibilities in the East, which were, it seemed, on the verge of being realized.[19] It is of interest that Meyer had been a member of both the Reich Farming Council (*Reichsbauernrat*) and the Staff Office of the Reich Ministry for Food and Agriculture.[20] As such, he would almost certainly have had experience of working with another planner of mass murder, Herbert Backe.

Meyer and his staff were able to produce a first draft in just three weeks, which Meyer presented to Himmler on 15 July.[21] Despite the speed at which Meyer and his staff worked in producing the draft, it would seem that military events had overtaken them. On the cover sheet to Meyer's draft there appears the simple handwritten comment 'superseded' (*überholt*), presumably from Himmler himself, though without any date or further explanation.[22] There is no evidence to suggest that the draft plan in its 15 July 1941 form was ever presented to Hitler,[23] although Himmler's extended presence at FHQ between 15 and 20 July would certainly have given him just such an opportunity.[24]

This draft from Meyer was in fact the second Generalplan Ost. The first had been produced by Meyer himself as early as January 1940, but this draft had dealt almost exclusively with those lands already occupied by Germany at that moment in time, in particular the former Polish territories.[25] Meyer's draft Generalplan Ost of 15 July 1941 has never been found,[26] which means that an examination of its contents, written at such a crucial point in time, is unfortunately not possible. The same fate appears to have befallen all copies of the next version of the Generalplan Ost, namely the RSHA version from the end of 1941.[27] In the case of this third draft of the Generalplan Ost, a commentary on it from Dr Erhard Wetzel, head of the section on race in the Reich Ministry for the Occupied Eastern Territories, dated 27 April 1942, does exist.[28] Referring to the draft, Wetzel noted that the five to six million Jews living in the USSR were expressly included by the RSHA in the total of thirty-one million people to be expelled from Eastern Europe and transported to western Siberia to make space for

4.5 million German settlers.[29] If, as Wetzel's commentary on it indicates, the aim in the RSHA's draft plan was to resettle the Soviet Jews further east – those Jews who, in the event, were the first of Europe's Jews to be murdered on a large scale – then this suggests not only that there was no pre-'Barbarossa' order to murder all Soviet Jews and that rather a territorial solution remained the aim,[30] but also that the final fate of the remaining Soviet Jews had not been determined by the end of 1941. For this reason, the RSHA's inclusion of the USSR's five to six million Jews in the total of those people who were to be expelled from Eastern Europe is astounding, given that whole communities of Soviet Jews were being slaughtered by the late summer of 1941, months before the RSHA plan was written.

If one is to accept Wetzel's commentary – and there is no reason not to do so – this is not the only instance of the RSHA version not being up to speed on issues of major importance. According to Wetzel, the RSHA had not taken into account the projected Germanization of several territories, one of which was the Crimea.[31] At a meeting of senior officials on 16 July 1941, discussed in more detail in chapter 9 of this study, Hitler had specifically instructed that the Crimea was to be cleared of 'all foreigners' and settled with Germans, and that it, along with a 'considerable hinterland' to the north, was to become Reich territory.[32] It is admittedly not entirely clear to what extent Hitler had a concrete time frame in mind. At the end of September 1941, he announced that he had a German protectorate of approximately twenty-five years' duration in mind for the Ukraine.[33] This, however, would indicate that the resettlement of the Ukraine, to which the Crimea was to be administratively attached,[34] and presumably the other occupied Soviet territories intended for this fate would take place only after these twenty-five years had passed.[35] In subsequently communicating Hitler's wishes in this matter to his staff, Himmler also appears to have referred to a 'later colonization' and not an immediate one.[36] Yet the Generalplan Ost should nevertheless have made reference to the intended Germanization of the Crimea and other territories, for the very reason that the plan was supposed to deal with the long-term intentions of the Nazi leadership.

In any case, the obvious errors and improbabilities in the RSHA plan led Himmler to turn once again to Meyer.[37] It is quite possible that the inadequacies of the RSHA plan had occurred to Himmler long before Wetzel's commentary appeared, as Meyer had already held a presentation on the matter at the end of January 1942,[38] and it is quite likely that he received instructions from Himmler on this occasion to redraft the plan. The result was the 'Generalplan Ost – Legal, Economic and Spatial Foundations for the Restructuring of the East', which Meyer submitted at the end of May 1942.[39] Himmler was on the whole pleased with Meyer's new version and intended to show it to Hitler.[40] By this time, however, almost a year into the war against the Soviet Union, the realization of these far-reaching resettlement plans was becoming increasingly unlikely.

Returning to the weeks immediately after the beginning of the eastern campaign, it was not only the Office of the RKFDV which was busying itself with plans for the future resettlement of territory in the process of being conquered from the Soviet Union. On 4 July 1941, the legal adviser and permanent representative of the Association of German Ethnic Groups in Europe (*Verband der Deutschen Volksgruppen in Europa*), Dr Werner Hasselblatt, sent a fifteen-page letter to Privy Councillor Georg Großkopf in the Foreign Office in Berlin.[41] Großkopf was Foreign Minister von Ribbentrop's permanent liaison officer to the Bureau Rosenberg. Hasselblatt's letter dealt with political and administrative questions concerning the East, in particular the Baltic, where he was from.[42] It constituted in effect a potential alternative to the Generalplan Ost, which was precisely at this moment in time in the process of being put together in the Office of the RKFDV.

As part of his Großraum conception of continental Europe united under the leadership of the German Reich, Hasselblatt proposed a twenty-year programme of complete Germanization of the land, which would be carried out 'without consideration of the West', by which he presumably meant Great Britain and the United States. The territories under consideration for this programme of Germanization were the southern strips of the Gaue of Lower Styria and Carinthia, Danzig-West Prussia, large parts of the Warthegau and Upper Silesia, Bohemia and Moravia, the area around Belgrade, the Crimea and northern Caucasus, western Lithuania and Courland, together with parts of Livonia. Like the authors of the various versions of the Generalplan Ost, Hasselblatt proposed a Germanization of the land, not of its inhabitants. Some thought would thus have to be given as to where to resettle those non-Germans who were to be ejected from the territories in question; the Germanization of Poles, Ukrainians, Czechs, Belarusians, Greater Russians, Karelians, Turks, Tartars or peoples of the Caucasus was not to be recommended.[43]

Hasselblatt then proceeded to allocate the various eastern territories, along with most of the other European states under either German occupation or German influence, to one of six groups, (a) to (f), each representing a different form of government or degree of control exercised by the Reich. The territories within the first group would be de jure sovereign, though permanently attached to Germany in 'intimate collaboration' through treaties. This group was made up of Denmark, Norway, Sweden, Finland, Romania, Belgium and, potentially, Hungary. Unsurprisingly, this group did not contain any of the Soviet territories. The second group consisted of those states with 'limited non-German sovereignty' – Slovakia, the Ukraine and the Caucasus (as a federal state). The territories within group (c) would possess both a German administration and a German upper class. Parts of the eastern Gaue, in the event that some Poles and Belarusians continued to reside there, were slated by Hasselblatt for this form of rule. Autonomous territories of the Reich constituted the fourth group, namely Estonia and two territories shifted further eastwards and inhabited by Latvians and Lithuanians. Territories which were to be administered permanently by a German apparatus made up group (e): the General Government, non-European colonies and those territories of the former USSR not already included in any of the other groups. The sixth and final group consisted of those territories which, 'in the course of the biological expansion of the German nation', represented the reserve for future German settlement. These territories were the parts of East Prussia, Danzig-West Prussia and the Warthegau which had not yet been naturally Germanized, along with the General Government, although the latter had already been included in group (e).[44]

Hasselblatt then listed the eight most important 'dividing elements' which he had used to assign the eastern territories to the six groups. These categories included nationhood, race, language, religion, cultural level and ideological and political alignment. A second list of six categories constituted those 'dividing elements' which were to be 'created' and included national frontiers, customs borders, police borders and the varying attitude of the territory and its inhabitants to the German nation corresponding to the scale 'oppressed peoples', 'ruled-over peoples', 'peoples devoted to the Reich' and 'friendly and allied peoples'.[45] Hasselblatt differentiated between the 'immediate programme' and the 'thousand-year programme'. The 'urgent' immediate programme aimed to achieve the maximum in economic production as quickly as possible. The key aspect of the thousand-year programme would be to prevent the divided parts of the 'huge Russian empire' from growing together again at some point in the future.[46]

Hasselblatt's recommendations were clearly much closer to the ideas propounded by Alfred Rosenberg than to those of other Nazis, who made in comparison only a limited differentiation (if any) between the various eastern peoples and sought merely to colonize and exploit the East. The similarities between the ideas of Hasselblatt and those of Rosenberg can be seen in particular in the former's assertion that the Ukraine and the Caucasus, as a federal state, would belong to that group of states with 'limited non-German sovereignty', that the Baltic States, in particular Estonia, would become integral territories of the Reich, and in the way these allocations were based on a series of categories such as language, religion and cultural value. Hasselblatt's proposal to prevent the divided parts of the Russian empire from growing together again at some point in the future was reminiscent of Rosenberg's desire to erect a 'cordon sanitaire'[47] against Greater Russia in the form of the Reich Commissariats of the Ukraine, the Baltic and Belarus, and the Caucasus, all of which would have a certain degree of autonomy, though remain dependent on Germany. Given the similarities between their respective ideas, it is perhaps not surprising that Hasselblatt subsequently became head of the special department German Eastern Policy in Rosenberg's East Ministry.[48]

In his letter, Hasselblatt went on to recommend the construction of a Reich Ministry for Eastern Administration (*Reichsministerium für Ostverwaltung*). As the 'instrument of the Führer', 'immense creative tasks' would be assigned to this central office. The Ministry would be necessary for lucid planning, the centralization of evacuation and resettlement work, and the administration of the limited human resources available for the occupied Soviet territories. All issues which affected the territories in the East or called for a decision from Hitler would require the participation of the Ministry.[49] Hasselblatt concluded his letter to Großkopf merely with the request that he be given the opportunity to visit the latter during the coming week.[50]

It is for several reasons unlikely that the proposals contained in Hasselblatt's letter exerted a significant influence on German policy in the East. First, his letter contained nothing very new; it was essentially a rerun of what Rosenberg had been recommending for the previous three months. Secondly, it is doubtful that the letter was even seen by anyone much higher in rank than Privy Councillor Großkopf, let alone the men who really made the decisions, such as Hitler, Göring and Himmler. Whether it even found its way to Head of the Reich Chancellery Lammers can be doubted. Thirdly, by the beginning of July 1941 the various offices of the SS were finally under way with the preparation of resettlement plans for the aftermath of what appeared to them at that moment in time to be a dazzlingly successful military campaign.

The Fate of the Soviet Jews: Pre-invasion Order for Genocide?

If the preparations of the RKFDV for recruiting Dutch and Flemish workers for resettlement in the East after the war, already being made in April and May 1941, constituted the 'positive' side of SS planning for policy in the occupied Soviet territories, then it was Reinhard Heydrich's Reich Security Main Office and its subordinate formations which would deal with the 'negative' side: the fate of racial and political 'undesirables'. As in Poland,[51] the Nazi leadership intended to physically remove the Soviet intelligentsia – or those they classed as belonging to this group – in an attempt, first, to hasten the collapse of the Soviet state (Goebbels: 'R[ussia] will fall apart like tinder'),[42] and, secondly, to ensure that no potential leaders remained who could form the nucleus of a future nationalistic resistance movement or ruling elite which could challenge German hegemony. Members of the so-called 'Jewish-Bolshevik intelligentsia', as the supposed core of Soviet power, were first in line for liquidation. This was to be the first task in the process of racial Neuordnung of the East under German domination. It was Himmler who possessed overall responsibility for these operations, though his forces would work in close collaboration with army units[53] and, later, increasingly with the civil administration.[54] His most senior representatives in the Soviet Union were the Higher SS and Police Leaders.

In late May 1941, following agreement with the Commander-in-Chief of the Army, Field Marshal von Brauchitsch, Himmler selected 'for the territory of the political administration' Higher SS and Police Leaders 'for the implementation of the special orders given to me by the Führer'. The HSSPF would thus be Himmler's representatives in the regions under civil administration once the handover of territories from military to civil jurisdiction had taken place. Until the handover of territory to the civil administration, the HSSPF would operate in the army rear areas and, along with the SS and police forces under Himmler's control, be subordinate to the respective army commander in questions of marching, provisioning and accommodation.[55] Among the units subordinated to the HSSPF were the Einsatzgruppen of the Security Police and the SD. Each of the four Einsatzgruppen comprised between 600 and 1,000 men and was subdivided into four or five *Einsatzkommandos* (task commandos) and *Sonderkommandos* (special commandos).[56] These mobile formations would advance immediately behind army units into occupied territory. With regard to their tasks, their primary function was to kill 'undesirable elements' or to incite sections of the native population to do their dirty work for them.

Due to an organizational blunder, Heydrich had not been able to inform Himmler's four HSSPF personally of the instructions for the operations of the Einsatzgruppen, instructions he had already issued to the Einsatzgruppen leaders themselves.[57] Thus, Heydrich was forced to pass this information on to the four HSSPF in a communication dated 2 July 1941. In his preliminary remarks, Heydrich announced that the short-term aim of the entire action was the political pacification of the soon-to-be-occupied territories, which was essentially a matter for the Security Police. The long-term aim, however, was the 'economic pacification' of the territories, which presumably meant the restructuring of the economy of the Soviet territories in accordance with the plans drawn up by the planners around Backe and Thomas. Although all security measures were to be geared towards this long-term aim, they were to be implemented with 'ruthless severity' in view of the decade-long shaping of the country in the Bolshevik mould. At the same time, the differences between the various indigenous peoples, especially the Balts, Belarusians, Ukrainians, Georgians, Armenians and Azerbaijanis, were 'naturally' to be taken as a basis for the action and to be used to the benefit of the objectives wherever possible. In another example of economic objectives occupying a position of priority in relation to other considerations, Heydrich concluded his preliminary remarks by stating unequivocally: 'The *political* pacification is the first prerequisite for the *economic* pacification.'[58] He then defined the groups of victims of the 'political pacification' very specifically:

> All of the following are to be executed[:]
> Functionaries of the Comintern (as with the Communist career politicians per se)
> [T]he higher-, medium-, and radical lower-level functionaries of the Party, the Central Committee [and] regional and district committees
> People's Commissars
> Jews in Party and state positions
> [O]ther radical elements (saboteurs, propagandists, snipers, assassins, agitators etc.[)][59]

Rosenberg had quite possibly exerted some influence here in declaring himself, as mentioned in the previous chapter, against 'a *general* annihilation of all state, local and village functionaries'. Hence, only 'radical' lower-level functionaries were to be killed.

This document probably remains the most informative that exists in efforts to determine whether a pre-invasion order was issued to the Einsatzgruppen to kill all Soviet Jews during the course of the war in the East. Given that Communist functionaries had already been mentioned at the top of the list, Heydrich's instructions did place particular emphasis on Jews by referring once more further down to 'Jews in Party and state positions'. Additionally, it is likely that Heydrich expected and indeed intended that his instructions be interpreted broadly; how, for example, were the terms 'propagandists' and 'agitators' to be defined? Even the last word on the list, 'etc.', demonstrates that those who came under the heading 'other radical elements' were by no means clearly specified.[60]

Nevertheless, the instructions can in no way be seen as an injunction to kill *all* Soviet Jews. The suggestion that Heydrich did not want to put anything more explicit down in black and white[61] is highly questionable. Why would he go to the trouble of contacting Himmler's most senior representatives in the Soviet Union with a precise list of those who should be murdered and then hold back when it came to the crunch? In any case, Heydrich explicitly stated in his communication of 2 July that he was informing the HSSPF of the 'most important instructions' he had already conveyed to the Einsatzgruppen chiefs in oral form.[62] Therefore, it can be presumed that, if Heydrich had in fact already issued an order to the heads of the four Einsatzgruppen to the effect that they should kill all Soviet Jews without distinction, it would have been included in his communication to the HSSPF.[63] This, however, was not the case. In addition, the almost daily 'incident reports' (*Ereignismeldungen*) compiled by the RSHA directly from information recorded by the Einsatzgruppen themselves and sent in writing back to Berlin, were very detailed; the SS had no compunction about putting their intentions down on paper.

The evidence of the first months of the invasion speaks in any case against the claim that the Einsatzgruppen were ordered from the beginning to kill all Soviet Jews, including women and children. On the contrary, during the first six weeks of the campaign, it was primarily men of military service age – Communists and members of the intelligentsia in particular – who were killed.[64] A sharp escalation in both the numbers killed and the range of victims – including women and children in substantial numbers and then entire Jewish communities – did not occur until August.[65] Let the following horrific examples suffice to illustrate this escalation: Einsatzkommando 3, part of Dr Walter Stahlecker's Einsatzgruppe A in the Baltic, reported 135 women (a little over 3 per cent) among 4,239 Jews 'executed' during the month of July 1941, but 26,243 women (over 46 per cent) and 15,112 children (almost 27 per cent) in the total of 56,459 Jews murdered in September.[66] On 20 August, two months into the campaign, Dr Dr [sic] Otto Rasch's Einsatzgruppe C, operating in northern and central Ukraine, gave a total number of 8,000 persons killed.[67] By the beginning of November, this number had increased tenfold to 80,000.[68] According to the statistics of Otto Ohlendorf's Einsatzgruppe D, operating in Bessarabia and southern Ukraine, 4,425 people were murdered by the unit up to and including 18 August (just under two months after the beginning of the campaign), whereas 8,890 'Jews and Communists' – i.e., twice as many – were 'executed' during the following four weeks.[69] In the next fifteen days they killed a further 22,467 people.[70]

Finally, one should for a moment abandon a position of hindsight and attempt to place oneself in the shoes of the Nazi leadership at the onset of 'Barbarossa'. According to the original plans, the minimum limit for the military advance was a theoretical line connecting Archangel in the north with Astrakhan on the Caspian Sea in the south, a line some 300 miles (over 480 km) *east* of Moscow. That would have meant that the Einsatzgruppen, with around 3,000 men, would have been expected to kill all Soviet Jews in an area three times as large as that which was actually conquered by the German army in 1941, all in the space of not longer than twelve weeks.[71]

The sharp escalation in killing mentioned above occurred, indeed could only have occurred, after Himmler massively increased the number of SS men operating behind the advancing German army. This build-up included reassigning on 23 July 1941 at least eleven battalions of Order Police (*Ordnungspolizei*), each of approximately 500 men, from various military commanders in the rear areas to the HSSPF in the north, centre and south of the Soviet territories. At the same time, two SS brigades, with a combined force of over 11,000, were attached to the HSSPF Centre and South. Thus, by the end of July, 5,500 to 6,000 members of the Order Police and 11,000 SS men had reinforced the 3,000 persons who constituted the Einsatzgruppen to provide a total of around 20,000 troops.[72] This build-up coincided with an increase in Himmler's trips to the East to visit his men in the field personally.[73] Taking all these factors into consideration, it is likely that the decision to extend the killing to all Soviet Jews was taken at some point between the middle and the end of July and passed on orally along the chain of command during the subsequent weeks. Himmler's presence at Führer Headquarters in East Prussia from 15 to 20 July would have given him the opportunity to discuss the operations of the Einsatzgruppen with Hitler,[74] and it is possible that decisions were taken here both to expand the scope of these operations to include the whole of Soviet Jewry and to provide the necessary manpower increases.

There is also no indication of a pre-invasion plan to begin wiping out all of Soviet Jewry during major hostilities and to complete it in the course of the occupation once the Soviet territories in question had been pacified. Although the killing of various groups of 'undesirables' would doubtless have continued in the wake of the defeat of the Red Army, to have killed hundreds of thousands of women and children after the cessation of hostilities, i.e., effectively in peacetime, would probably have been impossible even for the unscrupulous men in question. The initial combat phase was, on the contrary, seen by the Nazi leadership as a unique opportunity to annihilate Communist functionaries and the Jewish intelligentsia in the Soviet Union.[75] What it was not intended to constitute, at least prior to the invasion, was the moment in which all Soviet Jews were slaughtered, in spite of the horror which did occur after 22 June.[76]

Given that it remains unclear exactly when the decision was taken to expand the slaughter in the Soviet Union to include all Soviet Jews or indeed when this decision was communicated to those tasked with its implementation, determining the reason(s) for this escalation must necessarily be based largely on speculation. Surprisingly, given the import of the issue, many historians have neglected to venture an answer to the question as to why the killing in the Soviet Union was extended; a few, however, have. One historian appears to interpret the escalation as an attempt by Himmler to extend of his own accord the authority and jurisdiction he already possessed in the occupied Soviet territories.[77] Whilst Himmler may indeed have taken 'the decisive initiative'[78] in increasing the number of SS men operating in the killing zone, this would almost certainly have required a prior say-so from Hitler, and the question remains as to why this go-ahead was given.

Perhaps the most well-known explanation posits that in mid-July Hitler was convinced that the military campaign against the Soviet Union was almost over and, gripped by a feeling of 'victory euphoria', gave instructions to accelerate the killing, or racial 'cleansing', in preparation for a final settlement in the East.[79] This theory seems at first glance very plausible, but it is by no means clear that Hitler and his inner circle were in fact in a state of 'victory euphoria' at this point in time. As early as 24 July, four and a half weeks into the campaign and potentially only days after the decision was taken to escalate the killing of Soviet Jews, Joseph Goebbels noted in his diary: 'The mood in the Reich has become somewhat graver. It is gradually becoming clear that the eastern campaign is no stroll to Moscow.'[80]

A third historian has concluded that the Nazi leadership expanded the scope of the killing because, effectively, it could. The experiences of the first weeks of the campaign demonstrated that those charged with the task of eliminating the alleged core of Bolshevik power in the Soviet Union faced little serious opposition, either from the non-Jewish indigenous population or, crucially, from the Wehrmacht.[81] Indeed, it could well be the case that the Nazi leadership had the *intention* already prior to the invasion to wipe out Soviet Jewry in its entirety, but did not issue an explicit order to this effect due to its own uncertainty as to how feasible this would prove to be in practice. After the encouraging first few weeks of the campaign, however, the time for removing eastern Jewry root and branch was deemed to have come.

A Territorial Solution to the 'Jewish Question'

If immediate death was not intended for the majority of the Jewish population of the European part of the USSR prior to the onset of Operation Barbarossa, what then was to be their fate in the 'racially pure' German-occupied eastern territories? Up to the beginning of 1941, both the RKFDV and the RSHA had had their hands full with population shifts into and out of Poland,[82] where the former agency coordinated ethnic German resettlement whilst the latter handled expulsions eastwards.[83] The anticipated territorial solution to the 'Jewish Question'[84] (*Judenfrage*), the so-called Madagascar Plan (*Madagaskar-Plan*)[85] – the proposal to ship the bulk of continental Europe's Jews to the island of Madagascar off the southeastern coast of Africa – had also been on the agenda until the end of 1940. By that time it had become clear that, due to Great Britain's continued refusal to surrender and her ongoing control of the seas, the practical implementation of this scheme was not feasible. Thereafter, starting as early as the end of January or the beginning of February 1941,[86] much time was taken up with preparations for the tasks of the Einsatzgruppen during the military advance into Soviet territory, particularly drawn-out negotiations with the army leadership.[87] By piecing together the evidence available, however, it appears that Heydrich in particular found time alongside his other duties to prepare a territorial solution to the 'Jewish Question' to be implemented after the Soviet Union had been subdued and its European territories brought under German control.

A meeting between Heydrich and Reichsmarschall Göring on 26 March 1941 provides a suitable starting point. Following the meeting, Heydrich noted down in a series of points what had been discussed. One of these points read: '10. Regarding the solution to the "Jewish Question" I briefly reported to the Reichsmarschall ... and presented him with my draft, of which, with an alteration regarding the jurisdiction of Rosenberg, he approved and ordered resubmission.'[88] Heydrich forwarded the original version of these notes to Himmler and copies to Chief of Office IV (Gestapo) of the RSHA SS-Brigadeführer Heinrich Müller, 'also for Eichmann's information'; to head of Group E (Counter-Espionage) in Office IV SS-Sturmbannführer Walter Schellenberg; to Chief of Office I (Personnel) of the RSHA SS-Brigadeführer Bruno Streckenbach; and to Chief of Office III (SD Main Office) of the RSHA SS-Standartenführer Otto Ohlendorf, later head of the killing unit Einsatzgruppe D. The information contained was 'strictly confidential'.

The fact that SS-Obersturmbannführer Adolf Eichmann, the head of IV B 4, the RSHA's section on Jewish affairs, and principal organizer of transports, was to be informed of the contents of Heydrich's notes indicates that Heydrich and Göring discussed deportations. When this is combined with the knowledge that the two men also discussed 'the solution to the "Jewish Question"' in conjunction with the 'jurisdiction of Rosenberg', who, as discussed in the previous chapter, was at this point in time slated to head the civil administration in the territories later to be conquered from the Soviet Union, it becomes clear that Heydrich's reflections on a solution to the 'Jewish Question' were in terms of a territorial solution in the occupied Soviet territories after the war.[89] Thus, by the end of March 1941 at the latest, this course of action – the draft for which had been 'approved' by Göring – was the intended policy towards Europe's Jewish population.

Less than two weeks after the meeting between Göring and Heydrich, Rosenberg noted in a paper on the USSR that the 'total expulsion of Jewry' out of the Baltic States, which were intended for eventual incorporation into the Greater German Reich, would be necessary. As possible destinations for the Jewish expellees, Rosenberg suggested the territory eastwards of Lake Peipus on the Estonian–Russian border and declared that 'a great possibility for settlement' existed, above all, in Belarus.[90] Five days previously, on 2 April, he had noted that the core territory of Russia could be used as a deportation destination for 'undesirable elements of the population' from 'all other' territories.[91] The Soviet Jews would doubtlessly have come under the heading of 'undesirable elements'. Before this mass deportation further east could be effected, presumably after military hostilities had come to an end and damaged or destroyed railway lines been repaired, an interim solution to the 'Jewish Question' in the Soviet Union was deemed by Rosenberg to be necessary. In two subsequent papers, one from 29 April and the other from 7 May, he proposed ghettoization and forced labour.[92] Although Rosenberg was not necessarily at this point in time in contact with Heydrich and those around him regarding this issue, in his proposals for a long-term solution in the form of deportations further east he was evidently thinking along the same lines as the RSHA.

There must, however, be a prehistory to the 26 March meeting between Göring and Heydrich and indeed to the latter's draft. Two pieces of evidence indicate that Heydrich had been commissioned two months earlier to draw up this draft for 'the solution to the "Jewish Question"'. In notes from 21 January 1941 intended for Eichmann, Theodor Dannecker, the Gestapo's recently appointed 'Jewish expert' in Paris, wrote:

> In accordance with the will of the Führer, the 'Jewish Question' within those parts of Europe ruled over or controlled by Germany shall be brought to a final solution after the war. The Chief of the Security Police and the SD [i.e., Heydrich] has already received from the Führer via the RFSS [Reichsführer-SS Himmler] or through the Reichsmarschall [the] task of submitting a final solution project. ... It has been submitted to the Führer and the Reichsmarschall.
>
> It is certain that the implementation constitutes a mammoth task, the success of which can only be guaranteed through the most careful preparations. These must apply both to the tasks which precede a total deportation of the Jews and to the planning of a settlement operation established right down to the last detail in the yet to be fixed territory.[93]

Hence, the original commission had been given to Heydrich by Hitler himself, albeit via either Himmler or Göring, and as early as January 1941. It could feasibly have been earlier, depending on the accuracy of a statement made by Eichmann during a meeting on 20 March 1941 in the Propaganda Ministry between representatives of Joseph Goebbels's ministry and the RSHA. On this occasion Eichmann declared that Heydrich had been commissioned by Hitler 'with the final evacuation of the Jews', in response to which Heydrich had presented Hitler '8–10 weeks ago' with a suggestion. The suggestion had not yet been adopted, however, solely for the reason that 'the General Government is not at present in a position to receive one Jew or Pole from the old Reich'.[94] Thus, the destination of Europe's Jews, at least initially and perhaps only as a stop-off point en route to the Soviet territories, was to be Hans Frank's General Government, the part of occupied Poland not incorporated into the Reich. Perhaps Eichmann was not willing to divulge any more information. What is clear, however, is that, only six days later, Heydrich had the territories of the Soviet Union in mind as the final destination.

This inference is further supported by comments made by Hitler himself on 17 March, three days before the meeting in the Propaganda Ministry. As General Governor Frank told Party members in Krakow nine days later, Hitler had 'promised' him on this occasion that the General Government would be 'completely cleared of Jews in the foreseeable future'.[95] Goebbels had also been present at this meeting between Hitler and Frank, and recorded in his diary entry for 18 March what had passed between the three men over lunch the previous day: 'Vienna will soon be completely Jew-free. And it shall be Berlin's turn next. I am already arranging it with the Führer and Dr Franck [sic]. He puts the Jews to work, and they are even obedient. Later, they must get out of Europe completely.'[96] The territory which in January, according to Dannecker, was 'yet to be fixed' had now been decided upon.

Heydrich's original suggestion – potentially little more than a rough idea – had been presented to Hitler '8–10 weeks' prior to the meeting in the Propaganda Ministry. This provides us with an approximate date of mid-January 1941, which would also correspond to Dannecker's assertion on 21 January that the 'project' had already been submitted to Hitler and Göring. Heydrich would obviously have required a certain amount of time to prepare the 'suggestion' or 'project' after being commissioned to do so by 'the Führer via the RFSS or through the Reichsmarschall'. Realistically, then, Hitler could have set Heydrich the task at some point during the final weeks of 1940, by which time it had become clear within the Nazi leadership that the Madagascar Plan could not be implemented as a result of Great Britain's continued control of the oceans. By this time, the invasion of the Soviet Union had also been unalterably decided upon. This would indicate that the failure to achieve the prerequisite for the realization of the Madagascar Plan – namely control of the seas – and the expectation that a quick victory over the Soviet Union would make large, accessible tracts of land available, resulted in the proposal of the USSR as the location for a territorial solution to the 'Jewish Question'. Hence, it is more than likely that this idea developed out of the Madagascar Plan after this solution became impossible, rather than from a decision on the part of Hitler for a fundamental change of course regarding the fate of Europe's Jews. A territorial solution, as had been the case throughout 1940, remained the aim.

A statement made by the Romanian head of government, General Antonescu, on 16 August 1941 invites the assumption that those in the know regarding the intended territorial solution went beyond the likes of Heydrich, Eichmann, Goebbels and Frank.[97] Complaining about German troops driving Bessarabian Jews from the Ukraine back into Romania, after his own soldiers had driven them eastwards, Antonescu pointed out that this practice was in contrast to the guidelines regarding the treatment of the eastern Jews given to him by Hitler in Munich. The meeting in Munich had taken place two months earlier, on 13 June.[98] This apparent transition by mid-August 1941 from the intention to deport the surviving Soviet Jews (along with the rest of European Jewry) deep into the Soviet Union after the war, to attempts to keep them in the killing zone is a further argument against the existence of a pre-invasion order to the Einsatzgruppen to annihilate all Soviet Jews and in favour of a change of course in this respect towards the end of July.[99]

That the deportations and resettlement would take place during the post-war occupation period is also clear. Dannecker had stated in his letter to Eichmann that 'the "Jewish Question" within those parts of Europe ruled over or controlled by Germany shall be brought to a final solution after the war'. Additionally, the eastern campaign was intended to be short (six to twelve weeks) and there would be no available transport until after it was over due to the requirements of the German army.[100] Thus, it would basically have been impossible to deport Europe's Jews eastwards during the hostilities. When, on 19 June 1941, Goebbels met with Frank, the latter declared that he was 'looking forward to being able to deport the Jews' of the General Government.[101]

Reichsmarschall Göring's infamous commission of 31 July 1941 to Heydrich should be viewed in this context. With victory over the Soviet Union apparently imminent, Göring authorized Heydrich to 'make all necessary preparations with regard to organizational, technical and material matters for a complete solution of the "Jewish Question" in the German sphere of influence in Europe'.[102] This commission has often been interpreted as signalling the point at which the annihilation of European Jewry was ordered,[103] but there is no evidence for such an interpretation. Göring's commission supplemented the task given to Heydrich in a decree dated 24 January 1939 'to bring about the most suitable solution to the "Jewish Question", given the present conditions, by means of emigration or evacuation'.[104] Hence, a commission supplementing a task for emigration and evacuation – and 'evacuation' did not in January 1939 possess the meaning it would later acquire – would have constituted an extension and not a radical transformation of the instructions given two and a half years earlier, taking into consideration the massive increase in German-controlled territory and, consequently, in the number of Jews within reach, as well as the options available given the prevailing strategic and military situation. An authorization to organize the emigration of the Reich's Jews had now been extended to include all the Jews of occupied Europe.[105] Furthermore, the initiative originated not with Göring, but with the RSHA, as it was Eichmann who had drafted the document.[106] Göring only had to sign it.[107]

This was evidently not an order signalling a fundamental and radical change of course in Nazi Jewish policy.

The primary purpose of the document was to act as formal confirmation of Heydrich's and, by extension, of the RSHA's jurisdiction over the 'Jewish Question' and to enable the coordination of those state and Party agencies whose participation would be required for the realization of any far-reaching solution. This is clearly stated in the second sentence of the document: 'In so far as the jurisdictions of other central authorities are hereby affected, they are to be involved.'[108] The commission was indeed used to this effect when Heydrich attached a copy of the document to the invitations to the Wannsee Conference as proof of his authority.[109] In January 1942, at the conference itself, Heydrich once again made it clear that Göring had delegated to him responsibility for carrying out the preparations for the 'Final Solution' of the 'Jewish Question' in Europe.[110] By that time, of course, the term 'Final Solution' (*Endlösung*) could only have meant one thing, but it does not necessarily follow that it already possessed this distinct meaning in July 1941.

At the time when Madagascar was still on the agenda as a possible destination for at least a portion of Europe's Jews, the Nazi regime was well aware that the problems posed by climate, disease and a limited economic base would have rendered the island completely unsuitable for the settlement of four million Jews and, that if the plan was ever to have been implemented, it would, therefore, have claimed the lives of untold victims.[111] Similarly, whilst the anticipated solution to the 'Jewish Question' may in June 1941 have been a territorial one, as opposed to one which provided for the immediate and systematic mass murder of Europe's Jewish population or indeed of the Soviet Jews, for many of the Jews this so-called 'solution' would nevertheless have been a death sentence.[112] Although no preparations had been made before the start of Operation Barbarossa for mass murder, none had been made for a Jewish 'reservation' either.[113] As will be seen in chapter 7, those responsible for developing the Hungerpolitik foresaw by May 1941 the starvation of a large proportion of the inhabitants of the agricultural 'deficit territories' in the north and the east of the European part of the Soviet Union. This region was also to be the destination of Europe's Jews. What was to happen to Europe's Jews in territories where millions of people were to starve as a result of the wilful severance of their food supply by the German occupation forces? Those in the RSHA entrusted with the planning for this 'solution' would have been fully aware of the deadly implications of their proposals.

Although there is not an abundance of evidence pointing to the development of plans during the months prior to 22 June 1941 which paved the way for the deportation of the Jewish population of Europe into the former Soviet territories following the expected quick military victory over the Soviet Union, that evidence which is available is sufficient, as has been demonstrated, to determine what the likely intentions of the Nazi leadership were.

Post-invasion settlement policy would be formulated primarily within the offices of the RKFDV and related SS branches, even if confirmation that those powers relating to settlement and population policy conferred on Himmler as Reich Commissar for the Strengthening of German Nationhood in the decree of 7 October 1939 also applied to the occupied Soviet territories was not provided until the beginning of September 1941, two and a half months after the German invasion.[114] When confirmation of RKFDV Himmler's jurisdiction in the occupied Soviet territories did finally come, it was hardly a surprise, although Reich Minister Rosenberg contested the decision, apparently – at least initially – with the support of Reichsmarshall Göring, both of them clearly attempting to put a brake on the rapid growth in the power of the SS.[115] Whereas the form which the German civil or the military administration took might change from one territory to another, the form taken by SS and police control never varied, not even between the occupied territories and the Reich proper. The Higher SS and Police Leaders, for example, always retained the same status to Himmler, their immediate superior.[116] There was certainly some truth in the claim of the Chief of the SS Race and Settlement Main Office, SS-Gruppenführer Otto Hofmann, when he proclaimed: 'The East belongs to the Schutzstaffel.'[117]

SS planning for the forthcoming invasion and occupation followed for the most part a self-contained course. Its independence of action owed much to Hitler's trust in the faithful Himmler, the Reichsführer-SS's proximity to Hitler which came about in part as a result of this bond of loyalty, the highly secret nature of the organization's more far-reaching projects, and the size and power which the SS and its subordinate offices had attained by the launch of Operation Barbarossa, a development which would continue unabated over subsequent months and indeed years. At the same time, however, SS planning inevitably intertwined, both on a theoretical and on a practical level, with the work of the political and economic planners. Whether it was the resettlement of workers from Western Europe in the occupied Soviet territories, the transportation of Europe's Jews to the wastes of Siberia or the murder of tens of millions of Slavs, the SS had an increasingly influential finger in a whole host of proverbial pies.

Notes

1. Eichholtz, 'Institutionen und Praxis', p. 52.
2. For the text of the decree see *IMG*, vol. 26, pp. 255–257, doc. 686–PS, 'Erlaß des Führers und Reichskanzlers zur Festigung deutschen Volkstums'.
3. Heinemann, '*Rasse, Siedlung, deutsches Blut*', p. 191.
4. *IMG*, vol. 26, p. 255.
5. Quoted by Müller, *Hitlers Ostkrieg und die deutsche Siedlungspolitik*, p. 96.
6. For more on the HSSPF see 'The Fate of the Soviet Jews: Pre-invasion Order for Genocide?' in this chapter.
7. BA, R 49/2605, 'Betrifft: Ansiedlung von Reichsdeutschen in den Niederlanden', 4 April 1941, unsigned. On Rauter see Ruth Bettina Birn, 'Hanns Rauter – Höherer SS- und

Polizeiführer in den Niederlanden', in Ronald Smelser and Enrico Syring (eds), *Die SS: Elite unter dem Totenkopf* (Ferdinand Schöningh, Paderborn, 2000), pp. 408–417.
8. See BA, R 49/2606, 'Vermerk. Betrifft: Zusammenarbeit zwischen RJF und Stabshauptamt', *SS-Hauptsturmführer* Dr Günther Stier, 15 September 1941.
9. See BA, R 49/2607, 'Vermerk', from Hauptabteilung I des RKFDV to Presse-Abteilung des RKFDV, 1 November 1941. At the beginning of the war, it had been necessary for the Netherlands to import from abroad 33 per cent of the foodstuffs it required; Backe, *Um die Nahrungsfreiheit Europas*, Darstellung 1, inside front cover; BA-MA, RW 19/473, fo. 306.
10. BA, R 49/2605, 'Betrifft: Holländer-Siedlungen', 10 April 1941.
11. Ibid., 'Bericht über die Vorarbeiten zur Gewinnung von holländischen und flämischen Siedlern für die neuen Ost-Gebiete', pp. 1–8, 9 May 1941, unsigned.
12. Ibid., pp. 3–4.
13. Jeremy Noakes and Geoffrey Pridham (eds), *Nazism 1919–1945. A Documentary Reader, Vol. 3: Foreign Policy, War and Racial Extermination* (University of Exeter, Exeter, 1988), p. 895.
14. BA, R 49/2605, pp. 4–5 and 7–8.
15. BA, R 49/2606, letter from SS-Hauptsturmführer Dr Stier to the Higher SS and Police Leader North-West, 'Betrifft: Holländersiedlungen im Osten', 23 July 1941.
16. BA, R 6/34a, fo. 51.
17. On the Generalplan Ost see, above all, Karl Heinz Roth, '"Generalplan Ost" – "Gesamtplan Ost": Forschungsstand, Quellenprobleme, neue Ergebnisse', in Mechthild Rössler and Sabine Schleiermacher (eds), *Der "Generalplan Ost": Hauptlinien der nationalsozialistischen Planungs- und Vernichtungspolitik* (Akademie Verlag, Berlin, 1993), pp. 25–45 and 53–95.
18. Peter Witte et al. (eds), *Der Dienstkalender Heinrich Himmlers 1941/42* (Hans Christians Verlag, Hamburg, 1999), p. 179, entries for 23 and 24 June 1941.
19. Breitman, *The Architect of Genocide*, p. 168; Witte et al. (eds), *Dienstkalender*, p. 179, entry for 24 June 1941.
20. Heinemann, '*Rasse, Siedlung, deutsches Blut*', p. 626.
21. BA, NS 19/1739, fo. 2, letter from Meyer to Himmler, 15 July 1941.
22. Ibid.
23. Hans-Heinrich Wilhelm, 'Die Einsatzgruppe A der Sicherheitspolizei und des SD 1941/42 – Eine exemplarische Studie' in Krausnick and Wilhelm, *Die Truppe des Weltanschauungskrieges*, pp. 279–617, here p. 412.
24. See Witte et al. (eds), *Dienstkalender*, pp. 184–186, entries for 15–20 July 1941.
25. Roth, '"Generalplan Ost" – "Gesamtplan Ost"', p. 25.
26. For a reconstruction of how Meyer's plan of 15 July 1941 might have looked, see ibid., p. 65.
27. Ibid., p. 26; Uwe Mai, *"Rasse und Raum": Agrarpolitik, Sozial- und Raumplanung im NS-Staat* (Ferdinand Schöningh, Paderborn, 2002), p. 308; Heinemann, *"Rasse, Siedlung, deutsches Blut"*, p. 359.
28. For the full text of this commentary, see Heiber, 'Der Generalplan Ost', pp. 297–324, 'Stellungnahme und Gedanken zum Generalplan Ost des Reichsführers SS'.
29. Ibid., pp. 300–301.
30. See 'The Fate of the Soviet Jews: Pre-invasion Order for Genocide?' and 'A Territorial Solution to the "Jewish Question"' in this chapter.
31. Heiber, 'Der Generalplan Ost', p. 297.
32. *IMG*, vol. 38, pp. 87 and 90. On this, see Heinemann, *"Rasse, Siedlung, deutsches Blut"*, p. 364.
33. BA, R 43 II/688, fos. 126–127, 'Betrifft: Besetzte Ostgebiete', Lammers's notes, 1 October 1941; reproduced in *ADAP, Serie D: 1937–1941*, vol. 13/2 (Vandenhoeck & Ruprecht, Göttingen, 1970), pp. 487–488, doc. 372, 'Aufzeichnung des Chefs der Reichskanzlei', 1 October 1941.
34. Nbg. Dok. PS 1036, fo. 6.

35. On this, see Angrick, *Besatzungspolitik und Massenmord*, pp. 71–72.
36. BA, R 49/2607, p. 1, 'Betrifft: Besiedlung der Krim', SS-Gruppenführer Greifelt to Himmler, 11 December 1941.
37. Burleigh, *The Third Reich*, p. 547.
38. BA, NS 19/1739, fo. 4, 'Bezug: Vorlage vom 15.7.1941 u. Vortrag des Unterzeichneten am 27.1.1942', Meyer to Himmler, 28 May 1942.
39. Ibid. For the complete plan itself, dated June 1942, see BA, R 49/157a, pp. 1–84, 'Generalplan Ost. Rechtliche, wirtschaftliche und räumliche Grundlagen des Ostaufbaues'.
40. See Heiber, 'Der Generalplan Ost', p. 325.
41. PAAA, Pol. Abt. XIII, Nr. 27, R 105194, fos. 1–15, letter from Werner Hasselblatt to Georg Großkopf, 4 July 1941. On Hasselblatt, see Jacobsen, *Nationalsozialistische Außenpolitik*, p. 193.
42. Myllyniemi, *Die Neuordnung der baltischen Länder*, p. 58.
43. PAAA, Pol. Abt. XIII, Nr. 27, R 105194, fos. 1–3.
44. Ibid., fos. 4–5.
45. Ibid., fo. 6.
46. Ibid., fos. 1–2 and 5.
47. Dallin, *German Rule in Russia*, p. 49.
48. Gerlach, *Kalkulierte Morde*, p. 95.
49. PAAA, Pol. Abt. XIII, Nr. 27, R 105194, fos. 10–11.
50. Ibid., fo. 15.
51. See Martin Broszat, *Nationalsozialistische Polenpolitik 1939–1945* (Deutsche Verlags-Anstalt, Stuttgart, 1961), pp. 38–48.
52. *TBJG*, I/9, p. 330, entry for 23 May 1941: 'R[ußland] wird wie Zunder auseinanderfallen.'
53. On the close collaboration between SS formations and regular army units in the Soviet Union see *IMG*, vol. 32, pp. 473–475, doc. 3710-PS. For specific examples, see Wolfram Wette, *Die Wehrmacht: Feindbilder, Vernichtungskrieg, Legenden* (S. Fischer Verlag, Frankfurt am Main, 2002), pp. 108–133.
54. On collaboration in the Ukraine, see Dieter Pohl, 'Schauplatz Ukraine: Der Massenmord an den Juden im Militärverwaltungsgebiet und im Reichskommissariat 1941–1943', in Frei et al. (eds), *Ausbeutung, Vernichtung, Öffentlichkeit*, pp. 135–173, esp. pp. 172–173.
55. BA, R 58/241, fos. 305–306, 'Betr.: Sonderauftrag des Führers', Himmler, 21 May 1941; reproduced in Jacobsen, 'Kommissarbefehl', p. 219, doc. 9.
56. Krausnick, 'Die Einsatzgruppen', pp. 145–147. See also the post-war comments of Otto Ohlendorf, Chief of Einsatzgruppe D from 1941 to 1942, in *IMG*, vol. 4 (1947), pp. 360–361, 3 January 1946.
57. BA, R 70 Sowjetunion/32, fos. 4–10, 'Als Geheime Reichssache', 2 July 1941, here fo. 4.
58. Ibid., fo. 5: 'Die *politische* Befriedung ist die erste Voraussetzung für die *wirtschaftliche* Befriedung.'
59. Ibid., fos. 6–7: 'Zu exekutieren sind alle [:] Funktionäre der Komintern (wie überhaupt die kommunistischen Berufspolitiker schlechthin) [,] die höheren, mittleren und radikalen unteren Funktionäre der Partei, der Zentralkomitees, der Gau- und Gebietkomitees [,] Volkskommissare [,] Juden in Partei- und Staatsstellungen [,] sonstigen radikalen Elemente (Saboteure, Propagandeure, Heckenschützen, Attentäter, Hetzer usw. ()])'.
60. Peter Longerich, *The Unwritten Order: Hitler's Role in the Final Solution* (Tempus, Stroud, Glos., 2001), p. 66.
61. Krausnick, 'Die Einsatzgruppen', p. 164.
62. BA, R 70 Sowjetunion/32, fo. 4.
63. Ogorreck, *Die Einsatzgruppen*, pp. 101–102.
64. Christoph Dieckmann, 'Der Krieg und die Ermordung der litauischen Juden' in Ulrich Herbert (ed.), *Nationalsozialistische Vernichtungspolitik 1939–1945: Neue Forschungen*

und Kontroversen (Fischer Taschenbuch Verlag, Frankfurt am Main, 1998), pp. 292–329, here pp. 295–300.
65. Burrin, *Hitler und die Juden*, pp. 118–119.
66. Ibid., pp. 127–128.
67. Ibid., p. 128.
68. BA, R 58/218, fo. 341, 'Ereignismeldung UdSSR Nr. 128', Chef der Sicherheitspolizei und des SD, 3 November 1941.
69. BA, R 58/217, fo. 393, 'Ereignismeldung UdSSR Nr. 96', Chef der Sicherheitspolizei und des SD, 27 September 1941.
70. BA, R 58/218, fo. 3, 'Ereignismeldung UdSSR. Nr. 101', Chef der Sicherheitspolizei und des SD, 2 October 1941.
71. Streit, '*Wehrmacht, Einsatzgruppen*', pp. 105–106.
72. Christopher R. Browning, 'Beyond "Intentionalism" and "Functionalism": The Decision for the Final Solution Reconsidered', in Christopher R. Browning, *The Path to Genocide: Essays on Launching the Final Solution* (Cambridge University Press, Cambridge, 1992), pp. 86–121, here pp. 105–106. See also Gerlach, 'Die Ausweitung der deutschen Massenmorde', pp. 67–68.
73. Christopher R. Browning, *The Origins of the Final Solution: The Evolution of Nazi Jewish Policy, September 1939 – March 1942* (Arrow Books, London, 2005), pp. 310–312. See Witte et al. (eds), *Dienstkalender*, pp. 186–196, entries for 20 July to 16 August 1941.
74. Witte et al. (eds), *Dienstkalender*, pp. 184–186, entries for 15–20 July 1941. Michael Burleigh is right to point out, however, that – at least according to the minutes – no mention was made of the Jews during the high-level conference on 16 July; Burleigh, *The Third Reich*, p. 644. Himmler was in any case not present at the conference itself. See chapter 9 in this study.
75. See *IMG*, vol. 38, p. 88, for Hitler's comment during the conference of 16 July 1941 on the advantage of the Soviets waging a partisan war.
76. In the occupied Soviet territories in the six months between the beginning of the invasion and the end of 1941, approximately 800,000 Jewish people were murdered; Gerlach, 'Die Ausweitung der deutschen Massenmorde', p. 66.
77. Longerich, *The Unwritten Order*, pp. 72–73. For a similar argument, also emphasizing an exertion of pressure on Himmler's part, see Tobias Jersak, 'Die Interaktion von Kriegsverlauf und Judenvernichtung: Ein Blick auf Hitlers Strategie im Spätsommer 1941', *Historische Zeitschrift*, 268/2 (1999), pp. 311–374, here p. 328.
78. Longerich, *The Unwritten Order*, p. 72.
79. Most recently presented in Browning, *The Origins of the Final Solution*, pp. 309–314, esp. p. 313.
80. *TBJG*, II/1, p. 118, entry for 24 July 1941: 'Die Stimmung im Reich ist etwas ernster geworden. Man beginnt sich allmählich klarzumachen, daß der Ostfeldzug kein Spanziergang nach Moskau ist.' See also Franz Halder, *Kriegstagebuch, Band III: Der Rußlandfeldzug bis zum Marsch auf Stalingrad* (W. Kohlhammer Verlag, Stuttgart, 1964), p. 170, entry for 11 August 1941.
81. Herbst, *Das nationalsozialistische Deutschland*, pp. 378–379.
82. On developments in Poland between September 1939 and mid-March 1941, by which time military preparations for 'Barbarossa' had made the movement of ethnic Germans, Poles and Jews in and out of Poland impossible due to a lack of transport, see Aly, '*Endlösung*', pp. 29–268.
83. Christopher R. Browning, 'Nazi Resettlement Policy and the Search for a Solution to the Jewish Question, 1939–1941', in Browning, *The Path to Genocide*, pp. 3–27, here p. 9.
84. The term 'Jewish Question' will be placed in inverted commas throughout, as not to do so would suggest the author's acceptance that there was in fact a Jewish question (i.e., problem) which required solving, which is not the case.
85. On the Madagascar Plan see Irmtrud Wojak, *Eichmanns Memoiren: Ein kritischer Essay* (Fischer Taschenbuch Verlag, Frankfurt am Main, 2004) [2001], pp. 128–144; Hans

Jansen, *Het Madagascarplan: De voorgenomen deportatie van Europese joden naar Madagascar* (SDU Uitgevers, The Hague, 1996).
86. See Nbg. Dok. NG 5225, 'Aufzeichnung. Betr.: Einbau des Sonderkommandos AA in die SS', 4 February 1941, *SS-Sturmbannführer* Eberhard Freiherr von Künsberg.
87. On the negotiations between the army and the SS, see Breitman, *The Architect of Genocide*, pp. 147–150; *IMG*, vol. 32, pp. 471–475, doc. 3710–PS.
88. Quoted in Aly, '*Endlösung*', p. 270, 'Vermerk Heydrichs vom 26.3.1941': '10. Bezüglich der Lösung der Judenfrage berichtete ich kurz dem Reichsmarschall ... und legte ihm meinen Entwurf vor, dem er mit einer Änderung bezüglich der Zuständigkeit Rosenbergs zustimmte und Wiedervorlage befahl.'
89. Aly, '*Endlösung*', pp. 271–272.
90. Nbg. Dok. PS 1018, fos. 1–46, 'Denkschrift Nr. 2. Betrifft: UdSSR', n.d. (7 April 1941), here fos. 15 and 20–21. For the number of Jews resident in the Baltic States (c. 254,900) see IfZ, Fd 52, 'Verteilung d. jüd. Bevölkerung im ehem. Estland, Lettland, Litauen u. Nordpolen', 23 April 1941.
91. *IMG*, vol. 26, p. 549.
92. Ibid., pp. 561 and 571.
93. Quoted in Longerich, *Politik der Vernichtung*, p. 287: 'Gemäß dem Willen des Führers soll nach dem Kriege die Judenfrage innerhalb des von Deutschland beherrschten oder kontrollierten Teiles Europas einer endgültigen Lösung zugeführt werden. Der Chef der Sicherheitspolizei und des SD hat bereits vom Führer über den RFSS bezw. durch den Reichmarschall Auftrag zur Vorlage eines Endlösungsprojektes erhalten. ... Es liegt dem Führer und dem Reichsmarschall vor. Fest steht, dass es sich bei der Ausführung um eine Riesenarbeit handelt, deren Erfolg nur durch sorgfältigste Vorbereitungen gewährleistet werden kann. Diese müssen sich sowohl auf die einer Gesamtabschiebung der Juden vorausgehenden Arbeiten als auch auf die Planung einer bis ins einzelne festgelegten Ansiedlungsaktion in dem noch zu bestimmenden Territorium erstrecken.' On 24 January, three days after Dannecker made these notes, Heydrich presented to Göring, possibly on his 'final solution project', during a three-hour visit to Carinhall; IfZ, ED 180/5, Terminkalender Hermann Göring, fo. 13.
94. IfZ, MA 423, 'Notiz. Betrifft: Evakuierung der Juden aus Berlin', 21 March 1941; reproduced, with minor alterations, in H.G. Adler, *Der verwaltete Mensch* (J.C.B. Mohr, Tübingen, 1974), pp. 152–153.
95. Werner Präg and Wolfgang Jacobmeyer (eds), *Das Diensttagebuch des deutschen Generalgouverneurs in Polen 1939–1945* (Deutsche Verlags-Anstalt, Stuttgart, 1975), p. 338, entry for 26 March 1941: 'Der Führer hat mir versprochen, daß das Generalgouvernement in absehbarer Zeit von Juden völlig befreit sein werde.'
96. *TBJG*, I/9, p. 193: 'Wien wird nun bald ganz judenrein sein. Und jetzt soll Berlin an die Reihe kommen. Ich spreche das schon mit dem Führer und Dr. Franck ab. Der stellt die Juden zur Arbeit an, und sie sind auch fügsam. Später müssen sie mal ganz aus Europa heraus.'
97. *ADAP, Serie D: 1937–1941*, vol. 13/1 (Vandenhoeck & Ruprecht, Göttingen, 1970), p. 264, doc. 207, 'Der Gesandte in Bukarest an das Auswärtige Amt', 16 August 1941.
98. Longerich, *Politik der Vernichtung*, p. 292.
99. See 'The Fate of the Soviet Jews: Pre-Invasion Order for Genocide?' in this chapter.
100. Aly, "*Endlösung*", pp. 233–236.
101. *TBJG*, I/9, p. 390, entry for 20 June 1941: 'Dr. Franck [sic] erzählt vom Generalgouvernement. Dort freut man sich schon darauf, die Juden abschieben zu können.'
102. *IMG*, vol. 26, pp. 266–267, doc. 710–PS: '... alle erforderlichen Vorbereitungen in organisatorischer, sachlicher und materieller Hinsicht zu treffen für eine Gesamtlösung der Judenfrage im deutschen Einflußgebiet in Europa.'
103. See Lucy S. Dawidowicz, *The War against the Jews 1933–45* (Penguin, London, 1987) [1975], pp. 169–170; Graml, *Reichskristallnacht*, pp. 224–225; Browning, 'Beyond "Intentionalism" and "Functionalism"', p. 114.

104. *IMG*, vol. 26, p. 267: '... die Judenfrage in Form der Auswanderung oder Evakuierung einer den Zeitverhältnissen entsprechend möglichst günstigen Lösung zuzuführen.'
105. Herbst, *Das nationalsozialistische Deutschland*, p. 374.
106. Kershaw, *Hitler 1936–1945*, p. 471.
107. According to Göring's appointments diary, he was due to receive Heydrich at 6.15 p.m. on 31 July; IfZ, ED 180/5, Terminkalender Hermann Göring, fo. 107.
108. *IMG*, vol. 26, p. 267: 'Soferne hierbei die Zuständigkeiten anderer Zentralinstanzen berührt werden, sind diese zu beteiligen.'
109. Roseman, *The Villa, The Lake, The Meeting*, pp. 38 and 56.
110. For the minutes see PAAA, Inland II g, Nr. 177, R 100857, 'Besprechungsprotokoll', 16th of 30 copies, undated, fos. 166–180, here fo. 167; reproduced in *ADAP, Serie E: 1941– 1945*, vol. 1 (Vandenhoeck & Ruprecht, Göttingen, 1969), pp. 267–275, doc. 150, 'Undatiertes Protokoll der Wannsee-Konferenz'; reproduced in English translation in Roseman, *The Villa, The Lake, The Meeting*, Appendix A: Translation of the Protocol, pp. 108–118.
111. Leni Yahil, 'Madagascar – Phantom of a Solution for the Jewish Question', in Bela Vago and George L. Mosse (eds), *Jews and Non-Jews in Eastern Europe 1918–1945* (Halsted Press, New York, 1974), pp. 315–334, here pp. 317–319 and 326. The figure of four million featured in the RSHA's *Madagaskar-Plan* of 15 August 1940; Noakes and Pridham (eds), *Nazism 1919–1945, Vol. 3*, p. 1077. See also Jansen, *Het Madagascarplan*, pp. 532–533.
112. Wojak, *Eichmanns Memoiren*, pp. 138–139.
113. Longerich, *The Unwritten Order*, p. 61.
114. BA, R 6/9, fo. 17, letter from Dr Lammers to Reich Minister Rosenberg, 'Betrifft: Zuständigkeiten des Reichsführers SS in den besetzten Ostgebieten. Zum Schreiben vom 27 August 1941', 6 September 1941.
115. BA, R 6/21, fo. 232, letter from Rosenberg to Lammers, 'Stellungnahme über das Verhältnis des Reichsministers für die besetzten Ostgebiete und des Reichskommissars für die Festigung deutschen Volkstums', 23 September 1941; BA, R 6/21, fo. 191, letter from Rosenberg to Lammers, 27 August 1941.
116. Arnold Toynbee and Veronica M. Toynbee (eds), *Hitler's Europe* (Oxford University Press, London, 1954), p. 114. See also Noakes and Pridham (eds), *Nazism 1919–1945, Vol. 3*, pp. 918–919.
117. See Heiber, 'Der Generalplan Ost', p. 284: 'Der Osten gehört der Schutzstaffel.'

CHAPTER 7

RADICALIZING PLANS TO EXPLOIT SOVIET RESOURCES

The development of the 'starvation policy', the framework for which had been established in January and February 1941, entered a new phase of radicalization at the end of March. By the end of May, not only had the strategy been put down on paper in all its horrible detail, but wide-ranging agreement also reigned among the various economic, political and military agencies involved in or affected by the proposals. Of the soon-to-be-occupied Soviet territories, the Ukraine, widely regarded as the 'granary of Europe', played the most important role in the plans of the economic experts. Simultaneously, this region was also at the centre of political plans to form a defensive block against Greater Russia in an attempt to discourage future westward Russian expansion. Whether or not the perceived value of the Ukraine in fact corresponded to its actual worth, it retained its almost mystical status throughout and beyond the planning period.

Calculated Economic Considerations and Nazi Ideology

The relentless radicalization evident in the proposals of the economic planners during the spring of 1941 was based on carefully thought out and, at least in the eyes of the planners themselves, rational considerations. Thus, as the onslaught in the East grew ever nearer, and existing plans were fine-tuned, the watchword amongst the leading officials was 'rationality'. The extent to which this was kept in mind during the drafting and presentation of plans was directly proportional to the likelihood of a blueprint obtaining the seal of approval, just as approval for later policies advocating the feeding of sections of the Soviet civilian population depended not on 'mere' humanitarian arguments but rather on official backing and, in particular, the production of evidence that such an approach was of benefit to the German war effort.[1] In using the word 'rationality' here, reference is being made to an apparent reliance among the planners on detailed calculations and lengthy blueprints for the justification of their programmes, however barbaric and ill-judged, rather than simply on racial prejudices. One should by no means interpret this exposition as an attempt to rationalize Nazi policies themselves. What can be seen here is rather a series of endeavours by the Nazis to justify, or at least to endorse, their own policies on an economic or social basis, as opposed to simply reverting to arguments characterized by the savage and unyielding racism which was such an essential element of National Socialist ideological thinking.

Of course, racist attitudes towards the Soviet population were decisive in shaping the preparations for both the war itself and the subsequent occupation. This can clearly be seen if one compares German occupation policies in the Soviet Union with those in France, where there were also comprehensive economic and political aims. In fact, France ended up providing the Reich with far more in the way of economic produce and raw materials than the occupied Soviet territories did – indeed, seven times as much.[2] Such was the lowly position of the Soviet population in the racial pecking order of National Socialist ideology, however, that the awareness that the deaths of millions of human beings could be expected was not sufficient to prevent the Nazi planners from pursuing their agricultural-economic and political-structural objectives. Thus, any reservations which might have existed against policies which would inevitably result in millions of deaths were dispelled by Nazi racial thinking. Nevertheless, the mass murder of Slavs was not an explicit goal of National Socialism in itself, but rather a means of implementing economic-imperialist aims which could be justified, at least within Nazi circles, by science and economics. If these aims had the 'side effect' of bringing about the deaths of millions of supposedly biologically inferior beings, then – if only for the Nazis – so much the better.[3]

For comparative purposes, the distinction can be drawn between the treatment of the indigenous peoples during the German occupation of the Soviet Union and the policy pursued by the Nazi regime against Europe's Jewish population. In the latter case, ideological motivations were of primary importance, whereas economic considerations played a minor and often fleeting role. To be sure, if any further economic, political or social 'reasons' existed for doing away with the Jews, these were seen as additional proof of the authenticity of National Socialist racial-biological thinking.[4] By the same token, however, the requirements of the German economy, even in wartime, were rarely given priority when it came to the deployment and treatment of Jews over the primary objective of the Nazi regime, namely the removal of all Jews from the German sphere of control and, ultimately, their murder.[5]

At a meeting on 25 March 1941 of senior government officials in the General Government, General Governor Dr Hans Frank made it clear that the carrying out of 'great ethnic-political experiments' was not, at least for the time being, 'feasible' and referred to a recent comment made by

Reichsmarschall Göring: 'It is more important that we win the war than force through [our] racial policy.'⁶ Göring was not only the second most powerful man within the Nazi hierarchy, but was also heavily involved in the planning process at every step along the road to 'Barbarossa'. Given Göring's continuing influence and importance within the Third Reich during the winter and spring of 1941 before his later fall from grace,⁷ this expression can be taken as being representative of the sentiments of at least a section of those involved in the ongoing political and economic preparations for the war against the Soviet Union.

On 28 March 1941, the Staff Office of the Reich Farming Leader (*Stabsamt des Reichsbauernführers*), nominally under Darré as Reich Minister for Food and Agriculture and Reich Farming Leader but increasingly influenced by his deputy, Backe, completed an extensive study on the production and consumption of foodstuffs and fodder in the USSR. The authors argued that an across-the-board reduction in the consumption of foodstuffs from 250 kg per year to 220 kg (i.e., a reduction of 12 per cent) would provide a grain surplus of 8.7 million tons.⁸ In mid-February 1941, the Reich Food Estate had advocated a 10 per cent reduction in Soviet consumption, but this figure had now been increased to 12 per cent by the Staff Office of the Reich Farming Leader. The figures given in the study of 28 March would form the basis of the subsequent economic-political guidelines produced at the end of May, which described the 'starvation strategy' in full.

Regular contact between the chief exponents of the 'starvation strategy' continued to be maintained during this period, as demonstrated by a meeting on the last day of March 1941, at which Backe, Thomas, Schubert, Riecke, Hannecken and Ministerialrat Dr Friedrich Gramsch from Göring's Office of the Four-Year Plan were present.⁹ A day later, Reichsführer-SS Himmler entertained Göring's deputy, Staatssekretär Körner, though it is not known exactly what the two men discussed over their meal that afternoon.¹⁰ Progress on the 'starvation policy' during March and the beginning of April was in any case such that its initiator, Backe, felt able on 8 April to confide in his wife: 'My preparations for "Barbarossa" are moving along very well.'¹¹ Four days later, on 12 April, Backe – as head of the Task Force for Food in the VJPB – received complete powers over the agricultural exploitation of the soon-to-be-occupied Soviet territories from the Staatssekretär in the Office of the Four-Year Plan, Paul Körner, evidently acting on behalf of Göring, who had already been granted control over the entire economic administration in the Soviet territories. This was, 'on the order of the Führer', to remain strictly secret under all circumstances, from which it can be presumed that these powers related to the 'starvation strategy'.¹²

Before the end of the month, the other Staatssekretär in the Office of the Four-Year Plan, Erich Neumann, gave a talk to Berlin's Administrative Academy (*Verwaltungsakademie*) which, though nominally on the Four-Year Plan, effectively provided an assessment of the existing supply situation in German-occupied Europe. Neumann explained that the expansion of German-controlled territory and the extension of the war would in the long term have the effect of complicating the task of supplying these newly conquered territories and their inhabitants with raw materials and foodstuffs, particularly as certain articles were either not available in the occupied and dependent territories or not in sufficient quantities. As the supply of agricultural produce to those territories conquered by Germany in 1939 and 1940 was for the most part dependent on deliveries from overseas, deliveries which were no longer arriving due to the British naval blockade, the delivery of further substantial amounts of vital items from these territories to the Reich, with the possible exception of Denmark, was no longer feasible.[13]

At the time of its occupation, France, like the German Reich, required 17 per cent of its foodstuffs to be imported annually. The Netherlands and Belgium needed 33 and 49 per cent, respectively, whilst Norway, with a requirement of 57 per cent, imported more than it produced.[14] As the majority of the territories occupied by Germany themselves required deliveries, the German conquests of 1939 and 1940 had the overall effect of increasing rather than reducing the food deficit of the German sphere of influence.[15] The German leadership was adamant, however, that, if anyone was going to starve, it would not be the German people.[16] In order to avoid this, continued Neumann, it was Germany's 'allies' (*Bundesgenossen*) who would have to shoulder the burden and part with a portion of their resources not intended for export. In consequence, in the event of a longer-lasting war, these territories would gradually have to make the transition from being 'surplus territories' (*Überschussgebiete*) to being 'deficit territories' (*Zuschussgebiete*).[17]

This tendency of increased supply to the Reich can be seen in the example of Denmark. Whilst in 1939 some 23 per cent of Danish agricultural exports had gone to Germany, by 1941 – the country had been under German occupation since April 1940 – this had risen to 75 per cent, with Denmark covering between 10 and 15 per cent of Germany's foodstuffs.[18] Each of those European territories under either direct (i.e., military) or indirect (i.e., economic or political-diplomatic) German control would have its role to play within a German-dominated pan-European economy, or *Großraumwirtschaft*.[19] Given the scenario in the German-controlled territories of Western Europe, one can imagine what Germany's economic specialists had in mind for the territories of the Soviet Union, where the lives of the inhabitants were viewed by the Nazis as being pretty much worthless.

2 May 1941: the Meeting of the *Staatssekretäre*

The radicalization of Nazi plans for the exploitation of Soviet resources continued unabated into the month of May 1941. On 2 May the most important pre-invasion meeting of the economic specialists took place. The 'Memorandum on the Result of Today's Discussion with the Staatssekretäre

Regarding Barbarossa' recorded the shocking conclusions drawn by those attending the meeting. The men present did not mince their words:

> 1.) The war can only continue to be waged if the entire Wehrmacht is fed from Russia during the third war year.
> 2.) As a result, x million people will doubtlessly starve, if that which is necessary for us is extracted from the land.[20]

For the first time, the economic planners had explicitly stated in writing what the effect of their proposals to reduce Soviet consumption would actually be: the starvation of millions of people in the occupied eastern territories. The expectation that the invading troops would live off the land in order to avoid having to supply them with foodstuffs from the Reich could only have led to an increased understanding within the German army for the necessity of pursuing a 'starvation strategy' towards the Soviet population and indeed captured Soviet troops.[21] The German military was aware that Red Army units would have to be swiftly defeated, encircled and captured in large numbers in order to ensure a rapid advance in accordance with the envisaged aim of a Blitzkrieg campaign lasting no longer than six to twelve weeks. It was clear to the military planners that enormous numbers of Soviet prisoners would fall into German hands if all went to plan, yet they neglected to make the requisite preparations.[22] In their view, Soviet prisoners of war were to meet the same fate as the 'x million people' mentioned at the 2 May meeting. In fact, captured Soviet soldiers would constitute a part of these millions. Unlike sections of the Soviet civilian population, Soviet POWs would not have the opportunity to take to the country roads in order to procure food or to trade on the black market. This made them highly vulnerable and, in the twisted logic of the German planners, the perfect victims of the 'starvation policy'.[23]

Prior to the invasion, captured Soviet troops were not considered to be of any value to their German captors. In view of the expected quick victory, it was not deemed necessary to bolster the German war economy with an influx of politically and racially undesirable Soviet labour.[24] Therefore, plans to starve tens of millions of Soviets in order to free up food supplies were not being challenged at this moment in time by proposals to preserve Soviet prisoners of war as a valuable labour force. Only later, when the Blitzkrieg failed and became a war of attrition, did this become an important consideration. It might be added here that political commissars in the Red Army of course remained exempt from any ideas regarding the preservation of Soviet POWs for labour purposes, as the Nazi leadership viewed them as too great an ideological threat to be allowed under any circumstances into Germany or indeed – at least until Hitler's reluctant revoking of the so-called Commissar Order in the area of operations in May 1942[25] – to be left alive.

Soviet industry, the memorandum of 2 May continued, was to be restored or preserved only in cases where shortages existed for Germany, for example vehicle works, plants supplying iron, textiles factories and, in the event that there were production bottlenecks in Germany, armaments concerns.[26] Thus, only industrial sites which were of immediate use to Germany's war effort were to be maintained. Whatever Germany did not require should be left to deteriorate if it had not already been destroyed during the fighting. This mentality corresponded to the idea prevalent within the Nazi leadership that the Soviet territories were primarily agricultural lands and should not be allowed to develop industrially.

It is clear that the memorandum belonged to General Thomas, in whose files it was found.[27] Only two copies of the memorandum were made, and the second was for Lieutenant-General Schubert. Exactly who participated in the gruesome session is a little more difficult to ascertain. Two days earlier, on 30 April, a Major Günther in the Planning Staff Oldenburg (*Arbeitsstab Oldenburg*), which later became the Economic Staff East, telephoned General Thomas with the following message:

> Reichsleiter Rosenberg invites [the] General in an urgent matter to a discussion on Friday, 2.5.41, [at] 11 o'clock in the morning in the Office of the Reichsleiter.
> The Reichsleiter requests that [the] General keep as closely as possible to the appointment for the discussion, in order for him to be able to give the Führer a presentation on Friday afternoon.[28]

In accordance with this appointment, Rosenberg's diary records that he was due to 'receive' General Thomas and Staatssekretär in the Office of the Four-Year Plan Körner on 2 May,[29] all of which makes it very probable not only that it was indeed this meeting of the Staatssekretäre at which the three of them met but that Rosenberg hosted the discussion. This is significant in that Rosenberg's approval of the 'starvation strategy' at what was a relatively early stage in his involvement in the concrete planning for the forthcoming campaign and occupation can be confirmed.

It is quite probable that the Chief of the OKW Operations Staff, General Alfred Jodl, also attended the meeting. The entry for 2 May in the war diary of the High Command of the Wehrmacht contains the remark 'Chief at Reichsleiter Rosenberg's'.[30] It is unlikely that Rosenberg's meeting with Jodl was separate to that with Thomas and Körner, particularly since Rosenberg had an additional meeting to attend that day – with Hitler. Two days before the meeting of the Staatssekretäre, Rosenberg had spoken briefly with Hitler and the two of them had then arranged to discuss 'the questions of the East in more detail' on 2 May, which indeed they did.[31] This would, of course, have given Rosenberg the opportunity to report to Hitler on the outcome of the meeting of the Staatssekretäre.

Nevertheless, there is a possibility that Rosenberg was not present at the meeting of the Staatssekretäre on 2 May. In his first diary entry following this gathering, Rosenberg wrote that he had met with Körner and Thomas to discuss the work hitherto carried out by the Four-Year Plan organization on 3 May – a day later than he had been due to meet them according to his diary entry for 1 May. Gauleiter Dr Alfred Meyer, Rosenberg's deputy, was recorded as having had 'consultations' – presumably at the same time as Rosenberg met with Körner and Thomas – with Backe, Ministerialdirektor Gustav Schlotterer of the RWM and Ministerialdirektor Hans-Joachim Riecke of the RMEL.[32] It would, of course, be rather presumptuous to assume that this was an error on Rosenberg's part (although he made no reference to any alteration in the original plans) and that the discussion had in fact taken place on 2 May. The probability that this was a reference to a second meeting with Körner and Thomas, the first being in the company of the Staatssekretäre on 2 May, is not very high. Nevertheless, even if Rosenberg did not attend the meeting on 2 May, but rather discussed its results with Staatssekretär Körner and General Thomas the day after, it is certain that he approved of what he heard. He described the discussion as 'a good piece of general staff work founded on long experience'.[33]

The participation of other senior figures in the meeting of the Staatssekretäre should not be ruled out. It is almost certain that both Staatssekretär Backe and Lieutenant-General Schubert attended. As author of the 'starvation policy', Backe's absence would have been almost unthinkable. We can take the term 'the Staatssekretäre' to be a reference to those Staatssekretäre in the Wi Fü Stab Ost rather than those on the General Council for the Four-Year Plan. On 24 June 1941, Staatssekretär Körner opened the eleventh session of the General Council and informed the other participants that as a result of the preparations for 'Barbarossa', the convening of the General Council had 'up to now' not been able to take place.[34] The Wi Fü Stab Ost, on the other hand, had already had its fourth session on 26 May.[35] In view of this, the presence at the meeting of the Staatssekretäre Hermann von Hanneken, Friedrich Alpers and perhaps Friedrich Syrup is also likely. In addition, it is possible that Schlotterer and Riecke, both of whom held senior positions in the Wi Stab Ost, were there as well.[36]

It can be established with certainty that Reichsmarschall Göring, on the other hand, did not attend. In what appears to be a list of issues to be dealt with before the follow-up meeting to the discussion of 2 May, it was noted that: 'Decree of the Führer for the Reichsmarschall must finally be signed. Furthermore, the same applies to [the] Reichsmarschall's letter to the Army C-in-C.'[37] If Göring had been present, one would have expected him to have signed the letter to Field Marshal von Brauchitsch there and then. In any case, according to his appointments diary, Göring was in Paris on 2 May and it is fairly unlikely that the discussion took place in the French capital and not the German capital.[38]

Wide-ranging Agreement

All those present at the meeting of 2 May would have been very clear both as to the fact that the 'starvation strategy' had been decided on as an integral and vitally important part of German policy during the military campaign against the Soviet Union and the subsequent occupation, and also as to just how far-reaching such a strategy would be. In the days and weeks following the meeting, the activities of those agencies either directly involved in the economic planning or in related areas point to a wide-ranging agreement on the 'starvation policy', particularly on the part of Rosenberg and his political planners.

Although the 'starvation policy' had now been settled on, exactly where and how it would be applied in the different Soviet territories had yet to be determined. Three days after the meeting of the Staatssekretäre, General Thomas noted down several issues which still needed to be clarified by either Göring or Hitler, or for which an order from the Reichsmarschall or the Führer was required. Among the points he listed was the decision as to how the four future Reich Commissariats should be handled economically and the necessity of 'special instructions' being issued for each of the four territories.[39] Thomas made his own suggestions:

> *Baltenland*[40] must feed itself. Main task is exploitation of the shipyard and aluminium capacities and the oil deposits.
> *Ukraine* must – as agricultural surplus territory – be exploited as much as possible for industrial production. ...
> *Moscow*. The Moscow area, as agricultural deficit territory, is to be industrially exploited only in so far as the overall situation requires it. No accumulation of Wehrmacht tasks in the Moscow area.
> *Caucasus*. Quickest restart and increase of the mineral oil production and measures for the smooth evacuation of these quantities.[41]

It is evident here that the economic planners, as Rosenberg and his staff had originally proposed, intended to treat the four envisaged territories differently. The mineral oil of the Caucasus, which constituted almost 90 per cent of Soviet capacity, was required not only by the German war machine itself, but also for the highly mechanized Soviet agriculture, which consumed 60 per cent of the entire Soviet oil production, according to a paper from 4 May 1941 produced by the OKW's National Defence Section.[42] This made Soviet agriculture heavily dependent on the Caucasus. Almost three months earlier, during an internal discussion in Thomas's War Economy and Armaments Office, it had been pointed out that an exploitation of the occupied Soviet territories would only be possible if fuel supplies were to be secured, particularly given the extent to which agriculture was dependent on fuel. The men present came to the conclusion that the Soviet Union would only be valuable to them in the event that they controlled the Caucasus.[43] This judgement had also been made by Göring and Thomas on the occasion of their 26 February meeting.[44]

Thomas's reference in his notes of 5 May to there being no need for an 'accumulation of Wehrmacht tasks in the Moscow area' can be explained in that this region constituted the main 'deficit territory' in the context of the 'starvation strategy'. The Moscow area was thus to be sealed off from the source of its food supplies. In this territory, therefore, there would be precious little available to enable the German troops to 'live off the land'

and millions of Soviet citizens would face starvation. During a visit to the headquarters of Army Group Centre in July 1941, the Chief of the Advance Commando Moscow (*Vorkommando Moskau*) of Einsatzgruppe B, Professor Dr Franz Alfred Six, referred to an order given by Hitler to the effect that no member of the Wehrmacht would be allowed to enter Moscow. According to Six, after the encirclement of Moscow, his troops would force their way into the city and implement their 'security tasks'.[45]

By the time Backe expounded the food situation at the gathering of Reichs- and Gauleiter on 5 May, it is likely that at least the general direction in which these exploitation schemes were tending had been widely dispersed among the Nazi elite. Although Hitler was not present,[46] those who attended included future Reich Commissars in the Ukraine and the Baltic, respectively, Erich Koch and Hinrich Lohse, Rosenberg's deputy Alfred Meyer, Reichsführer-SS Heinrich Himmler[47] and Joseph Goebbels, who had been treated to a private presentation from Backe five days earlier, at which Backe had informed the Propaganda Minister that the expected reduction of meat rations would take place on 2 June 1941 to the amount of 100 g – from 500 g down to 400 g[48] – per week.[49] Goebbels recorded in his diary entry for 6 May what most, if not all, of those present at the session of the Reichs- and Gauleiter must have been thinking: 'If only this year's harvest is good. And then we want to line our pockets in the East.'[50]

The forthcoming reduction of meat rations was also one of the topics discussed at a meeting on 14 May 1941 between Ministerialdirigent Dr Julius Claussen, a colleague of Backe's and Riecke's in the RMEL, and an Eicke, one of General Thomas's subordinates in the War Economy and Armaments Office.[51] Claussen described the food situation as 'strained and difficult'. As the grain production in almost all European countries fell far short of what was required to feed each population, those territories occupied by Germany had for the most part to be supplied by the Reich.[52] One European state which could be of more support when it came to food supplies, continued Claussen, was the Soviet Union, more specifically the Ukraine, 'the granary of Russia [sic]'. According to Claussen, the Ukraine produced forty million tons of grain annually, 40 per cent of the entire Soviet harvest of 100 million tons. Germany, on the other hand, without the newly incorporated Polish territories, had produced 23.5 million tons the previous year. Claussen then claimed that the Ukrainian population could make do with ten to fifteen million tons of grain – he did not need to spell out what would happen to the remaining twenty-five to thirty million tons produced by the Ukraine.[53]

Although the Ukraine produced 40 per cent of the Soviet Union's grain, its population constituted less than a fifth of the entire Soviet population (33.5 million people from a total of 173 millions),[54] which meant that the territory also supplied other parts of the Soviet Union with grain. Thus, the Germans would be removing grain which was intended for Soviet citizens, not for export. It was not a 'surplus', as Claussen claimed; it was required in order to feed part of the Soviet population. The figure of twenty-five to thirty million tons of grain per year to be plundered by the invaders appears to have been the largest amount mentioned by anyone involved in these preparations, dwarfing as it did the earlier figures of four and 8.7 million tons calculated by the Reich Food Estate and the Staff Office of the Reich Farming Leader, respectively. It was admittedly uncommon for the economic planners to set the target quite so high, indicating that, even in their inflated view of what was possible, Claussen's colleagues were aware that such an expectation was completely unrealistic. By this stage in the preparations, the figure cited was more often than not around a third of that given by Claussen.

In the week following the meeting of the Staatssekretäre on 2 May, Alfred Rosenberg produced three papers relating to his preparations for the future administration in the occupied East. The first, dated 7 May, was entitled 'Instruction for a Reich Commissar in the Ukraine'.[55] The second, produced a day later, was its equivalent for the area of 'Baltenland', as the Baltic States and Belarus were at this stage being collectively referred to. In his drafting of the paper, Rosenberg crossed through 'Balten' and replaced it with 'Ost'.[56] The designation 'Ostland' would stick. The third paper, also bearing the date of 8 May, was called 'General Instruction for all Reich Commissars in the Occupied Eastern Territories'.[57]

The opening paragraph of the 'Instruction for a Reich Commissar in the Ukraine' bore the unmistakable influence of the economic experts and, more specifically, the meeting of 2 May – a further indication that Rosenberg either attended the meeting itself or, at the very least, was briefed on its key talking points soon afterwards: 'Aim of the work of a German Reich Commissar in the Ukraine is first of all the securing of foodstuffs and raw materials for the German Reich [and] with it the strengthening of the German prosecution of the war, then the establishment of a free Ukrainian state in closest alliance with the Greater German Reich.'[58] Rosenberg in fact considered these two issues – the securing of foodstuffs and raw materials on the one hand and Ukrainian independence on the other hand – to be closely, indeed inextricably, linked, as the final paragraph of the paper demonstrates:

> The tasks of a German Reich Commissar in the Ukraine can be of world historical consequence. If the setting up of a free Ukrainian state as far as Saratov through the application of all political, psychological and cultural methods proves to be successful, then the century-long nightmare which the German nation has experienced due to the Russian Empire is destroyed, then Germany is not endangered through any overseas blockade and the provision of foodstuffs and raw materials [is] secured for all time.[59]

Thus, to make Germany free from the danger of any future naval blockade and to secure its foodstuffs and raw materials, Rosenberg believed it was necessary to set up a free Ukrainian state which would act as a barricade against any expansion of Greater Russia and hence remove the 'nightmare' of the Russian Empire. Did Rosenberg not realize that the majority of his colleagues in the Party leadership anticipated that Germany itself, and not the Ukraine, would take on the task of removing the perceived Russian threat? From their point of view, there was no sensible reason to allow, let alone encourage, the establishment of an independent Ukraine. It would only complicate matters. There was to be only one master in the East and there would not be any room for partners in the enterprise. As Hitler later put it: 'It is never to be permitted that anyone other than the German carries weapons!'[60] Rosenberg's proposal to extend the territory of the Ukraine as far as Saratov on the River Volga would have meant the Ukraine's eastern border reaching the imaginary AA line between Archangel in the north and Astrakhan in the south – an eastward expansion at the expense of Russia of almost 300 miles (around 480 km)![61]

This paper from 7 May was at least Rosenberg's fifth since the beginning of April 1941. It was not the first to refer to the Soviet territories as Germany's future supplier of food and raw materials,[62] but it was the first in which Rosenberg so explicitly pointed to the importance of providing for the food requirements of the German people as the prerequisite for a successful prosecution of the war and attached so much weight to the task. It is unlikely to have been a coincidence that on the very day that Rosenberg wrote the first of the three papers mentioned, 7 May 1941, he hosted Staatssekretär Backe in his office at Margaretenstrasse 17 in Berlin-Tiergarten. The meeting between the two of them took place at 4 p.m. Earlier that day Backe had met with his colleague in the RMEL Hans-Joachim Riecke (10.30 a.m.) and visited Reich Economics Minister Walther Funk (11.30 a.m.).[63] This is a further indication of the close and regular collaboration which took place between the political planners around Rosenberg and the economic planners around Backe and Thomas during the spring of 1941.

A further step in the accommodation of the respective interests of the economic and the political planners occurred the following day, on 8 May, when Rosenberg and his deputy, Gauleiter Dr Meyer, hosted Staatssekretär Körner. Körner had proposed an alteration in paragraph six of the draft decree for the civil administration of the soon-to-be-occupied Soviet territories to the effect that the passage stating that the Reich Commissars would receive instructions 'exclusively' from Rosenberg be deleted. Rosenberg recognized, however, that this would make the implementation of his own commission almost impossible, and therefore stood his ground. The two men eventually concluded that the relevant sections of the draft decree drawn up by Head of the Reich Chancellery Lammers should be left unaltered.[64] Rosenberg and Körner also agreed that, for the duration of the work of the Bureau Rosenberg, Gustav Schlotterer of the RWM and Hans-Joachim Riecke of the RMEL would be delegated to collaborate with the Bureau Rosenberg on questions relating to trade and industry and food supply, respectively.[65] This decision was noteworthy not only in that it marked a significant move towards increased interagency cooperation, but also in that the two men selected were far from being nobodies. On the contrary, they were of considerable importance. Schlotterer was the leading planner in the Reich Economics Ministry for the future European Neuordnung,[66] whilst Riecke was Backe's right-hand man. Both Schlotterer and Riecke would go on to occupy senior positions in the Reich Ministry for the Occupied Eastern Territories.[67]

Just to underline his new approach, Rosenberg concluded his 'General Instruction for all Reich Commissars in the Occupied Eastern Territories' of 8 May by describing the coming campaign as 'a struggle for the sustenance and provisioning with raw materials both of the German Reich and of the whole European area'.[68] Such was his commitment to this aspect of the forthcoming campaign and occupation, that he was even prepared to renounce in the same paper the immediate abolition of the Soviet collective farms – a measure guaranteed to gain the approval of the vast bulk of the Soviet population – on the basis that the existing agricultural system could not be fundamentally altered from one day to the next if one did not want to bring about 'incalculable consequences', indeed 'chaos'. All farmers and employees should initially continue just as before.[69] Either Rosenberg had been persuaded by Backe's arguments or he had realized that Backe and his colleagues had the ear not only of Göring but also of Hitler himself and that the wise thing to do would be to fall in with their schemes, or more than likely a combination of these two explanations. Whichever of these interpretations most closely represents the truth, it is apparent that, from the beginning of May 1941, Rosenberg became increasingly vocal in his promotion of the economic aspects of the forthcoming eastern campaign.

One of the most crucial reasons that the 'starvation policy' was able so smoothly to gain wide-ranging acceptance from leading Party and state agencies was its perceived status as a necessary prerequisite for the operational plans of the German military leadership.[70] It was abundantly clear to the military leadership that the success of the campaign depended on the speed with which the German advance could be carried out. The speed of the advance was in turn dependent on the ability of the supply apparatus to provide the troops with fuel, ammunition and food. The advancing troops could only be supplied with vehicle fuel for a maximum of two months following the invasion.[71] It was only possible to make available the 250,000 tons of diesel oil required for the forthcoming operations as a result of immediate and severe cutbacks in the construction industry, in agriculture and in the economies of occupied Europe.[72] Ironically, the bulk of the fuel to be transported eastwards would be required by the trucks themselves which were transporting it.[73] Baku, the supplier of 89 per cent of Soviet mineral oil and one of the major targets of the German advance, was situated on the Caspian Sea at the eastern edge of the area planned for occupation, and could not be reached and occupied in the first weeks of the campaign, if in fact at all. The advance would, therefore, have to fall back on the Soviet railways.

In accordance with this expectation Colonel-General Halder recorded the following in his war diary entry of 28 January 1941: 'Spaciousness – no delays; only that guarantees victory. Delay-free implementation is a supply question. Everything must assist in solving it. Distances! ... Railways are the only way to make headway without facing a shortage of transport capacity.'[74] Similar sentiments were to be found three days later in the diary of a staff officer in the 4th Army, Captain Dr Hans Meier-Welcker, who noted: 'The supply determines the limit of the operational possibilities with regard to the depth.'[75] Despite Halder's belief that the Soviet rail network would provide a solution to the Wehrmacht's transport problems, the railway lines running in a west–east direction were in fact few in number and their capacity was therefore limited.[76] Additionally, Soviet railways had a gauge of 1.524 m, 8.9 cm broader than the 1.435 m gauge in use in most European countries, including Germany.[77] Even if engineers attached to the advancing troops succeeded in rapidly relaying the track, this task would inevitably slow down the advance – a development which could not be contemplated. Furthermore, it was by no means guaranteed that those few west-east lines could be protected from destruction during the initial military advance.[78] Therefore, in order to keep to a minimum those military supplies which had to be transported from central Europe, thereby relieving the strain on the limited transport routes, the transportation of food supplies was to be drastically restricted and the German troops were expected to feed themselves – as clearly stated at the meeting of the Staatssekretäre on 2 May 1941 – 'from the land'.

Thus, Germany's chances of victory were directly related to the extent to which the troops succeeded in providing for themselves with agricultural produce from the occupied Soviet territories, clearly to the disadvantage of the indigenous population. In that sense, pursuing the 'starvation policy' was in the interests of the Wehrmacht.[79] This became clear to the military from an early stage in the preparations. In February 1941, Army Quartermaster-General Wagner, the man responsible for supplying the troops, recognized and recorded the following points: 'The supplies must be limited through extensive exploitation of the land, [and] the capture must be tightly controlled. The country's stocks are not to be utilized through indiscriminate pillaging, but rather through seizure and collection according to [the] well thought out plan.'[80] Wagner's reference to a 'well thought out plan' almost certainly points to his knowledge of Backe's 'starvation strategy', which, though already aired at meetings with Hitler and Göring and certain other senior officials, does not appear from the available documentation, however, to have yet been at an advanced stage.

An order on the organization and tasks of the forthcoming military occupation issued on 3 April 1941 in the name of the Commander-in-Chief of the Army, Field Marshal von Brauchitsch, made it clear to the troops themselves what was at stake. Safeguarding the major transport routes and exploiting the land for the requirements of the troops was described in the order as being 'of decisive importance for the operations'. For this reason, all those regular soldiers in the rear areas were to be deployed exclusively for these tasks, although the 'systematic administration and exploitation' of the occupied territories, which would come later, was not the responsibility of the army.[81] In a letter dated 14 May 1941, Staatssekretär Backe reminded

Field Marshal Keitel how significant the 'complete provisioning of the army from [the] occupied territories' was for the economic situation.[82] Accordingly, the OKW's 'Special Instructions to Directive No. 21 (Case Barbarossa)', issued five days later, went further in its clarity than Brauchitsch's order of 3 April: 'The exceptional conditions in the area "Barbarossa" necessitate the *comprehensive and tightly conducted exploitation of the land* for supplying the troops, especially in the rations area. The troops must realize that *every reduction in supplies*, particularly in rations, increases the scope of the operations.'[83]

Hitherto, references to the 'starvation strategy' and its constituent parts, whilst leaving very little doubt as to the far-reaching consequences of what was being proposed, had stopped short of describing either exactly how the plan would be applied geographically or how it would in fact be implemented. The Wi Stab Ost's economic-political guidelines of 23 May 1941 would go some way towards answering many lingering questions and constitute not only the most detailed exposition of the Nazi Hungerpolitik that exists, but indeed the most comprehensive blueprint in history for mass murder.

The *Hungerpolitik* in Writing

Indicative of the 'rational' approach of the planning staffs discussed earlier were the economic-political guidelines for the coming invasion produced by the agricultural section – headed by Hans-Joachim Riecke – of the Economic Staff East.[84] These guidelines appeared on 23 May 1941 and clearly represented the written version of the conclusions reached by the Staatssekretäre at their meeting three weeks earlier, on 2 May. The 'starvation policy' developed over the preceding months was now delineated in all detail; nothing was left to the imagination. This probably accounts for the limited number of copies of the guidelines passed on to other agencies. Backe's Task Force for Food within the Four-Year Plan organization, for example, received just two.[85]

The study of the Staff Office of the Reich Farming Leader from 28 March 1941, mentioned earlier, formed the basis of these guidelines. In accordance with the findings of this study, it was stated in the 23 May guidelines that a reduction in the annual Soviet consumption of grain and potatoes from 250 kg to 220 kg (i.e., 12 per cent) per person would create annual surpluses of 8.7 million tons. Thus, the assumption on which the 'starvation strategy' was to be based was that Soviet grain surpluses would not be determined through the size of the harvest in the East but rather through the size of individual consumption.[86] In other words, the German occupiers intended to manipulate the distribution of grain supplies amongst the Soviet population, thereby creating 'surpluses' for themselves. However, the guidelines recognized that the Germans would be more than likely to gain little from an attempt to reduce the consumption of the Soviet population across the board due to their inability to control either the movement of large numbers of the civilian population or trade on the black market. Devising an alternative method of implementing this concept was made easier for the planners by the fact that the 'surplus territories' lay in the so-called 'black earth' areas of the south and the south-east and in the Caucasus, whereas the 'deficit territories' lay predominantly in the so-called 'wooded zone' of the north. Thus, a sealing off of the 'surplus territories' from the 'deficit territories', it was hoped, would make large amounts of grain available to the Germans. The consequence of this would be the non-delivery of agricultural produce to the whole 'wooded zone', including the important industrial centres of Moscow and Leningrad. Only the oil-rich region of Transcaucasia (comprising present-day Georgia, Armenia and Azerbaijan) was to be exempted from this fate, although it constituted a 'deficit territory'.[87] These tactics could have only one outcome: the starvation of large sections of the Soviet population. A little further on in the guidelines, this was indeed explicitly stated: 'The population of these areas, particularly the population of the cities, will have to face the most terrible famine. It will be a case of diverting the population to the Siberian spaces. As railway transport is out of the question, this problem will also be an extremely difficult one.'[88]

The perceived importance of this strategy for Germany, German-occupied Europe and the German war effort itself was then emphasized, along with a warning for those who might entertain thoughts of not implementing it:

> Many tens of millions of people in this territory will become superfluous and will die or must emigrate to Siberia. Attempts to rescue the population there from death through starvation by obtaining surpluses from the black earth zone can only be at the expense of the provisioning of Europe. They prevent the possibility of Germany holding out till the end of the war, they prevent Germany and Europe from resisting the blockade. With regard to this, absolute clarity must reign.[89]

Such attempts would in any case fail, according to the guidelines, in consequence of the prevailing transport conditions, more specifically the weakness of the Soviet rail network. The existing railway lines would be required for supplying the troops and exporting goods to continental Europe.[90]

In the future, the 'surplus territories' in the south of the Soviet Union would have to turn their eyes towards Europe. Their food surpluses could only be bought, however, when they in turn obtained their consumer goods from Germany or other parts of Europe, as the case may be. The destruction of the Soviet manufacturing industry in the 'wooded zone' in the north, which constituted a competitor, was thus 'an absolute necessity' for Germany's future.[91] The grain-producing Soviet territories would be forced into a position of dependency on the Reich. The incorporation of the Soviet food economy into the continental European framework would 'inevitably' result in both the industry in the 'deficit territories' and a large proportion of their inhabitants dying out.[92]

Obtaining grain surpluses and surpluses of oil crops, especially sunflowers, and guaranteeing the supply of the entire Eastern Army from the land constituted the concrete objectives of the economic operation.[93] The 'minimum aim' set by the economic planners was the feeding of the Wehrmacht from enemy land during the third year, and perhaps additional years, of the war. This had to be achieved under all circumstances. It was foreseen in the guidelines that at least two-thirds of the Wehrmacht (i.e., the Eastern Army) had to be completely provided for out of the Eastern space – a requirement totalling four and a half to five million tons of grain – whilst the remaining third would be supplied from French contributions. This expectation diverged from the meeting of the Staatssekretäre three weeks earlier in that the feeding of the entire Wehrmacht from 'Russia' during the third war year had on that occasion been foreseen. This is to be explained in so far as the fraction given in the guidelines of 23 May was a 'minimum aim' – the planners expected this amount to be comfortably exceeded. By expecting the entire invading army of more than three million men to live off the land, the planners hoped to ease the strain on the lines of transport, which had to carry both goods from the East to Germany and certain military supplies going the other way.[94] Moreover, Germany would be relieved of the burden of providing for three million people who received particularly high rations. Fighting troops, for example, received 1,700 g of meat per week compared with 500 g for an average consumer. From 1 June 1941 these amounts were cut to 1,400 g and 400 g, respectively.[95] Unlike other foodstuffs, meat would have to be obtained from the 'wooded zone', in particular from Belarus and the industrial regions around Moscow, for both the German army and the Reich. This would have to take place from the beginning in order to avoid the livestock in these territories – cut off from their grain supplies – being slaughtered in no time by the hungry local population and consequently leaving nothing available for German requirements.[96] Only when the requirements of the German army had been covered would deliveries to the civilian population in Germany begin.[97] Thus, the needs of the German population were logically subordinated to those of the German soldiers fighting in the East. The needs of the Soviet population were subordinated to both. Indeed, the indigenous population was even relegated to a position behind other, non-German Europeans, as the economic planners deemed it necessary to make supplies of the most important foodstuffs – oil crops, grain and meat – available on the largest possible scale in order to guarantee not only the supply of the German troops and Greater Germany, but also of the occupied territories in northern and western Europe which were dependent on overseas supplies.[98]

What is, in some respects, remarkable about the 23 May 1941 guidelines is that, despite this document's considerable length (almost twenty pages), the programme of annihilation contained within its pages is described and justified without a single racial-ideological remark being made. Thus, though the authors had not suddenly abandoned their beliefs and prejudices regarding what they saw as the subhuman Slavic hordes, the purpose of whose existence – provided they were considered useful enough to be spared in the programme of mass slaughter – was to work as helots for their German masters, it was not deemed necessary to revert to such utterances. As they saw it, there were quite enough rational justifications for their proposals.

In view of the fact that the principal victims of the 'starvation strategy' were to be those living in the 'wooded zone' of northern and central Russia and those living in the cities, it has been argued that, as almost all Soviet Jews lived in urban areas, it was planned prior to the German invasion of June 1941 to kill the bulk of the Soviet Union's Jewish population by means of those measures which were to be carried out in implementing the 'starvation strategy'.[99] It is indeed the case that most – almost 85 per cent of – Soviet Jews lived in towns and cities[100] and, moreover, the Nazi planners were well aware of this fact.[101] However, one must be careful about drawing conclusions where there is no evidence that the Nazis themselves drew the same conclusions. Just because almost all Soviet Jews lived in the cities and the urban population of the Soviet Union constituted one of the primary groups of envisaged victims of the 'starvation strategy', it does not automatically mean that the intention of the National Socialist regime was in fact to annihilate the Soviet Jews in the course of implementing the 'starvation strategy'. It is unclear, and was indeed unclear to the Nazi planners themselves, how the 'starvation policy' was to be carried out in practice or exactly how the anticipated millions of victims were to be 'selected'. Furthermore, there is no mention of the Jewish population of the Soviet Union in the guidelines of 23 May 1941.

That the strategy illustrated in the guidelines had received the explicit 'approval of the highest authorities', which could only have meant Göring, Himmler and Hitler himself, was confirmed in the document.[102] On 16 May 1941, one week before the guidelines were issued, Backe had held a presentation for Hitler on the Obersalzberg above Berchtesgaden.[103] The subject of Backe's presentation is not known, but work on the guidelines would by that time have been at an advanced stage and Backe's meeting with Hitler would have provided him with an opportunity to report on them. The reason given in the guidelines for the 'approval of the highest authorities' was that their content was in accordance with the political tendencies: 'preservation of the little Russians, preservation of the Caucasus, of the Baltic provinces, [and] Belarus at the expense of the driving back of the greater Russians'.[104] The term 'little Russians' (*Kleinrussentum*) is used here to refer to the Ukrainians, and contrasts with the term 'greater Russians' (*Großrussentum*). Although references to the Ukraine as 'little Russia' (*Kleinrußland*) or its people as 'little Russians' are not widespread in Nazi planning papers, they are to be found on occasion, including elsewhere in the 23 May guidelines themselves.[105] The passage gives the impression that the political aims, at least at this stage in the preparations, were being given priority over the economic aims and that the latter had to agree with the former in order to find approval with Germany's supreme leadership. Although such an impression is somewhat misleading, it is clear from the passage quoted above that by the second half of May 1941 the various political and economic proposals corresponded closely to one another. Similar sentiments are to be found a little further on in the guidelines: 'As the political line of thought is directed against the greater Russians, it will be a case of driving the greater Russians into the wooden zone and occupying the freed-up collective farms with the remaining little Russians.'[106]

One proposal which did not find the agreement of the economic planners, however, was Rosenberg's cherished wish to abolish the collective farms, which were despised by the vast bulk of the Soviet population, as was widely known. This idea was rejected by the authors of the guidelines. The collective farms (*kolkhozy*) accounted for over 95 per cent of those employed in Soviet agriculture, whilst the remainder were divided between state-owned estates (*sovkhozy*) and establishments providing machinery services (*MTS*).[107] Keeping these *kolkhozy* was seen by the authors of the guidelines as a prerequisite for both an increase in agricultural production in the 'surplus territories' and the actual seizure of agricultural surpluses.[108] The potential disorder involved in converting the collective farms into smaller, private enterprises was deemed to be highly detrimental and thus too risky to be undertaken.

Whilst Rosenberg appreciated the necessity of initially retaining the collective farms, as a successful exploitation of the Soviet lands during the first stages of the occupation was not possible without them, he also expected, as did officials within the German Foreign Office, that the Soviet farmers would be assured that their grievances would not be overlooked.[109] Following a meeting on 29 May 1941 with members of Rosenberg's staff and military officers, Privy Councillor Großkopf, Foreign Minister von Ribbentrop's permanent liaison officer to the Bureau Rosenberg, wrote:

> We must realize that, through our efforts and slogans to maintain the collective and national estates (for economic reasons which are for us decisive) in their present condition, we give up the most powerful means of political agitation.
>
> The Bolsheviks carried out the revolution [in] 1917 with the slogan 'All land to the peasants' and crushed all white counter-revolutionaries with this slogan, which secured them the help of the peasants.
>
> The peasants thus expect from us [the] dissolution of the hated collective economies.[110]

It is not difficult to understand why Großkopf refers to the issue of the collective farms as 'the most powerful means of political agitation'. Although its contribution ultimately turned out to be substantial, if any class constituted a potentially weak link in the Soviet war effort it was the peasantry. After all, peasants – mostly consisting of embittered and alienated collective farmers – comprised 60 per cent of the Soviet population, and more than 60 per cent of the Soviet armed forces in the Second World War came from the countryside.[111] If it had been implemented, the dissolution of the collective farms would more than likely have proved to be a very large carrot indeed. The issue of the collective farms would become one of the most hotly debated points of dispute within German occupation policy.[112]

At some time during the planning phase for the eastern campaign, Backe made it quite clear to Reichsmarschall Göring that he did not want to be bothered with any ideological ideas, above all those which concerned settlement of farmers, land reform or related issues, declaring that he absolutely could not depart from the use of collective farms. He had heard such ideas from Rosenberg's bureau. Göring promised him in this respect a completely free hand, which is what he got.[113] However, in an order to various ministers dated 27 July 1941, Göring indicated that the collective farms could have a limited shelf life. He stated that the highest economic performance could not be expected in the long term from the 'Bolshevik collective economy' but rather only on the tried and tested foundations of private ownership, albeit guided by the state. The collective system, he declared, would continue to be used only as long as it was absolutely necessary in order to avoid a breakdown in the supply of the Wehrmacht and the German economy from the Soviet territories, a development which could occur as a result of such a sudden change in the agricultural system.[114] Backe responded only days later at a session of the Wi Fü Stab Ost by requesting that any notions about altering the form of the collective farms be put on the back burner, as no other method of running the farms existed.[115]

Backe's extensive influence on the contents of the 23 May guidelines can most clearly be seen in the final pages of the document, where Nazi intentions for the future relationship between Europe and the occupied Soviet territories are outlined. The incorporation into Europe of the food-producing economy of 'Russia' was envisaged and with it the substitution of overseas imports by imports from the fertile lands of the East. The Soviet territories would, therefore, not replace but rather supplement agricultural production in continental Europe. With this development, the eastern regions would enable German-occupied Europe to overcome its food shortages both during the war itself and in the post-war period. It was anticipated that, through the intensification of agricultural production in the agriculturally valuable territories of the East and a resulting increase in the yields, these territories would constitute in the future a lasting and considerable addition to the productive capacity of continental Europe.[116]

Thus, the subjugation of the Soviet Union and the merging of its economic capacity with that of continental Europe would equip its Nazi masters to wage world war against the Anglo-Saxon powers. The emphasis in the guidelines on increasing agricultural production in the fertile areas in the south and south-east of the Soviet territories, however, demonstrates that German plans for the 'granary of Europe' were not just limited to a no-holds-barred wartime exploitation, but rather to a long-term economic merging of these territories with German-dominated continental Europe.[117]

As far as the Nazi leadership was concerned, it was not only victory in the war which was dependent on the success of this strategy, but also the winning of the peace.[118] As Hitler put it a few months later: 'The struggle for the hegemony of the world will be decided in favour of Europe by the possession of the Russian space. Thus Europe will be an impregnable fortress, safe from all threat of blockade. All this opens up economic vistas which, one may think, will incline the most liberal of the Western democrats towards the New Order.'[119]

Hitler rejected a colonial policy of overseas exports and imports, as had been practised by Wilhelmine Germany, and sought instead to deal with Germany's supposed inability to support itself from its existing land mass by 'adapting' the German living space to the size of the population – in other words, by incorporating territory bordering the German Reich, more specifically, 'the East'.[120] Autarky on a purely national level, which had been an aim in the mid- to late 1930s, had gradually been replaced by a more far-reaching concept. Hitler summed up this approach a matter of days before the beginning of the eastern campaign when he declared that 'what one requires but does not have, one must conquer'.[121] Conquest of territory rich in economic resources unavailable in sufficient quantity in the territory already occupied by the conqueror would thus enable a group of affiliated nations to become collectively autarkic. This design, taken as a whole, was the concept of Großraumwirtschaft – the harnessing of the combined economic resources of a single, large, autarkic land mass. The function of the Soviet Union within this arrangement, or at least its European part, would be the production and delivery of raw materials and foodstuffs; it would not have any industrial capacity or manufacturing capabilities to speak of.[122] As Hitler rather typically expressed it in mid-September 1941: 'We will be a grain exporter for all those in Europe who are dependent on grain. In the Crimea we have citrus fruits, rubber plants (with 40,000 ha we will make ourselves independent), cotton. The Pripet Marshes provide us with reeds. To the Ukrainians we will deliver headscarves, glass necklaces as jewellery and whatever else pleases colonial peoples.'[123] The actual implementation of these far-reaching plans would fortunately prove to be far less straightforward than their formulation.

Soviet Labour: Deployment in the Reich?

Given the importance that the question of labour procurement would assume for Germany from the beginning of 1942 onwards, it is perhaps surprising that this issue does not appear to have been addressed in detail by the economic planners in the guidelines of 23 May 1941 or indeed at any stage prior to the commencement of Operation Barbarossa. The matter was also neglected by Rosenberg in his memoranda of April and May 1941. Indeed, it can be stated with confidence that, during the planning phase for 'Barbarossa', no serious consideration was given to the employment of

Soviets – whether prisoners of war or civilians – in the Reich.[124] Furthermore, there existed an explicit ban from Hitler, no less, on the deployment of Soviet POWs for work in the Reich.[125]

This stance can be explained in that the German leadership, in view of the expected quick victory over the Red Army, deemed it not only unnecessary but also highly dangerous to bolster the German war economy with an influx of politically and racially undesirable Soviet forced labour.[126] There were admittedly labour shortages in German armaments factories, but these were expected to be filled by German soldiers returning from the East after a successful military campaign.[127] Hitler anticipated that it would be necessary to retain only forty to fifty divisions in the occupied Soviet territories following the expected victory and that the size of the German army could be reduced accordingly.[128] Guidelines were issued by Hitler which accorded with this line of thinking: 'The military control over the European space following the defeat of Russia will soon allow a significant reduction in the size of the army.'[129] In mid-August 1941, the OKW was planning to dissolve fifty German divisions after the anticipated victory against the Soviet Union; as a result, 300,000 men would have been freed up for employment in the armaments industry.[130] This whole approach was motivated by the firm belief that the military campaign against the USSR would be successfully concluded within a matter of months.

As for labour in the occupied Soviet territories themselves, the indigenous population would be required primarily in agriculture, to harvest the crops so as to fulfil the expectations of the Nazi leadership, which have already been discussed in detail above. There was never any debate in the corridors of power as to what might be the fate of Soviet farmers and farm workers. Such a debate was indeed entirely unnecessary, at least until the time came to implement the long-term resettlement plans of the SS.[131] Achieving the production targets set by Germany's economic planners required the existence of a large agricultural workforce in the occupied Soviet territories. Pre-invasion discussions about Soviet agricultural workers revolved not around what to do with the farmers but rather around the question of whether or not to maintain the collective farms.

In contrast to agriculture, Soviet industry would only be maintained or restored, as the case may be, if it was situated in the so-called 'surplus territories' and even then only in those areas which were of crucial importance to the German war economy.[132] The productive capacity of the 'wooded zone' was of no interest to the German leadership.[133] In the blueprints of the economic planners, it was those working in industry and manufacturing in the so-called 'deficit territories' of the 'wooded zone' and in the large cities – not the agricultural workers – who would be the principal victims of starvation.[134] Thus, no pre-invasion conflict existed between plans to starve tens of millions of Soviets in order to free up food supplies and the idea of preserving Soviet citizens as a valuable labour force. This is for the simple reason that there was not a pre-invasion intention, let alone a plan, to harness Soviet labour for the benefit of the German war machine because the Soviet population at that point in time was for the most part not viewed in these terms.

The change of course on this issue started to occur only in the autumn of 1941, by which time it had become clear that the German Blitzkrieg had failed and that victory in the East would not be achieved before the end of the year. Despite the potential risks from the political and racial viewpoint of the Nazi leadership, the enormous calls on domestic manpower caused by the continuation of the war against the Soviet Union and a reluctance to conscript German women required a change of mind in this matter. Of decisive importance for the shift to the use in the Reich of workers from the occupied eastern territories was Hitler's order of 31 October 1941 on the deployment of Soviet prisoners of war in the German war economy.[135]

> The Führer has now ordered that the labour of the Russian [sic] prisoners of war should also be utilized extensively through large-scale assignment for the requirements of the war industry. Prerequisite for production is adequate nourishment. In addition, very low wages are to be paid for the most modest supply of a few consumer goods for everyday life, with potential rewards for satisfactory work.[136]

At the beginning of November 1941, the Reich Minister for Labour announced that a large number of foreign workers, including some from the occupied eastern territories, would 'soon' be put to use in the Reich.[137] At a session of the Economic Staff East on 7 November, Reichsmarschall Göring announced that the Soviet labour force, by order of Hitler, was to be utilized in Germany. In the occupied Soviet territories, Soviet civilians would be required to carry out heavy manual work. German skilled workers, on the other hand, belonged in the armaments industry. Shovelling and breaking rocks was not for them, according to Göring; 'that's what the Russian is there for'.[138] Göring's regulations of 7 November 1941 constituted the green light for the extensive use of Soviet workers in Germany.[139] On 19 December, Reich Minister Rosenberg issued a general edict on labour service which compelled Soviet civilians to work for the occupation authorities.[140]

The Special Status of the Ukraine

Several strands of this study so far have led to one territory of the Soviet Union in particular: the Ukraine. Clearly, Hitler was convinced of the importance for Germany of obtaining Lebensraum, foodstuffs and raw materials, only 'available' in sufficient quantities in the East, and cherished the idea of accomplishing this goal. As time went on, his eyes came to rest more and more on the Ukraine, the apparent long-term solution to the Reich's alleged problems.

Some years after the Second World War, the former League of Nations High Commissioner in the Free City of Danzig, Carl J. Burckhardt, recorded

Hitler saying to him on 11 August 1939: 'Everything I undertake is directed against Russia; if the West is too dumb and too blind to grasp this, I will be forced to reach an agreement with the Russians, to strike down the West and then after its defeat to turn against the Soviet Union with my assembled forces. I need the Ukraine, in order that no one is able to starve us again, like in the last war.'[141] In very clear words – Burckhardt was so surprised that he scarcely believed what he had just heard – Hitler announced his intention to seize the Ukraine by force and, significantly, the specific justification for this: to maintain the sustenance of the German people. At the beginning of December 1940, Colonel-General Halder remarked to Hitler that the Soviet Union's most important armaments centres were situated in the Ukraine, in Moscow and in Leningrad. The Ukraine, he continued, was moreover an agricultural 'surplus territory'.[142] In his January 1941 presentation, Herbert Backe assured Hitler that 'the occupation of the Ukraine would liberate us from every economic worry' and then pointed out that the Ukraine was indeed the only 'surplus territory' in the Soviet Union, i.e., the only one producing a surplus of grain.[143] At the beginning of August 1941, the Commander of Army Group North, Field Marshal Wilhelm Ritter von Leeb, recorded in his diary Backe's view that the Ukraine had to be utilized for the purpose of supplying 'the European space'.[144]

In summing up the main points of the prevailing war situation in his diary entry of 2 March 1941, Ulrich von Hassell, the former German Ambassador to Rome, began by noting the growing danger of food supplies, a danger which would become 'alarming' in the event that Hitler would indeed march on 'Russia' in the spring. This 'madness' was being justified, according to Hassell, on the following basis: '1. with the necessity to occupy the Ukraine, 2. to finish off the "potential allies" of the opposing side "as a precaution"!'[145] Thus, according to Hassell, the main justification being used within the Nazi leadership for an invasion of the Soviet Union was 'the necessity to occupy the Ukraine', accompanied by all the rewards that it was believed would ensue. Hassell, who was normally well informed about such matters, was in regular and close contact during this period with, amongst others, General Thomas, and indeed dined with the latter only a matter of days after the quoted diary entry was written.[146] In contrast to the view held by the Nazi leadership, Hassell felt that the real consequences of a German invasion would be very different: '1. cutting off of supplies from Russia, whilst the Ukraine will only be usable after a longer time; 2. new, most serious strain on all war resources and forces; 3. complete encirclement, wilfully brought about.'[147]

There were also others, like Hassell, who questioned the sagacity of a policy which pinned all hopes on the supposed 'granary of Europe', whilst effectively disregarding the loss of vital deliveries from the Soviet Union which an invasion would inevitably trigger – the dangers of which had been pointed out by Göring's economic advisers at the end of January 1941 and indeed by Thomas in his otherwise optimistic study of February.[148] This time around, the critical assessment came from someone who, unlike

Hassell, continued to occupy a senior position in the German government. On 19 April 1941, when most of the major policy decisions regarding operations in the East had admittedly already been made, long-time Finance Minister Lutz Graf Schwerin von Krosigk wrote a letter to Reichsmarschall Göring, responding to points made by the latter during their 'last discussion'.[149] Echoing Gebhardt von Walther's negative assessment of the economic and agricultural gains to be made from an occupation of Soviet territories, and questioning the apparently widespread belief within the Nazi leadership that such an occupation would prove decisive in supplying Germany with sufficient foodstuffs, Schwerin von Krosigk commented:

> I do not believe that the conquest of Russian territories would significantly help [us] on the food front. In this connection, I take it for granted – about which I do not presume to make a judgement – that, militarily, this victory will be achieved without too many difficulties. Nevertheless, the Russian ... would leave us with burnt fields and barns, which would scarcely bring us the grain amounts this year which we would receive automatically from Russia at present on the basis of the current delivery contracts. It could be, if one reckons with a war of several years against the united England-America [sic] ..., that perhaps more than the 1½–2½ mill[ion] t[ons], which Russia should deliver, could be obtained from the southern Russian territories. But, even if one assumes this to be the case, I request to be allowed to point out three things.[150]

He then proceeded to strengthen his argument against an invasion by drawing attention to three major issues. First, the transport difficulties involved in making deliveries from the Soviet Union would not disappear only because of a German occupation of large areas of Soviet territory. Secondly, the benefits to be had from a policy of economic exploitation would always be outweighed by the negative effect on German production caused by an extension of the war. Thirdly, a 'complication' with the Soviet Union would lead to the loss of the highly important supply of soybeans from Manchuria in north-eastern China.[151]

Schwerin von Krosigk drew the conclusion that, all in all, Germany's food situation, certainly for the coming year and in all probability for a longer period of time, would more probably deteriorate than improve in the event of an invasion of the USSR.[152] Significantly, Schwerin von Krosigk added:

> It could be that all these grave misgivings must be accepted in the event that the Russians do not keep to the Pact with us, do not provide the promised deliveries etc. Hitherto, however, no signs exist to warrant such an attitude. Moreover, I believe that the Russians, as a result of a perfectly understandable fear, would give us the shirts off their backs in their efforts to fulfil our delivery wishes, even if these were to be increased.[153]

For Hitler and the Nazi leadership, however, it was the very fact – and growing awareness – of Germany's increasing reliance on the Soviet Union for vital food and raw materials supplies that made it necessary to end this economic dependence.[154] On more than one occasion during the months prior to the launch of Operation Barbarossa, Colonel-General Halder noted in his war diary both the uncertainty of future Soviet deliveries and the increase in Soviet demands.[155] Germany was heavily dependent on the Soviet Union for deliveries of both raw materials with which to fight the war and foodstuffs. The supreme leadership was not prepared to run the risk of Stalin pulling the plug on these supplies at a crucial moment. They preferred the alternative of mounting a massive invasion rather than allowing the continuation of Germany's uncertain dependence on Stalin's adherence to his treaty obligations. Effectively, they believed Stalin to be just as treacherous and opportunistic as they themselves were.

Due to either his unwillingness or his inability to do so, Göring left Schwerin von Krosigk's letter unanswered.[156] This may of course be explained by a belief on Göring's part that it was simply unnecessary to reply to the letter, but one might also draw the conclusion that Göring – or indeed anyone for that matter – was incapable of presenting economic counter-arguments to the points raised in the German Finance Minister's letter. The highly questionable prerequisite for ultimate victory was, after all, a successful completion of the military campaign in the space of two or three months, which was in turn dependent on the ability of the German supply apparatus to provide the troops with sufficient fuel, ammunition and food. In no way was the undertaking based on economic certainties. Nobody, for example, had been able to provide an effective solution to the transport difficulties facing the German army. This was indicative of the whole approach of those responsible for the planning. Since the frank but limited exchange of views in January 1941 as to the economic repercussions of waging war against the Soviet Union,[157] at a time when the decision to invade had in any case already been taken by Hitler, there had been no serious attempt within the corridors of power to engage in a critical analysis of the economic implications of an invasion and occupation of the European USSR or, crucially, the existence of potential alternative scenarios should the military campaign and, therefore, the programme of economic exploitation not go to plan. The insistence of Germany's supreme leadership that potential difficulties be 'worked around' effectively dismissed any air of uncertainty which had existed within the ranks of the economic planners, particularly the Office of the Four-Year Plan, at the beginning of 1941.

Schwerin von Krosigk's letter of 19 April 1941 also raises the question: how did the conservative Finance Minister – not a member of Hitler's inner circle – know about the preparations for 'Barbarossa', which were supposed to be secret? More generally, how large (or small) must the planning group be for such a covert undertaking? In a diary entry from the end of May 1941, Joseph Goebbels mentioned a 'wave of camouflage' and stated that 'only a few people' in the entire state and military apparatus were in the picture regarding the true intentions hidden behind their mobilization. According to Goebbels, the 'other civil ministries have no idea what it is about', whilst his own ministry – nearly all of whom were also in the dark –

had to play up the theme of the invasion of Britain.[158] It was probably inevitable, however, that leaks regarding German intentions occurred during the planning period. In fact, Soviet Foreign Minister Molotov had been made aware of German preparations for war as early as February 1941, two months before Schwerin von Krosigk wrote his letter to Göring.[159] The Commander of Army Group Centre, Field Marshal Fedor von Bock, discovered 'how hard it is to keep something secret in wartime' when his Polish cleaning lady asked him to see to it that she kept her position because Bock was 'after all going away'![160]

Another senior official, this time the Staatssekretär in the Foreign Office, Ernst Freiherr von Weizsäcker, followed Schwerin von Krosigk's example nine days later with a letter of his own.[161] On 21 April, Weizsäcker had already taken the opportunity to tell his immediate superior, Foreign Minister Joachim von Ribbentrop, that he believed a war against the Soviet Union would be a 'disaster'.[162] A week later, he sent Ribbentrop a letter in which he gave reasons for his 'rejection' of such a war.[163] Like Schwerin von Krosigk, Weizsäcker began his letter by arguing in economic terms: 'If every burnt down Russian city was for us worth just as much as a sunken English warship, then I would support the German–Russian war in the summer; I believe, however, that we would only win militarily against Russia, on the other hand lose economically.'[164] Weizsäcker then turned to the much-heard claim that the military defeat of the Soviet Union, as Britain's last potential ally on the Continent, would be a crushing blow for Britain and indeed hasten her collapse.[165] As early as the beginning of August 1940, Weizsäcker had noted: 'To defeat England in Russia is not a plan.'[166] It was for him decisive whether the undertaking would indeed hasten Britain's collapse or not. If Britain was on the verge of collapse, then the engaging of a new opponent would only encourage the British, who expected nothing from the Soviets: 'Hope in Russia does not delay the English collapse. We don't destroy any English hopes with Russia.'[167] On the other hand, if an impending British collapse was not forthcoming and a continuation of the blockade could thus be expected, 'the thought could suggest itself' that Germany would have to 'feed' itself from the Soviet land mass through the use of force.[168] This thought had been more than suggested. It was indeed now part of German policy for the forthcoming campaign and occupation, even if Weizsäcker himself was not privy to this information. As an active member of the opposition to Hitler, one might expect him, like Ulrich von Hassell, to have been in contact with General Thomas, though it might be presuming too much to believe that Thomas would have shared his deep involvement in the development of the 'starvation strategy' with Weizsäcker and the other conspirators.[169]

Like Schwerin von Krosigk, Weizsäcker expressed certainty – no less could be expected from someone in his position – that Germany would be militarily victorious and that its forces would reach Moscow and beyond. What he doubted, however, was that the Germans would be able to exploit what they had won in the face of the 'well-known passive resistance of the

Slavs'.[170] In summing up, Weizsäcker argued that a German attack on the Soviet Union would be seen in Britain as a lack of belief on the part of the Germans in victory over the island nation.[171] Weizsäcker's clearly expressed argument that a German invasion of the Soviet Union would actually bolster British fortitude was simply common sense, and the failure of Hitler and the rest of the Nazi leadership to recognize this further indicates an absence of logical analysis within the state and Party hierarchy when it came to the likely effects, both political and economic, of a German invasion of the European USSR. Their viewpoint was, of course, based on the presumption that a military campaign would be without doubt an overwhelming success, and therefore failed to give due consideration to the possibility that events might in fact take a different course. Two days after Weizsäcker had written his letter to Ribbentrop, Hitler set the start date of 'Barbarossa' for 22 June.[172]

Although it would appear from a postscript attached to Weizsäcker's letter that Ribbentrop himself had requested that Weizsäcker write the statement,[173] if Ribbentrop's circular of 26 August 1941 is anything to go by, Weizsäcker's letter of four months earlier had been wasted on the Foreign Minister. Ribbentrop's note – confidently predicting success against the Soviet Union during 1941 – summed up the significance of Operation Barbarossa for the Nazi leadership:

> The victory over Russia [sic] is of particular importance for Germany because
> 1.) for all the future, by means of the seizure of the Ukrainian territories, there will no longer be a food problem;
> 2.) as a result of the seizure of the territories rich in raw materials and the industrial centres, the German raw materials question will all in all likewise no longer be a problem and the German war capacity [will be] hugely increased in the future;
> 3.) and above all Germany now has its rear free as a result of [the] removal of the threat from the East. It can now turn against its final opponent England with the force of its entire national strength.[174]

As Ribbentrop saw it, then, the importance of, and hence stimulus for, the German invasion of the Soviet Union could be summed up in three aims: to solve the food problem in the German-occupied territories; to bolster the German war capacity through the influx of raw materials; and to remove the Soviet Union with a view to turning once more, though this time immeasurably stronger than before, against Great Britain. These different strands of argumentation were not separate, but rather inextricably intertwined. The failure of the objections raised by Schwerin von Krosigk and Weizsäcker to have an impact on policy was not so much due to the fact that both letters were sent during the second half of April 1941, when most of the major policy decisions regarding operations against the Soviet Union had already been made, but rather because they did not carry enough weight. The policy of agricultural exploitation developed over the preceding months had too much high-level support.

In a letter to Benito Mussolini on the eve of the launch of the military campaign, Hitler himself, effectively confirming Ulrich von Hassell's assessment of three and a half months earlier, stressed the central importance of the Ukraine in his plans: 'I hope above all that it is then possible for us to secure in the long term a common food-supply basis in the Ukraine which will provide us with those surpluses which we will perhaps need in the future. I might add here however, that – as far as can presently be seen – this German harvest promises to be a very good one.'[175] If further proof of the significance of the Ukraine is (or was at the time) required, then one must look no further than Hitler's own comment about the region at the conference of 16 July 1941 at FHQ, three and a half weeks after the beginning of the eastern campaign. This important meeting is discussed later in more detail,[176] but it is worth mentioning the remark here, particularly as it was one of the few Hitler made in which a time frame for events in the occupied Soviet territories was envisaged. Hitler emphasized that the most important territory for the next three years would be, without a doubt, the Ukraine.[177]

In addition to his emphasis on the agricultural benefits to be gained from an occupation and exploitation of the Ukraine, Hitler made his political views on the future of the territory – at least once the military campaign was under way – very clear. His opinion of the people themselves gave a good indication of how he envisaged their role and the treatment to be meted out to them. He considered them 'just as lazy, disorganized and nihilistic-Asiatic as the Greater Russians'.[178] Indeed, ever since writing *Mein Kampf*, Hitler had regarded the Slavic peoples as a whole as 'an inferior race', incapable of organizing themselves into a state.[179] He thus rejected the notion of a 'free Ukraine', as did the most senior administrative official in the Ukraine, Reich Commissar Erich Koch.[180] Hitler had 'no interest ... in creating an independent Ukraine'.[181] In perhaps his most concrete statement on the long-term future of any one of the occupied Soviet territories, Hitler announced at the end of September 1941 in the presence of Reich Minister Rosenberg, Reichsleiter Bormann and Head of the Reich Chancellery Lammers what he had in mind for the Ukraine: a German protectorate of approximately twenty-five years' duration. As he saw it, an independent Ukraine was – and would for decades remain – out of the question.[182]

These views on the future of the Ukraine were quite different to those of the Reich Minister for the East, Alfred Rosenberg. He declared on many occasions during the pre-invasion preparation period that the Ukraine should become an 'independent state' and announced that one of the aims of the Reich Commissar in the Ukraine would be the establishment of a 'free Ukrainian state in closest alliance with the Greater German Reich'.[183] One of Rosenberg's cherished projects was the construction of a major university in the Ukrainian capital Kiev.[184] Given Hitler's belief – expressed on one occasion in the presence of Erich Koch – that the destruction of the Soviet Union's large cities constituted the prerequisite for the endurance of German hegemony in Europe and that 'hardly anything of the city of Kiev will remain',[185] the realization of Rosenberg's wish was highly unlikely. In any case, Hitler stated explicitly on another occasion that he was not in favour of a university in Kiev.[186] Lammers informed Rosenberg shortly afterwards that Hitler had declared the erection of a university in Kiev – 'the prospect of which has apparently been held out and is being pursued by some departments' – to be 'out of the question'.[187]

The Ukraine was the major area of disagreement within the schemes of the political and economic planners. The treatment of this territory was rightly described by Dr Werner Koeppen, Rosenberg's liaison officer at FHQ, as being 'a very critical question' which would decisively and for the duration determine the degree of respect accorded to the East Ministry both by its subordinate offices (i.e., the Reich Commissariats) and external agencies (e.g., the OKW).[188] The importance of this issue lay not only in the centrality of the Ukraine within Nazi eastern policy but also in the extent of the quasi-positive attention afforded the territory by Rosenberg and his staff. They wanted to give the Ukraine special status amongst the eastern territories and treat the population with a certain degree of consideration. The economic experts, on the other hand, saw the Ukraine as the most important 'surplus territory' and ripe for ruthless exploitation. They believed, indeed, that it was vital that they obtain as much from the Ukraine as possible – both a successful prosecution of the war and the securing of the basis of Germany's future sustenance depended on it.

Rosenberg's subsequent problems with the Reich Commissar in the Ukraine, Erich Koch – a man who, like Hitler, Göring and Bormann, made no differentiation between the different peoples in the East – stemmed from this fundamental difference in approach. Thus, it becomes clear why someone like Koch, who was particularly brutal, even by Nazi standards, was entrusted by Hitler, with the support of Göring and the economic planners,[189] with control over the Ukraine and its people. In terms of the policy ultimately followed by Germany, however, there was never any real doubt where Hitler's sympathies lay, except perhaps among the staff of the Bureau Rosenberg. Hitler's blessing had already been bestowed on Backe's plans and the establishment of an economic organization under Göring and Thomas for the ruthless exploitation of the occupied Soviet territories before Rosenberg was even commissioned to sketch out the future political administration. On this matter, then, Rosenberg had been sidelined right from the start.

Notes

1. See Schulte, *The German Army*, pp. 98–99.
2. Mulligan, *The Politics of Illusion and Empire*, p. 116. Even Belgium contributed over twice as much to the Reich as could be squeezed out of the Soviet territories during their occupation (roughly 9.3 billion RM as compared with about 4.5 billion RM); Ericson, *Feeding the German Eagle*, p. 173.
3. See the excellent discussion in Ulrich Herbert, 'Racism and Rational Calculation: The Role of "Utilitarian" Strategies of Legitimation in the National Socialist "Weltanschauung"', *Yad Vashem Studies*, 24 (1994), pp. 131–145, esp. pp. 143–144.

4. Ibid., pp. 144–145.
5. On the Nazis' 'irrational' use of Jewish workers, see Daniel Jonah Goldhagen, *Hitler's Willing Executioners: Ordinary Germans and the Holocaust* (Alfred A. Knopf, New York, 1996), chaps. 10–12.
6. Präg and Jacobmeyer (eds), *Das Diensttagebuch des deutschen Generalgouverneurs*, p. 336, entry for 25 March 1941: 'Es ist wichtiger, daß wir den Krieg gewinnen, als Rassenpolitik durchsetzen.'
7. Alfred Kube's contention that the decisive turning point in Göring's demise occurred already in the years 1938 and 1939 cannot, in light of his prominent role in the preparations for 'Barbarossa' and indeed in the first weeks of the campaign itself, be accepted; Kube, *Pour le mérite und Hakenkreuz*, p. 324. See also pp. 335–339.
8. See Gerlach, *Kalkulierte Morde*, pp. 67–68.
9. BA-MA, RW 19/165, fo. 2, 'Aktennotiz über Besprechung am 31.3.', Stab Ia, 2 April 1941. Colonels John and Becht, Major von Gusovius and Captain Meendsen-Bohlken, all of whom were from Thomas's War Economy and Armaments Office, were also present.
10. Witte et al. (eds), *Dienstkalender*, p. 143, entry for 1 April 1941: '14.00 Essen im Amt mit Staatssekretär Körner.'
11. BAK, N 1075/1, Mappe 3, handwritten letter to Ursula Backe: 'Meine Vorbereitungen für "Barbarossa" gehen sehr gut weiter.'
12. BAK, N 1094/II 20, Mappe III.
13. BA, R 26 I/6, fos. 1–25, 'Der Vierjahresplan', 29 April 1941, here fos. 22–23. The speech was written by Oberregierungsrat Dr Otto Donner.
14. Backe, *Um die Nahrungsfreiheit Europas*, Darstellung 1, inside front cover; BA-MA, RW 19/473, fo. 306. Between 1933/34 and 1938/39, the extent of Germany's self-sufficiency was increased from 80 to 83 per cent; Joachim Lehmann, 'Die deutsche Landwirtschaft im Kriege', in Dietrich Eichholtz, *Geschichte der deutschen Kriegswirtschaft 1939–1945, Band II/2: 1941–1943*, 2nd edition (K.G. Saur, Munich, 1999) [1985], pp. 570–642, here p. 573.
15. Gerlach, 'Die Ausweitung der deutschen Massenmorde', p. 14.
16. Hitler made such a comment to Mussolini on the occasion of their meeting in Florence on 28 October 1940; *ADAP, Serie D: 1937–1941*, vol. 11/1, p. 350, doc. 246.
17. BA, R 26 I/6, fo. 23.
18. Burleigh, *The Third Reich*, p. 458.
19. On the thinking behind the European economic Neuordnung and the concept of a Großwirtschaftsraum, see Umbreit, 'Kontinentalherrschaft', pp. 210–216; Noakes and Pridham (eds), *Nazism 1919–1945, Vol. 3*, pp. 884–900.
20. *IMG*, vol. 31, p. 84, doc. 2718-PS, 'Aktennotiz über Ergebnis der heutigen Besprechung mit den Staatssekretären über Barbarossa', 2 May 1941: '1.) Der Krieg ist nur weiter zu führen, wenn die gesamte Wehrmacht im 3. Kriegsjahr aus Rußland ernährt wird. 2.) Hierbei werden zweifellos zig Millionen Menschen verhungern, wenn von uns das für uns Notwendige aus dem Lande herausgeholt wird.'
21. On this, see Gerlach, *Kalkulierte Morde*, pp. 71–75.
22. Gerlach, *Kalkulierte Morde*, p. 783; Ulrich Herbert, *Fremdarbeiter: Politik und Praxis des 'Ausländer-Einsatzes', in der Kriegswirtschaft des Dritten Reiches* (Dietz, Bonn, 1999), p. 156.
23. See Gerlach, 'Die Ausweitung der deutschen Massenmorde', pp. 40 and 82–83.
24. Gerlach, *Kalkulierte Morde*, pp. 456–457; Herbert, *Fremdarbeiter*, p. 158.
25. See Warlimont, *Inside Hitler's Headquarters*, pp. 169–170; Percy Ernst Schramm (ed.), *Kriegstagebuch des Oberkommandos der Wehrmacht (Wehrmachtsführungsstab) 1940–1945: Geführt von Helmuth Greiner und Percy Ernst Schramm*, vol. II/1: 1 January 1942–31 December 1942 (Bernard & Graefe Verlag, Frankfurt am Main, 1963), p. 341, entry for 6 May 1942.
26. *IMG*, vol. 31, p. 84.
27. Gerlach, *Kalkulierte Morde*, p. 46, fn. 59.

28. BA-MA, RW 4/ v. 759, fol. 14: 'Herr Reichsleiter Rosenberg bittet Herrn General in einer dringenden Angelegenheit zu einer Besprechung am Freitag, 2.5.41, 11,00 Uhr vormittags in das Amt von Herrn Reichsleiter. Der Herr Reichsleiter bittet Herrn General möglichst um Einhaltung des Termins der Besprechung, um am Freitagnachmittag dem Führer Vortrag halten zu können.'
29. Rosenberg's diary entry for 1 May 1941, published in the *Frankfurter Rundschau*, no. 140, 22 July 1971.
30. Schramm (ed.), *KTB des OKW*, I, p. 390: '2. Mai 1941 (Chef bei Reichsleiter Rosenberg).'
31. Rosenberg's diary entries for 1 and 6 May 1941, published in the *Frankfurter Rundschau*, no. 140, 22 July 1971.
32. Rosenberg's diary entry for 6 May. On Riecke see Aly and Heim, *Vordenker der Vernichtung*, p. 386; on both Riecke and Schlotterer, see Müller, 'Ausbeutungskrieg', p. 174.
33. Rosenberg's diary entry for 6 May: 'Es war eine jetzt auf großer Erfahrung beruhende gute Generalstabsarbeit.'
34. BA-MA, RW 19/177, fos. 163–169, '11. Sitzung des Generalrats vom 24.6.1941 unter Vorsitz von Staatssekretär Körner', here fo. 163.
35. BA-MA, RW 19/739, fos. 130–136, 'Niederschrift zur 4. Sitzung des Wirtschafts-Führungsstabes Ost unter Vorsitz von Staatssekretär Körner vom 26. Mai 1941'.
36. See Eichholtz, *Geschichte der deutschen Kriegswirtschaft*, I, p. 240.
37. BA-MA, RW 19/739, fo. 306, Stab Ia, 'Besprechung Staatssekretäre 2.5.41': '1.) Weisung des Führers an Reichsmarschall muß endlich unterschrieben werden. Ferner ebenfalls Brief des Reichsmarschalls an den Ob d H.' The letter was in fact signed by Göring, sent to and received by Brauchitsch by 14 May at the latest; BA-MA, RW 19/739, fo. 267, 'Aktenvermerk. Betr.: Wirtschaftsorganisation Barbarossa', 14 May 1941.
38. IfZ, ED 180/5, Terminkalender Hermann Göring, fo. 62, entry for 2 May 1941.
39. See Rolf-Dieter Müller, 'Industrielle Interessenpolitik im Rahmen des "Generalplans Ost": Dokumente zum Einfluß von Wehrmacht, Industrie und SS auf die wirtschaftspolitische Zielsetzung für Hitlers Ostimperium', *Militärgeschichtliche Mitteilungen*, 29 (1981), pp. 101–141, here doc. 4, p. 118, 'Fragen, die durch den Herrn Reichsmarschall noch befohlen bzw. beim Führer geklärt werden müssen', 5 May 1941.
40. 'Baltenland' was how the Baltic States and Belarus were being collectively referred to at this stage.
41. Müller, 'Industrielle Interessenpolitik', p. 118: '*Baltenland* muß sich selbst ernähren. Hauptaufgabe ist Ausnutzung der Werft- und Aluminiumkapazitäten und der Ölvorkommen. *Ukraine* muß – da landwirtschaftliches Überschußgebiet – möglichst stark für die industrielle Fertigung ausgenutzt werden. ... *Moskau*. Das Gebiet Moskau als landwirtschaftliches Zuschußgebiet ist industriell nur insoweit ausnutzen, als es die Gesamtsituation verlangt. Keine Anhäufung von Wehrmachtaufträgen im Moskauer Gebiet. *Kaukasus*. Schnellste Ingangsetzung und Erhöhung der Mineralölförderung und Maßnahmen zum glatten Abtransport dieser Mengen.'
42. Moritz (ed.), *Fall Barbarossa*, pp. 178–181, doc. 47, 'Planungsunterlage der Abteilung Landesverteidigung im OKW für die Eroberung des Erdölgebiets im Kaukasus'.
43. BA-MA, RW 19/164, fo. 153, 'Vortrag Obstlt. Tietze, Major Sadewasser, Hptm. Emmerich, Herr Biedermann beim Amtschef', 13 February 1941.
44. BA-MA, RW 19/185, fo. 170. See chapter 4, 'Thomas's Study of Mid-February 1941', in this study.
45. Rudolf-Christoph Freiherr von Gersdorff, *Soldat im Untergang* (Ullstein, Frankfurt am Main/Berlin/Vienna, 1977), p. 93; Christian Gerlach, 'Deutsche Wirtschaftsinteressen, Besatzungspolitik und der Mord an den Juden in Weißrußland 1941–1943', in Herbert (ed.), *Nationalsozialistische Vernichtungspolitik*, pp. 263–291, here pp. 270–271. On Six, see Lutz Hachmeister, *Der Gegnerforscher: Die Karriere des SS-Führers Franz Alfred Six* (C.H. Beck, Munich, 1998).

46. Moll, 'Steuerungsinstrument im "Ämterchaos"?', p. 233. This was the last scheduled conference of the Reichs- and Gauleiter before the beginning of the invasion.
47. Witte et al. (eds), *Dienstkalender*, p. 155, entry for 5 May 1941.
48. Halder, *KTB*, II, p. 408, entry for 12 May 1941.
49. *TBJG*, I/9, pp. 283–284, entry for 1 May 1941.
50. Ibid., pp. 293–294: 'Wenn nur die diesjährige Ernte gut wird. Und dann wollen wir uns ja im Osten gesundstoßen.'
51. BA-MA, RW 19/473, fos. 177–179, 'Dr. Claussen über die Ernährungslage', 14 May 1941.
52. Ibid., fos. 177–178. See also BA-MA, RW 19/177, fol. 19, 'Kriegswirtschaftlicher Lagebericht Nr. 21, Mai 1941', signed by General Thomas, 10 June 1941.
53. BA-MA, RW 19/473, fo. 178.
54. BA, NS 43/41, fos. 130–131, Sammlung politischer und wirtschaftlicher Studien geleitet von Luigi Lojacono; Enrico Insabato, 'Die Ukraine: Bevölkerung und Wirtschaft', undated (1940?). Compare these figures with the report of the *Volkswirtschaftliche Abteilung* of the Deutsche Reichsbank, which gives the Ukrainian population as thirty-one million people from a total of 168 million (also less than a fifth), but states that the Ukraine produced only 20 per cent of the entire grain harvest; BA, R 2/30921, 'Die sowjetische Landwirtschaft', 21 May 1941.
55. *IMG*, vol. 26, pp. 567–573, doc. 1028–PS, 'Instruktion für einen Reichskommissar in der Ukraine'.
56. Ibid., pp. 573–576, doc. 1029–PS, 'Instruktion für einen Reichskommissar im Ostland'.
57. Ibid., pp. 576–580, doc. 1030–PS, 'Allgemeine Instruktion für alle Reichskommissare in den besetzten Ostgebieten'.
58. Ibid., p. 567: 'Ziel der Arbeit eines deutschen Reichskommissars in der Ukraine ist zunächst die Sicherung von Nahrungsmitteln und Rohstoffen für das Deutsche Reich, damit Festigung der deutschen Kriegsführung, sodann die Errichtung eines freien ukrainischen Staates im engsten Bündnis mit dem Großdeutschen Reich.'
59. Ibid., p. 573: 'Die Aufgaben eines deutschen Reichskommissars in der Ukraine können von weltgeschichtlicher Tragweite sein. Gelingt es unter Einsetzung aller politischen, psychologischen und kulturellen Mittel einen freien ukrainischen Staate bis *nach* Saratow zu gründen, dann ist der jahrhundertelange Albdruck, den das deutsche Volk durch das russische Imperium empfinden müsste, gebrochen, dann ist Deutschland durch keine überseeische Blockade gefährdet und die Nahrungsmittel- und Rohstoffversorgung für alle Zukunft gesichert.'
60. *IMG*, vol. 38, p. 88: 'Nie darf erlaubt werden, dass ein Anderer Waffen trägt, als der Deutsche!'
61. See Appendix 3.
62. See *IMG*, vol. 26, p. 551 and doc. 1024–PS, 'Allgemeiner Aufbau und Aufgaben einer Dienststelle für die Zentrale Bearbeitung der Fragen des Osteuropäischen Raumes', 29 April 1941, pp. 560–566, here p. 562.
63. BAK, N 1075/9, 'Termine am Mittwoch, dem 7. Mai 1941'. The Margaretenstrasse is today called the Scharounstrasse. I am grateful to Dr Ernst Piper for this piece of information.
64. Nbg. Dok. PS 1018, fos. 64–73, 'Aktennotiz über die Unterredung mit Staatssekretär Körner', 8 May 1941, here fos. 64–65 and 70–71.
65. Ibid., fol. 69.
66. Herbst, *Der Totale Krieg und die Ordnung der Wirtschaft*, pp. 129 and 133–134; Marc Buggeln, 'Währungspläne für den europäischen Großraum: Die Diskussion der nationalsozialistischen Wirtschaftsexperten über ein zukünftiges europäisches Zahlungssystem', *Beiträge zur Geschichte des Nationalsozialismus, Band 18: Europäische Integration*, Sonderdruck (Wallstein Verlag, Göttingen, 2002), pp. 41–76, here p. 51. I am grateful to Paolo Fonzi for making a copy of this article available to me.
67. See chapter 9, 'The Concept of a Territorial Ministry in the East'.

68. *IMG*, vol. 26, p. 580: 'Dieser kommende Kampf ist ein Kampf um die Ernährung und Rohstoffversorgung sowohl für das Deutsche Reich als auch für den ganzen europäischen Raum ....'
69. Ibid., p. 578.
70. Gerlach, 'Die Ausweitung der deutschen Massenmorde', p. 19.
71. BA-MA, RW 19/185, fos. 171 and 175.
72. BA-MA, RW 19/164, fo. 119, 'Besprechung General von Hanneken und Oberst John beim Amtschef (mit Oberstlt. Tietze, Reg. Rat Mureck, Major Sadewasser)', 25 January 1941.
73. Klaus A. Friedrich Schüler, *Logistik im Russlandfeldzug: Die Rolle der Eisenbahn bei Planung, Vorbereitung und Durchführung des deutschen Angriffs auf die Sowjetunion bis zur Krise vor Moskau im Winter 1941/42* (Peter Lang, Frankfurt am Main, 1987), pp. 164 and 166–167.
74. Halder, *KTB*, II, p. 258: 'Großräumigkeit – kein Stocken; das allein verbürgt den Sieg. Stockungslose Durchführung ist eine Nachschubfrage. Alles muß zusammen helfen, sie zu lösen. Entfernungen! ... Bahnen sind das einzige Mittel, um ohne Transportraumzuschuß weiterzukommen.'
75. Hans Meier-Welcker, *Aufzeichnungen eines Generalstabsoffiziers 1939–1942* (Rombach, Freiburg im Breisgau, 1982), p. 103, entry for 31 January 1941: 'Die Versorgung bestimmt die Grenze der Operationsmöglichkeiten nach der Tiefe.'
76. See Ihno Krumpelt, *Das Material und die Kriegführung* (E.S. Mittler & Sohn, Frankfurt am Main, 1968), p. 142. Dr Krumpelt and a small staff were commissioned by Army Quartermaster-General Eduard Wagner at the beginning of October 1940 with the planning for supplying the troops during the eastern campaign; see pp. 140–156, esp. pp. 140 and 149.
77. BA, R 26 IV/33a, 'Richtlinien für die Führung der Wirtschaft in den neubesetzten Ostgebieten (Grüne Mappe)', Teil I (2. Auflage), July 1941, p. 12. See also Schüler, *Logistik im Russlandfeldzug*, p. 114.
78. For General Thomas's fears in this respect see BA-MA, RW 19/185, fol. 170.
79. Gerlach, 'Die Ausweitung der deutschen Massenmorde', p. 20.
80. Quoted in Gerlach, 'Militärische "Versorgungszwänge"', p. 184: 'Der Nachschub muß durch weitgehende Ausnutzung des Landes eingeschränkt, das Erfassungswesen straff geregelt werden. Nicht durch wahlloses Zugreifen, sondern durch Beschlagnahme und Beitreibung nach wohldurchdachtem Plan sind die Bestände des Landes nutzbar zu machen.'
81. Norbert Müller (ed.), *Okkupation, Raub, Vernichtung: Dokumente zur Besatzungspolitik der faschistischen Wehrmacht auf sowjetischen Territorium 1941 bis 1944* (Militärverlag der Deutschen Demokratischen Republik, Berlin, 1980), pp. 35–42, doc. 4, 'Anordnung des Oberbefehlshabers des Heeres über Organisation und Aufgaben des militärischen Okkupationsregimes in den zu erobernden Gebieten der UdSSR (Besondere Anordnungen für die Versorgung, Teil C)', 3 April 1941, here pp. 35 and 39.
82. BA-MA, RW 19/739, fos. 124–125, here fo. 124.
83. Ueberschär and Wette (eds), *"Unternehmen Barbarossa"*, pp. 308–312, doc. 7, 'Besondere Anordnungen Nr. 1 zur Weisung Nr. 21 (Fall "Barbarossa") vom 19.5.1941 mit Anlage 1: Gliederung und Aufgaben der im Raum "Barbarossa" einzusetzenden Wirtschaftsorganisation, und Anlage 3: Richtlinien für das Verhalten der Truppe in Rußland', here p. 308: 'Die besonders gelagerten Verhältnisse im Raum "Barbarossa" machen die *umfassende und straff geleitete Ausnutzung des Landes* für die Versorgung der Truppe gerade auf dem Verpflegungsgebiet erforderlich. Die Truppe muß sich bewußt sein, daß *jede Einsparung im Nachschub*, besonders von Verpflegung, die Reichweite der Operationen vergrößert.'
84. *IMG*, vol. 36, pp. 135–157, doc. 126-EC, 'Wirtschaftspolitische Richtlinien für Wirtschaftsorganisation Ost, Gruppe Landwirtschaft', 23 May 1941. Götz Aly and Susanne Heim mistakenly refer to this document as the '*Grüne Mappe*'; Aly and Heim, *Vordenker der Vernichtung*, p. 372.

85. BA, R 26 IV/9, 'Geheime Ostsachen 1941', serial no. 13, 23 May 1941.
86. *IMG*, vol. 36, pp. 137–138.
87. Ibid., pp. 138 and 140.
88. Ibid., p. 141: 'Die Bevölkerung dieser Gebiete, insbesondere die Bevölkerung der Städte, wird größter Hungersnot entgegensehen müssen. Es wird darauf ankommen, die Bevölkerung in die sibirischen Räume abzulenken. Da Eisenbahntransport nicht in Frage kommt, wird auch dieses Problem ein äußerst schwieriges sein.'
89. Ibid., p. 145: 'Viele 10 Millionen von Menschen werden in diesem Gebiet überflüssig und werden sterben oder nach Sibirien auswandern müssen. Versuche, die Bevölkerung dort vor dem Hungertode dadurch zu retten, dass man aus der Schwarzerdezone Überschüsse heranzieht, können nur auf Kosten der Versorgung Europas gehen. Sie unterbinden die Durchhaltemöglichkeit Deutschlands im Kriege, sie unterbinden die Blockadefestigkeit Deutschlands und Europas. Darüber muß absolute Klarheit herrschen.'
90. Ibid., p. 145.
91. Ibid., p. 144.
92. Ibid., p. 156.
93. Ibid., p. 147.
94. Ibid., pp. 148–149 and 154.
95. BA-MA, RW 19/473, fo. 177.
96. *IMG*, vol. 36, p. 151.
97. Ibid., p. 150.
98. Ibid., p. 154.
99. Gerlach, *Kalkulierte Morde*, pp. 93 and 630–631; Gerlach, 'Deutsche Wirtschaftsinteressen', p. 272.
100. Gert Robel, 'Sowjetunion', in Wolfgang Benz (ed.), *Dimension des Völkermords: Die Zahl der jüdischen Opfer des Nationalsozialismus* (R. Oldenbourg Verlag, Munich, 1991), pp. 499–560, here p. 501.
101. See IfZ, Fd 52, 'Verteilung d. jüd. Bevölkerung im ehem. Estland, Lettland, Litauen u. Nordpolen', 23 April 1941. Here it is stated that 'Juden wohnen fast ausschl[ießlich] in den Städten' ('Jews live almost exclusively in the cities').
102. *IMG*, vol. 36, p. 140.
103. BAK, N 1094/II 20, Mappe III, letter from Backe to Darré, 9 October 1941.
104. *IMG*, vol. 36, p. 140: 'Aus dieser Lage, die die Billigung der höchsten Stellen erfahren hat, da sie auch im Einklang mit den politischen Tendenzen steht (Erhaltung des Kleinrussentums, Erhaltung des Kaukasus, der Baltischen Provinzen, Weißrußlands auf Kosten der Zurückdrängung des Großrussentums), ergeben sich folgende Konsequenzen ....'
105. Ibid., pp. 139 and 147. See also BA, R 70 Sowjetunion/32, fo. 10; here Heydrich instructs the German security forces to talk only of 'Russen (nicht Großrussen)', 'Ukrainern (nicht Kleinrussen), Weissruthenen (nicht Weissrussen)', and the 'Sowjetunion (nicht Russland schlechthin)'.
106. *IMG*, vol. 36, p. 147: 'Da die politische Richtung gegen das Großrussentum geht, wird es darauf ankommen, Großrussen in die Waldzone zu verdrängen und die freiwerdenden Kolchose mit den übrigen Kleinrussen zu besetzen.'
107. Harrison, *Accounting for War*, pp. 98, 100 and 266–267. See also BA, 99 US 7/1085, fo. 141, post-war comments of Hans-Joachim Riecke, 13 August 1948.
108. *IMG*, vol. 36, pp. 146 and 153.
109. Müller, 'Ausbeutungskrieg', p. 195.
110. PAAA, Pol. Abt. XIII, Nr. 25, R 105192, fos. 198850–198858, 'Betr.: Sitzung im Außenpolitischen Amt am 29. Mai über Ost-Fragen', Georg Großkopf, 30 May 1941, here fo. 198852: 'Wir müssen uns darüber klar sein, dass wir durch unsere Bemühungen und Parolen, die Kollektive und Staatsgüter (aus für uns maßgebenden wirtschaftlichen Gründen) in ihrem gegenwärtigen Zustand zu erhalten, das schlagkräftigste Agitationsmittel aus der Hand geben. Die Bolschewiken haben mit der Parole "Alles Land den Bauern" 1917 die Revolution gemacht und alle weißen Gegenrevolutionen mit

dieser Parole, die ihnen die Hilfe der Bauern sicherte, niedergeworfen. Die Bauern erwarten von uns daher eine Auflösung der verhassten Kollektivwirtschaften.'
111. John Barber and Mark Harrison, *The Soviet Home Front, 1941–1945: A Social and Economic History of the USSR in World War II* (Longman, Harlow, 1991), p. 99.
112. On the collective farms see Gerlach, *Kalkulierte Morde*, pp. 342–371.
113. Hans Kehrl, *Krisenmanager im Dritten Reich, 6 Jahre Frieden – 6 Jahre Krieg: Erinnerungen* (Droste Verlag, Düsseldorf, 1973), p. 223.
114. BA, R 26 I/13, fo. 4.
115. BA, R 94/9, 'Niederschrift über die Sitzung des Wirtschaftsführungsstabes Ost vom 31. Juli 1941', p. 4.
116. *IMG*, vol. 36, pp. 156–157.
117. See Brandt, *Management*, pp. 57–58.
118. *IMG*, vol. 36, p. 156.
119. Trevor-Roper (ed.), *Hitler's Table Talk*, p. 32, entry for 17/18 September 1941.
120. See Hitler's speech to army commanders on 10 February 1939; BA, NS 11/28, fos. 86–119, 'Rede am 10. Februar 1939 in Berlin an die Truppenkommandeure des Heeres', esp. fos. 92–94.
121. *IMG*, vol. 27, pp. 220–221, doc. 1456-PS, 'Aktennotiz', signed by General Thomas, 20 June 1941, here p. 220: 'Man muß einen anderen Weg gehen und muß das, was man benötigt und nicht hat erobern.'
122. See Müller, 'Raubkrieg', p. 178.
123. Jochmann (ed.), *Monologe im Führerhauptquartier*, p. 63, entry for 17/18 September 1941: 'Wir werden ein Getreide-Exportland sein für all in Europa, die auf Getreide angewiesen sind. In der Krim haben wir Südfrüchte, Gummipflanzen (mit 40 000 ha machen wir uns unabhängig), Baumwolle. Die Pripjet-Sümpfe geben uns Schilf. Den Ukrainern liefern wir Kopftücher, Glasketten als Schmuck und was sonst Kolonialvölkern gefällt.'
124. Herbert, *Fremdarbeiter*, p. 156; Streit, *Keine Kameraden*, p. 192.
125. See *IMG*, vol. 27, pp. 63–64, doc. 1199-PS, 'Vermerk über Besprechung bei Wi Rü Amt am 4.7.[19]41, betr. Verwendung und Arbeitseinsatz der russischen Kriegsgef.', 4 July 1941, Lieutenant Colonel Dr Krull, here p. 63.
126. Gerlach, *Kalkulierte Morde*, pp. 456–457; Herbert, *Fremdarbeiter*, p. 158; Rolf-Dieter Müller, 'Menschenjagd: Die Rekrutierung von Zwangsarbeitern in der besetzten Sowjetunion', in Hannes Heer and Klaus Naumann (eds), *Vernichtungskrieg: Verbrechen der Wehrmacht 1941–1944* (Hamburger Edition, Hamburg, 1995), pp. 92–103, here p. 94.
127. Müller, 'Menschenjagd', p. 93.
128. Schramm (ed.), *KTB des OKW*, I, p. 258, entry for 9 January 1941.
129. Hubatsch (ed.), *Hitlers Weisungen für die Kriegsführung*, pp. 136–139, doc. 32b, 'Richtlinien für die personelle und materielle Rüstung', 14 July 1941, here p. 136: 'Die militärische Beherrschung des europäischen Raumes nach der Niederwerfung Rußlands erlaubt es, den Umfang des Heeres demnächst wesentlich zu verringern.'
130. Herbert, *Fremdarbeiter*, p. 158.
131. See chapter 6.
132. See chapter 4, 'Thomas's Study of Mid-February 1941'.
133. *IMG*, vol. 36, pp. 140–141.
134. Ibid., pp. 141, 145 and 156.
135. *Trials of War Criminals before the Nuernberg Military Tribunals under Control Council Law No. 10, Nuernberg, October 1946–April 1949*, vol. VIII (United States Government Printing Office, Washington, 1952), pp. 398–400, 'Subject: Use of Prisoners of War in the War Industry', signed by Field Marshal Keitel.
136. Ibid., p. 399; quoted in part in Herbert, *Fremdarbeiter*, p. 163. A combination of the original, though incomplete, German quotation and the complete English language translation has been used here.

137. BA, R 1501/3646, 'Betrifft: Seuchenhygienische Überwachung von Arbeitslagern', RMI, 4 November 1941.
138. N. Müller (ed.), *Okkupation, Raub, Vernichtung*, doc. 113, pp. 282–285, 'Aufzeichnung im Wirtschaftsstab Ost über die von Göring gegebenen Richtlinien für den Arbeitseinsatz von Sowjetbürgern', 7 November 1941, here p. 282.
139. Herbert, *Fremdarbeiter*, p. 165.
140. Burleigh, *The Third Reich*, p. 551; Nova, *Alfred Rosenberg*, p. 47.
141. Burckhardt, *Meine Danziger Mission*, p. 348: 'Alles was ich unternehme, ist gegen Rußland gerichtet; wenn der Westen zu dumm und zu blind ist, um dies zu begreifen, werde ich gezwungen sein, mich mit den Russen zu verständigen, den Westen zu schlagen, und dann nach seiner Niederlage mich mit meinen versammelten Kräften gegen die Sowjetunion zu wenden. Ich brauche die Ukraine, damit man uns nicht wieder wie im letzten Krieg aushungern kann.'
142. *IMG*, vol. 28, p. 393, doc. 1799–PS.
143. See BA-MA, RW 19/164, fo. 126.
144. Meyer (ed.), *Generalfeldmarschall Wilhelm Ritter von Leeb: Tagebuchaufzeichnungen*, p. 320, entry for 5 August 1941.
145. Hassell, *Die Hassell-Tagebücher*, p. 230: '1. mit der Notwendigkeit, die Ukraine zu besetzen, 2. den "potentiellen Alliierten" der Gegenseite "vorsorglich" zu erledigen!'
146. See ibid., pp. 232 and 276–277, entries for 16 March 1941, 20 September 1941 and 4 October 1941.
147. Ibid., p. 230: '[In Wirklichkeit sind die Folgen:] 1. Abschneiden der Zufuhren aus Rußland, während die Ukraine erst nach langer Zeit nutzbar wird; 2. neue schwerste Belastung aller Kriegsmittel und Kräfte; 3. willentlich herbeigeführte, volle Einkreisung.'
148. See BA, 99 US 7/1074, fo. 69; Thomas, *Geschichte*, p. 531.
149. BA, R 2/24243, fos. 34–41, 19 April 1941, here fo. 34.
150. Ibid., fo. 35: 'Ich glaube nicht, daß auf dem Ernährungsgebiet die Eroberung russischer Gebiete wesentlich helfen würde. Ich setzte hierbei voraus – worüber ich mir kein Urteil anmaße –, daß militärisch diese Gewinnung ohne allzugroße Schwierigkeiten sich erreichen ließe. Trotzdem würde wohl der Russe ... uns verbrannte Felder und Scheunen hinterlassen, die für dieses Jahr uns wohl kaum die Beträge an Getreide bringen würden, die wir jetzt auf Grund der laufenden Lieferungsverträge ohne weiteres von Rußland bekommen würden. Es mag sein, daß, wenn man mit einem mehrjährigen Krieg gegen das vereinigte England-Amerika rechnet ..., dann aus den südrussischen Gebieten vielleicht mehr als die 1½–2½ Mill. to, die Rußland uns liefern soll, herausgeholt werden könnten. Aber selbst wenn man dies annimmt, bitte ich auf drei Dinge hinweisen zu dürfen.'
151. Ibid., fos. 35–36.
152. Ibid.
153. Ibid., fo. 40: 'Es kann sein, daß alle diese schweren Bedenken in den Kauf genommen werden müssen, wenn die Russen den Pakt mit uns nicht einhalten, die versprochenen Lieferungen nicht erfüllen usw. Bisher sind aber doch für eine solche Haltung keine Anzeichen vorhanden. Ich glaube vielmehr, daß die Russen aus einer durchaus begreiflichen Angst sich das Hemd ausziehen würden, um Lieferungswünsche von uns zu erfüllen, auch wenn sie noch gesteigert würden.'
154. See Rich, *Hitler's War Aims*, pp. 207–208.
155. Halder, *KTB*, II, pp. 207 and 311, entries for 3 December 1940 and 13 March 1941.
156. BA, 99 US 7/1077, fo. 63, post-war comments of Paul Körner, 3 August 1948.
157. See chapter 4, 'Working around Potential Difficulties'.
158. *TBJG*, I/9, p. 346, entry for 31 May 1941: 'Die anderen Zivilministerien haben keine Ahnung, worum es geht.'
159. See chapter 4, 'Soviet Awareness of German Intentions'.
160. Gerbet (ed.), *Generalfeldmarschall Fedor von Bock: The War Diary*, p. 223, entry for 20 June 1941.

161. *ADAP*, Serie D: 1937–1941, vol. 12/2, pp. 550–551, doc. 419, 'Der Staatssekretär an den Reichsaußenminister'.
162. Hill (ed.), *Die Weizsäcker-Papiere*, p. 248, notes from 21 April 1941.
163. Ibid., p. 249, notes from 28 April 1941.
164. *ADAP*, Serie D: 1937–1941, vol. 12/2, p. 550: 'Wäre jede niedergebrannte russische Stadt für uns ebenso viel wert wie ein versenktes englisches Kriegsschiff, dann würde ich den deutsch-russischen Krieg in diesem Sommer befürworten; ich glaube aber, daß wir gegen Rußland nur militärisch gewinnen, dagegen wirtschaftlich verlieren würden.'
165. For examples of this assertion, see Halder, *KTB*, II, pp. 21, 31 and 443, entries for 13 and 22 July 1940, 4 June 1941; Below, *Hitlers Adjutant*, p. 254; Meyer (ed.), *Generalfeldmarschall Wilhelm Ritter von Leeb: Tagebuchaufzeichnungen*, p. 251, entry for 14 August 1940; Schramm (ed.), *KTB des OKW*, I, p. 257, entry for 9 January 1941. Contrast with Halder, *KTB*, II, p. 261, entry for 28 January 1941: '*Barbarossa*: Sinn nicht klar. Den Engländer treffen wir nicht' ('*Barbarossa*: Purpose is not clear. We don't affect the English').
166. Hill (ed.), *Die Weizsäcker-Papiere*, p. 216, notes from 4 August 1940: 'England in Rußland schlagen, ist doch kein Programm.'
167. *ADAP*, Serie D: 1937–1941, vol. 12/2, p. 551: 'Die Hoffnung auf Rußland hält den englischen Zusammenbruch nicht auf. Mit Rußland vernichten wir keine englische Hoffnung.'
168. Ibid.
169. The role, character and motivations of those involved both in planning – and in some cases carrying out – mass murder and, at the same time, in the conspiracy against Hitler deserve to be investigated more closely. Alongside Thomas, others who would also fall into this category are the Chief of the Reich Criminal Police and of Einsatzgruppe B, Arthur Nebe, and Chief of the Army General Staff Franz Halder, who was deeply involved not only in the military planning for 'Barbarossa' but also in the formulation of the so-called 'criminal orders'. Worth mentioning here is Christian Gerlach, 'Männer des 20. Juli und der Krieg gegen die Sowjetunion', in Heer and Naumann (eds), *Vernichtungskrieg: Verbrechen der Wehrmacht*, pp. 427–446.
170. *ADAP*, Serie D: 1937–1941, vol. 12/2, p. 551: 'Ich bezweifle aber durchaus, daß wir das Gewonnene gegen die bekannte passive Resistenz der Slawen ausnutzen könnten.'
171. Ibid.
172. *IMG*, vol. 26, p. 399, doc. 873-PS.
173. *ADAP*, Serie D: 1937–1941, vol. 12/2, p. 551: 'Diese Stellungnahme ist ganz kurz gefasst, da der Herr Reichsaußenminister sie binnen kürzester Frist gewünscht hat.'
174. *ADAP*, Serie D: 1937–1941, vol. 13/1, pp. 319–321, doc. 244, 'Runderlaß des Reichsaußenministers', here p. 320: 'Für Deutschland ist der Sieg über Rußland von besonderer Bedeutung, denn 1.) wird es durch die Inbesitznahme der ukrainischen Gebiete für alle Zukunft ein Ernährungsproblem nicht mehr geben; 2.) ist infolge der Inbesitznahme der reichen Rohstoffgebiete und Industriezentren die deutsche Rohstofffrage im großen gesehen ebenfalls kein Problem mehr und das deutsche Kriegspotential weiterhin gewaltig gesteigert; 3.) und vor allem aber hat Deutschland durch Wegfall der Bedrohung im Osten nunmehr den Rücken frei. Es kann sich nunmehr mit der Wucht seiner gesamten Volkskraft gegen seinen letzten Gegner England wenden.'
175. *ADAP*, Serie D: 1937–1941, vol. 12/2, pp. 889–892, doc. 660, 'Der Führer an den Duce', 21 June 1941, here p. 891: 'Ich hoffe vor allem, daß es uns dann möglich ist, in der Ukraine auf längere Sicht hin eine gemeinsame Ernährungsbasis zu sichern, die uns jene Zuschüsse liefern wird, die wir vielleicht in der Zukunft benötigen. Ich darf aber hier einfügen, daß – soweit es bis jetzt zu übersehen ist – die diesmalige deutsche Ernte eine sehr gute zu werden verspricht.'
176. See chapter 9, '16 July 1941: the Conference at FHQ'.
177. *IMG*, vol. 38, p. 91.
178. BA, R 6/34a, fo. 28, 24 September 1941. This comment comes from notes made by Dr Werner Koeppen, Alfred Rosenberg's liaison at FHQ, on Hitler's 'table talk' of 1941.

179. Hitler, *Mein Kampf*, pp. 654–655.
180. BA, R 6/34a, fo. 12, 19 September 1941. Hitler's lunch guests on 18 September, when the comment was made, were Koch and Dr Lammers.
181. Trevor-Roper (ed.), *Hitler's Table Talk*, p. 34, entry for 17/18 September 1941.
182. BA, R 43 II/688, fos. 126–127, 'Betrifft: Besetzte Ostgebiete', Lammers's notes, 1 October 1941; reproduced in *ADAP, Serie D: 1937–1941*, vol. 13/2, pp. 487–488, doc. 372, 'Aufzeichnung des Chefs der Reichskanzlei'.
183. *IMG*, vol. 26, pp. 567 and 577. See also p. 551.
184. For examples, see Nbg. Dok. PS 1018, fo. 34; *IMG*, vol. 26, pp. 568 and 619, and vol. 38, p. 89.
185. BA, R 6/34a, fo. 12. See chapter 9, 'Ordering the Destruction of Leningrad and Moscow', in this study.
186. Jochmann (ed.), *Monologe im Führerhauptquartier*, p. 63, entry for 17/18 September 1941.
187. BA, R 43 II/690b, fo. 13, letter from Lammers to Rosenberg, 'Betrifft: Universität Kiew', 25 September 1941: 'Der Führer hat sich dahin ausgesprochen, daß die Errichtung einer Universität in Kiew, die anscheinend von irgendwelchen Stellen in Aussicht genommen worden ist und betrieben wird, nicht in Frage kommt.'
188. BA, R 6/34a, fo. 26, 23 September 1941.
189. See *IMG*, vol. 38, pp. 90–91. On 14 July 1941, three days before the high-level meeting to appoint the Reich and General Commissars in the East (see chapter 9, '16 July 1941: the Conference at FHQ', in this study) and over a month prior to Koch's official appointment as Reich Commissar for the Ukraine, Hans-Joachim Riecke visited Koch at his estate in Krasne to discuss 'questions relating to the deployment in Russia'; BA-MA, RW 31/42, fo. 160, war diary of the Wi Stab Ost, entry for 14 July 1941.

Chapter 8

Expectations and Official Policy on the Eve of the Invasion

All those concerned with the preparations for the imminent invasion and subsequent occupation, particularly those involved in planning the economic exploitation of the Soviet Union, were banking on a rapid and successful conclusion to the military campaign and a consequentially early start for the implementation of their occupation policy itself. The success of the whole operation depended on it. If the Blitzkrieg developed into a war of attrition, then the deficiencies of the German war economy would be laid bare, with potentially fatal consequences. Therefore, the presumption that the campaign would be won in the allotted time frame – indeed, that it had to be – was built into both the invasion and the occupation plans. The expected duration for accomplishing the military objectives of the eastern campaign ranged from six weeks to three months. Meeting this target would ensure an end to major hostilities prior to the onset of the autumn rains and well before the start of the notoriously cold Russian winter. Few among the political and military elite believed that the target would not be met. All those directly involved in the planning for the campaign and subsequent occupation were in agreement that the aims could be achieved in the time frame envisaged.

With the formulation and distribution of the economic-political guidelines of 23 May 1941, the central aim of the campaign against the Soviet Union – to obtain as much as possible in the way of agricultural produce from the Soviet territories – had been clearly established and approved by Germany's supreme leadership. With barely a month till the invasion date of 22 June, the moment for setting official policy had indeed now arrived. The various and, at times, contrasting proposals from the planning staffs within the VJPB, RMEL, Wi Rü Amt, Bureau Rosenberg, RSHA and Office of the RKFDV would have to be weighed up and evaluated whilst the planners themselves continued with their machinations. As so often, however, things were not quite so straightforward in the Nazi regime. Conflicts over such vital issues as the allocation of power in the occupied Soviet territories, the policies to be pursued there and both the shape and the staffing of the future civil administration were still raging into the final pre-invasion days. The economic planners once again led the way in continuing to push their own agenda, whilst Himmler's SS began to assert itself both in support of the annihilatory objectives of those around Backe as well as against the anticipated jurisdiction of Rosenberg and his staff. This conflict between the SS and the civil administration would drag on well beyond 22 June.

Counting on a Swift Victory

Speculation as to the likelihood of a swift victory against the Red Army was widespread among senior figures in both the political and the military leaderships. Reichsmarschall Göring, 'just like the Führer', was 'of the view that the whole Bolshevik state would collapse' when German troops entered the Soviet Union.[1] Four days before the launching of the campaign, Joseph Goebbels noted in his diary that, like Reichsleiter Rosenberg and Dr Fritz Todt, Reich Minister for Armaments and Munitions, he anticipated a 'very quick collapse'. They hoped that the Soviets would amass their forces on the other side of the border – this, it was believed, would then allow for a rapid destruction of the Soviets' fighting forces, with the probability that the German army would capture large numbers of enemy soldiers.[2] This expectation in itself, widely held within the German leadership, tells us much about the reasons for the massive death rate amongst Soviet POWs in German captivity, estimated at 3.3 million from a total of 5.7 million captured between June 1941 and February 1945.[3] Far from it being a case of the German authorities being taken by surprise at the capture of tens of thousands of Soviet soldiers during the first weeks of the campaign and their inability to deal logistically with such numbers, they were in fact well aware that, if military operations went according to plan, captured Soviet troops would be flooding into German POW camps from day one. Despite this knowledge, they neglected to make anything like sufficient preparations for the provisioning of captured enemy troops. This was intentional and is to be explained in the context of the 'starvation strategy'. If the German troops had to supply themselves from Soviet resources – clearly to the detriment of the Soviet population – there would be no food left over for Soviet troops who fell into German hands. In the event of surpluses being available, they would be sent back to the Reich, as had been repeatedly stated during the run-up to the campaign. The German troops themselves were directly, and not inconsiderably, affected by Hitler's patent unwillingness to make winter preparations in view of the expectation that the campaign would be at an end before the onset of winter.[4] This inevitably resulted in the German troops being wholly insufficiently kitted out with winter clothing – such was the self-assuredness and the extreme irresponsibility of the German leadership.

In a communication with the Section for Wehrmacht Propaganda in the OKW Operations Staff from the day before the invasion, the National Defence Section, headed by General Warlimont, expressed similar sentiments to those conveyed by Goebbels in his diary entry of three days earlier:

> The *opponent*, in accordance with the hitherto existing picture regarding this, has deployed the bulk of his forces in the border regions and because of this fits in with German intentions. This Russian concentration is to be made use of in the compiling of reports to the effect that the Russians had deployed themselves 'all set to go' and the German action was thus an absolute military necessity.[5]

As shown earlier,[6] the concept of a 'preventive war' has no basis in reality and indeed, as demonstrated by this internal OKW communication, finds its origins in the Nazi regime's own pre-invasion propaganda.

The members of Germany's military leadership were no less confident of a swift victory than their political counterparts. At the end of April 1941, Army Commander-in-Chief Brauchitsch judged the likely course of military operations as follows: 'Fierce border battles anticipated, duration up to 4 weeks. Afterwards, only minor resistance is to be expected.'[7] At the beginning of May, over six weeks before the beginning of the campaign, Colonel-General Halder was already discussing with fellow senior officers duties to be carried out in the autumn of 1941 'after [the] completion of our European tasks' (i.e., the military defeat of the Soviet Union).[8] A month later, Halder stated in his war diary that work on the organizational foundations for the conversion of the army for tasks within Germany following 'Barbarossa' had already been in progress 'for a long time'.[9] There was no doubting the confidence of this man or of those around him. Ernst von Weizsäcker, who was in close contact with Halder,[10] noted on 2 June that the German military expected the action against the Soviet Union to be over 'within 4, 8, at the most 10 weeks'.[11]

It was not only the army leadership which was very optimistic about a quick end to hostilities; the most senior officers of the Wehrmacht, as could be expected, were also certain of the inferiority of their opponent. The Chief of the OKW Operations Staff, General Jodl, was recorded as declaring that 'the Russian colossus' would 'be proved to be a pig's bladder; prick it and it will burst'. Hitler had also described the Soviet armed forces as a colossus, but a 'headless colossus with feet of clay'. Hitler did, however, add that 'we cannot with certainty foresee what they might become in the future. The Russians must not be underestimated.'[12] The Soviet Union and its military were, however, being underestimated, and indeed by the majority of Germany's military and political leadership, Hitler included, despite his occasional expressions of concern and uncertainty. The reference to the Soviet armed forces being 'headless' was not a judgement on Stalin's leadership capacity, for Hitler held Stalin, the self-styled 'Man of Steel', in high esteem. It was rather an allusion to the purges of the Soviet officer corps carried out by Stalin during the late 1930s. Given the almost universal feeling amongst the German leadership – both political and military – of racial superiority towards the Slavic peoples, it is highly likely that the same confidence (or foolishness) would have been in evidence even if no purges had taken place. In contrast to the misgivings voiced in the autumn of 1939 within the army leadership regarding the success of a campaign against France, no doubts were expressed by the military leadership at the time of the preparations for 'Barbarossa' to the effect that the undertaking could fail.[13]

The German leadership was not alone in its expectation of a quick victory over the Red Army. Though not tinged with the same sense of racial superiority as its German counterpart, the British government did not rate the chances of a successful Soviet defence against German attack highly. The Ministry of Economic Warfare believed that the Germans would not incur heavy casualties or any high degree of military exhaustion in defeating the Red Army. On 9 June 1941, less than two weeks before 'Barbarossa' got under way, the Joint Intelligence Committee produced a paper dealing with the military, political and economic effects of a Soviet–German war. According to this paper, the Germans could hope to occupy the Ukraine and possibly to reach Moscow in four to six weeks.[14] Members of the US government expressed similar views. Secretary of War Henry Stimson and Secretary of the Navy Frank Knox spoke of six to eight weeks and one to three months, respectively, for the length of time which would elapse between the beginning of the German invasion and the collapse of the Soviet Union.[15]

By the first week of June 1941 at the latest, the tasks of the four principal agencies in the forthcoming campaign – or at least their broad boundaries – had become clear to those involved in the preparations. At a two-day meeting in Berlin of officers from the army and the *Abwehr*, the Wehrmacht's counter-intelligence department, on 5 and 6 June, Major Johann Schmidt von Altenstadt gave a presentation on the 'cooperation' between the four central pillars of German occupation policy. In addition to being head of the department War Administration attached to the Quartermaster-General in the OKH, Altenstadt was also the first port of call for the Bureau Rosenberg's liaison officer to the OKH, attached to the staff of the Quartermaster-General,[16] Otto Bräutigam, who doubled as the designated deputy leader of the Policy Department in the future Reich Ministry for the Occupied Eastern Territories.[17] In his presentation, Altenstadt summed up the fundamental areas of competence of the four pillars as follows:

>4 representatives: *Wehrmacht*: Overpowering of the enemy
>*Reichsführer SS*: Political-police fight against the enemy
>Reichsmarschall: Economy
>Rosenberg: Polit[ical] reconstruction.[18]

In Major von Altenstadt's summing up of the main players and their broadly defined tasks, Reichsführer-SS Himmler was denoted as possessing responsibility not only for police and security measures against the enemy, but also for political measures. This automatically encroached upon the intended sphere of authority of Reichsleiter Rosenberg, whose jurisdiction was defined by Altenstadt perhaps as accurately as had hitherto been the case. According to Altenstadt, Rosenberg and the Reich Commissars subordinated to him would be responsible for 'political reconstruction' – their function lay in the reorganization and re-establishment of administrative institutions and structures, though self-evidently under German and not indigenous control. It is apparent from Himmler's correspondence from the end of May and the beginning of June 1941, which is discussed later in this chapter, that the Reichsführer-SS expected his jurisdiction in the East to cover political as well policing tasks. Exactly what was meant by 'political' tasks is not entirely clear, but Himmler was evidently not the only person under this impression, as Altenstadt's presentation demonstrates.

A meeting on 10 June 1941 between Backe and Himmler indicates the harmony which existed between the ideas of the author of the 'starvation strategy' on the one hand and those of the man who would later be the 'architect'[19] of the so-called 'Final Solution' on the other. It should come as no surprise that Backe held the rank of Gruppenführer in the SS (roughly equivalent to Lieutenant-General in the army) or that he was a friend of Himmler's right-hand man, Reinhard Heydrich, Chief of the Reich Security Main Office.[20] Himmler and Backe met on 10 June ostensibly to discuss agriculture in the soon-to-be-occupied territories of the USSR. However, although Himmler had been a poultry farmer in Munich in the late 1920s, one can be sure that it was not this aspect of agriculture which the two men discussed. Backe requested Himmler's permission that the two to three thousand ethnic German settlers in Bessarabia who were capable as farmers be used for the administration of large estates in the aftermath of Operation Barbarossa. Himmler 'naturally' granted Backe his permission and instructed the relevant orders to be issued.[21] In this case, Himmler was acting in his capacity as Reich Commissar for the Strengthening of German Nationhood.[22]

It would be highly surprising, however, if Backe and Himmler did not also discuss the plans for mass murder in which the two of them were deeply involved. A post-war statement from Erich von dem Bach-Zelewski points in this direction. Bach-Zelewski was at the time SS-Gruppenführer and designated Higher SS and Police Leader for Russia-Centre, and was present at the get-together of 12–15 June 1941 of senior SS officers at the Wewelsburg, a Renaissance castle which was the scene of Himmler's attempts to provide the SS with a scientific and ritualistic centre.[23] Alongside Himmler and Bach-Zelewski, Reinhard Heydrich, Chief of the Order Police Kurt Daluege and designated Higher SS and Police Leader for Russia-North Hans-Adolf Prützmann, among others, were also present.[24] At Nuremberg after the war, Bach-Zelewski recalled Himmler speaking of the purpose of the Soviet campaign as being 'the decimation of the Slavic population by thirty million'.[25] Karl Wolff, the former Chief of the Personal Staff of the

Reichsführer-SS, qualified this assertion somewhat by claiming that Himmler had stated that the death of thirty million people was not to be the aim, but rather the result, of the war against the USSR.[26]

The anticipated number of Soviet deaths quoted by Bach-Zelewski and attributed to Himmler may well have originated with Backe, as the figure of circa thirty million emerged on several other occasions and appears to have been the standard expectation amongst the economic planners of the human cost of the 'starvation strategy'. Thirty million was the amount by which the Soviet population – exclusively the urban population – had grown between the beginning of the First World War in 1914 and the beginning of the Second World War in 1939.[27] It is worth recalling that it was in fact 'particularly the population of the cities', according to the economic-political guidelines of 23 May 1941, which would 'have to face the most terrible famine' in the Soviet Union.[28] Twenty to thirty million was also the figure later given by Reichsmarschall Göring in a discussion with the Italian Foreign Minister, Count Galeazzo Ciano, for the number of people in the Soviet Union who would starve during 1941.[29]

According to a statement made by the Chief of the Advance Commando Moscow of Einsatzgruppe B, Professor Dr Franz Alfred Six, in July 1941 at the headquarters of Army Group Centre, thirty million people would starve in a 'blazing strip' (*Brandstreifen*) between Moscow and the Ural Mountains as a result of the removal of all foodstuffs from this territory.[30] Moscow was in the 'wooded zone' of the north and constituted, therefore, a so-called 'deficit territory'. When Bach-Zelewski referred to Himmler's comments at the Wewelsburg, he neglected to mention that it was he, as Higher SS and Police Leader for Russia-Centre, who was responsible for the extermination of twenty million people in Belarus and the territories further east, including Moscow and the surrounding area.[31] He had received this order from Himmler.[32] Exactly when he received it, however, is unclear. The fact that responsibility for the killing of two-thirds of the thirty million fell to Bach-Zelewski can be explained in that a significant chunk of the so-called 'wooded zone' was located in his geographical area of competence.[33] For the most easterly of the Russian General Commissariats, beyond the Ural Mountains, Rosenberg envisaged the notorious SS and Police Leader in Lublin, Odilo Globocnik,[34] who would later be appointed to run 'Aktion Reinhardt', the murder of the General Government's Jews in the extermination camps of Belzec, Sobibór and Treblinka.[35]

Already before the beginning of the war, continental Europe needed imports of twelve to thirteen million tons of grain a year, equivalent to the food requirements of over twenty-five million people.[36] Supplying the inhabitants of continental Europe with the foodstuffs they required and thereby making continental Europe – in other words, German-occupied Europe – immune from naval blockade was the purpose of the intended starvation of thirty million Soviet citizens. In the process, the industrial and urban development which had taken place in the Soviet Union over the previous thirty years was to be reversed.

Economic and Agricultural Guidelines

In the four weeks between the production of the economic-political guidelines of 23 May 1941 by the agricultural section of the Economic Staff East and the commencement of 'Barbarossa', a further set of guidelines was produced which would serve as the official handbook for the economic administration of the occupied Soviet territories. These instructions, known as the 'Green Folder' (*Grüne Mappe*) because of the colour of their binding, were issued on 16 June, just six days before the invasion began.[37] The folder served in the first place to orient those in the highest leadership and command positions down as far as divisional level.[38] Given its official nature, the language used in this document – 1,000 copies of which were distributed – was slightly more restrained than that used in the economic-political guidelines of 23 May, but the message was nonetheless clear: the resources of the newly occupied territories were to be immediately and comprehensively fleeced to the advantage of Germany and its invading troops.[39]

In a preamble to the document, dated 16 June, Field Marshal Keitel gave his express approval, and thus in effect that of the whole military, to the instructions and their contents. This was, of course, to be expected, as the military had worked closely with the economic experts in setting the parameters of the guidelines and indeed the policy contained therein. In addition, the Green Folder contained directives for the provisioning of the troops 'off the land', something in which the army leadership had a vested interest. Economic sections would be at the disposal of the Wehrmacht authorities for the purpose of satisfying the immediate supply requirements of the troops. During the operations, the Economic Staff East would remain in direct proximity to the High Command of the Army and the Army's Quartermaster-General, Eduard Wagner, the latter being responsible both for supplying the troops and for matters of military administration in the occupied territories.[40] Indeed, such was the closeness of the relationship between the Economic Staff East and the Office of the Army Quartermaster-General that, until the end of 1941, Lieutenant-General Schubert was housed in General Wagner's quarters in Bartenstein in East Prussia. At Schubert's request, he was given the room next to Wagner's.[41] Tellingly, Wagner's wife was under the impression that her husband had in fact himself created the Economic Staff East![42]

Perhaps more clearly than hitherto, the guidelines stated that the winning 'for Germany' of as much as possible in the way of foodstuffs and mineral oil was the 'main economic aim of the campaign'. The first task, indeed, was to ensure as soon as possible that the German troops were fed 'completely' from the occupied area, with the intention of alleviating Europe's food situation and easing the strain on transport routes. In terms of the seizure of foodstuffs, stress was laid in particular on oil crops and grain.[43] Thus, the guidelines confirmed the vital importance of the appropriation of foodstuffs and thus implicitly approved the 'starvation policy' drawn up over the preceding months. Furthermore, with regard to the treatment to be meted out to the local population, the cities of Leningrad and Moscow and the territory eastwards of the latter constituted a 'difficult problem' according to the author(s) of the guidelines, particularly as the two cities required substantial food surpluses. The measures to be taken in this respect would be contained in further instructions, which were to be issued on the strength of the experiences of the first weeks of the campaign.[44] The economic-political guidelines of 23 May had already made it abundantly clear, however, what the fate of the inhabitants of these territories was likely to be.

As for industrial raw materials, the Green Folder placed emphasis on mineral oil.[45] The exploitation of the remainder of Soviet industrial capacity, including the armaments industry, would only be considered in so far as the implementation of the projected main tasks of the campaign would not be impaired as a result. A breakdown in industrial production in the agricultural 'deficit territories' of north and central Russia due to a migration of workers into the countryside – doubtlessly in search of food – was to be fully accepted.[46] As has already been discussed, in the conception of the Nazi planners, Russia would in the future no longer possess any industrial capacity or manufacturing capabilities to speak of.[47] As northern and central Russia possessed only a very limited agricultural capacity, and therefore required relatively small numbers of workers to cultivate the crops, it would be no great shame in the eyes of the occupiers if an exodus of workers were to occur. In such regions, which were unable to sustain themselves, the economic organization was in any case to restrict itself to exploiting only what it found following the capture of the area by German troops.[48]

This programme and the guidelines as a whole appear once again to have obtained the express approval of Hitler: 'According to the orders issued by the Führer, all measures are to be taken which are necessary to bring about the immediate and most extensive exploitation of the occupied territories for the benefit of Germany. On the other hand, all measures which could endanger this aim are to be omitted or set aside.'[49] In fact, according to a revealing report dating from the end of June 1941 and produced by the War Economy and Armaments Office, an extensive economic exploitation of the Soviet territories was not only the main aim of the undertaking, but also the main *reason* for the decision to invade the Soviet Union. The report, entitled 'Thoughts on the Topic: "Economic War of Attrition Instead of War with a Rapid Military Conclusion"', stated: 'The main reason for the operation against Russia lies without doubt in the pressure on Germany's supreme leadership to broaden at all costs the economic basis of Germany's prosecution of the war.'[50] In other words, the necessity to strengthen Germany's war economy in view of the looming confrontation against the Anglo-Saxon powers was decisive in motivating the German leadership to launch a full-scale invasion of the Soviet Union prior to the defeat of Great Britain, thereby bringing about a two-front war.

In addition to Hitler's approval, the Green Folder had also received the approval of Göring in the sense that the guidelines were issued in his name, even if he had not necessarily contributed directly to their production. In fact, it was Colonel, later Major-General, Hans Nagel of the Wi Rü Amt who 'compiled' the Green Folder.[51] Nagel had been armaments inspector in Prague and in the General Government during the course of 1939 and was appointed the following June as head of the economy attached to the military commander in Belgium and northern France. From the beginning of the Soviet campaign till the end of 1941 Nagel was the liaison officer between Göring and Thomas, Chief of the War Economy and Armaments Office. In this capacity Nagel's duties included forwarding to Göring any demands from Thomas and, vice versa, to Thomas any decisions taken by Göring.[52] He was requested by Thomas to report to him twice a month on all the important happenings in the economic sphere.[53]

At almost thirty pages, the Green Folder was even more substantial than the guidelines of 23 May 1941. Once more, however, racial-ideological remarks were scarce. On page eighteen, the Belarusians were described as lagging intellectually far behind the Greater Russians, Jews and Poles resident in Belarus,[54] a comment similar to the sentiments expressed by Rosenberg on the subject in his paper of 2 April 1941.[55] For the most part, though, as in the guidelines of 23 May, the 'logic of economic circumstances'[56] sufficed to justify the programme of annihilation. Generally speaking, the Green Folder had little to offer that was not already contained, and expressed more explicitly, in the 23 May guidelines from Riecke's Group La of the Economic Staff East. The Green Folder constituted the official version of an economic programme which had already been approved by Germany's supreme leadership several weeks, if not months, earlier.

On the first day of June – that is, between the appearance of the economic-political guidelines on 23 May 1941 and the Green Folder on 16 June – Backe issued his so-called '12 Commandments' (*12 Gebote*) as part of the 'Folder for District Agricultural Leaders' (*Kreislandwirtschaftsführermappe*).[57] He evidently deemed it necessary to explain in writing how the agricultural leaders should behave towards the Soviet population. Nevertheless, it was important for these men once in the occupied eastern territories to take independent action and not be afraid of making decisions which could be wrong – better to act and make a mistake than not to act at all. Anyone who did nothing out of fear of taking responsibility was 'of no use'.[58] Allowing the agricultural administrators a good deal of independence corresponded to Hitler's expectations of the men appointed to the civil administration in the occupied Soviet territories. He wished only broad instructions to be sent out from Berlin; 'the settlement of day-to-day issues can safely be left in the hands of the respective regional Commissars'.[59]

The central importance of agriculture, and hence of the agricultural leaders, to the German occupation is indicated by the huge numbers sent to the East. In total, around 13,000 agricultural leaders were deployed in the occupied Soviet territories, aside from Galicia and Bialystok,[60] under the charge of Backe's right-hand man, Hans-Joachim Riecke.[61] In his instructions of 1 June, Backe claimed – rather unconvincingly – that the Russian was 'effeminate and sentimental' and wanted foreigners to come and rule his land in order to provide order. This had apparently always been the case, from the Normans and the Mongols right up to the present day. It was not the aim of the occupiers to convert the Soviet population to National Socialism, but rather to transform the 'Russians' into their tool.[62] The eleventh commandment served as a reminder, if one was needed, of the Nazi plan to starve large sections of the Soviet population: 'The Russian has already endured poverty, hunger and frugality for centuries. His stomach is elastic, hence no false sympathy. Do not attempt to apply the German standard of living as [your] yardstick and to alter the Russian way of life.'[63] In his paper of February 1941, General Thomas had in a similar vein attempted to justify his proposal that the Soviet consumption per head be reduced by arguing that 'the Russian is accustomed to adapting his needs to poor harvests'.[64] Backe concluded his 12 Commandments by reiterating that the agricultural leaders had to fend entirely for themselves. There should be no complaints or cries for help from the top. 'Help yourself, then God will help you!'[65]

The Standpoint of the Political Planners

In response to Dr Lammers having forwarded to him the draft decrees for the organization of the occupied eastern territories, Himmler sent Lammers a 'Draft of a new §2 for the decree of the Führer, re.: intended appointment of Rosenberg' on the day of his 10 June meeting with Backe.[66] Lammers, as Head of the Reich Chancellery and one of Hitler's principal advisers on legal problems, was responsible for formulating and preparing so-called 'Führer decrees' (*Führererlasse*).[67] In the absence of cabinet discussions (since 1937), a flood of legislation emanating independently from each ministry had to be formulated by a process whereby drafts were circulated and recirculated among the relevant parties until some agreement was reached. Only at that stage would Hitler, provided he approved after its contents had been briefly summarized for him, put his name to the decree. Lammers, as the sole link between the ministers and Hitler, naturally attained considerable influence over the way legislation and other business of ministers were presented to Hitler.[68]

In his covering letter of 10 June, Himmler argued amongst other things for the issuing of a 'special regulation' for the police, similar to those being prepared for the military and for the Four-Year Plan organization (eventually issued on 25 and 29 June 1941, respectively). This was particularly necessary, according to Himmler, in view of the 'difficulties' which the police had faced in the General Government, the Protectorate of Bohemia and Moravia and in other occupied territories in carrying out the measures dictated by his directives. Accordingly, Himmler also enclosed a draft of a 'special decree of the Führer'.[69] This issue had already been on Himmler's mind for several weeks, as demonstrated by his letter to Head of the Party Chancellery Martin Bormann, in which he posed the question as to whether or not he would be 'under Rosenberg's command' when it came to his (Himmler's) tasks for the 'political securing' of the territory under occupation.[70] As mentioned above, Himmler was at this point in time evidently expecting to be commissioned by Hitler not only with policing tasks in the East, but also with tasks of a more political nature.

Upon reading the altered draft for the administration of the occupied eastern territories, Alfred Rosenberg wrote to Lammers, complaining of the apparent inconsistency between Lammers's original, 'completed' draft of this 'Führer decree' and Himmler's more recent version:

> In your completed draft ..., it states that the setting down of the law in the eastern territories is to be carried out by the Reich Minister, furthermore that the Reich Commissars are subordinated to the Reich Minister for the Occupied Eastern Territories, receive their directives *exclusively* from him and that they are to manage the *entire* administration in those territories entrusted to them.[71]

In Rosenberg's view, a further distribution of authority within the occupied Soviet territories – beyond the accustomed division between the military commander and the civil administration – would be 'completely unbearable'. Yet this was exactly what Himmler's own draft was proposing. Rosenberg clearly feared for his own position: 'According to the draft of the Reichsführer SS and Chief of the German Police, there remains absolutely nothing left for the Reich Minister for the Occupied Eastern Territories and the Reich Commissars to do, except perhaps to take note of the orders of other authorities, as, alongside the military commander, the economy and the police would represent independent powers ....'[72] Here is evidence that Rosenberg, a full month before his official appointment as Reich Minister in the East, was well aware of how the hierarchical picture was developing and what the chances were of his coming out of the scramble for power with any kind of meaningful authority. In part, the 'power struggle' seen in the occupied East after the German–Soviet war was under way had already begun during the preparations for that conflict. This was how the Nazi state functioned. The overlapping duties, competences and areas of authority in the dual Party–state system, consciously encouraged by Hitler as a means of preserving his own rule and fostering loyalty and initiative,[73] led to both radicalism and, ultimately, chaos – hence the 'organized chaos' subsequently seen during the German occupation itself.[74] Rosenberg recognized the logical implications of such a system. In his view, the outcome of the realization of such proposals as those put forward by Himmler would not be to assist Hitler in the implementation of 'a great political conception', but rather to produce power struggles between different agencies, which would mutually cancel each other out and leave not an 'organized eastern space under German rule' in their wake but 'unparalleled chaos'.[75]

Further difficulties for the members of the Bureau Rosenberg arose some time shortly after 16 June 1941, the day the Green Folder was issued. A copy of this document fell into the hands of Otto Bräutigam, designated deputy of

Georg Leibbrandt in the Policy Department of the RMO. Disgusted, as he later claimed, with the 'policy of unscrupulous exploitation' contained in its pages, Bräutigam, along with Leibbrandt, went directly to Rosenberg to complain. Rosenberg, seemingly more bothered by his relatively modest position on the distribution list – he received copy thirty-three of the guidelines – than by the contents of the document, nevertheless instructed Bräutigam to draw up a draft of political guidelines which would accompany Göring's economic instructions. Bräutigam completed the draft by the following day and laid it before Rosenberg, who, with merely minor modifications, accepted it and circulated it with a covering letter.[76]

The opening statements of Bräutigam's declaration, entitled 'General Guidelines for the Political and Economic Administration of the Occupied Eastern Territories', portrayed 'Barbarossa' as a struggle against the dangers of Bolshevism and Soviet imperialism.[77] As well as removing this threat, wrote Bräutigam, a German defeat of Soviet forces would make both Germany and Europe immune from blockade. In order to realize these objectives, it would be necessary to win the sympathy and with it the cooperation of the broad mass of the populations of the Baltic States, Belarus, the Ukraine and the Caucasus; Russia was conspicuous by its absence. Bräutigam then summed up the thrust of his arguments in two sentences: 'The war against the Soviet Union is a political campaign, not an economic raid. The conquered territory is not as a whole to be regarded as an object of exploitation, even when the German food and war economy must lay claim to more extensive territories.'[78] Given that the programme of ruthless economic exploitation and mass starvation had received 'the approval of the highest authorities',[79] Bräutigam's analysis of the nature of the operation was way off the mark.

Bräutigam then stated his acceptance that the abolition of the collective farms was, 'for well-known economic reasons' (i.e., that such a wholesale rearrangement of the Soviet agricultural system could well create major difficulties when it came to reaping and distributing the harvest), 'for the time being' out of the question.[80] Bräutigam quickly sprang once more from the defensive, however, and dealt directly with the concepts of the economic experts themselves, challenging the wisdom of approaching the tasks in hand with a fixed plan for seizing a certain amount of grain from the forthcoming harvest. He even went so far as to suggest that the scenario that Germany would have to use its own supplies to help the Soviet population out ('with the exception of the Russian territories') was just as likely to be the case as there being grain surpluses available to the Germans. This kind of statement was, of course, sacrilege to the economic planners who had dreamed up the 'starvation strategy'. Bräutigam did not stop there. Towards the end of the guidelines he argued that it would be an 'enormous achievement' if the German army succeeded in provisioning itself to a large extent from the land, something considered by those present at the meeting of the Staatssekretäre on 2 May 1941 as a prerequisite for the continuation of the war![81]

That Bräutigam argued against exactly these concepts hints at his knowledge of the meeting of 2 May. In his memoirs, written over twenty years after the war, though nevertheless very detailed, he wrote that he had been influenced in his drafting of the political guidelines by a session in the Reich Ministry for Food and Agriculture, from which a participant had shown him a copy of the minutes. Bräutigam recalled that Staatssekretär Backe had declared that ten million tons of grain would have to be delivered from the occupied eastern territories to Germany.[82] On two separate occasions in his guidelines, Bräutigam referred to 'figures of 7 and 10 million tons of grain' as being the amounts already named for intended seizure in the East. Although the meeting of 2 May was not a standard session of the RMEL (General Thomas was present, for example), Bräutigam may have been talking about the same meeting, and Rosenberg could feasibly have been the participant who showed him a copy of the minutes. It is clear from his guidelines that he for one did not subscribe to the conclusions drawn there.

Almost immediately after the beginning of the German invasion, the Office of the Four-Year Plan not surprisingly raised objections to Bräutigam's guidelines for policy in the East and Rosenberg was forced to withdraw them.[83] Bräutigam's statement was in part a rejection of the premises on which Germany's intended economic policy in the occupied Soviet territories, approved by Hitler, was based. 'Complete exploitation' (*restlose Ausbeutung*) was a phrase used repeatedly in the various guidelines issued by the VJPB and the Wi Stab Ost and the core 'concept' of their plans. Yet here were the men most responsible for planning the political administration of the occupied eastern territories raising objections to the very notion of 'complete exploitation'. Drafted by Bräutigam, supported by Leibbrandt and approved by Rosenberg without the initial knowledge or influence of the economic planners, it is reasonable to describe the 'General Guidelines for the Political and Economic Administration of the Occupied Eastern Territories' as the 'clearest expression of the political objectives of the East Ministry that is available to us'.[84]

How far the future East Minister, Rosenberg, was in fact prepared to go in promoting and defending this set of ideas, however, is another question. His lacklustre response to the objections raised against Bräutigam's guidelines by the VJPB does not speak in his favour. He does not appear to have defended the statement and its ideas, but rather withdrew it at the first sign of trouble. This could, of course, have a lot to do with Rosenberg's dawning realization that Göring was to have far greater power in the administrative set-up in the East and that there would only be one winner in any confrontation between the Reichsmarschall and the Reichsleiter. It can also be explained by the fact that the Bureau Rosenberg – hence presumably Rosenberg himself – had already a month earlier declared itself 'in agreement' with the Green Folder, the very guidelines against which Bräutigam's paper, approved by Rosenberg, was directed! Towards the end of the fourth session of the Wi Fü Stab Ost on 26 May 1941, three weeks before the Green Folder was issued (and only three days after the release of the 23 May guidelines), talk turned to this document:

> Following the last 'B[arbarossa]' session, the 'green folder' compiled by Colonel Nagel was passed on to the [other] departments for comment. The departments are to coordinate their requests for alterations, in so far as this has not already taken place, directly with Colonel Nagel. Fundamental objections have not been raised. Oberbereichsleiter Malettke [sic] from the Staff Rosenberg has also declared himself to be in agreement. He has likewise agreed with the Staff Schubert upon the leaflets put together by the Staff Rosenberg.[85]

The fact that the acquiescence of Rosenberg's representative received a special mention in the minutes of the session indicates not only its importance but also that this acquiescence was explicitly given and not simply presumed. Additionally, the minutes also make it clear that the various departments involved were given the opportunity to comment on, request alterations to and even raise objections to the contents of the Green Folder, should they so wish.

Rosenberg's own position with regard to these questions can be better seen in a speech he gave on 20 June 1941, two days before the opening of the eastern campaign. Although it is very often referred to as being a speech before his closest colleagues in the Bureau Rosenberg,[86] it is known that Reinhard Heydrich, who was not only Chief of the RSHA but would be appointed four days later as Himmler's liaison officer to Rosenberg,[87] was also present.[88] In addition, Rosenberg's request towards the end of his speech that 'wishes of other departments' be referred to him suggests that representatives of other bodies also attended.[89] Rosenberg spoke of the necessity of setting up state structures 'organically' in order to erect them against 'Moscow'. The four large blocks which would 'shield' Germany would be 'Greater Finland', the Baltic (*Baltenland*), the Ukraine and the Caucasus. The 'freedom of the Ukrainian people' was stressed as being one of Germany's aims, to be adopted 'absolutely' as a 'political item on the agenda'. However, there was no sense at this point in time, argued Rosenberg, 'to speak about in which form and extent a Ukrainian state can later come into being',[90] thus suggesting, as his written statements from April and May had done, that the creation of an independent Ukraine was for him a long-term goal, which would follow a period of preparation. At this point, about halfway through the speech, Rosenberg came to perhaps the most important passage, one which summed up his concept of how policy should be pursued in the East:

> If the economic leadership of the Reichsmarschall must aim at pulling as much as possible out of this territory [i.e., the Ukraine], then it [i.e., the economic leadership] will truly be able to support this [i.e., Rosenberg's] political stance and this political leadership; for there is a difference, as to whether after a few years I have won 40 million people to voluntary cooperation or whether I must place a soldier behind every peasant. I believe that, when both sides recognize

these necessities, then the political [leadership] will be an aid to the economic leadership and, vice versa, the economic leadership can adjust itself very well to the political objective.[91]

At the same time as stressing the importance of winning the native population to 'voluntary cooperation', however, Rosenberg emphasized that the nourishment of the German population 'stands during these years doubtlessly at the top of German demands in the East'. It would be the job of the 'southern territories' and northern Caucasus to balance out the German food requirements.[92]

The sentences from Rosenberg which followed demonstrate that he could compete with the economic planners when it came to callous articulation of the consequences of their starvation policies: 'We see by no means the obligation to feed the Russian people as well [as ourselves] from these surplus territories. We know that that is a harsh necessity which is beyond every emotion. A very extensive evacuation will doubtlessly be necessary and very difficult years will certainly be in store for the Russian people.'[93] This, without doubt, was a wholehearted acceptance on Rosenberg's part of the consequences of the policy of ruthless requisitioning of foodstuffs from the 'surplus territories' of the Soviet Union. These consequences have been portrayed during the course of this study. Rosenberg's use of the word 'evacuation' (*Evakuierung*) in this context can only be taken as an example of the use of camouflage language, in this case alluding to the intentional starvation of the people in question. Rosenberg had in fact made a similar comment in a speech given at a Nazi Party rally on 22 February 1941. On this occasion he had claimed that it was not Germany's duty to supply all the peoples of occupied Europe with its (i.e., Germany's) foodstuffs.[94] The final words of Rosenberg's 22 June speech confirmed the two 'immense tasks' facing the Reich. Reichsmarschall Göring's 'great task' would be the securing of the German food supply and the consolidation of the war economy whilst the liberation of Germany 'forever from the political pressure coming from the East' would be 'the political aim in this struggle'.[95]

What conclusions can be drawn from the various facets of this most revealing of speeches from Rosenberg? He remained determined to follow through his aim of establishing three substantial buffer states – the Ukraine, the Caucasus and a single Baltic state – in order to act as a protective barrier against Greater Russia, which he saw as the core of the Bolshevik menace. The Baltic States would be united to form a protectorate in anticipation of later annexation to the Reich; the Ukraine would eventually attain independence, though all the while maintaining close relations with Germany; and the Caucasus would take the form of a federal state. Rosenberg's embracement of Göring's 'great task' – the ruthless economic exploitation of the occupied territories (above all, the Ukraine) – is likely to have been genuine rather than a matter of awareness on Rosenberg's part that any attempt to deflect his colleagues in the Nazi leadership from this cause would be futile. The enthusiasm with which he appears to have espoused its necessity certainly points in this direction. In a report on the preparatory work for the occupation of the Soviet territories compiled just under a week after the commencement of 'Barbarossa', Rosenberg confirmed that the 'most extensive agreement' had been reached regarding 'eastern questions' during talks over the preceding two months with Schlotterer, Thomas, Körner, Backe, Riecke, Schubert and others concerning the economic objectives of the Wi Fü Stab Ost.[96]

What marked Rosenberg out more than anything from the likes of Göring, Backe and Riecke was his realization that the best way to maximize the amount of grain which Germany could obtain from the East whilst at the same time minimizing the destruction of agricultural produce and the dislocation of production was to win the bulk of the native population over to voluntary cooperation. Hence his declaration during his speech that the Germans 'are no enemies of the Russian people',[97] despite his wish to cut 'Greater Russia' off from the rest of the Soviet lands in an attempt to force it to 'turn eastwards'. Rosenberg had no qualms about the nature of the policy developed by the economic planners; his conception differed regarding methods of approach and implementation. Although not the 'man of action' that Göring, for example, was and certainly not so adept when it came to prevailing in the power struggles inherent in the nature of the Nazi state, Rosenberg was nonetheless 'brutal and cruel'. This was the assessment of Douglas M. Kelly, the American military doctor and psychiatrist in the Nuremberg prison.[98] Rosenberg was the man who declared that the regulations of the Hague Convention on Land Warfare were not valid in the East and that all Jewish civil servants in the occupied eastern territories should disappear completely.[99] In mid-September 1941 he advocated 'the dispatching of all the Jews of central Europe' to the East in retaliation for the deportation of the Volga Germans by Stalin,[100] a suggestion acted upon by Hitler only days later.[101] A little over two months afterwards he announced in a speech to the German press that the so-called 'Jewish Question' could only be solved 'by the complete biological annihilation of all Jews, from the entire area of Europe'.[102] In creed, if not in manner, Rosenberg fitted in well with the other men about to be let loose on the Soviet Union.

Notes

1. BA-MA, RW 19/185, fo. 170.
2. *TBJG*, I/9, p. 386, entry for 18 June 1941.
3. For the calculations, see Streit, *Keine Kameraden*, pp. 128–137 and 244–249, esp. pp. 244–246.
4. Oberst i.G. a.D. Wilhelm von Rücker, 'Die Vorbereitungen für den Feldzug gegen Russland', in Wagner (ed.), *Der Generalquartiermaster*, Appendix, pp. 313–318, here p. 317. See also Klink, 'Die militärische Konzeption des Krieges', p. 318; Kershaw, *Hitler 1936–1945*, pp. 439 and 447.
5. BA-MA, RW 4/v. 578, fos. 85–89, Abteilung Landesverteidigung, 'Betr.: Barbarossa', 21 June 1941, here fo. 87: 'Der *Gegner* ist nach dem bisher darüber vorliegenden Bild mit der Masse seiner Kräfte in den Grenzzonen aufmarschiert und kommt hierdurch den

deutschen Absichten entgegen. Bei der Berichterstattung wird diese russische Massierung dahin auszunutzen sein, dass der Russe "sprungbereit" aufmarschiert war und somit das deutsche Vorgehen eine absolute militärische Notwendigkeit war.'
6. See chapter 4, 'Soviet Awareness of German Intentions'.
7. *IMG*, vol. 26, p. 400: 'Voraussichtlich heftige Grenzschlachten, Dauer bis zu 4 Wochen. Im weiteren Verlauf wird dann aber nur noch mit geringerem Widerstand zu rechnen sein.'
8. Halder, *KTB*, II, p. 394, entry for 5 May 1941: '[General] Erfurth, [Oberst] Ziehlberg: Aufgaben der kriegsgeschichtlichen Arbeiten ab Herbst 1941 nach Erledigung unserer europäischen Aufgaben.'
9. Ibid., p. 444, entry for 5 June 1941: 'Organisatorische Grundlagen für Umbau des Heeres für deutsche Aufgaben nach Barbarossa sind seit langem in Arbeit.'
10. Hill (ed.), *Die Weizsäcker-Papiere*, p. 54.
11. Ibid., p. 257, notes from 2 June 1941.
12. Warlimont, *Inside Hitler's Headquarters*, p. 140. Jodl's comment was made on 18 January 1941 and Hitler's on 9 January.
13. Hillgruber, *Hitlers Strategie*, pp. 210–211.
14. Llewellyn Woodward, *British Foreign Policy in the Second World War*, vol. 1 (Her Majesty's Stationery Office, London, 1970), pp. 615 and 619–620.
15. Andreas Hillgruber, 'Das Rußland-Bild der führenden deutschen Militärs vor Beginn des Angriffs auf die Sowjetunion', in Hans-Erich Volkmann (ed.), *Das Rußlandbild im Dritten Reich* (Böhlau Verlag, Cologne/Weimar/Vienna, 1994), pp. 125–140, here p. 139.
16. Bräutigam, *So hat es sich zugetragen*, pp. 309–310.
17. Ibid., p. 322. Altenstadt's own adviser in all administrative questions was Ministerialdirigent Dankwerts of the Reich Interior Ministry.
18. BA-MA, RH 19 III/722, fos. 82–86, here fo. 83: '4 Beauftragte: *Wehrmacht*: Niederringen des Feindes[;] *Reichsführer SS*: Politisch-polizeil. Bekämpfung des Feindes[;] Reichsmarschall: Wirtschaft[;] Rosenberg: Polit. Neuaufbau.'
19. See Breitman, *The Architect of Genocide*.
20. See Joachim Lehmann, 'Herbert Backe – Technokrat und Agrarideologe' in Ronald Smelser, Enrico Syring and Rainer Zitelmann (eds), *Die Braune Elite II: 21 weitere biographische Skizzen* (Wissenschaftliche Buchgesellschaft, Darmstadt, 1993), pp. 1–12, here p. 9.
21. BA, NS 19/3874, fo. 9, letter from Himmler to SS-Brigadeführer Ulrich Greifelt, Head of the Staff Main Office of the Reich Commissar for the Strengthening of German Nationhood, 11 June 1941.
22. See chapter 6, 'Germanic Resettlement'.
23. Benz et al. (eds), *Enzyklopädie des Nationalsozialismus*, p. 806. This gathering has often been dated to the beginning of 1941, even since the correct date was established in the literature in 1982; Karl Hüser, *Wewelsburg 1933 bis 1945 – Kult- und Terrorstätte der SS. Eine Dokumentation* (Verlag Bonifatius-Druckerei, Paderborn, 1982), p. 3. As recently as 1994 (Gerhart Hass, 'Zum Rußlandbild der SS' in Volkmann (ed.), *Das Rußlandbild im Dritten Reich*, pp. 201–224, here p. 214) and even 1998 (Longerich, *Politik der Vernichtung*, p. 298), the date of the gathering was given as 'January 1941'.
24. Witte et al. (eds), *Dienstkalender*, p. 172, entry for 12 June 1941.
25. *IMG*, vol. 4, pp. 535–536, 7 January 1946.
26. Jochen von Lang, *Der Adjutant. Karl Wolff: Der Mann zwischen Hitler und Himmler* (Herbig, Munich/Berlin, 1985), pp. 50–51.
27. Backe, *Um die Nahrungsfreiheit Europas*, p. 162.
28. *IMG*, vol. 36, p. 141; see chapter 7, 'The *Hungerpolitik* in Writing', in this study.
29. Czesław Madajczyk, *Die Okkupationspolitik Nazideutschlands in Polen 1939–1945* (Akademie-Verlag, Berlin, 1987), p. 92.
30. Gersdorff, *Soldat im Untergang*, p. 93; Gerlach, 'Deutsche Wirtschaftsinteressen', pp. 270–271.

31. BA D-H, ZM 1683, Bd. 1, fo. 105, post-war questioning in Riga of Friedrich Jeckeln, former Higher SS and Police Leader for Russia-South and, later, for Russia-North, 2 January 1946; Gersdorff, *Soldat im Untergang*, p. 93.
32. BA D-H, ZM 1683, Bd. 1, fo. 105.
33. Gerlach, *Kalkulierte Morde*, p. 53.
34. Nbg. Dok. PS 1036, fo. 14. The name of the General Commissariat was Sverdlovsk (Yekaterinburg).
35. Gerlach, *Kalkulierte Morde*, p. 712.
36. Aly and Heim, *Vordenker der Vernichtung*, p. 366. See also BA-MA, RW 19/473, fos. 306–307, 'Die Ernährungsbilanzen Festlandeuropas' (nach Berechnungen der Studiengesellschaft für bäuerliche Rechts- und Wirtschaftsordnung e.V.), Wi Rü Amt/Stab I b 5, 10 December 1940.
37. Robert J. Gibbons, 'Allgemeine Richtlinien für die politische und wirtschaftliche Verwaltung der besetzten Ostgebiete', *Vierteljahrshefte für Zeitgeschichte*, 25 (1977), pp. 252–261, here p. 254; Brandt, *Management*, p. 69.
38. BA-MA, RW 19/739, fo. 77, 'Vortragsnotiz über die Besprechung betr. Vorbereitungen Barbarossa am 29.4. nachmittags', 9 May 1941.
39. BA, R 26 IV/33a, 'Richtlinien für die Führung der Wirtschaft in den neubesetzten Ostgebieten (Grüne Mappe)', Teil I (2. Auflage), July 1941. The second edition was printed 2,000 times.
40. BA, R 26 IV/33a, pp. 3 and 5–6. See Gerlach, 'Militärische "Versorgungszwänge"', pp. 177–182.
41. Gerlach, 'Militärische "Versorgungszwänge"', p. 180.
42. Wagner (ed.), *Der Generalquartiermeister*, p. 215.
43. BA, R 26 IV/33a, pp. 3–4 and 9. Cooking oil is extracted from the oil-bearing part of the crop, whether it be a fruit (e.g., olive), a seed (e.g., sesame) or a nut (e.g., walnut). Today, Russia is one of the world's largest sunflower seed producers.
44. Ibid., p. 18. See chapter 9, 'Ordering the Destruction of Leningrad and Moscow', in this study.
45. BA, R 26 IV/33a, p. 4.
46. Ibid., pp. 4–5.
47. See chapter 7, 'The *Hungerpolitik* in Writing'.
48. BA, R 26 IV/33a, p. 3.
49. Ibid.: 'Nach den vom Führer gegebenen Befehlen sind alle Maßnahmen zu treffen, die notwendig sind, um die sofortige und höchstmögliche Ausnutzung der besetzten Gebiete zugunsten Deutschlands herbeizuführen. Dagegen sind alle Maßnahmen zu unterlassen oder zurückzustellen, die dieses Ziel gefährden könnten.'
50. BA-MA, RW 19/473, fos. 167–176, 'Gedanken zu dem Thema: "Wirtschaftlicher Durchhaltekrieg statt Krieg der schnellen militärischen Entscheidung"', June 1941, here fo. 174: 'In dem Zwang für die deutsche Oberste Führung, um jeden Preis das [W]irtschaft-Fundament der deutschen Kriegsführung zu verbreite[r]n, liegt zweifellos der Hauptgrund für die Aktion gegen Rußland.'
51. See BA-MA, RW 19/739, fo. 135. Within a month, Nagel had been promoted to Major-General; see BA-MA, RW 19/175, fo. 100, 'Namensbezeichnung in der Wi-Organisation Ost', 25 June 1941.
52. BA, 99 US 7/1110, fo. 176, post-war comments of Hans Nagel, 8 September 1948. See also *IMG*, vol. 36, pp. 105–106 and 109.
53. BA, 99 US 7/1112, fo. 19, post-war comments of Hans Nagel, 9 September 1948.
54. BA, R 26 IV/33a, p. 18.
55. See *IMG*, vol. 26, pp. 549–550.
56. Götz Aly, 'The Planning Intelligentsia and the "Final Solution"', in Michael Burleigh (ed.), *Confronting the Nazi Past: New Debates on Modern German History* (Collins & Brown, London, 1996), pp. 140–153, here p. 148. See also Aly and Heim, 'Deutsche Herrschaft "im Osten"', pp. 100–101.

57. *IMG*, vol. 39 (1949), pp. 367–371, doc. 089–USSR, '12 Gebote', Herbert Backe, 1 June 1941.
58. Ibid., pp. 367–368.
59. Trevor-Roper (ed.), *Hitler's Table Talk*, p. 590, entry for 22 July 1942.
60. Gerlach, *Kalkulierte Morde*, pp. 168–169; Eichholtz, 'Institutionen und Praxis', p. 51. See Müller, *Hitlers Ostkrieg und die deutsche Siedlungspolitik*, p. 99, where the number of agricultural leaders is given as 'more than ten thousand'.
61. Mai, '*Rasse und Raum*', p. 306. Here, the number of agricultural leaders is given as 'around 10,000'.
62. *IMG*, vol. 39, pp. 370–371.
63. Ibid., p. 371: 'Armut, Hunger und Genügsamkeit erträgt der russische Mensch schon seit Jahrhunderten. Sein Magen ist dehnbar, daher kein falsches Mitleid. Versucht nicht, den deutschen Lebensstandard als Masstab anzulegen und die russische Lebensweise zu ändern.'
64. Thomas, *Geschichte*, p. 517.
65. *IMG*, vol. 39, p. 371: 'Hilf Dir selbst, dann hilft Dir Gott!'
66. BA, R 6/21, fol. 60, 'Entwurf eines neuen §2 zum Erlaß des Führers betr. beabsichtigte Einsetzung Rosenbergs', 10 June 1941.
67. A comprehensive biographical study of Lammers remains outstanding.
68. Kershaw, *Hitler 1889–1936*, p. 533.
69. BA, R 6/21, fos. 59–60, letter from Himmler to Lammers, 10 June 1941, here fo. 59.
70. BA, NS 19/3874, fos. 12–13, here fo. 12; reproduced in Heiber (ed.), *Reichsführer!*, pp. 87–88, here p. 87.
71. BA, R 6/21, fos. 62–73, letter from Rosenberg to Lammers, 14 June 1941, here fos. 62–63: 'In den von Ihnen fertiggestellten Entwurf ... steht, daß die Rechtsetzung in den Ostgebieten durch den Reichsminister erfolgt, ferner daß die Reichskommissare dem Reichsminister für die besetzten Ostgebiete unterstehen, *ausschließlich* von ihm ihre Weisungen erhalten und daß sie die *gesamte* Verwaltung in den ihnen anvertrauten Gebieten zu führen haben.'
72. BA, R 6/21, fos. 66–67: 'Nach dem Entwurf des Reichsführers SS und Chef der Deutschen Polizei bleibt für den Reichsminister für den besetzten Ostgebiete und die Reichskommissare überhaupt nichts zu tun übrig als höchstens die Befehle anderer Stellen zur Kenntnis zu nehmen, denn neben dem Militärbefehlshaber würden die Wirtschaft und die Polizei selbständige Gewalten darstellen ....'
73. The application of the 'divide and rule' tag to Hitler's method of governing is nothing new; see Karl Dietrich Bracher, *Die deutsche Diktatur: Entstehung, Struktur, Folgen des Nationalsozialismus*, rev. 4th edition (Kiepenheuer & Witsch, Cologne, 1972), pp. 251–258 and, esp. pp. 375–379.
74. See chapter 1, 'Organized Chaos: the German Occupation, 1941–1944'.
75. BA, R 6/21, fos. 67–68.
76. Bräutigam, *So hat es sich zugetragen*, pp. 315–316; Gibbons, 'Allgemeine Richtlinien', p. 255.
77. For the full text of the guidelines see BA, NS 19/2808, fos. 2–8, 'Allgemeine Richtlinien für die politische und wirtschaftliche Verwaltung der besetzten Ostgebiete', n.d.; reproduced in Gibbons, 'Allgemeine Richtlinien', pp. 257–261, which is used here. The fact that a copy of Bräutigam's guidelines is to be found in the files of the Personal Staff of Reichsführer-SS Himmler makes it clear that members of Himmler's staff, and perhaps Himmler himself, had knowledge of the guidelines and hence the stance of the Bureau Rosenberg with regard to the issues addressed in the guidelines.
78. Gibbons, 'Allgemeine Richtlinien', p. 259: 'Der Krieg gegen die Sowjetunion ist ein politischer Feldzug, kein wirtschaftlicher Raubzug. Das eroberte Gebiet darf also als Ganzes nicht als ein Ausbeutungsobjekt betrachtet werden, selbst wenn auch die deutsche Ernährungs- und Kriegswirtschaft größere Gebiete beanspruchen muß.'
79. See chapter 7, 'The *Hungerpolitik* in Writing'.

80. Gibbons, 'Allgemeine Richtlinien', p. 259. See also Bräutigam, *So hat es sich zugetragen*, p. 306; BA, R 26 I/13, fo. 2, order from Göring to various ministers, 27 July 1941.
81. Gibbons, 'Allgemeine Richtlinien', pp. 260–261.
82. Bräutigam, *So hat es sich zugetragen*, p. 316.
83. Ibid., p. 323.
84. Gibbons, 'Allgemeine Richtlinien', p. 253: '… es ist die wohl klarste Darlegung der politischen Zielsetzung des Ostministeriums, die uns zur Verfügung steht.'
85. BA-MA, RW 19/739, fos. 130–136, 'Niederschrift zur 4. Sitzung des Wirtschafts-Führungstabes Ost unter Vorsitz von Staatssekretär Körner vom 26. Mai 1941', here fos. 135–136: 'Die von Oberst Nagel zusammengestellte "grüne Mappe" ist im Anschluss an die letzte "B"-Sitzung den Ressorts zur Stellungnahme zugeleitet worden. Die Ressorts stimmen ihre Abänderungswünsche, soweit dies nicht bereits geschehen ist, unmittelbar mit Oberst Nagel ab. Auch Oberbereichsleiter Malettke vom Stabe Rosenberg hat sich einverstanden erklärt. Er hat die vom Stabe Rosenberg zusammengestellten Flugblätter ebenfalls mit dem Stabe Schubert abgestimmt.' Including Staatssekretär Körner, seventeen men were present at the session. The minutes were taken by Dr Joachim Bergmann of the VJPB. After the invasion of the Soviet Union, Oberbereichsleiter Walter Malletke became head of the Department for Special Measures in the Main Department III (Economy) of the RMO; Gerlach, *Kalkulierte Morde*, p. 158, fn. 201.
86. See Cecil, *The Myth of the Master Race*, p. 203; Krausnick, 'Die Einsatzgruppen', p. 114; Aly and Heim, *Vordenker der Vernichtung*, p. 378.
87. BA, NS 19/2803, fo. 1, letter from Himmler to Rosenberg, 24 June 1941. See also BA, NS 19/3874, fo. 3, letter from Himmler to Lammers, 28 May 1941, for Himmler's appointment of SS-Brigadeführer Heinrich Müller, Chief of Office IV (Gestapo) in the RSHA, as liaison officer to Rosenberg.
88. See *IMG*, vol. 11 (1947), p. 528, for Rosenberg's statement of 16 April 1946 at Nuremberg.
89. *IMG*, vol. 26, pp. 610–627, doc. 1058–PS, 'Rede des Reichsleiters A. Rosenberg vor den engsten Beteiligten am Ostproblem am 20. Juni 1941', here p. 625.
90. Ibid., pp. 616 and 618–619: 'In welcher Form und in welchem Umfang dann später ein ukrainischer Staat entstehen kann, darüber zu sprechen, hat jetzt noch keinen Sinn.'
91. Ibid., pp. 619–620: 'Wenn die Wirtschaftsführung des Reichsmarschalls darauf ausgehen muss, möglichst viel aus diesem Gebiet herauszuziehen, dann wird sie diese politische Haltung und politische Führung erst recht unterstützen können; denn es ist ein Unterschied, ob ich 40 millionen Menschen nach einigen Jahren zur freiwilligen Mitarbeit gewonnen habe oder hinter jeden Bauern einen Soldaten stellen muss. Ich glaube, wenn beide Seiten diese Notwendigkeiten sehen, dann wird die Politik eine Helferin für die Wirtschaftsführung sein und umgekehrt sich die Wirtschaftsführung sehr gut auf die politische Zielsetzung einstellen können.'
92. Ibid., p. 622: 'Die deutsche Volksernährung steht in diesen Jahren zweifellos an der Spitze der deutschen Forderungen im Osten ….'
93. Ibid.: 'Wir sehen durchaus nicht die Verpflichtung ein, aus diesen Überschussgebieten das russische Volk mit zu ernähren. Wir wissen, dass das eine harte Notwendigkeit ist, die ausserhalb jeden Gefühls steht. Zweifellos wird eine sehr umfangreiche Evakuierung notwendig sein und dem Russentum wird sicher sehr schwere Jahre bevorstehen.'
94. BA, NS 8/90, fos. 54–61, 'Aus der Rede des Reichsleiters Alfred Rosenberg bei der Kundgebung der NSDAP. Gau Hamburg bei Sagebiet am 22. Februar 1941', *Hansische Hochschul-Zeitung*, vol. 22, March 1941, here fo. 55.
95. *IMG*, vol. 26, pp. 626–627: 'Deutschland für immer von dem politischen Druck aus dem Osten zu befreien; das ist das politische Ziel in diesem Kampf.'
96. Ibid., pp. 584–592, doc. 1039–PS, 'Bericht über die vorbereitende Arbeit in Fragen des osteuropäischen Raumes', 28 June 1941, here p. 586: 'In den Ostfragen wurde, was die unmittelbare fachliche Arbeit jetzt und für die Zukunft anbetrifft, weitgehendste Übereinstimmung erzielt.'
97. Ibid., p. 621.

98. Joachim C. Fest argued that 'that is certainly wrong'; Fest, 'Alfred Rosenberg', p. 174.
99. BA, R 90/256a, pp. 25 and 28.
100. H.D. Heilmann, 'Aus dem Kriegstagebuch des Diplomaten Otto Bräutigam' in Götz Aly (ed.), *Biedermann und Schreibtischtäter: Materialien zur deutschen Täter-Biographie* (Rotbuch Verlag, Berlin, 1987), pp. 123–187, here p. 144, entry for 14 September 1941. For a contrasting interpretation, see Gerlach, 'Die Ausweitung der deutschen Massenmorde', pp. 77–78.
101. Kershaw, *Hitler 1936–1945*, pp. 478–479.
102. See Arad, 'Alfred Rosenberg and the "Final Solution"', p. 280.

CHAPTER 9

POST-INVASION DECISIONS

The preparations for German occupation policy in the Soviet Union, which, at least in the case of military planning, had effectively started in July 1940, were not concluded until after the invasion was launched and hostilities were under way. Certain key decisions had not been made prior to the onset of 'Barbarossa'. That these decisions related largely, though not exclusively, to the setting up of a civil administration in the occupied Soviet territories is hardly surprising, given that, of the four pillars of the occupation – army, economic organization, civil administration and SS/police – this was both the last to be initiated into the invasion plans and the last for which the necessary preparations commenced. Those decisions made after 22 June 1941, such was their import, could only be made by Hitler himself. They related to the appointment of the most senior civil administrators in the soon-to-be-occupied Soviet territories and to the form which the Berlin-based coordinating body, headed by Alfred Rosenberg, would ultimately take. These issues were addressed at a small but high-level meeting at the Führer Headquarters on 16 July, attended by a handful of senior figures from the military, the Reich government and the Party. The relevant decrees would be signed by Hitler the following day.

Another significant issue addressed by Hitler in mid-July 1941 was the treatment of the heavily populated, industrial cities of Moscow and Leningrad. Although this subject had been broached on several occasions during the previous two or three months by various high-ranking officials, it was only in mid-July that a final decision was made as to what should be done with these large cities and their inhabitants. It now came to the fore in conjunction with the progress of the military campaign and the pressing need to establish a policy, particularly with regard to Leningrad, which was rapidly reached by German troops during their initial advance into Soviet territory.

16 July 1941: the Conference at FHQ

The day after Himmler's receipt of Konrad Meyer's draft Generalplan Ost – three and a half weeks into military operations against the Soviet Union – an important meeting took place at the 'Wolf's Lair' (*Wolfsschanze*), the Führer Headquarters just outside Rastenburg in East Prussia (present-day Poland).[1] The opening phase of the campaign had gone so well that Colonel-General Halder was induced to record in his diary entry of 3 July: 'It is thus not saying too much when I claim that the campaign against Russia has been won within 14 days.'[2] In this moment of apparent triumph Hitler evidently felt the time had come to formally confirm the shape of the civil administration soon to be deployed in the pacified areas of the East. Moreover, both the OKH and the OKW had been pressing Reichsleiter Rosenberg to assist in freeing up military manpower being used to administer the occupied territories by providing 'partial solutions' in setting up a civil administration in certain territories.[3] Pressure may also have been exerted by senior SS and police officials keen to see a political administration established to replace the existing military administration.[4] Some senior figures were even under the impression that Göring, and not Rosenberg, was in fact to receive control over the political administration of the occupied Soviet territories.[5] A civil administration, regardless of who sat at its head, could not be set up, however, until the proposed appointments for the positions of Reich and General Commissar had been approved by Hitler himself. Thus, the most concrete reason for the meeting of 16 July was the necessity to confirm the selection of, and to appoint, the senior civil administrators.

The discussion at FHQ lasted five hours, from three in the afternoon till eight in the evening, with a coffee break part-way through. Joining Hitler were Reichsleiter Rosenberg, Head of the Reich Chancellery Lammers, Field Marshal Keitel, Reichsmarschall Göring and, taking the minutes, Reichsleiter Bormann, Head of the Party Chancellery. All of these men have been encountered during the course of this study. Rosenberg was there representing the future civil administration, Keitel the military and Göring the economic organization. Lammers, who would be called upon to draw up the decrees resulting from the discussion, and Bormann were often present at such meetings in their capacities as heads of the Reich and Party chancelleries, respectively.

Hitler began by stating that the Germans should not announce their aims in the occupied Soviet territories to the whole world; it sufficed that they themselves knew what they wanted. No superfluous policy declarations should be made which could make their tasks more difficult. It should not be clear to others that German measures in the East were leading to a 'final settlement'. 'All necessary measures – shootings, evacuations etc. – we will take and can take in spite of this.'[6] It was not desirable to make enemies prematurely and unnecessarily:

But it must be clear to us that we will never again leave these territories. Accordingly, it is a matter of:
1.) Doing nothing to obstruct the final settlement, but rather preparing this on the quiet;
2.) emphasizing that we are the bringers of freedom. ...
Essentially, it is thus a matter of conveniently carving the giant cake up, in order that we can firstly rule it, secondly administer it, and thirdly exploit it.[7]

Göring emphasized once more the importance of the third of these undertakings – exploitation – by declaring that 'we must first of all think about the securing of our sustenance, everything else can be dealt with only much later'.[8] These general expressions of intent were interspersed now and then with more concrete statements of policy. The Crimea, according to Hitler, had to be cleared of all 'foreigners' and settled with Germans, whilst both the Crimea, 'with a considerable hinterland', and the entire 'Balten-Land' had to be incorporated into the Reich. Hitler wanted the city of Leningrad, on the other hand, to be 'razed to the ground' before being handed over to Finland, one of Germany's military partners in the invasion of the Soviet Union.[9]

Talk then turned to the appointment of the senior civil administrators. The suitability of Hinrich Lohse for the post of Reich Commissar in the Baltic was discussed at length, Lohse having already been charged by Rosenberg with the 'central treatment of questions' concerning the former Baltic republics and Belarus as early as 23 April 1941.[10] Göring proposed either that the Baltic should be handed over to Erich Koch, for the reason that Koch knew the area very well, or that Koch should become Reich Commissar in the Ukraine, because, given his initiative and experience in such matters, he would do the best job of managing the territory. Rosenberg, who had earmarked the Gauleiter of Thuringia, Fritz Sauckel, for the Ukraine, responded to Göring's suggestion by protesting that Koch would not comply with his (Rosenberg's) directives and that Koch had said as much. Göring, however, told Rosenberg that the appointed men could not be treated like children but must, on the contrary, be very independent.

Despite Göring's doubts that he would fulfil his task 'very well', as Rosenberg had asserted, Arno Schickedanz was accepted as Reich Commissar in the Caucasus, with the proviso that the former Mayor of Vienna, SA-Gruppenführer Dr Hermann Neubacher, be installed alongside him to take care of economic matters.[11] Neubacher had in fact been proposed two months earlier as Reich Commissar for the Caucasus by Göring's deputy in the VJPB and the Wi Fü Stab Ost, Staatssekretär Körner.[12] At the beginning of April 1941, Rosenberg had already recommended that Göring, as Plenipotentiary for the Four-Year Plan, appoint the head of an 'oil commission' to work alongside the Reich Commissar in the Caucasus.[13]

Hitler himself expressed the desire that both the deputy Gauleiter of Franconia, Karl Holz, and former Gauleiter Alfred Eduard Frauenfeld be employed in the occupied Soviet territories, the latter to administer the

Crimea. The Crimea was slated by Rosenberg for inclusion in the Reich Commissariat Ukraine.[14] Hitler furthermore suggested that Wilhelm Kube, also a former Gauleiter, be appointed as Reich Commissar for Moscow and the surrounding area. After both Rosenberg and Göring had expressed the opinion, however, that Kube, who was in his mid-fifties,[15] was too old for such a post, SA-Obergruppenführer Siegfried Kasche, the German envoy in Zagreb,[16] was chosen in lieu of him. Kube would instead fill the position of General Commissar in Belarus, termed by the Nazis as 'Weißruthenien'. On Göring's suggestion, the Kola Peninsula was entrusted for 'exploitation' to the Gauleiter of Essen, Josef Terboven, who already held the additional post of Reich Commissar for the Occupied Norwegian Territories. Hitler concluded that Lohse should be appointed to administer the Baltic 'if he feels that he is up to the task', but that Koch be given the Ukraine, as this would 'undoubtedly be the most important territory for the next three years'.[17] The appointment of Koch as Reich Commissar in the Ukraine constituted in effect both a rejection of the policy Rosenberg sought to pursue in this territory and at the same time a fundamental blow to his overall conception of the future configuration of the occupied eastern territories, within which the Ukraine functioned as the most important part.[18]

After the coffee break, Dr Lammers read out the draft decrees which he had prepared during the preceding weeks[19] and presumably amended as the discussion progressed or during the break.[20] In all likelihood in response to these draft decrees, talk turned to the jurisdiction of Reichsführer-SS Himmler. A month earlier to the day, Bormann had written to Lammers in support of Himmler's claims – already put forward in Himmler's own 10 June letter to Lammers – to extended powers in the occupied eastern territories and requested Lammers to take into consideration his (Bormann's) 'line of thought' on the occasion of his next presentation to Hitler.[21] Even if Lammers did pass Bormann's arguments on to Hitler, they are unlikely to have been decisive in forming the latter's conception of Himmler's forthcoming role in the East. Hitler's ideas as to the 'special tasks' assigned to Himmler and the powers necessary in order for them to be carried out were by this time already largely fixed. In the event, both Hitler and Göring stressed the importance that Himmler should possess exactly the same powers in the occupied Soviet territories as those he already possessed in the Reich itself. This meant the authority he exercised as Reichsführer-SS and Chief of the German Police, but also in his capacity as Reich Commissar for the Strengthening of German Nationhood. Additional political powers, which Himmler appears to have been hankering after in his letter to Lammers,[22] and which could only have been at the expense of Rosenberg's own expected powers, were not transferred to him. At the close of the meeting, Hitler expressed the hope that any disputes would quickly sort themselves out in the field.[23] Before leaving, Göring shook Rosenberg's hand, accompanying the gesture with the words 'Here's to our collaboration.'[24]

Rosenberg's reaction to the proceedings of the meeting was a mixed one. He believed he had received a huge task, indeed the greatest that the Reich had to offer: making Europe independent from overseas.[25] This was obviously a reference to the attempt to make German-controlled Europe immune to naval blockade by achieving self-sufficiency in foodstuffs and vital raw materials. He recognized, however, that he would have to share this authority with Göring, who, as Plenipotentiary for the Four-Year Plan, controlled 'economic interventions'. Rosenberg mistakenly believed Göring's privilege to be temporary, though perceived the possibility that these 'economic interventions', if they were not implemented with clear coordination, could endanger the political objectives.[26] Otto Bräutigam, having been filled in by Rosenberg the same evening, recognized that it would be difficult for the civil administration to govern the territories without the police and the economic apparatus being completely under its control.[27]

Bräutigam's misgivings were confirmed the following day. He lunched with Himmler, Rosenberg and Lammers in Himmler's special train, 'Heinrich', before the party travelled to FHQ. Those decrees drawn up by Lammers, drafts of which had been read out by him at the conference the day before, were then signed to fix in writing the decisions reached.[28] Lammers had been assisted in the formulation of the 'Führer decree' on the administration of the newly occupied territories (i.e., the decree appointing Rosenberg as East Minister) by Staatssekretär Stuckart from the Interior Ministry and by his colleague in the Reich Chancellery, Ministerialdirektor Wilhelm Kritzinger. Following a discussion with Stuckart just under a week before the 16 July meeting, Kritzinger had redrafted this decree.[29] All the documents were ready by about six o'clock on the evening of 17 July.[30] Rosenberg was officially appointed 'Reich Minister for the Occupied Eastern Territories', though it was explicitly stated in §3 of the decree that the respective jurisdictions of Göring and Himmler in the newly occupied territories, regulated in separate decrees, would be left untouched. The Reich Commissars were to be directly subordinate to Rosenberg and to receive instructions exclusively from him unless §3 found application – in other words, unless it was deemed necessary for either Göring or Himmler to issue orders to the Reich Commissars. This immediately provided Göring and Himmler, as well as the Reich Commissars themselves, with a loophole to be exploited. The purpose of the decree, and thus the role of the newly appointed minister, was 'to re-establish and maintain public order and public life in the newly occupied eastern territories'.[31]

Göring, whose role in the occupation of the Soviet territories had been clear for several months, had already been officially appointed as economic supremo by Hitler at the end of June 1941. He was empowered to order 'all measures which are required for the most extensive exploitation possible of the available supplies and economic capacities and for the expansion of economic forces in favour of the German war economy'.[32] On the same day, Göring was appointed as Hitler's deputy in the event that the latter, through illness or due to other events, was unable to fulfil his duties.[33]

One notable absentee from the 16 July conference was Reichsführer-SS Himmler, who would be responsible for security and policing measures during the coming campaign and subsequent occupation. That Himmler did not attend the meeting, despite being in the vicinity between 15 and 20 July,[34] suggests that most of the key decisions regarding future policy in the East had been made prior to the conference and that his presence was, therefore, not required. He was, however, informed of what had been discussed during the five-hour meeting, and sent the author of the minutes, Martin Bormann, his 'very special thanks' for having been provided with a copy.[35]

The securing of the newly occupied eastern territories by the police, so ran the relevant decree of 17 July, was 'a matter for the Reichsführer-SS and Chief of the German Police'.[36] Himmler would already have discussed his 'special tasks' with Hitler over the preceding weeks and months. It was not necessary to give details in the decree – presumably the 'special decree of the Führer' referred to by Himmler in his 10 June letter to Lammers – of what exactly those tasks entailed. Himmler was entitled to issue orders to the Reich Commissars. If of a general nature or possessing political significance, Himmler was to run these orders by Reich Minister Rosenberg, unless the issuance of such orders concerned the averting of an immediately threatening danger. This caveat was crucial, as it was presumably down to Himmler to define what did and what did not fall under this heading. It meant that he could consult Rosenberg as much or as little as he liked, even with regard to issues of a political nature.

In addition to the aforementioned decrees, Hinrich Lohse was appointed in a separate decree as Reich Commissar for the 'Ostland', to be based in Riga. The districts of Bialystok and eastern Galicia were cut out of what had formerly been eastern Poland and on 1 August 1941 formally handed over to the Gauleiter of East Prussia, Erich Koch, and the General Governor Hans Frank, respectively.[37] Frank had for some time been endeavouring to obtain approval for the extension of his General Government at the expense of that part of Poland which had been annexed by the USSR in 1939 and part of the Belarusian territories.[38] Koch would not be officially appointed as Reich Commissar for the Ukraine, based in Rovno, until 20 August 1941, in anticipation of the handing over to civilian rule of the first of those territories intended to constitute the Reich Commissariat Ukraine, which took place on 1 September.[39] The award of Bialystok to Koch was apparently intended as compensation for him not receiving control over the Reich Commissariat 'Ostland', which he himself had been hoping for.[40] On Rosenberg's suggestion – made as early as 7 April 1941[41] – Hitler appointed Dr Alfred Meyer, Gauleiter of North Westphalia,[42] as Rosenberg's 'permanent representative', with the rank of Staatssekretär.[43] For the next four months, however, these appointments would all remain secret. Hitler had intended to wait for a suitably triumphant moment to publicize the establishment of a civil administration for the pacified parts of the occupied Soviet territories, a hoped-for juncture which would never arrive.[44]

Ultimately, the unanticipated course of military events would mean that, of the four Reich Commissariats planned by Rosenberg and approved by Hitler,[45] only two – 'Ostland' and 'Ukraine' – would be established. The others – 'Russia' and 'Caucasus' – remained on paper. Originally, five Reich Commissariats had been envisaged, but the different parties involved in the planning for the shape of the future political administration in the East had come to an agreement by the second half of May 1941 at the latest to limit the number to four.[46] The territory initially foreseen as a fifth administrative unit, the Don-Volga region with its seat in Rostov-on-Don,[47] was dropped because it did not possess a specific political objective.[48] Rosenberg's suggestion to divide the territory which would have comprised this fifth administrative unit between the Reich Commissariat Ukraine and the Reich Commissariat Caucasus was approved by Hitler.[49]

If Himmler's absence from the 16 July meeting is viewed as an indication that most of the key decisions regarding future policy in the East had already been made prior to the conference and that his presence was therefore not required, wherein lies the significance of this gathering of senior members of the Nationalist Socialist hierarchy? The most concrete result of the conference was the confirmation of appointments to the civil administration in the occupied eastern territories. Of particular importance to the historian, however, are, first, the evidence of the growing impotence of the designated Minister for the East Rosenberg in questions of major policy and, secondly, that the minutes represent probably our best example of Hitler's own overview and enunciation of the intended approach to future occupation policy in the occupied Soviet territories. Though, as so often, painted in broad brushstrokes, his colonial and settlement plans were expressed more clearly than had hitherto been the case.[50]

Ordering the Destruction of Leningrad and Moscow

The economic-political guidelines of the agricultural group in the Economic Staff East from 23 May 1941 had stated that Moscow and Leningrad, as a result of their location in the so-called 'wooded zone', would not receive deliveries of agricultural produce.[51] In the Green Folder, issued three and a half weeks later, the cities of Leningrad and Moscow were described as a 'difficult problem', particularly as they required substantial food surpluses. However, the Green Folder merely declared that the measures to be taken in this respect would be contained in further instructions which were to be issued on the strength of the experiences of the first weeks of the invasion.[52] Following the rapid advance of Army Group North towards Leningrad, Hitler began to contemplate the fate of the city. As mentioned above, he declared at the conference of 16 July that he wanted Leningrad to be 'razed to the ground' before being handed over to the Finns.[53] A little over a week earlier, he had already announced his intention to deal with both Leningrad and Moscow in this way. His reasons were recorded by Colonel-General Halder:

> It is the Führer's fixed decision that Moscow and Leningrad be razed to the ground in order to prevent people remaining there, whom we would then have

to feed in the winter. The cities should be destroyed by the Luftwaffe. Tanks are not to be employed for this purpose. 'National catastrophe which deprives not only Bolshevism, but also Muscovy, of its centres.'[54]

On the same day, 8 July, Hitler reiterated his intention to 'erase' 'cities like' Moscow and Leningrad to Joseph Goebbels during the Propaganda Minister's visit to Führer Headquarters. Nothing was to be allowed to remain of Bolshevism.[55] It would not be long before Kiev would join Moscow and Leningrad as one of the targets of this all-consuming destructiveness.[56]

A whole range of senior figures in the political and military leaderships voiced their support for this approach to the Soviet Union's major urban centres. These men included Field Marshal Wilhelm Ritter von Leeb, who, as the Commander of Army Group North, was responsible for laying siege to Leningrad ('The emphasis must first of all be placed on reaching the narrow line of encirclement in order to lay the foundations for a bombardment of Leningrad');[57] Quartermaster-General Wagner ('For the time being, Petersburg will have to sweat it out[;] what are we supposed to do with a city of 3½ mill[ions], which just rests itself on our supply pouch[?] There are no sentimentalities here');[58] Reichsmarschall Göring ('For economic reasons, the conquest of large cities is not desirable. Their encirclement is more advantageous');[59] Erich Koch ('The intention of the Führer, who sees the destruction of the large Russian cities as [the] prerequisite for the permanence of our power in Russia, was strengthened further by the Reich Commissar');[60] and Reinhard Heydrich ('In my opinion, in such cases, vast numbers of incendiary and high-explosive bombs must be used').[61] In mid-October 1941, the OKW gave explicit orders to the effect that a surrender on the part of the inhabitants of Leningrad was not to be accepted.[62]

It is possible that the recommendation that the populations of large Soviet cities should not be fed in the event of the capture of these cities originally came from the Reich Ministry for Food and Agriculture in April 1941, more specifically, from Hans-Joachim Riecke.[63] It is hardly surprising that the proposal came from the ministry whose employees were most responsible for the conception and development of the 'starvation strategy'. The destruction of Leningrad and the substantial reduction of its population were certainly taken on board by the SS as long-term aims. In the fourth version of the Generalplan Ost from 28 May 1942,[64] SS-Oberführer Meyer gave the urban population of the intended German settlement territory of 'Ingermanland' (i.e., Leningrad and the surrounding area) as 200,000 in comparison with a pre-war population in Leningrad of 3.2 million.[65] The planned eradication of Leningrad was clearly included in Meyer's calculations.

As can be seen from Göring's and Hitler's comments, from 16 September and 8 July 1941, respectively, the course of action described was pursued for 'economic reasons' and, more specifically, 'in order to prevent people remaining there, whom we must then feed in the winter'. In other words, when it came to the allocation of foodstuffs, senior Nazis viewed the millions of inhabitants of the Soviet Union's largest cities merely as competition for the German troops and Germans back in the Reich. For Hitler and his lieutenants, it was preferable to starve the millions of inhabitants of these cities than to feed them with valuable foodstuffs which could be put, as they saw it, to better use. From their point of view, it was apt that the vast majority of these envisaged victims were not rural agricultural workers, who were required by the Germans to tend to the crops, but urban industrial workers and their families, who were deemed to be largely superfluous to requirements. The starving out of Leningrad between 1941 and 1943, to which at least 600,000 people fell victim, turned out, however, to be something of an exception in the context of the 'starvation strategy'. Elsewhere in the occupied Soviet territories it proved more difficult to cordon off whole regions and bring about the deaths of hundreds of thousands of people through starvation. In the event, thousands of Soviet civilians took to the country roads in search of food and trade on the black market thrived, just the thing the economic planners had sought to avoid.[66]

Economic factors were of such significance in both the planning and the implementation of the eastern campaign that they even influenced a decision which, at first sight, would appear to be of a purely military nature. The determination within the German leadership to wipe out the large Soviet cities and their inhabitants was also influenced by other factors, such as the cities' industrial capacity and their political and ideological role. Of crucial importance, however, was the perceived necessity to eliminate as many consumers as possible who could endanger officially sanctioned plans to artificially create vast surpluses of foodstuffs in order to feed the invading army and assist in making German-occupied Europe immune from blockade.

The Concept of a Territorial Ministry in the East

The 'Decree of the Führer regarding the Administration of the Newly Occupied Eastern Territories' of 17 July 1941 not only appointed Alfred Rosenberg as administrative head in the East, but also set up a new type of governmental institution: a territorial ministry. Of the fifteen Reich ministries in existence at the time, this was the only ministry responsible for a specific geographical region.[67] The interposition of a minister between Hitler and the chiefs of the civil administration in the occupied territories (in this case, Erich Koch and Hinrich Lohse as Reich Commissars) was an innovation. Instead of being directly answerable to Hitler, as was the case for all the other administrative heads in the various German-occupied territories of Europe, the Reich Commissars, at least officially, were subordinated to Reich Minister Rosenberg. Norway and the Netherlands were both governed by a Reich Commissar, Josef Terboven and Arthur Seyß-Inquart, respectively, but did not possess a Reich Minister. The senior administrative figure in Bohemia and Moravia, the rump of Czechoslovakia, carried the title Reich Protector. The rump of Poland, the General Government, was ruled by the General Governor, Hans Frank. Both Belgium and northern France were under the control of a military commander. In Denmark, also an administrative exception, both the king and the government remained in office, their activities, however, regulated by a representative of the German Foreign Office.[68] Although the Reich Commissariat in Norway was officially accorded the status of a Reich Ministry[69] and both Reich Commissar Seyß-Inquart and General Governor Frank held the rank of Reich Minister,[70] it was only for the territories conquered from the Soviet Union that an actual ministry was erected.

As seen earlier, Rosenberg had already highlighted in his paper of 2 April 1941 the necessity of 'a different treatment' of the USSR to that employed in the occupied territories of Western Europe. He justified this in view of the 'enormous spaces' and the consequential 'difficulties of administration', as well as the completely different living conditions supposedly brought about by Bolshevism.[71] Five days later, he argued that, in order to deal with what he saw as the unique problems in the East, 'a central leadership of the work of the different Reich Commissariats is urgently necessary'. This would, first, relieve the strain on Hitler, who would not constantly have to deal with four or five eastern administrations and, secondly, enable the whole area to be supervised from one position, thus making sure that the assigned tasks would be correctly carried out. As 'Protector-General for the occupied eastern territories', with his seat in Berlin, Rosenberg proposed himself. All official business between the authorities in the 'old Reich' and the Reich Commissariats would go through the Protector-General. Rosenberg, at least at this point in time, did not foresee the establishment of a new, large Reich authority as being necessary.[72]

The first references to the post of Reich Minister for the Occupied Eastern Territories – and hence to an East Ministry – appeared in a paper from Rosenberg himself, dated 25 April 1941 and entitled 'Memorandum No. 3. Re.: USSR',[73] and not in fact in Rosenberg's 'General Instruction for all Reich Commissars in the Occupied Eastern Territories' from 8 May, a belief which is nevertheless widespread in the literature on the subject.[74] In view of the fact that Rosenberg referred here to the 'Reich Minister and Protector-General for the occupied eastern territories' and that he had recommended himself for the post of Protector-General two and a half weeks earlier, it is likely that he now saw himself as the future Reich Minister. One of the leitmotivs running through Rosenberg's pre-invasion writings on the administration of the occupied eastern territories was the idea that the Reich Commissariats had to be treated differently whilst remaining in the same framework. Hence, in his view, the (Protector-General's or) Minister's job was to coordinate the Reich Commissars and their tasks. Rosenberg had admittedly at the beginning of April 1941 rejected the idea of the establishment of a new, large Reich authority – what could only have meant a ministry. The idea of an East Ministry seems, however, to have grown on him.

Rosenberg's proposal of 25 April does not appear to have garnered much initial attention within the political leadership. Perhaps this was because Rosenberg's memoranda were intended only for Hitler himself; perhaps it was because the suggestion had come from Rosenberg, who was widely regarded as a doctrinaire.[75] Whatever the reason, substantial objections to the proposal were only raised at the beginning of July 1941, less than two weeks before Rosenberg's official appointment as East Minister. The strongest case against the creation of a separate ministry was made in a comprehensive four-page letter, dated 4 July, to Head of the Reich Chancellery Lammers.[76] The author was Dr Wilhelm Stuckart, Staatssekretär in the Ministry of the Interior. Stuckart, co-author of the Nuremberg Laws of 1935 and a member of the General Council for the Four-Year Plan, was subsequently to assist Lammers and Ministerialdirektor Wilhelm Kritzinger in the formulation of the 'Führer decree' on the administration of the newly occupied territories (i.e., the decree appointing Rosenberg as East Minister). Like many of the Staatssekretäre, Stuckart was much more than a civil servant; he was ideologically reliable and growing in power. It is arguable that he was by this time the most important man in the Interior Ministry.

Stuckart had heard about the draft 'Führer decree' regarding the administration of the occupied eastern territories, which was in the process of being passed around those concerned. As Stuckart himself remarked, the political objective for the four 'territorial complexes' envisaged was in each case a different one. Both the resulting treatment of the four territories and the economic structure within them would be correspondingly disparate. For this very reason, Stuckart deemed it questionable whether it was necessary to create 'a uniform, all-embracing territorial ministry for all 4 territories'. Furthermore, it would be quite out of the question for the occupied eastern territories to be exempt from the uniform economic policy which existed for all of German-controlled Europe and was set by the Plenipotentiary for the Four-Year Plan. Likewise, control over the police forces in the 'entire European space' could only be exercised by one official in the Reich, and that was the Reichsführer-SS and Chief of the German Police. Stuckart came to the conclusion that an East Ministry claiming total control over the occupied eastern territories 'would not have a positive effect'.[77] The knowledge of the eastern territories possessed by the members of Rosenberg's staff, he believed, could be put to more effective use. Stuckart proposed the following:

> Reichsleiter Rosenberg and his staff should in my opinion be included in the form that they contribute in *political* terms to the measures of the supreme Reich authorities ... as well as to the measures of the Reich Commissars. ... In this way, the political influence of Reichsleiter Rosenberg and his staff would in my opinion be safeguarded, without the danger arising of the work being duplicated and in the end of officials working against one another. The Reich Commissars of the individual large territorial complexes would, as is the case with all other Reich Commissars, be directly subordinate to the Führer.[78]

Rosenberg's bureau would, in other words, act as a liaison between the Reich Commissars in the East and the authorities in the 'old Reich'. This scenario, Stuckart believed, would allow the work of Rosenberg and his staff to have a really productive effect without strength and energy being wasted with arguments over jurisdiction.[79] Although Stuckart was clearly unaware that the powers of Göring and Himmler would be left untouched by the appointment of Rosenberg as East Minister, thus ensuring uniform economic and police policies in all territories under German control, his assessment of the likely effect of the creation of a territorial ministry and the insertion of a minister between Hitler and the Reich Commissars was very astute. Dr Peter Kleist, head of the regional department 'Ostland' in Georg Leibbrandt's 'Main Department I: Policy' in the RMO, similarly suggested – albeit after the war – that the construction of a small, highly qualified command staff following the pattern of the Four-Year Plan organization would have been a possible alternative. This command staff would have then been responsible for giving the relevant Reich authorities binding instructions for the wording of their respective measures affecting the new territories.[80]

The creation of a territorial ministry for the occupied eastern territories was clearly a polarizing issue. The decision as to what kind of governing apparatus to set up in the East lay at the end of the day with Hitler. As documentary evidence recording Hitler's expression of his own personal feelings regarding an East Ministry in the weeks and months prior to its establishment is not available, his feelings on the matter can only be pieced together using subsequent statements from him. Staatssekretär Stuckart feared that the erection of a territorial ministry would have the effect of loosening the grip of the 'old Reich' and its authorities on the East. Perhaps this is exactly what Hitler wanted: 'Let me issue a word of warning to our legal gentlemen [of whom doctor of law Stuckart was one]; that they should refrain from attempting to impose their mania for regulations on the administration of our Eastern territories.'[81] In this connection, Hitler laid particular emphasis on the point that 'there is nothing more harmful to the organisation of a State than over-centralisation and limitation of local power. The lawyers among us hanker constantly for such limitation.'[82]

Comments Hitler made at the beginning of August 1941 could have been a direct response to Stuckart's call for a 'uniform' policy coming out of the 'old Reich' for all occupied territories. Referring to German bureaucrats, Hitler remarked:

> Their fixed idea is that legislation should be the same for the whole Reich. Why not a different regulation for each part of the Reich? They imagine that it's better to have a regulation which is bad, but uniform, rather than a good regulation that would take account of particular circumstances. ... One favourable circumstance, in view of the changes of method that are called for, is that we are going to have a continent to rule. When that happens, the different positions of the sun will bar us from uniformity![83]

The 'changes of method' referred to by Hitler were self-evident. The slaughter carried out in Poland would be pursued in the Soviet Union on a much wider scale against a backdrop of general lawlessness. Both the military campaign itself and the subsequent occupation would be markedly different to experiences in Western Europe.

Three months later, in November 1941, Hitler continued in the same vein: 'One mustn't suppose that a regulation applicable to the old Reich or a part of it is automatically applicable to the Kirkenes, say, or the Crimea. There's no possibility of ruling this huge empire from Berlin, and by the methods that have been used hitherto.'[84] By appointing Rosenberg as Reich Minister for the Occupied Eastern Territories, however, with his seat in Berlin,[85] the 'huge empire' in the East *was* in effect being ruled from the German capital. These two aspects of Hitler's policy – limited regulation from Berlin whilst at the same time creating a Berlin-based territorial ministry – could be reconciled only if Hitler intended from the beginning to limit Rosenberg's power as East Minister. The East Ministry would not constitute in any way an independent power base but rather a deflecting mechanism: the authorities in the 'old Reich' would deal directly with Rosenberg's ministry, whilst the true powers in the occupied Soviet territories – Göring's economic organization, Himmler's SS and the Reich Commissars – would be given a free hand to implement their important tasks. As Hitler put it: 'Under no circumstances at all are we allowed to lapse into the mistake of eternal regimentation in the occupied Eastern territories. … As regards the Eastern territories, therefore, I wish only broad instructions to be issued from Berlin; the settlement of day-to-day issues can safely be left in the hands of the respective regional Commissars.'[86]

If one should be wary of attaching too much importance to Hitler's so-called 'table talk', which often constituted vague night-time ramblings on any and every topic, depending on his mood, there exist in addition Martin Bormann's minutes for the 16 July 1941 conference at FHQ. On this occasion, Hitler stated:

> We will thus emphasize once more that we were forced to occupy, to put in order and to secure a territory; in the interest of the inhabitants we had to provide for peace, food, transport etc. etc.; for this reason, our regulation. It should thus not be apparent that a final settlement develops along with it! All necessary measures – shootings, evacuations etc. – we will take and can take in spite of this.[87]

This passage makes it clear that any attempts on the part of the German occupiers to re-establish daily life in the eastern territories – in so far as this in fact took place – should be for the purpose of disguising the development of a 'final settlement' in the East. The 'regulation' of the East Ministry, therefore, served these ends and was quite possibly the reason for it being set up.

In practice, then, the RMO was to shield or disguise the more important 'special tasks' of Göring and Himmler and their subordinate agencies. The

East was to be detached further from the troublesome bonds of the administrative and legal principles of the 'old Reich'.[88] Despite all 'coordinating measures' (*Gleichschaltungsmassnahmen*) which had been carried out in Germany, the bureaucratic structure there remained entrenched.[89] Courts and law codes, though diluted, continued to exist in the 'old Reich'. In the East, on the other hand, all legal restrictions were stripped away.[90] This was deemed necessary by the Nazi occupiers in view of the far-reaching tasks to be carried out there.

Whether Rosenberg was himself aware of the role intended by Hitler for the RMO is unlikely, though the matter is not entirely clear. On 22 July 1941, five days after being appointed as Reich Minister for the Occupied Eastern Territories, Rosenberg gave an address for the German weekly newsreel in which he declared that he saw the purpose of his appointment as being to continue the struggle in the East 'which Adolf Hitler began one day as [an] unknown soldier and completes as Führer of the Reich' and, importantly, to secure 'welfare and public order for the peoples of the East coming under German administration'.[91] It is more likely that Rosenberg genuinely saw the (limited) restoration of civil society in the occupied eastern territories as being at least one of his tasks and that this statement to the press was sincere, rather than him being in the know regarding Hitler's real intentions for the RMO and intentionally providing a false picture of his duties in the East, and one that was in fact less than flattering to him. Indeed, the purpose of his appointment was described in the relevant decree of 17 July 1941 as being 'to re-establish and maintain public order and public life in the newly occupied eastern territories'.[92]

Whatever it was that persuaded Hitler to order the creation of a territorial ministry, it appears that he was not entirely convinced of its desirability. During a meeting with Rosenberg in May 1942, at which Lammers was also present, Hitler said that at the beginning he had not at all been completely in favour of 'making a ministry out of the eastern commission'. Rosenberg was 'astounded, because Dr Lammers had indeed made the establishment of a ministry out to me to be the wish of the Führer. I said to the Führer that at the time I would have made special suggestions. I then requested Dr Lammers to support me in this matter.'[93] It cannot be determined whether Lammers did indeed support Rosenberg or, for that matter, the extent to which Hitler had originally had misgivings regarding the establishment of a ministry. It could be that he decided that this was the best alternative available whilst not being unreservedly in favour of it (much like the selection of Rosenberg himself, perhaps). Although it appears that the original suggestion for the setting up of a ministry came from Rosenberg, this episode indicates not so much that Hitler allowed himself to be talked into it by Rosenberg, but rather that the decision for the creation of a ministry was in fact very much Hitler's own. This would tally with the analysis made here of the reasons for the creation of a territorial ministry in the East and its purpose during the occupation period.

Turning briefly to look at the make-up of the East Ministry, without it becoming an examination of the structure of the ministry itself, as this is not an institutional study, what one sees reinforces the idea of a coordinating ministry, lacking any real power or influence. It was divided into three 'main departments' (*Hauptabteilungen*): policy, administration and economics.[94] As demonstrated above, major policy decisions had essentially been made during the first months of 1941. In any case, Hitler requested Rosenberg in the autumn of 1941, following the latter's problematic visit to Erich Koch's Reich Commissariat Ukraine, 'not to meddle in the internal administration of the Reich Commissariats, but to confine yourself to broad, general directives, which are first to be agreed on with me'![95] The 'Main Department II: Administration', responsible for legal questions, was headed by Ministerialdirektor Dr Ludwig Runte, formerly Regierungspräsident in Arnsberg.[96] The 'Main Department III: Economics' could only have had a coordinating function, as economic policy had been concentrated in the person of Reichsmarschall Göring by mid-February 1941 at the latest, a fact explicitly acknowledged by Rosenberg at the end of April of that year.[97] This probably explains why the 'Main Department III', in contrast to the other two main departments, does not appear to have had an official at its head.[98]

Like the other main departments, the 'Main Department III' consisted of several sub-departments, in this case 'Economic–Political Cooperation', 'Food and Agriculture', 'Forestry and Timber Industry' and 'Special Tasks'.[99] Gustav Schlotterer of the Reich Ministry for Economics and Hans-Joachim Riecke of the Reich Ministry for Food and Agriculture, who were both senior members of the Wi Stab Ost alongside their ministerial functions, headed the first and the second of these departments, respectively. In addition to the expertise they possessed, they were clearly selected for the RMO in order to represent and promote the interests of Göring's economic organization and to avoid work being duplicated. In a 'Report on the Preparatory Work in Questions of the Eastern European Space', written just under a week after the launch of Operation Barbarossa, Rosenberg wrote that the purpose of the appointment of Schlotterer and Riecke was 'to coordinate the political aims with the economic necessities'.[100] This once more demonstrates the balancing act which was incumbent on Rosenberg from the moment Hitler commissioned him to work on concrete preparations for the eastern campaign. Despite his numerous political objectives, which were for him of the utmost importance, Rosenberg (increasingly) recognized – indeed, could not fail to recognize – both the crucial position occupied by, and the considerable high-level support which existed in favour of, economic factors, and was forced constantly to take these into consideration.

The fourth department within the 'Main Department III' of the East Ministry, 'Special Tasks', was led by Oberbereichsleiter Walter Malletke, who, as shown earlier, was the member of Rosenberg's staff who declared himself to be in agreement with the contents of the Green Folder at the fourth session of the Wi Fü Stab Ost on 26 May 1941.[101] The department

'Forestry and Timber Industry' was headed by Ministerialdirigent Johannes Barth.[102] At the end of April 1941, five 'departments', made up of several 'branches', had been envisaged for the future ministry.[103] These departments probably corresponded to what later became the three 'main departments', which were themselves subdivided into 'departments'. Oberbereichsleiter Malletke had initially been foreseen by Rosenberg as the head of the department 'Economic-Political Coordination',[104] one of the five original departments. This department – in effect a main department – most probably became the department 'Economic-Political Cooperation' within the 'Main Department III: Economics', control of which was awarded not to Malletke but to Gustav Schlotterer. These alterations were indicative of the nature of the RMO, the structure of which proved to be very fluid and underwent a series of major changes during the course of its existence. This state of affairs constituted an extension of the pre-invasion situation in which the planning for the future civil administration in the occupied Soviet territories was begun only late in the day as compared with other policy areas and subordinated from day one to the economic planning and the objectives contained therein.

Notes

1. For the minutes of the meeting, see *IMG*, vol. 38, pp. 86–94, doc. 221–L, 'Aktenvermerk'. On the FHQ, a few miles east of Rastenburg, used by Hitler as his command centre from 24 June 1941 onwards, see Warlimont, *Inside Hitler's Headquarters*, pp. 172–178.
2. Halder, *KTB*, III, p. 38, entry for 3 July 1941: 'Es ist also wohl nicht zuviel gesagt, wenn ich behaupte, daß der Feldzug gegen Rußland innerhalb [von] 14 Tagen gewonnen wurde.' Compare this comment with those made in Halder's entry for 11 August 1941; p. 170. See also *TBJG*, II/1, p. 118, entry for 24 July 1941.
3. BA, R 6/21, fo. 101. See also BA-MA, RW 19/164, fos. 139–140, 'Besprechungsnotiz über die Besprechung General Thomas mit General Wagner am 8.7.41 in Quelle', 11 July 1941.
4. See Meyer (ed.), *Generalfeldmarschall Wilhelm Ritter von Leeb: Tagebuchaufzeichnungen*, p. 290, entry for 9 July 1941.
5. BA-MA, RW 19/164, fos. 139–140. See chapter 5, 'Selecting an Administrative Chief', in this study.
6. *IMG*, vol. 38, p. 87: 'Alle notwendige Massnahmen – Erschiessen, Aussiedeln etc. – tun wir trotzdem und können wir trotzdem tun.'
7. Ibid., pp. 87–88: 'Uns muss aber dabei klar sein, dass wir aus diesen Gebieten nie wiederherauskommen. Demgemäss handelt es sich darum: 1.) Nichts für die endgültige Regelung zu verbauen, sondern dieser unter der Hand vorzubereiten; 2.) wir betonen, dass wir die Bringer der Freiheit wären. ... Grundsätzlich kommt es also darauf an, den riesenhaften Kuchen handgerecht zu zerlegen, damit wir ihn erstens beherrschen, zweitens verwalten und drittens ausbeuten können.'
8. Ibid., p. 89: 'Der Reichsmarschall stellt ... fest, dass wir doch zunächst an die Sicherung unserer Ernährung denken müssen, alles andere könne doch erst viel später kommen.' See also p. 90.
9. Ibid., pp. 87 and 89–90. On Leningrad see 'Ordering the Destruction of Leningrad and Moscow' in this chapter.
10. BA, R 6/24, fo. 2, letter from Rosenberg to Lohse, 23 April 1941.

11. Bräutigam, *So hat es sich zugetragen*, p. 340. On Neubacher, see Heilmann, 'Aus dem Kriegstagebuch des Diplomaten Otto Bräutigam', pp. 173–174.
12. BA-MA, RW 4/v. 759, fo. 29.
13. See chapter 5, 'Selecting an Administrative Chief'.
14. See *IMG*, vol. 26, pp. 572–573.
15. Gerlach, *Kalkulierte Morde*, p. 161, fn. 217.
16. For basic information on Kasche, see Heilmann, 'Aus dem Kriegstagebuch des Diplomaten Otto Bräutigam', pp. 172–173. For Himmler's opinion of Kasche see BA, R 43 II/684a, fo. 78, 'Aktennotiz', 15 November 1941.
17. *IMG*, vol. 38, pp. 90–92.
18. Myllyniemi, *Die Neuordnung der baltischen Länder*, p. 62.
19. See BA, R 6/21, fos. 62–63 and 66–67.
20. *IMG*, vol. 38, p. 93.
21. BA, NS 19/3874, fos. 6–7, 'Betrifft: Verwaltung der osteuropäischen Gebiete im Falle ihrer Besetzung', 16 June 1941. See also BA, NS 19/3874, fo. 8, letter from Himmler to Bormann, 21 June 1941.
22. See chapter 8, 'The Standpoint of the Political Planners'.
23. *IMG*, vol. 26, pp. 93–94.
24. Rosenberg's diary entry for 16 July 1941, published in 'Der Kampf gegen die Kirche: Aus unveröffentlichten Tagebüchern Alfred Rosenbergs', *Der Monat*, 1 (1949), no. 10, pp. 26–38, here p. 37: 'Auf gute Zusammenarbeit.' I am grateful to Marc Svetov for providing me with a copy of this article.
25. Ibid., p. 36.
26. Ibid.
27. Heilmann, 'Aus dem Kriegstagebuch des Diplomaten Otto Bräutigam', pp. 136–137, entry for 16 July 1941.
28. Ibid., pp. 137–138, entry for 17 July 1941; Witte et al. (eds), *Dienstkalender*, p. 185, entry for 17 July 1941.
29. BA, R 43 II/688, fos. 20–24, letter from Kritzinger to Reichskabinettsrat Hermann von Stutterheim (Reich Chancellery), 11 July 1941, here fo. 20.
30. Bräutigam, *So hat es sich zugetragen*, p. 343.
31. *IMG*, vol. 29 (1948), pp. 235–237, doc. 1997–PS, 'Erlaß des Führers über die Verwaltung der neu besetzten Ostgebiete', 17 July 1941: 'Um die öffentliche Ordnung und das öffentliche Leben in den neu besetzten Ostgebieten wiederherzustellen und aufrecht zu erhalten, ordne ich an: ...' (p. 235).
32. Moll (ed.), *"Führer-Erlasse"*, pp. 179–180, doc. 93, 'Erlaß des Führers über die Wirtschaft in den neu besetzten Ostgebieten', 29 June 1941, here p. 179: 'In den neu besetzten Ostgebieten ordnet Reichsmarschall Hermann Göring ... alle Maßnahmen an, die zur höchstmöglichen Ausnutzung der vorgefundenen Vorräte und Wirtschaftskapazitäten und zum Ausbau der Wirtschaftskräfte zu Gunsten der deutschen Kriegswirtschaft erforderlich sind.'
33. Ibid., p. 180, doc. 94, 'Erlaß über die Stellvertretung des Führers', 29 June 1941.
34. Witte et al. (eds), *Dienstkalender*, pp. 184–186, entries for 15–20 July 1941. Without providing any supporting evidence, Uwe Mai claims that Himmler was in fact present at the 16 July meeting; Mai, *"Rasse und Raum"*, p. 305.
35. BA, NS 19/3873, fo. 10, letter from Himmler to Bormann, 22 July 1941.
36. Moll (ed.), *"Führer-Erlasse"*, p. 188.
37. Ibid., pp. 189–190, doc. 101, 'Erster Erlaß des Führers über die Einführung der Zivilverwaltung in den neu besetzten Ostgebieten', 17 July 1941, and pp. 191–192, doc. 103, decree from Hitler, 22 July 1941; BA-MA, RW 4/v. 578, fos. 121–122, decree from Hitler, 22 July 1941.
38. PAAA, Pol. Abt. XIII, Nr. 25, R 105192, fos. 198841–198842, 'Betrifft: Stellenbesetzungen für den Fall einer erweiterten Aktion nach Osten', Georg Großkopf, 4 June 1941.

39. Moll, *"Führer-Erlasse"*, p. 195, doc. 107, 'Zweiter Erlaß des Führers über die Einführung der Zivilverwaltung in den neu besetzten Ostgebieten', 20 August 1941; BA-MA, RW 19/175, fos. 203–204, decree from Hitler, 20 August 1941.
40. Bräutigam, *So hat es sich zugetragen*, p. 341.
41. *IMG*, vol. 26, p. 559.
42. On Meyer see Pätzold and Schwarz, *Tagesordnung*, pp. 230–232.
43. BA, R 43 II/690a, fo. 5, 17 July 1941, attachment to letter from Dr Lammers to Reich Minister Rosenberg dated 18 July 1941.
44. Dallin, *German Rule in Russia*, p. 85.
45. *IMG*, vol. 26, p. 587.
46. BA-MA, RW 4/v. 759, fo. 29, attachment to letter from Dr Lammers to Field Marshal Keitel, 20 May 1941; *ADAP, Serie D: 1937–1941*, vol. 12/2, doc. 573, p. 772, 'Aufzeichnung des Vortragenden Legationsrats Großkopf (Abt. Deutschland)', 30 May 1941. See also Müller, 'Industrielle Interessenpolitik', p. 118.
47. BA-MA, RW 4/v. 759, fo. 29; *IMG*, vol. 26, pp. 556–557. In his memoirs, Otto Bräutigam states that Soviet Turkistan was to have been the fifth administrative unit; Bräutigam, *So hat es sich zugetragen*, pp. 301–302.
48. BA, R 43 II/688, fo. 33, letter from Rosenberg to Dr Wilhelm Frick, 9 July 1941.
49. BA-MA, RW 4/v. 759, fo. 29.
50. Hillgruber, *Hitlers Strategie*, p. 539.
51. *IMG*, vol. 36, p. 138; see chapter 7, 'The *Hungerpolitik* in Writing', in this study.
52. BA, R 26 IV/33a, p. 18; see chapter 8, 'Economic and Agricultural Guidelines', in this study.
53. *IMG*, vol. 38, p. 90; see '16 July 1941: the Conference at FHQ' in this chapter.
54. Halder, *KTB*, III, p. 53, entry for 8 July 1941: 'Feststehender Entschluß des Führers ist es, Moskau und Leningrad dem Erdboden gleich zu machen, um zu verhindern, daß Menschen darin bleiben, die wir dann im Winter ernähren müssten. Die Städte sollen durch die Luftwaffe vernichtet werden. Panzer dürfen dafür nicht eingesetzt werden. "Volkskatastrophe, die nicht nur den Bolschewismus, sondern auch das Moskowitertum der Zentren beraubt.".'
55. *TBJG*, II/1, p. 33, entry for 9 July 1941.
56. BA, R 6/34a, fo. 12, 19 September 1941.
57. Meyer (ed.), *Generalfeldmarschall Wilhelm Ritter von Leeb: Tagebuchaufzeichnungen*, pp. 302–303 and 360, entries for 21 July and 20 September 1941: 'Der Schwerpunkt muß zunächst auf die Gewinnung der engen Einschließungslinie gelegt werden, um die Grundlage für eine Beschießung von Leningrad zu schaffen' (p. 360).
58. Quoted in Gerlach, 'Militärische "Versorgungszwänge"', pp. 196–198, from a letter from Wagner to his wife, Elisabeth, dated 9 September 1941: 'Zunächst muß man ja Petersburg schmoren lassen, was sollen wir mit einer 3½ Mill. Stadt, die sich nur auf unser Verpflegungsportemonnaie legt. Sentimentalitäten gibt's dabei nicht' (pp. 196–197).
59. *IMG*, vol. 36, p. 109: 'Aus wirtschaftlichen Überlegungen ist die Eroberung großer Städte nicht erwünscht. Ihre Einschließung ist vorteilhafter.'
60. BA, R 6/34a, fo. 12: 'Die Tendenz des Führers, der die Zerstörung der russischen Großstädte als Voraussetzung der Dauer unserer Macht in Russland ansieht, wurde durch den Reichskommissar noch gefestigt.'
61. BA, NS 19/3882, fos. 13–14, Heydrich to Himmler, 20 October 1941, here fo. 14: 'Meines Erachtens muss in solchen Fällen massenhaft mit Brand- und Sprengbomben gearbeitet werden.'
62. Meyer (ed.), *Generalfeldmarschall Wilhelm Ritter von Leeb: Tagebuchaufzeichnungen*, p. 373, entry for 12 October 1941.
63. See Aly and Heim, *Vordenker der Vernichtung*, pp. 384–385 and 504.
64. BA, NS 19/1739, fos. 4–5, 'Vorgang: Generalplan Ost – Rechtliche, wirtschaftliche u. räumliche Grundlagen des Ostaufbaus', cover sheet from SS-Oberführer Professor Konrad Meyer to Himmler, 28 May 1942.

65. BA, R 49/157a, 'Generalplan Ost – Rechtliche, wirtschaftliche und räumliche Grundlagen des Ostaufbaues', Meyer, pp. 71 and 73.
66. See Gerlach, 'Die Ausweitung der deutschen Massenmorde', pp. 29–32; *IMG*, vol. 36, p. 138.
67. Benz et al. (eds), *Enzyklopädie des Nationalsozialismus*, pp. 622–623.
68. On occupation arrangements in Denmark, see Burleigh, *The Third Reich*, pp. 457–460.
69. Toynbee and Toynbee (eds), *Hitler's Europe*, p. 102.
70. Ibid., p. 100.
71. *IMG*, vol. 26, p. 554; see chapter 5, 'Selecting an Administrative Chief', in this study.
72. *IMG*, vol. 26, pp. 557 and 559; see chapter 5, 'Selecting an Administrative Chief', in this study.
73. Nbg. Dok. PS 1020, fos. 1–15, 'Denkschrift No. 3. Betrifft: UdSSR', 25 April 1941, here fos. 2, 4 and 15.
74. See, for example, Rebentisch, *Führerstaat und Verwaltung*, p. 314.
75. See *TBJG*, I/9, p. 330, entry for 23 May 1941.
76. BA, R 43 II/688, fos. 10–12.
77. Ibid., fos. 10–11.
78. Ibid., fo. 11: 'Reichsleiter Rosenberg und sein Stab sollten m.E. in der Form eingeschaltet werden, dass sie in *politischer* Beziehung sowohl an den Massnahmen der obersten Reichsbehörden ... als auch an den Massnahmen der Reichskommissare mitwirken. ... Auf diese Weise wäre m.E. der politische Einfluss des Reichsleiters Rosenberg und seines Stabes sichergestellt, ohne dass daraus die Gefahr einer Doppelarbeit und schliesslich einer Gegeneinanderarbeit aufträte. Die Reichskommissare der einzelnen grossen Gebietskomplexe würden, wie dies auch bei allen übrigen Reichskommissaren der Fall ist, dem Führer unmittelbar unterstellt.'
79. Ibid.
80. Peter Kleist, *Zwischen Hitler und Stalin 1939–1945* (Athenäum-Verlag, Bonn, 1950), p. 147.
81. Trevor-Roper (ed.), *Hitler's Table Talk*, p. 585, entry for 22 July 1942.
82. Ibid., p. 533, entry for 24 June 1942.
83. Ibid., pp. 18–19, entry for 1–2 August 1941.
84. Ibid., p. 104, entry for 1–2 November 1941. The original reads 'Kirkenaes'. This should be 'Kirkenes' (a town in northern Norway near the borders with Russia and Finland).
85. *IMG*, vol. 29, p. 236. The Reich Commissars had their seats in the East.
86. Henry Picker (ed.), *Hitlers Tischgespräche im Führerhauptquartier 1941–42* (Athenäum-Verlag, Bonn, 1951), p. 117, entry for 22 July 1942: 'In den Fehler des ewigen Reglementierens dürften wir in den besetzten Ostgebieten unter gar keinen Umständen verfallen'; Trevor-Roper (ed.), *Hitler's Table Talk*, p. 590, entry for 22 July 1942.
87. *IMG*, vol. 38, p. 87: 'Wir werden also wieder betonen, dass wir gezwungen waren, ein Gebiet zu besetzen, zu ordnen und zu sichern; im Interesse der Landeseinwohner müssten wir für Ruhe, Ernährung, Verkehr usw. usw. sorgen; deshalb unsere Regelung. Es soll also nicht erkennbar sein, dass sich damit eine endgültige Regelung anbahnt! Alle notwendigen Massnahmen – Erschiessen, Aussiedeln etc. – tun wir trotzdem und können wir trotzdem tun.'
88. Rebentisch, *Führerstaat und Verwaltung*, p. 313.
89. See ibid., p. 326.
90. Jonathan Steinberg, 'The Third Reich Reflected: German Civil Administration in the Occupied Soviet Union, 1941–4', *English Historical Review*, 40 (1995), pp. 620–651, here pp. 632 and 634. For an example of the lack of uniformity in the laws of the 'old Reich' and those of the occupied eastern territories see Steinberg's discussion of the debate over the definition of a Jew, pp. 643–647.
91. BA, NS 8/71, fos. 2–4, 'Ansprache für die deutsche Wochenschau', 22 July 1941, here fo. 3.
92. *IMG*, vol. 29, p. 235; see '16 July 1941: the Conference at FHQ' in this chapter.

93. *IMG*, vol. 27, pp. 283–294, doc. 1520-PS, 'Vermerk über eine Unterredung mit dem Führer im Führerhauptquartier am 8.5.42', 13 May 1942, here p. 294: 'Ich war erstaunt, weil mir Dr. Lammers gerade die Gründung eines Ministeriums als den Wunsch des Führers hingestellt hatte. Ich sagte dem Führer, dass ich noch seinerzeit Sondervorschläge gemacht hätte. Ich bat dann Dr. Lammers, mich in dieser Angelegenheit zu unterstützen.'
94. In a discussion on 3 July 1941 and again in a letter dated 8 July, Finance Minister Lutz Graf Schwerin von Krosigk had recommended to Rosenberg that three 'large groups' be set up: administration, economics, technical matters; BA, R 2/30518.
95. Bräutigam, *So hat es sich zugetragen*, pp. 612–613: 'Ich bitte Sie daher, sich in die innere Verwaltung der Reichskommissariate nicht einzumischen, sondern sich auf die mit mir vorher abzustimmenden großen generellen Richtlinien zu beschränken' (p. 613).
96. See *IMG*, vol. 26, p. 564; Gerlach, *Kalkulierte Morde*, p. 158, fn. 203.
97. *IMG*, vol. 26, p. 563.
98. See ibid.; BA, R 6/30, fo. 12, 'Reichsministerium für die besetzten Ostgebiete', 20 December 1941.
99. Gerlach, *Kalkulierte Morde*, p. 158, fn. 201.
100. *IMG*, vol. 26, p. 586. See also PAAA, Pol. Abt. XIII, Nr. 25, R 105192, fol. 198823, letter from Privy Councillor Großkopf to Gustav Hilger, 19 November 1941.
101. See chapter 8, 'The Standpoint of the Political Planners'.
102. BA, R 6/30, fo. 12.
103. *IMG*, vol. 26, pp. 560–565.
104. Ibid., p. 563.

CHAPTER 10

CONCLUSIONS

The evaluation and analysis of the findings of this study have been ongoing during its course. Simply repeating all the arguments raised and points made in the study and the conclusions reached is not the purpose of this final chapter. To do so would have little merit in itself and, furthermore, run the risk of being tiresome for the reader. The purpose of this chapter is rather to summarize the main arguments and draw such conclusions which relate directly to the aims of the study and the principal reasons for which the study was undertaken in the first place.

At the outset, this study set itself three central aims: (1) to trace the development of both the political and the economic planning by senior bodies within the state and Nazi Party apparatuses for the German occupation policy in the Soviet Union; (2) to examine the extent to which these two aspects of planning and the approaches and objectives contained therein were compatible with each other; and (3) to thoroughly consider the role of Alfred Rosenberg, not only in the political preparations for the occupation – for which he was responsible – but also with regard to his awareness of the economic plans, his involvement in their formulation and the extent of his support for them. In drawing conclusions from the work carried out in order to accomplish these three aims, the main arguments contained in the study will now be summarized and evaluated.

Neither the political nor the economic planning for German occupation policy in the conquered Soviet territories took place over the entire twelve-month period which this study has examined. As has been demonstrated, the economic planning only started to take shape at the end of 1940, approximately halfway through the period in question. The concrete political planning was carried out over an even shorter period of time, beginning as it did essentially only three and a half months before the commencement of the German invasion and, hence, four and a half months prior to the official appointment of the civil (i.e., political) administrators in the occupied Soviet territories. However, Hitler took his 'definite decision' to invade the Soviet Union during the first half of 1941 at the end of July 1940, and reached what was for him effectively the point of no return some time during the first two weeks of November, confirming this resolution in writing in his 'Directive No. 21: Case Barbarossa', issued on 18 December 1940. Thus, as this study has dealt with the development of political and economic planning for the German occupation of the European USSR, it has been necessary to examine the period between July and December 1940, during which the decision to invade was taken.

The highly questionable prerequisite for ultimate victory in the German–Soviet war was a successful completion of the military campaign in the space of two or three months, which was in turn dependent on the ability of the German supply apparatus to provide the troops with sufficient fuel, ammunition and food. Although economic gain was the key motivation for waging war against the Soviet Union in mid-1941, the undertaking was in no way based on economic certainties. Subsequent to the frank but limited exchange of views between Reichsmarschall Göring's economic advisers in January 1941 as to the economic repercussions of waging war against the Soviet Union, at a time when the decision to invade had in any case already been taken by Hitler, there was no serious attempt within the corridors of power to engage in a critical analysis of the economic implications of an invasion and occupation of the European USSR or, crucially, the existence of potential alternative scenarios should the military campaign and, therefore, the programme of economic exploitation not go according to plan. In the case of the Soviet Union, where ideological motives combined with what were perceived as strategic and economic necessities, Hitler's mindset was such that potential difficulties were expected to be 'worked around'. It was up to the economic planners to find a solution, whatever that might be, to the perceived problem. This insistence effectively dismissed any air of uncertainty which had existed within the ranks of the economic planners at the beginning of 1941 and assisted in paving the way for the acceptance and advancement of the concept of starving millions of Soviet citizens for agricultural gain. The assertion, present in recent literature on the subject,[1] that Herbert Backe was the instigator of the Hungerpolitik and the driving force behind its development and radicalization, has been reinforced in this study and the case for taking this line of argument has been strengthened.

Hitler's choice of Alfred Rosenberg, first of all to plan the future political structure of the occupied Soviet territories and then to act as chief administrator of the region indicates the deficiencies of any other potential candidate rather than the aptness of Rosenberg for the position, as Hitler's claim that he had 'no better man than Rosenberg' demonstrates. A separate but related decision on Hitler's part was the creation of a ministry for the territories in question. Although Hitler instructed that a Berlin-based territorial ministry be set up, he opted at the same time for limited regulation of the occupied Soviet territories from Berlin. These two aspects of Hitler's policy could be reconciled only if Hitler intended from the beginning to limit Rosenberg's power as East Minister. In accordance with this line of thinking, the East Ministry would not constitute in any way an independent power base but rather a deflecting mechanism: the central authorities in the 'old Reich' would deal directly with Rosenberg's ministry, whilst the true powers in the occupied Soviet territories – Göring's economic organization, the SS and the Reich Commissars – would be given a free hand to implement their more important 'special tasks'. Detaching the occupied Soviet territories further from the bureaucratic bonds of the 'old Reich' was deemed necessary by the Nazi leadership in view of the far-reaching tasks to be carried out there.

These far-reaching occupation tasks included undertakings which can be classified neither as being of a specifically political-administrative nature nor as being directly related to economic policy. These tasks, which consisted of the murder of racial and political 'undesirables', the expulsion of substantial sections of the indigenous population from their homes and the resettlement of peoples of 'Germanic' racial stock in the occupied Soviet territories, can essentially be summed up as 'population policy' and have been dealt with in chapter 6 of this study. The responsibility for the preparation and implementation of these policies fell, above all, to Heinrich Himmler's SS. Though separate, there are clear links, both theoretical and practical, between this aspect of National Socialist eastern policy and the work of the political and economic planners. Examples dealt with in this study are the work of the Bureau Rosenberg for the resettlement of certain population groups, particularly the Soviet Jews, and the congruity of plans for mass murder, as the oft-cited figure of thirty million Soviet deaths indicates. With regard to National Socialist 'population policy' in the occupied Soviet territories, this study has confirmed the historiographical position that no pre-invasion order was given for the genocide of Soviet Jewry, but that rather a territorial solution – though not planned out in detail at the time of the launch of Operation Barbarossa – was initially envisaged and had been approved by Germany's supreme leadership.

In view of the substantial time discrepancy in the point at which concrete planning began for the economic aspects of the future occupation and for the political aspects, and the preference enjoyed by the economic objectives, it is clear – a point repeated throughout this study – that the economic objectives of the occupation were given precedence over the political objectives by Germany's supreme leadership. This can be seen, to name but a handful of examples, in the repeated and explicit approval given by Hitler to the plans formulated by the economic experts,[2] something which he failed to grant the political plans drawn up by the Bureau Rosenberg; in the report produced by the War Economy and Armaments Office at the end of June 1941, which gave the main reason for the decision to invade the Soviet Union as being the necessity 'to broaden at all costs the economic basis of Germany's prosecution of the war';[3] in Reinhard Heydrich's assertion, made at the beginning of July, that the political pacification of the Soviet territories was a prerequisite for the economic pacification, and not vice versa;[4] and in Göring's declaration at the 16 July conference in FHQ – a conference hosted by Hitler, who did not contradict Göring's statement – that Germany must 'first of all' think about securing her sustenance, whereas everything else could be left until 'much later'.[5]

That economic aims were of crucial importance within the strategy for the invasion and occupation of the Soviet Union cannot be doubted. A further context in which this importance can be seen is the way in which the economic objectives of the campaign and occupation affected – and to a large extent dictated – what initially appear to have been purely military issues. Two telling examples of this are the decision not to conquer large cities, but rather to lay siege to them in order to starve the population before razing the cities to the ground; and the disagreement between Hitler and his senior generals during July and August 1941 over whether Moscow – politically of primary concern – or the economically vital areas of the Ukraine and the Caucasus should be the military priority. Hitler, arguing for the latter, succeeded in carrying the day.

Although economic objectives occupied a position of pre-eminence from the beginning of 1941 onwards, it is important to make clear that the consensus between the different groups of planners regarding the content of the political and economic plans themselves was in fact more wide-ranging and extensive than has hitherto been thought. The Economic Staff East's economic-political guidelines of 23 May 1941 constitute the most detailed and explicit exposition of the economic proposals that exists. An attempt has been made here to emphasize the harmony between the Hungerpolitik described in its pages and the political considerations of the envisaged occupation policy. The economic policy contained in the guidelines had 'received the approval of the highest authorities, as it is in accordance with the political tendencies (preservation of the little Russians, preservation of the Caucasus, of the Baltic provinces, [and] Belarus at the expense of the driving back of the greater Russians)'.[6] This passage demonstrates the agreement that existed in the economic and political plans for the various territories whose occupation was foreseen: the Ukraine, the Caucasus, the Baltic States, Belarus and Russia. The extent of agreement on major issues among the economic planners, the political planners and those who ultimately made the final decisions on state policy, above all Hitler, was in fact substantial.

The most important issues where wide-ranging agreement was reached should be remarked on here. The fundamental decision to break the occupied territory up into administrative subdivisions under the jurisdiction of political, and not military, officials appears to have been made by Hitler in early March 1941. This decision was accepted as a matter of course by Rosenberg in his very first planning paper of 2 April and not only made more specific but also elaborated on by the proposal that the treatment of the different territories should vary.[7] By the second half of May 1941 at the latest, with Rosenberg setting the pace, the different parties involved in planning the shape of the future political administration in the occupied

Soviet territories had come to an agreement to limit the number of Reich Commissariats to four,[8] a decision which subsequently found the agreement of Hitler.[9] Thereafter, this whole approach was taken on board and repeatedly advocated from all sides.[10]

The specifics of these administrative units which were planned by Rosenberg, particularly their geographical layout, were undoubtedly convenient for the purposes of Hitler and the rest of the National Socialist leadership. Not only was it agreed that the four Reich Commissariats – 'Ostland', Ukraine, Caucasus and Russia – would all be treated differently, but in many cases the nature of the treatment itself was agreed upon. The Baltic States would be united with Belarus to form a protectorate in anticipation of later annexation to the Reich.[11] As the Soviet Union's most oil-rich area, the protection of the Caucasus from the worst effects of military hostilities was viewed by all concerned as being of vital importance and the maintenance of high oil production as being the number one priority in that region.[12] The Caucasus was to take the form of a federal state.[13] According to the instructions of the economic planners, even Belarus – despite being a so-called 'deficit territory' in terms of its grain production – was to be handled 'carefully', in part for political reasons.[14]

Agreement between Rosenberg's staff, the economic planners, the security forces of the SS and police and the senior political leadership regarding the treatment to be meted out to the fourth Reich Commissariat, Russia, and its people was near universal.[15] In addition to preventing the Russian empire from rising again in the future, the planners intended to significantly weaken the Reich Commissariat Russia itself through an extremely harsh treatment of the territory. Its inhabitants should suffer more than those of any other region. It would not be going too far to describe the central Russia envisaged by the National Socialist leadership and planning staffs, particularly Moscow and the surrounding area, as a zone of death. As its administrative chief, this territory required 'an absolutely *ruthless* personality',[16] who would completely annihilate 'the Bolshevik-Jewish state administration', carry out 'a very extensive economic exploitation' and allocate large swathes of Russian land to the neighbouring territories.[17] Russia's major cities were to be razed to the ground. 'No accumulation of Wehrmacht tasks'[18] was intended in the Moscow area because the region was to be sealed off from the source of its food supplies and would, therefore, be unable to support German troops stationed there. The population of this territory would 'face the most terrible famine'[19] and thirty million people would starve in a 'blazing strip' between Moscow and the Ural Mountains as a result of the removal of all foodstuffs from the area.[20] In this matter, Rosenberg and his staff did not require any persuasion from the officials in the Reich Ministry for Food and Agriculture or the Office of the Four-Year Plan. The nature of the treatment foreseen by Rosenberg for this territory was highly compatible with the plans drawn up by the economic experts and was indeed recognized as such by the latter.[21] If the division of the occupied territory into Reich Commissariats and the formulation of differing policies for each region are examples of the economic planners agreeing with proposals put forward and developed by Rosenberg, then the acknowledgement of the primary importance in German occupation policy of an extensive exploitation of Soviet agricultural produce and raw materials is an example of an aspect – or, rather, *the* aspect – of the proposed economic policy being approved of and indeed championed by Rosenberg. This will be returned to shortly.

When it came to the fundamental aspects of 'population policy', there was also consensus between the leading figures. This can be seen in the proposal to transport the Soviet Jews further eastwards,[22] and, in the long term, to resettle people of 'Germanic' stock in the East.[23i] Even when it came to the hotly disputed question of whether to maintain or abolish the Soviet Union's collective farms, agreement was eventually reached by most of the key players, if only in the short term.[24] Five weeks after the military campaign began, however, it was economics supremo Göring who indicated that the life of the collective farms would be limited,[25] a stance which was fully in accordance with the position held by the political planners around Rosenberg. Such was the extent of agreement on important aspects of policy that one can in fact talk of a wide-ranging consensus on the key short-term issues relating to the occupation of the conquered Soviet territories.

In addition to dealing with the aspects of proposed occupation policy over which agreement was reached by the planning groups, it is also necessary to deal with the issues regarding which wide-ranging agreement was not reached. The political aims of the planners around Rosenberg and the economic aims of Backe and his colleagues were not entirely in accordance with each other when it came to the Ukraine, and the treatment of this territory constituted the principal point of dispute amongst the political and economic planners. The Ukraine was not only the place where the economic and political objectives diverged most significantly but also the most important territory for both groups of planners, as well as for Hitler himself, as he explicitly stated during the conference at FHQ on 16 July 1941.[26]

On the part of Rosenberg and his staff, the central political aim for the Ukraine was future independence, whatever this actually meant for them in concrete terms.[27] This, however, was later rejected out of hand by Hitler,[28] for whom nurturing an independent Ukraine as one of several buffer states against Greater Russia was not necessary – the job of keeping the rump of Russia at bay would be done by Germany alone. In any case, Hitler made no differentiation between the different Soviet peoples; for him, they were all 'subhumans'. Although the establishment of 'independence' in the Ukraine was Rosenberg's long-term aim for the territory,[29] he nevertheless anticipated a period of preparation leading up to that. Hitler's appointment of Erich Koch as Reich Commissar in the Ukraine, however, thwarted from the outset Rosenberg's hopes of exerting any significant influence on the policy pursued there.

Although Rosenberg's ideas and his role in the planning in general have already been repeatedly referred to above whilst dealing with the extent to which the different plans were compatible, it is necessary to address Rosenberg's position directly. It is evident from the various papers he produced at the time that he was aware by early May 1941 at the latest of at least the general nature of the main proposals being put forward by the economic planners, though quite feasibly a great deal more, and was clearly in agreement with them regarding the harshness necessary in the occupied Soviet territories in order to provide the German people with additional foodstuffs. Although certain members of his staff expressed reservations when it came to the proposed policy of complete exploitation of the economic resources of the occupied Soviet territories,[30] Rosenberg ultimately made explicit his own approval of the Hungerpolitik.[31]

What marked Rosenberg out more than anything from the likes of Göring, Backe and Riecke was his awareness that the best way to maximize the amount of grain which Germany could obtain from the occupied Soviet territories whilst at the same time minimizing the destruction of agricultural produce and the dislocation of production was to win the bulk of the native population over to voluntary cooperation. His approach can be summed up in the following quote from his speech of 20 June 1941: '... there is a difference, as to whether after a few years I have won 40 million people to voluntary cooperation or whether I must place a soldier behind every peasant.'[32] Rosenberg had no qualms about the *nature* of the policy developed by the economic planners; his conception differed regarding methods of approach and implementation. His belief in winning over the vast bulk of the indigenous population for cooperation with Germany, shared by members of his staff,[33] was one which he held throughout the entire planning period and is particularly apparent in his speech of 20 June 1941. Even combined with a more measured approach from the economic organization, however, this would not have been an easy task, given Rosenberg's own ostracism of Russians, the largest group within the Soviet population. Indeed, around half of the population were ethnic Russians.[34] Something else that Rosenberg apparently failed to recognize was the price that not only Russia but also the Ukraine and its inhabitants would pay if the Hungerpolitik was in fact implemented. All concerned foresaw a particularly ruthless treatment of Moscow and the surrounding area, but, although it was far from being a 'deficit territory', the Ukraine would also inevitably suffer a great deal, precisely because the supposed grain 'surpluses' which were to be obtained from the occupied Soviet territories could only be obtained, if indeed at all, by the employment of severe measures in this very territory, which was widely believed to be the Soviet Union's most grain-rich.

Significantly, Rosenberg perceived these two issues – the securing of foodstuffs and raw materials on the one hand and Ukrainian independence on the other – to be closely, indeed inextricably, linked. In order to secure Germany's foodstuffs and raw materials and make it free from the danger of any future naval blockade, Rosenberg believed it was necessary to set up a free Ukrainian state, which would act as a barricade against any future expansion of Greater Russia and hence remove the perceived 'nightmare' of the Russian empire from Germany's eastern border.³⁵ Either he was not aware of, or refused to take on board, the fact that the majority of his colleagues in the state and Party leadership anticipated that Germany itself, and not the Ukraine, would assume the task of removing the supposed Soviet threat from the European arena. From their point of view, allowing, let alone encouraging, the establishment of an independent Ukraine would only complicate matters.

Now that the three aims of this study have been dealt with separately, it is worth bringing the various conclusions together. Collaboration and cooperation between the economic and political planners were more systematic, sustained and extensive than has hitherto been thought. In a report on his preparatory work for the occupation of the Soviet territories compiled just under a week after the commencement of Operation Barbarossa, Rosenberg confirmed that the 'most extensive agreement' had been reached regarding 'eastern questions' during talks concerning the objectives of the Economic Command Staff East which had taken place over the preceding two months with the leading figures in the realm of agricultural and economic planning – Backe, Thomas, Riecke, Körner, Schubert and Schlotterer – as well as others. Rosenberg's talks with Schlotterer, for example, had taken place 'almost daily'.³⁶ Although political considerations remained of primary importance for him throughout, Rosenberg nevertheless showed a keen interest in the economic aspects of the forthcoming occupation and demonstrated a willingness both to involve himself in the preparations and to seek conformity between his own aims and those of the economic planners.

If the German military campaign against the Soviet Union had in fact gone to plan and been successfully brought to an end in the space of six to twelve weeks, would Rosenberg's long-term aims for a Neuordnung of the occupied Soviet territories have stood any chance of realization? Given the central role of an 'independent' Ukraine in Rosenberg's plans to establish a substantial buffer against the remains of Greater Russia in the form of three state structures on the one hand, and Hitler's declaration that he had a German protectorate of approximately twenty-five years' duration in mind for the Ukraine on the other,³⁷ the answer would probably have to be 'no'. Indeed, it was above all with regard to the long-term political future of the occupied Soviet territories where Hitler and Rosenberg's respective concepts most fundamentally diverged.³⁸ For the very reason that those issues on which the two men clearly did not see eye to eye related to the long-term and not to the immediate future, Hitler presumably deemed it unnecessary to clarify such issues with Rosenberg prior to a campaign which all concerned expected to be brought to a victorious conclusion within three months. Perhaps Rosenberg would have had to elaborate on exactly what he meant by Ukrainian 'independence', which was self-evidently not used in the same sense as non-Nazis might use the term, either then or now.

By the same token, however, it would have been necessary for the economic planners to expand on their own proposal that a Hungerpolitik be pursued in the occupied Soviet territories. The Hungerpolitik was merely a concept – there was no clear idea among the economic planners as to how this policy was in fact to be implemented. The whole idea was too insufficiently thought through to be described as a 'plan'. Thus, in the absence of a detailed programme of action developed by Germany's economic planners, it is almost impossible to determine how realistic such a concept indeed was. A further problem is the fact that the German–Soviet war took a very different course to that which had been expected, indeed, taken for granted, by the German planning apparatus. Predictably, no contingency plans existed for such an eventuality. Given that German projections for grain hauls and economic gain in general were based on a scenario in which major hostilities were rapidly brought to an end and the European USSR was occupied and pacified, it is clear that the results did not correspond to the projections, but it is far more problematic to determine whether or not they would have done if the war had progressed as planned. Ultimately, however, even if the invasion had proceeded in accordance with German expectations, major transport difficulties and the dislocation and disruption caused by military hostilities, particularly in Soviet agriculture, would have been enough to ensure that economic gain, at least in the first year of the occupation and quite possibly in subsequent years, would have been significantly less than the economic planners had envisaged.

As an extension of the policy of sealing off the 'deficit territories' of the north and west of the European Soviet Union from the 'surplus territories' of the south and east, the Hungerpolitik envisaged that the resources of the latter would be incorporated in the long term into the economic system of German-occupied Europe. The aim of this incorporation was the substitution of overseas imports to the Continent by imports from the food-producing economy of the former Soviet territories, which would supplement agricultural production in German-occupied Europe and constitute a lasting and considerable addition to its productive capacity. The creation of such a Großraumwirtschaft, so National Socialist thinking went, would make German-occupied Europe safe from all threat of blockade and enable Germany to avoid the fate which had befallen it during the First World War twenty-five years earlier.

In theory, Rosenberg would almost certainly have welcomed such a development, given that he had repeatedly stressed during the months of April to June 1941 the importance of securing Germany's sustenance,[39] and referred in his diary entry of 16 July 1941 to the task he had received from Hitler as that of making Germany independent from overseas imports.[40] In practice, however, it would undoubtedly have involved massive economic and social upheaval in the Ukraine and, given traditional National Socialist methods, countless deaths. Thus, we return to the question of methods of approach and implementation and the evident discrepancy between those advocated by Rosenberg and the political planners and those proposed by the economic planners. In any case, it is quite likely that, once the victory against the Soviet Union had been won, Rosenberg would ultimately have demonstrated that he lacked the requisite pragmatism and ruthlessness in furthering his own interests to stay the course in the German-occupied Soviet territories and been replaced by someone judged more suitable for the tasks at hand.

In conclusion, it can be stated that German occupation policy in the Soviet Union was built from the beginning on shaky foundations due to a fundamental disagreement regarding the practical approach to policy implementation. Unlike most of the other key figures, Rosenberg differentiated between the different peoples in the Soviet Union and argued for the importance of winning over the bulk of the native population in most of the territories to voluntary cooperation in order to ease the implementation of both the political and the economic objectives. Moreover, a consensus on the Ukraine which satisfied both the economic and the political planners was, crucially, never reached. Whether it influenced his efforts to coordinate his plans with those of the economic experts or not, it is clear that Rosenberg recognized in advance of the invasion that he was not going to have the kind of power which he had originally expected at the time of his initiation into the proceedings by Hitler at the beginning of April 1941.[41] Thus, it was inevitable that the failure prior to the invasion to reach agreement on all major policy areas and on the exact jurisdiction of each of the key figures in the German occupation regime resulted in an atmosphere of mistrust and competition when the time came for theory to be put into practice. Whilst the unexpected course of the German–Soviet war and the necessity to adapt policy to the ever-shifting military situation played a major role in bringing about the administrative chaos, power struggles and wide-ranging policy disputes witnessed during the German occupation, it is fair to say that the roots of this discord can be found in the planning phase for the occupation.

In the introduction to this study, it was argued that recent literature on the pre-invasion planning for German occupation policy in the Soviet Union has for the most part failed to provide a clear and structured picture of the gradual development of these plans, that an examination of the simultaneous development of plans by the economic planners on the one hand and the political planners on the other, the extent of agreement between those involved and the compatibility of their respective plans has not yet been systematically undertaken, and that, as a result, collaboration between different groups of planners and the extent to which this took place have been barely touched upon. The details and analysis provided in the main body of this study and the evaluation of the evidence supplied in this conclusion have hopefully gone some way towards remedying the existence of such gaps in the secondary literature. Furthermore, this study should not – and hopefully does not – occupy a place on its own in the existing secondary literature on Germany during the years 1933 to 1945. Both the research carried out for the study and the conclusions drawn here contribute to some of the major and ongoing debates in this field. These include the concept prevalent in nationalist circles of Germany's right to colonial land in 'the East'; the dispute regarding the extent to which a polycratic form of rule existed in National Socialist Germany; the question as to how much importance was attached in the decision-making process at all levels of governance to argumentation on a perceived 'rational' basis on the one hand and to ideology on the other hand; and the issues surrounding the Nazi genocide in the occupied Soviet territories, not least its motivations and progressive radicalization, explored here in the planning rather than the practice.

As a result of the findings of this study, it is now clear that there was close and constant intercommunication between those responsible for preparing a workable administrative and political structure for the occupied Soviet territories, above all Rosenberg and his staff, and those charged with formulating the economic policy to be pursued there, with senior members of the RMEL and the VJPB at the forefront of preparations in this area. Furthermore, it has been established that there was explicit and enthusiastic agreement between both sets of planners and the supreme political and military leadership on a wide range of central aspects of policy. The involvement of planners in areas which were not their customary realms of expertise and the overlap between different spheres of jurisdiction have also been shown to have been more extensive than hitherto thought. Although this study has concentrated, above all, on those 'specialists' who were responsible for formulating German policy in the occupied territories of the Soviet Union, it is clear that the coordination of all major strands of planning ultimately took place via the authoritative voice in National Socialist Germany, particularly in matters pertaining to the Soviet Union and its envisaged future as German colonial land, Hitler.

Further work is naturally required on individual aspects of the subject matter addressed by this study, as well as on cooperation in general between different state and Party agencies in National Socialist Germany. One such aspect relating directly to the work carried out here is the extent or lack of opposition in the various ministries and offices involved in the preparations for 'Barbarossa' and its aftermath to the plans being formulated, whilst another pertinent issue is how many – and which – officials were in fact initiated into the political and economic planning for the invasion and occupation of the Soviet Union and when. Whilst these and other such topics lie beyond the scope of this particular study and cannot, therefore, be addressed by it, it is to be hoped that the content and conclusions found here contribute to stimulating further research in the area.

Notes

1. See, above all, Gerlach, *Kalkulierte Morde*, pp. 46–76.
2. For examples see *IMG*, vol. 36, p. 140; BA, R 26 IV/33a, p. 3.
3. BA-MA, RW 19/473, fo. 174.
4. BA, R 70 Sowjetunion/32, fo. 5.
5. *IMG*, vol. 38, p. 39.
6. Ibid., vol. 36, p. 140.
7. Ibid., vol. 26, pp. 548 and 577.
8. For Thomas (5 May 1941): Müller, 'Industrielle Interessenpolitik', p. 118; for Rosenberg/Stuckart/the SD (20 May 1941): BA-MA, RW 4/v. 759, fo. 29; for Leibbrandt (29 May 1941): *ADAP, Serie D: 1937–1941*, vol. 12/2, p. 772.

9. See BA-MA, RW 4/v. 759, fo. 29 (20 May 1941); *IMG*, vol. 26, p. 587.
10. For Thomas (5 May 1941): Müller, 'Industrielle Interessenpolitik', p. 118; for Bräutigam (June 1941): Gibbons, 'Allgemeine Richtlinien', p. 261; for Himmler (24 June 1941): BA, NS 19/2803, fo. 2; for Stuckart (4 July 1941): BA, R 43 II/688, fo. 10; for Rosenberg (16 July 1941): *IMG*, vol. 38, p. 89.
11. See BA D-H, ZM 1683, Bd. 1, fos. 105–106; for Rosenberg (8 May 1941): *IMG*, vol. 26, pp. 574 and 577; for Hitler (16 July 1941): *IMG*, vol. 38, p. 89.
12. For Rosenberg (2 April 1941): *IMG*, vol. 26, p. 552; for Thomas (5 May 1941): Müller, 'Industrielle Interessenpolitik', p. 118.
13. For Rosenberg (8 May, 20 June 1941): *IMG*, vol. 26, pp. 578 and 624; for the Foreign Office (29 May 1941): *ADAP, Serie D: 1937–1941*, vol. 12/2, p. 772.
14. *IMG*, vol. 36, pp. 142–143.
15. For the Wi Stab Ost (23 May 1941): *IMG*, vol. 36, pp. 138, 141, 145 and 156; for Rosenberg (7 April, 20 June 1941): *IMG*, vol. 26, pp. 557 and 622; for Bräutigam (June 1941): Gibbons, 'Allgemeine Richtlinien', p. 260.
16. *IMG*, vol. 26, p. 557.
17. Ibid., p. 549.
18. Müller, 'Industrielle Interessenpolitik', p. 118.
19. *IMG*, vol. 36, p. 141.
20. Gersdorff, *Soldat im Untergang*, p. 93; Gerlach, 'Deutsche Wirtschaftsinteressen', pp. 270–271.
21. See *IMG*, vol. 36, p. 147.
22. For Rosenberg (7 April 1941): Nbg. Dok. PS 1018, fos. 15 and 20–21.
23. For Rosenberg (2 April, 8 May 1941): *IMG*, vol. 26, pp. 550 and 574.
24. For Thomas (20 February 1941): Thomas, *Geschichte*, p. 517; for Rosenberg (25 April, 8 May 1941): Nbg. Dok. PS 1020, p. 6; *IMG*, vol. 26, p. 578; for the Wi Stab Ost (23 May 1941): *IMG*, vol. 36, p. 146; for Bräutigam (June 1941): Gibbons, 'Allgemeine Richtlinien', p. 259; for Heydrich: BA, R 70 Sowjetunion/32, fo. 10; for Backe: Kehrl, *Krisenmanager im Dritten Reich*, p. 223.
25. BA, R 26 I/13, fo. 4.
26. *IMG*, vol. 38, p. 91.
27. For Rosenberg (2 & 7 April, 7 & 8 May 1941): *IMG*, vol. 26, p. 551; Nbg. Dok. PS 1018, fo. 30; *IMG*, vol. 26, pp. 567, 573 and 577–578; for Bräutigam: Gibbons, 'Allgemeine Richtlinien', p. 258.
28. See BA, R 6/34a, fo. 12 (18 September 1941); BA, R 43 II/688, fos. 126–127 (1 October 1941).
29. See *IMG*, vol. 26, pp. 567 (7 May 1941) and 619 (20 June 1941).
30. For Bräutigam (June 1941): Gibbons, 'Allgemeine Richtlinien', p. 259.
31. See BA-MA, RW 19/739, fos. 135–136 (26 May 1941); *IMG*, vol. 26, p. 622 (20 June 1941).
32. *IMG*, vol. 26, pp. 619–620.
33. For Rosenberg (29 April, 7 May 1941): *IMG*, vol. 26, pp. 562 and 567–568 (Ukraine); for Bräutigam (June 1941): Gibbons, 'Allgemeine Richtlinien', pp. 259 and 261. This approach was not to be taken with the Reich Commissariat Russia.
34. Burleigh, *The Third Reich*, p. 537.
35. *IMG*, vol. 26, p. 573.
36. Ibid., p. 586.
37. BA, R 43 II/688, fos. 126–127 (1 October 1941).
38. On this see Dallin, *German Rule in Russia*, p. 49.
39. See *IMG*, vol. 26, pp. 551 (2 April 1941), 562 (29 April 1941), 567, 573 (7 May 1941), 622 and 626 (20 June 1941).
40. 'Der Kampf gegen die Kirche', p. 36.
41. See BA, R 6/21, fos. 66–67 (14 June 1941).

Appendices

1. Timeline of Key Events, July 1940–July 1941

1940

3 July	Colonel-General Halder assigns Colonel von Greiffenberg, Chief of the Operations Department in the Army General Staff, to examine how to carry out a military strike against the Soviet Union in order to force recognition of Germany's dominant role in Europe.
21 July	Hitler meets with the commanders-in-chief of the three branches of the armed forces, Field Marshal Keitel and General Jodl and speaks for the first time about the possibility of an invasion of the USSR. Hitler refers for the first time to the post-invasion occupation of Soviet territories.
28 July	Rear Admiral Fricke, the Chief of the Operations Department in the Naval War Staff, presents his 'Reflections on Russia' to Grand Admiral Raeder; Fricke argues that obtaining Lebensraum in the Soviet Union would secure Germany for the future by providing both 'the necessary living space' and 'those goods which are vital in wartime'.
31 July	Hitler, addressing the heads of the OKW, army and navy, announces his 'definite decision to deal with Russia' in the spring of 1941.
10 August	A military-geographical study of the European USSR produced by the Army General Staff judges the Ukraine to be 'both agriculturally and industrially the most valuable part of the Soviet Union'.

26 September	During a one-to-one presentation for Hitler, Raeder proposes a Mediterranean strategy as an alternative to an invasion of the Soviet Union.
10 October	In a report sent to Hasso von Etzdorf, the representative of the Foreign Office with the OKH, Gebhardt von Walther, an official in the German embassy in Moscow, argues that an occupation of the Ukraine, the Baltic and Belarus would be more of a burden for Germany's economic position than a help. The report is then passed on by Etzdorf to Halder, who, despite meeting with Hitler on 4 November, two days after receipt of the document, does not appear to bring it up.
1 November	Lieutenant-General Erich Stud, head of the section Industrial Armaments of the Army in the Army Weaponry Office, meets with officers from various departments within the Wi Rü Amt to discuss the setting up of an organization to take care of the seizure of 'the most important military-economic industrial plants and raw material deposits' in the European USSR.
6 November	Göring informs the top functionaries of the Four-Year Plan organization of the intentions of the political leadership towards the Soviet Union.
12–13 November	Soviet Foreign Minister Molotov visits Berlin for two days of discussions with Hitler, Ribbentrop and Göring.
18 December	Hitler issues 'Directive No. 21: Case Barbarossa', in which he instructs the German armed forces to be prepared, even before the end of the war against Britain, to crush the Soviet Union in a rapid campaign. Rosenberg gives Georg Leibbrandt, head of the Eastern Office in the APA, the task of drafting a plan for the possible future administration of the Soviet Union.
Christmas holidays	Backe redrafts the RMEL's annual report on the food situation in Germany; he feels that the first and second versions, produced in November and December 1940, respectively, do not portray the food situation dramatically enough.

1941

9 January	In a speech to the military leadership, Hitler declares that the destruction of the Soviet Union, whose land offers 'immense riches', will leave Germany 'unassailable'.

	Backe passes the RMEL's annual report on the food situation in Germany on to his superior, Reich Minister Darré, for the latter's signature; that same day, Darré forwards the report, just like every year, to Hitler via Head of the Reich Chancellery Lammers.
13 January	Backe gives Göring a presentation on the food situation.
	Göring issues a circular announcing a reduction in meat rations, which is to come into effect on 2 June 1941.
21 January	In a letter to Eichmann, the Gestapo's 'Jewish expert' in Paris, Theodor Dannecker, writes: 'In accordance with the will of the Führer, the "Jewish Question" within those parts of Europe ruled over or controlled by Germany shall be brought to a final solution after the war' in a 'yet to be fixed territory'. Heydrich, who had already received the task from Hitler, has submitted his suggestion for a 'Final Solution'.
22 January	In response to doubts raised in the Wi Rü Amt regarding the consequences of even a short interruption in the delivery of raw materials from the USSR, Thomas informs Keitel of his intention to prepare a paper detailing his misgivings.
29 January	Göring presides over a meeting of his economic advisers and requests from those present their view as to the economic repercussions of waging war with the Soviet Union. With the exception of Backe, all respond negatively, arguing that the 'tremendous consumption of economic goods of all types that would be entailed by such a war [is] in no ratio whatsoever to the difficulties arising'. Backe, on the other hand, claims that large amounts of grain could be extracted from the Soviet territories.
Before 30 January	During a presentation on the food situation, Backe assures Hitler that 'the occupation of the Ukraine would liberate us from every economic worry'.
8 February	Thomas warns Keitel and Jodl that in the event of an eastern campaign, supplies of aviation fuel will only last until autumn 1941 and those of vehicle fuel only until mid-August.
20 February	Keitel presents Hitler with a report (dated 13 February) from Thomas entitled 'The Military-Economic Consequences of an Operation in the East'; a second copy is sent to Göring.
26 February	Göring transfers the preparation for the entire administration of the economic organization in the

	Soviet Union to Thomas; the exploitation of the food sector is to be taken over by Backe.
3 March	Jodl gives instructions as to how the 'Guidelines for Special Fields to Directive No. 21 (Case Barbarossa)' are to be altered in accordance with the wishes of Hitler, who has rejected a draft of the guidelines that same day; the appointment of Reich Commissars is envisaged.
13 March	The OKW's 'Guidelines for Special Fields', now conforming to Hitler's wishes, are issued.
16 March	Brauchitsch and Wagner present the draft of a set of administrative instructions for 'Barbarossa' in an attempt to persuade Hitler to appoint a military administration in the style of France or Belgium; Hitler rejects the proposal.
19 March	Thomas presents the Wi Rü Amt's proposals for a military-economic organization to Göring, who declares himself 'fully in agreement'.
20 March	At a meeting in the Propaganda Ministry, Eichmann declares that Heydrich has been commissioned by Hitler 'with the final evacuation of the Jews', in response to which Heydrich presented a suggestion to Hitler '8–10 weeks ago'.
26 March	Göring and Heydrich discuss the future of the Soviet territories, including Rosenberg's jurisdiction within the administration.
28 March	The Staff Office of the Reich Farming Leader completes an extensive study on the production and consumption of foodstuffs and fodder in the USSR, in which it is argued that a 12 per cent reduction in the Soviet consumption of foodstuffs would provide a grain surplus of 8.7 million tons.
31 March	Rosenberg is appointed by Hitler as head of a 'Political Central Office for Eastern Questions'.
2 April	During a two-hour meeting, Hitler and Rosenberg discuss the political administration of the soon-to-be-occupied Soviet territories.
7 April	In a paper on personnel in the future civil administration, Rosenberg proposes himself as 'Protector-General for the occupied eastern territories', with his seat in Berlin.
10 April	Meeting between Hitler and Rosenberg.
12 April	Backe receives complete powers over the agricultural exploitation of the soon-to-be-occupied Soviet territories; on Hitler's orders, this is under all circumstances to remain strictly secret.

19 April	In a letter to Göring, Schwerin von Krosigk questions the likelihood of economic gain through an attack on the Soviet Union; his letter remains unanswered.
20 April	Rosenberg is appointed as Hitler's 'Plenipotentiary for the Central Treatment of Questions of the Eastern European Space'.
23 April	Rosenberg charges Lohse with the 'central treatment of questions' concerning the former Baltic republics and Belarus.
25 April	Rosenberg refers for the first time to the post of Reich Minister for the Occupied Eastern Territories in a paper entitled 'Memorandum No. 3. Re.: USSR'.
30 April	During a presentation on the food situation, Backe informs Goebbels that the expected reduction of meat rations will take place on 2 June.
2 May	At a meeting of the Staatssekretäre on the food situation and the war against the Soviet Union, those present conclude that 'x million people will doubtlessly starve, if that which is necessary for us is extracted from the land'. Meeting between Hitler and Rosenberg.
5 May	Backe gives a speech on the food situation at a gathering of Reichs- and Gauleiter.
7 May	Meeting between Rosenberg and Backe.
8 May	Meeting between Rosenberg and Körner.
14 May	During a meeting with an Eicke from the Wi Rü Amt, Julius Claussen from the RMEL claims that, from the Ukraine's annual production of forty million tons of grain, the Ukrainian population can make do with ten to fifteen million tons, thus leaving twenty-five to thirty million tons to be plundered by Germany.
16 May	Backe gives Hitler a presentation in Berchtesgaden.
23 May	The agricultural section of the Wi Stab Ost produces the 'Economic-Political Guidelines for the Economic Organization East', which represent the detailed written version of the conclusions reached by the Staatssekretäre at the meeting of 2 May.
26 May	At a session of the Wi Fü Stab Ost, the representative of the Bureau Rosenberg declares himself to be in agreement with the Green Folder.
2 June	Meat rations are reduced for every category of consumer.
10 June	Backe and Himmler meet to discuss agriculture in the soon-to-be-occupied Soviet territories.
12–15 June	Meeting of senior SS officers at the Wewelsburg; Himmler describes the purpose (or result) of the Soviet

	campaign as being 'the decimation of the Slavic population by thirty million'.
20 June	Rosenberg gives a speech in which he declares: 'We see by no means the obligation to feed the Russian people as well [as ourselves] from these surplus territories.'
21 June	In a letter to Mussolini, Hitler stresses the economic gains to be made by occupying the Ukraine.
22 June	Operation Barbarossa, the German invasion of the Soviet Union, commences.
24 June	During a forty-five-minute meeting, Himmler requests Konrad Meyer to draw up a sketch for the resettlement possibilities in the East, which are, it seems, on the verge of being realized.
4 July	In a letter to Lammers, Stuckart registers misgivings about the establishment of a ministry for the occupied Soviet territories.
15 July	Meyer presents Himmler with a first draft of the plan requested three weeks earlier; the draft plan is declared to have been 'superseded'.
16 July	Meeting at FHQ attended by Rosenberg, Göring, Keitel, Lammers and Bormann; the selections are made for the posts of Reich and General Commissar in the occupied Soviet territories.
17 July	Rosenberg is officially appointed as Reich Minister for the Occupied Eastern Territories.

2. Envisaged Chain of Command in the Occupied Soviet Territories*

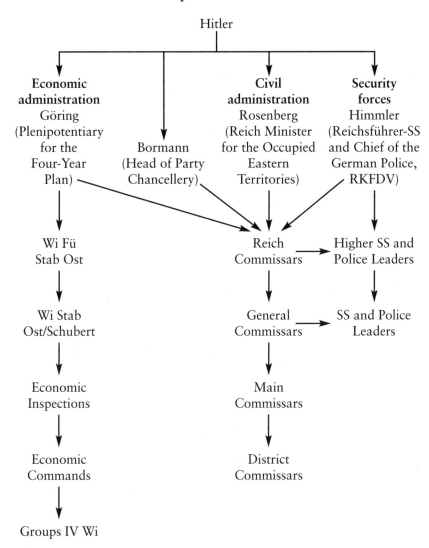

KEY

 = Direct institutional chain of command (indicating direction in which orders were to be given).

 = Inter-institutional authority to give orders (indicating direction in which orders could be given).

* Not including regular military formations. All sources used to put this diagram together have been referenced in the main text.

3. Maps

(a) Intended reordering of the occupied Soviet territories according to the plans of the Bureau Rosenberg, April–June 1941*

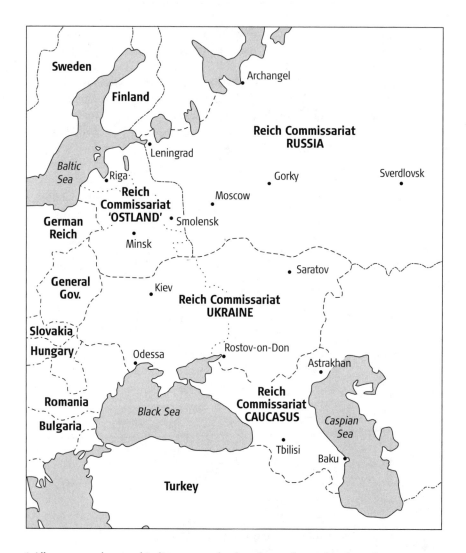

* All sources used to put this diagram together have been referenced in the main text.

(b) Intended separation of 'deficit territories' from 'surplus territories' in the occupied Soviet territories according to the plans of the Economic Staff East, May 1941*

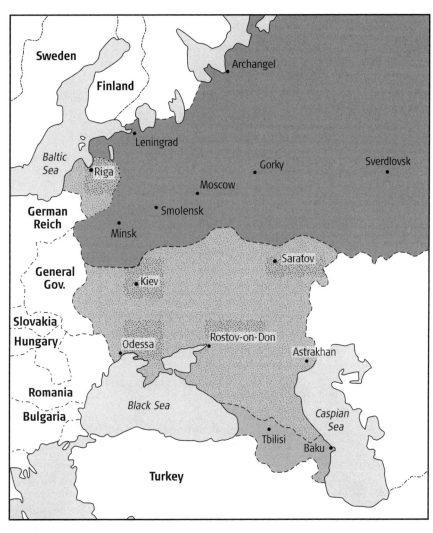

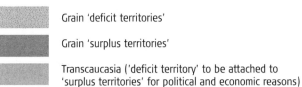

Grain 'deficit territories'

Grain 'surplus territories'

Transcaucasia ('deficit territory' to be attached to 'surplus territories' for political and economic reasons)

* All sources used to put this diagram together have been referenced in the main text.

Glossary

AA line	imaginary line stretching from Archangel in the north of the Soviet Union to Astrakhan in the south; the designated minimum limit for the German military advance
Barbarossa	German code name for the invasion of the Soviet Union
Blitzkrieg	'lightning war'
Einsatzgruppen	mobile 'task forces' of the Security Police and the SD
Ereignismeldungen	'incident reports' compiled directly from information recorded by the Einsatzgruppen in the occupied Soviet territories and sent back in writing to the RSHA
Gauleiter	head of the main Nazi administrative district, or *Gau* (plural: *Gaue*)
Generalplan Ost	'General Plan East'
Großraum	'greater space'; denoting in this case continental Europe under German domination
Großraumwirtschaft	'greater space economy' (also Großwirtschaftsraum, 'greater economic space'); a concept advocating the combining of the economic resources of a single, large, autarkic land mass (in this case, continental Europe under German domination)
Hungerpolitik	'starvation policy'
Lebensraum	'living space'
Luftwaffe	German air force
Neuordnung	'New Order'
Reichsleiter	coveted title for senior members of the NSDAP appointed by Hitler to specific areas of expertise, e.g., Reichsleiter for Propaganda Joseph Goebbels

Reichsmarschall	'Reich Marshal'; a title created especially for Hermann Göring following the fall of France in June 1940 and affording him the status of the highest-ranking officer in the Wehrmacht
Staatssekretär	'permanent secretary'
Wehrmacht	German armed forces between 1935 and 1945

BIBLIOGRAPHY

1. Archival Sources

I. Bundesarchiv, Berlin-Lichterfelde (BA)

Reichsfinanzministerium
  R 2/24243, 30518, 30921
Reichsministerium für die besetzten Ostgebiete
  R 6/4, 9, 21, 24, 30, 34a, 60a
Reichsnährstand
  R 16/1299
Chef der Bandenkampfverbände, Truppen und Schulen der Ordnungspolizei
  R 20/45b
Beauftragter für den Vierjahresplan
  R 26 I/6, 13, 35
Beauftragter für den Vierjahresplan – Geschäftsgruppe Ernährung
  R 26 IV/9, 33a, 51
Alte Reichskanzlei
  R 43 I/1476
Reichskanzlei
  R 43 II/684a, 686a, 688, 690a, 690b
Reichskommissar für die Festigung deutschen Volkstums
  R 49/157a, 2605, 2606, 2607
Reichssicherheitshauptamt
  R 58/217, 218, 241
Polizeidienststellen in der Sowjetunion
  R 70 Sowjetunion/32
Reichskommissariat Ostland
  R 90/16, 256a
Generalkommissariat Lettland
  R 92/2
Reichskommissariat Ukraine
  R 94/9

Reichsministerium des Innern
  R 1501/3646
Reichsministerium für Ernährung und Landwirtschaft
  R 3601/3371
Reichsarbeitsministerium
  R 3901/20136
Kanzlei Rosenberg
  NS 8/63, 71, 90, 167, 175
Adjutantur des Führers
  NS 10/107
Parteiamtliche Prüfungskommission zum Schutz des NS-Schrifttums
  NS 11/28
Reichsführer-SS, Persönlicher Stab
  NS 19/1739, 2696, 2803, 2808, 2822, 3873, 3874, 3882
Reichsorganisationsleiter der NSDAP
  NS 22/1042
Außenpolitisches Amt der NSDAP
  NS 43/3, 41, 49
Nürnberger Nachfolgeprozesse Fall XI – Wilhelmstraßen-Prozeß
  99 US 7/1074, 1077, 1085, 1106, 1108, 1110, 1112

II. Bundesarchiv-Militärarchiv, Freiburg im Breisgau (BA-MA)

Heeresgruppe Nord
  RH 19 III/722
OKW/WFSt/Qu
  RW 4/v. 578, v. 759
OKW/Wehrwirtschafts- und Rüstungsamt
  RW 19/164, 165, 175, 177, 185, 473, 739
Wirtschaftsstab Ost
  RW 31/42
Ergänzungsfilmbestand aus DDR Zeit
  WF-01/15885

III. Bundesarchiv, Koblenz (BAK)

Nachlaß Herbert Backe
  N 1075/1, 5, 9
Nachlaß Richard Walther Darré
  N 1094/I 65a, II 20

IV. Bundesarchiv-Zwischenarchiv, Dahlwitz-Hoppegarten (BA D-H)

ZM 1683, Bd. 1

V. Institut für Zeitgeschichte, Munich (IfZ)

ED 180/5   Terminkalender Hermann Göring
Fd 52   Heeresgruppe Nord, EGr. Kroatien, 1941 und 1944
MA 423   Reichsring für Volksaufklärung und Propaganda/Hauptamt
Nuremberg documents:
NG 5225, NI 7291, PS 1018, PS 1020, PS 1036

VI. Politisches Archiv des Auswärtigen Amts (PAAA)

R 27334   Handakten Etzdorf, Vertrauliche Aufzeichnungen des Vertreters des Auswärtigen Amts beim OKH, Nr. 1
R 27335   Handakten Etzdorf, Vertrauliche Aufzeichnungen des Vertreters des Auswärtigen Amts beim OKH, Nr. 2
R 27336a   Handakten Etzdorf, Vertrauliche Aufzeichnungen des Vertreters des Auswärtigen Amts beim OKH, Nr. 3
R 100857   Inland II g, Nr. 177
R 105192   Pol. Abt. XIII, Nr. 25
R 105194   Pol. Abt. XIII, Nr. 27

VII. Militärgeschichtliches Forschungsamt, Potsdam (MGFA)

'Erster Entwurf zu einer militärgeographischen Studie über das europäische Rußland', Generalstab des Heeres, Abteilung für Kriegskarten und Vermessungswesen (IV. Mil.-Geo.), abgeschlossen am 10. August 1940.

2. Printed Sources

Akten zur deutschen auswärtigen Politik 1918–1945. Serie C: *1933–1936*, vol. 5/2, Vandenhoeck & Ruprecht, Göttingen, 1977. Serie D: *1937–1941*, vol. 8, P. Keppler, Baden-Baden/Frankfurt am Main, 1961; vols. 11/1 & 11/2, Gebr. Hermes KG, Bonn, 1964; vols. 12/1 & 12/2, Vandenhoeck & Ruprecht, Göttingen, 1969; vols. 13/1 & 13/2, Vandenhoeck & Ruprecht, Göttingen, 1970. Serie E: *1941–1945*, vol. 1, Vandenhoeck & Ruprecht, Göttingen, 1969.

Backe, Herbert. *Um die Nahrungsfreiheit Europas: Weltwirtschaft oder Großraum*, 2nd edition. Goldmann, Leipzig, 1943 [1942].

Below, Nicolaus von. *Als Hitlers Adjutant 1937–45*. von Hase & Koehler, Mainz, 1980.

Benz, Wolfgang, Konrad Kwiet and Jürgen Matthäus, eds. *Einsatz im "Reichskommissariat Ostland": Dokumente zum Völkermord im Baltikum und in Weißrußland 1941–1944*. Metropol, Berlin, 1998.

Boberach, Heinz, ed. *Meldungen aus dem Reich 1938–1945: Die geheimen Lageberichte des Sicherheitsdienstes der SS*, vols. 5 & 6. Pawlak Verlag, Herrsching, 1984.

Bräutigam, Otto. *So hat es sich zugetragen ... Ein Leben als Soldat und Diplomat*. Holzner-Verlag, Würzburg, 1968.

Burckhardt, Carl J. *Meine Danziger Mission, 1937–1939*. Georg D.W. Callwey, Munich, 1960.

Domarus, Max, ed. *Hitler: Reden und Proklamationen 1932–1945*, vols. I/1 & I/2. Süddeutscher Verlag, Munich, 1965.

Fröhlich, Elke, ed. *Die Tagebücher von Joseph Goebbels. Sämtliche Fragmente, Teil I: Aufzeichnungen 1924–1941*, vol. 2. K.G. Saur, Munich, 1987.

———. *Die Tagebücher von Joseph Goebbels. Teil I: Aufzeichnungen 1923–1941*, vol. 9, K.G. Saur, Munich, 1998. *Teil II: Diktate 1941–1945*, vol. 1, K.G. Saur, Munich, 1996.

Gerbet, Klaus, ed. *Generalfeldmarschall Fedor von Bock: The War Diary 1939–1945*. Schiffer, Atglen, PA, 1996.

Gersdorff, Rudolf-Christoph Freiherr von. *Soldat im Untergang*. Ullstein, Frankfurt am Main/Berlin/Vienna, 1977.

Gibbons, Robert J. 'Opposition gegen "Barbarossa" im Herbst 1940', *Vierteljahrshefte für Zeitgeschichte*, 23 (1975): 332–340.

———. 'Allgemeine Richtlinien für die politische und wirtschaftliche Verwaltung der besetzten Ostgebiete', *Vierteljahrshefte für Zeitgeschichte*, 25 (1977): 252–261.

Halder, Franz. *Kriegstagebuch. Band I: Vom Polenfeldzug bis zum Ende der Westoffensive*, W. Kohlhammer Verlag, Stuttgart, 1962. *Band II: Von der geplanten Landung in England bis zum Beginn des Ostfeldzuges*, W. Kohlhammer Verlag, Stuttgart, 1963. *Band III: Der Rußlandfeldzug bis zum Marsch auf Stalingrad*, W. Kohlhammer Verlag, Stuttgart, 1964.

Hassell, Ulrich von. *Die Hassell-Tagebücher 1938–1944: Aufzeichnungen vom Andern Deutschland*. Goldmann, Berlin, 1994.

Heiber, Helmut. 'Aus den Akten des Gauleiters Kube', *Vierteljahrshefte für Zeitgeschichte*, 4 (1956): 67–92.

———. 'Der Generalplan Ost', *Vierteljahrshefte für Zeitgeschichte*, 6 (1958): 281–325.

———. *Reichsführer!... Briefe an und von Himmler*. Deutsche Verlags-Anstalt, Stuttgart, 1968.

Heilmann, H.D. 'Aus dem Kriegstagebuch des Diplomaten Otto Bräutigam'. In Götz Aly, ed. *Biedermann und Schreibtischtäter: Materialien zur deutschen Täter-Biographie*. Rotbuch Verlag, Berlin, 1987: 123–187.

'Herbert Backe'. *Das Reich*, No. 23, Berlin, 7 June 1942: 1.

Hill, Leonidas E., ed. *Die Weizsäcker-Papiere 1933–1950*. Propyläen Verlag, Frankfurt am Main/Berlin/Vienna, 1974.

Hitler, Adolf. *Mein Kampf*. Mariner Books, New York, 1999 [1925/1926].

Hubatsch, Walter, ed. *Hitlers Weisungen für die Kriegsführung 1939–1945*, 2nd edition. Bernard & Graefe Verlag, Koblenz, 1983 [1962].

Jacobsen, Hans-Adolf. 'Kommissarbefehl und Massenexekutionen sowjetischer Kriegsgefangener'. In Hans Buchheim, Martin Broszat, Hans-Adolf Jacobsen and Helmut Krausnick. *Anatomie des SS-Staates, Band II*. Walter-Verlag, Olten, 1965.

Jochmann, Werner, ed. *Adolf Hitler: Monologe im Führerhauptquartier 1941–1944. Die Aufzeichnungen Heinrich Heims*. Albrecht Knaus Verlag, Hamburg, 1980.

'Der Kampf gegen die Kirche: Aus unveröffentlichten Tagebüchern Alfred Rosenbergs', *Der Monat*, 1 (1949), no. 10: 26–38.

Kárný, Miroslav, Jaroslava Milotova and Margita Kárná, eds. *Deutsche Politik im "Protektorat Böhmen und Mähren" unter Reinhard Heydrich 1941–1942: Eine Dokumentation*. Metropol, Berlin, 1997.

Kehrl, Hans. *Krisenmanager im Dritten Reich, 6 Jahre Frieden – 6 Jahre Krieg: Erinnerungen.* Droste Verlag, Düsseldorf, 1973.
Kempner, Robert M.W. '"Rosenberg, jetzt ist Ihre große Stunde gekommen". Aufzeichnungen über Eroberungspläne Hitlers', *Frankfurter Rundschau*, no. 140, 22 June 1971.
———. 'Der Führer hat mir einen Kontinent anvertraut: Aus geheimen Aufzeichnungen zum Überfall auf Rußland', *Vorwärts*, no. 28, 2 July 1981: 20.
Kleist, Peter. *Zwischen Hitler und Stalin 1939–1945.* Athenäum-Verlag, Bonn, 1950.
Kotze, Hildegard von, ed. *Heeresadjutant bei Hitler 1938–1943: Aufzeichnungen des Majors Engel.* Deutsche Verlags-Anstalt, Stuttgart, 1974.
Krumpelt, Ihno. *Das Material und die Kriegführung.* E.S. Mittler & Sohn, Frankfurt am Main, 1968.
Meier-Welcker, Hans. *Aufzeichnungen eines Generalstabsoffiziers 1939–1942.* Rombach, Freiburg im Breisgau, 1982.
Meyer, Georg, ed. *Generalfeldmarschall Wilhelm Ritter von Leeb: Tagebuchaufzeichnungen und Lagebeurteilungen aus zwei Weltkriegen.* Deutsche Verlags-Anstalt, Stuttgart, 1976.
Moll, Martin, ed. *"Führer-Erlasse" 1939–1945.* Franz Steiner Verlag, Stuttgart, 1997.
Moritz, Erhard, ed. *Fall Barbarossa: Dokumente zur Vorbereitung der faschistischen Wehrmacht auf die Aggression gegen die Sowjetunion (1940/41).* Deutscher Militärverlag, Berlin, 1970.
Müller, Norbert, ed. *Okkupation, Raub, Vernichtung: Dokumente zur Besatzungspolitik der faschistischen Wehrmacht auf sowjetischem Territorium 1941 bis 1944.* Militärverlag der Deutschen Demokratischen Republik, Berlin, 1980.
Müller, Rolf-Dieter. 'Industrielle Interessenpolitik im Rahmen des "Generalplans Ost": Dokumente zum Einfluß von Wehrmacht, Industrie und SS auf die wirtschaftspolitische Zielsetzung für Hitlers Ostimperium', *Militärgeschichtliche Mitteilungen*, 29 (1981): 101–141.
Müller, Rolf-Dieter, ed. *Die deutsche Wirtschaftspolitik in den besetzten sowjetischen Gebieten 1941–1943: Der Abschlußbericht des Wirtschaftsstabes Ost und Aufzeichnungen eines Angehörigen des Wirtschaftskommandos Kiew.* Harald Boldt Verlag, Boppard am Rhein, 1991.
Noakes, Jeremy and Geoffrey Pridham, eds. *Nazism 1919–1945. A Documentary Reader, Vol. 3: Foreign Policy, War and Racial Extermination.* University of Exeter, Exeter, 1988.
Picker, Henry, ed. *Hitlers Tischgespräche im Führerhauptquartier 1941–42.* Athenäum-Verlag, Bonn, 1951.
Präg, Werner and Wolfgang Jacobmeyer, eds. *Das Diensttagebuch des deutschen Generalgouverneurs in Polen 1939–1945.* Deutsche Verlags-Anstalt, Stuttgart, 1975.
Der Prozess gegen die Hauptkriegsverbrecher vor dem Internationalen Militärgerichtshof, Nürnberg, 14 November 1945 – 1 October 1946, vols. 4, 9, 11, 26–32, 34, 36 and 38–39. Sekretariat des Gerichtshofs, Nuremberg, 1947–1949.
Rücker, Wilhelm von. 'Die Vorbereitungen für den Feldzug gegen Russland'. In Elisabeth Wagner, ed. *Der Generalquartiermaster: Briefe und Tagebuchaufzeichnungen des Generalquartiermeisters des Heeres, General der Artillerie Eduard Wagner.* Günter Olzog Verlag, Munich, 1963: 313–318.

Salewski, Michael. *Die deutsche Seekriegsleitung 1935–1945, Band III: Denkschriften und Lagebetrachtungen 1938–1944*. Bernard & Graefe Verlag, Frankfurt am Main, 1973.
Schmidt, Paul. *Statist auf diplomatischer Bühne 1923–45*. Athenäum-Verlag, Bonn, 1953.
Schramm, Percy Ernst, ed. *Kriegstagebuch des Oberkommandos der Wehrmacht (Wehrmachtsführungsstab) 1940–1945: Geführt von Helmuth Greiner und Percy Ernst Schramm*, vol. I: 1 August 1940 – 31 December 1941, Bernard & Graefe Verlag, Frankfurt am Main, 1965; vol. II/1: 1 January 1942 – 31 December 1942, Bernard & Graefe Verlag, Frankfurt am Main, 1963.
Seraphim, Hans-Günther, ed. *Das politische Tagebuch Alfred Rosenbergs aus den Jahren 1934/35 und 1939/40*. Musterschmidt-Verlag, Göttingen, 1956.
Thomas, Georg. *Geschichte der deutschen Wehr- und Rüstungswirtschaft (1918–1943/45)*. Harald Boldt Verlag, Boppard am Rhein, 1966.
Trevor-Roper, Hugh R., ed. *Hitler's Table Talk, 1941–1944: His Private Conversations*, 3rd edition. Enigma Books, New York, 2000 [1953].
Trials of War Criminals before the Nuernberg Military Tribunals under Control Council Law No. 10, Nuernberg, October 1946 – April 1949, vols. VIII & XII. United States Government Printing Office, Washington, 1951–1952.
Ueberschär, Gerd R., and Lev A. Bezymenskij, eds. *Der deutsche Angriff auf die Sowjetunion 1941: Kontroverse um die Präventivkriegsthese*. Primus Verlag, Darmstadt, 1998.
Wagner, Elisabeth, ed. *Der Generalquartiermaster: Briefe und Tagebuchaufzeichnungen des Generalquartiermeisters des Heeres, General der Artillerie Eduard Wagner*. Günter Olzog Verlag, Munich, 1963.
Wagner, Gerhard, ed. *Lagevorträge des Oberbefehlshabers der Kriegsmarine vor Hitler 1939–1945*. J.F. Lehmanns Verlag, Munich, 1972.
Warlimont, Walter. *Inside Hitler's Headquarters 1939–1945*. Weidenfeld & Nicolson, London, 1964.
Weinberg, Gerhard L., ed. *Hitlers Zweites Buch: Ein Dokument aus dem Jahr 1928*. Deutsche Verlags-Anstalt, Stuttgart, 1961.
Witte, Peter, Michael Wildt, Martina Voigt, Dieter Pohl, Peter Klein, Christian Gerlach, Christoph Dieckmann and Andrej Angrick, eds. *Der Dienstkalender Heinrich Himmlers 1941/42*. Hans Christians Verlag, Hamburg, 1999.

3. Secondary Literature

Adler, H.G.. *Der verwaltete Mensch*. J.C.B. Mohr, Tübingen, 1974.
Aly, Götz. *"Endlösung": Völkerverschiebung und der Mord an den europäischen Juden*. S. Fischer, Frankfurt am Main, 1995.
———. 'The Planning Intelligentsia and the "Final Solution"'. In Michael Burleigh, ed. *Confronting the Nazi Past: New Debates on Modern German History*. Collins & Brown, London, 1996: 140–153.
Aly, Götz and Susanne Heim. 'Deutsche Herrschaft "im Osten": Bevölkerungspolitik und Völkermord'. In Peter Jahn and Reinhard Rürup, eds. *Erobern und Vernichten: Der Krieg gegen die Sowjetunion 1941–1945, Essays*. Argon, Berlin, 1991: 84–105.
———. *Vordenker der Vernichtung: Auschwitz und die deutschen Pläne für eine neue europäische Ordnung*. Hoffmann & Campe Verlag, Hamburg, 1991.

Angrick, Andrej. *Besatzungspolitik und Massenmord: Die Einsatzgruppe D in der südlichen Sowjetunion 1941–1943*. Hamburger Edition, Hamburg, 2003.
Arad, Yitzhak. 'Alfred Rosenberg and the "Final Solution" in the Occupied Soviet Territories'. *Yad Vashem Studies on the European Jewish Catastrophe and Resistance*, 13, 1979: 263–286.
Barber, John, and Mark Harrison. *The Soviet Home Front, 1941–1945: A Social and Economic History of the USSR in World War II*. Longman, Harlow, 1991.
Benz, Wolfgang, Hermann Graml and Hermann Weiß, eds. *Enzyklopädie des Nationalsozialismus*, 4th edition. Deutscher Taschenbuch Verlag, Munich, 2001 [1997].
Birn, Ruth Bettina. 'Hanns Rauter – Höherer SS- und Polizeiführer in den Niederlanden'. In Ronald Smelser and Enrico Syring, eds. *Die SS: Elite unter dem Totenkopf*. Ferdinand Schöningh, Paderborn, 2000: 408–417.
Bollmus, Reinhard. 'Alfred Rosenberg – "Chefideologe" des Nationalsozialismus?'. In Ronald Smelser and Rainer Zitelmann, eds. *Die braune Elite: 22 biographische Skizzen*. Wissenschaftliche Buchgesellschaft, Darmstadt, 1989: 223–235.
Boog, Horst, Jürgen Förster, Joachim Hoffmann, Ernst Klink, Rolf-Dieter Müller and Gerd R. Ueberschär. *Der Angriff auf die Sowjetunion*. Fischer Taschenbuch Verlag, Frankfurt am Main, 1991.
Bracher, Karl Dietrich. *Die deutsche Diktatur: Entstehung, Struktur, Folgen des Nationalsozialismus*, rev. 4th edition. Kiepenheuer & Witsch, Cologne, 1972.
Bramwell, Anna. *Blood and Soil: Richard Walther Darré and Hitler's 'Green Party'*. The Kensal Press, Abbotsbrook, Bucks., 1985.
Brandt, Karl. *Management of Agriculture and Food in the German-Occupied and Other Areas of Fortress Europe: A Study in Military Government*. Stanford University Press, Stanford, CA, 1953.
Breitman, Richard. *The Architect of Genocide: Himmler and the Final Solution*. The Bodley Head, London, 1991.
Broszat, Martin. *Nationalsozialistische Polenpolitik 1939–1945*. Deutsche Verlags-Anstalt, Stuttgart, 1961.
Browning, Christopher R. 'Nazi Resettlement Policy and the Search for a Solution to the Jewish Question, 1939–1941'. In Christopher R. Browning. *The Path to Genocide: Essays on Launching the Final Solution*. Cambridge University Press, Cambridge, 1992: 3–27.
———. 'Beyond "Intentionalism" and "Functionalism": The Decision for the Final Solution Reconsidered'. In Christopher R. Browning. *The Path to Genocide: Essays on Launching the Final Solution*. Cambridge University Press, Cambridge, 1992: 86–121.
———. *The Origins of the Final Solution: The Evolution of Nazi Jewish Policy, September 1939 – March 1942*. Arrow Books, London, 2005.
Buggeln, Marc. 'Währungspläne für den europäischen Großraum: Die Diskussion der nationalsozialistischen Wirtschaftsexperten über ein zukünftiges europäisches Zahlungssystem', *Beiträge zur Geschichte des Nationalsozialismus, Band 18: Europäische Integration*, Sonderdruck. Wallstein Verlag, Göttingen, 2002: 41–76.
Burleigh, Michael. *Germany Turns Eastwards: A Study of Ostforschung in the Third Reich*. Pan Books, London, 2002 [1988].
———. '"See you again in Siberia": the German–Soviet War and Other Tragedies'. In Michael Burleigh, ed. *Ethics and Extermination: Reflections on Nazi Genocide*. Cambridge University Press, Cambridge, 1997: 37–110.

———. *The Third Reich: A New History*. Pan Books, London, 2001.

Burrin, Philippe. *Hitler und die Juden: Die Entscheidung für den Völkermord*. S. Fischer, Frankfurt am Main, 1993 [1989].

Carr, William. *Arms, Autarky and Aggression: A Study in German Foreign Policy 1933–1939*. W.W. Norton & Company, New York, 1973.

Cecil, Robert. *The Myth of the Master Race: Alfred Rosenberg and Nazi Ideology*. B.T. Batsford, London, 1972.

———. *Hitler's Decision to Invade Russia 1941*. David McKay Company, New York, 1975.

Dallin, Alexander. *German Rule in Russia, 1941–1945: A Study of Occupation Policies*. Macmillan, London, 1957.

Dawidowicz, Lucy S. *The War against the Jews 1933–45*. Penguin, London, 1987 [1975].

Dieckmann, Christoph. 'Der Krieg und die Ermordung der litauischen Juden'. In Ulrich Herbert, ed. *Nationalsozialistische Vernichtungspolitik 1939–1945: Neue Forschungen und Kontroversen*. Fischer Taschenbuch Verlag, Frankfurt am Main, 1998: 292–329.

Eichholtz, Dietrich. 'Institutionen und Praxis der deutschen Wirtschaftspolitik im NS-besetzten Europa'. In Richard J. Overy, Gerhard Otto and Johannes Houwink ten Cate, eds. *Die 'Neuordnung' Europas: NS-Wirtschaftspolitik in den besetzten Gebieten*. Metropol, Berlin, 1997: 29–62.

———. *Geschichte der deutschen Kriegswirtschaft 1939–1945, Band I: 1939–1941*, 4th edition. K.G. Saur, Munich, 1999 [1969].

Ericson, Edward E. *Feeding the German Eagle: Soviet Economic Aid to Nazi Germany, 1933–1941*. Praeger, Westport, CT, 1999.

Europa unterm Hakenkreuz. Die Okkupationspolitik des deutschen Faschismus (1938–1945). Achtbändige Dokumentenedition, edited by a committee under the direction of Wolfgang Schumann and Ludwig Nestler. *Band 5: Die faschistische Okkupationspolitik in den zeitweilig besetzten Gebieten der Sowjetunion (1941–1944)*. Deutscher Verlag der Wissenschaften, Berlin, 1991, document selection and introduction by Norbert Müller.

Ferguson, Niall. *Empire: How Britain Made the Modern World*. Penguin, London, 2004.

Fest, Joachim C. 'Alfred Rosenberg – The Forgotten Disciple'. In Joachim C. Fest. *The Face of the Third Reich: Portraits of the Nazi Leadership*. Da Capo Press, New York, 1999 [1963]: 163–174.

———. *Hitler: Eine Biographie*. Ullstein, Frankfurt am Main, 1973.

Förster, Jürgen. 'Hitlers Entscheidung für den Krieg gegen die Sowjetunion'. In Horst Boog, Jürgen Förster, Joachim Hoffmann, Ernst Klink, Rolf-Dieter Müller and Gerd R. Ueberschär. *Der Angriff auf die Sowjetunion*. Fischer Taschenbuch Verlag, Frankfurt am Main, 1991: 27–68.

———. 'Das Unternehmen "Barbarossa" als Eroberungs- und Vernichtungskrieg'. In Horst Boog, Jürgen Förster, Joachim Hoffmann, Ernst Klink, Rolf-Dieter Müller and Gerd R. Ueberschär. *Der Angriff auf die Sowjetunion*. Fischer Taschenbuch Verlag, Frankfurt am Main, 1991: 498–538.

———. 'Hitlers Wendung nach Osten: Die deutsche Kriegspolitik 1940–1941'. In Bernd Wegner, ed. *Zwei Wege nach Moskau: Vom Hitler-Stalin-Pakt bis zum 'Unternehmen Barbarossa'*. Piper, Munich, 1991: 113–132.

Gerlach, Christian. 'Männer des 20. Juli und der Krieg gegen die Sowjetunion'. In Hannes Heer and Klaus Naumann, eds. *Vernichtungskrieg: Verbrechen der Wehrmacht 1941–1944*. Hamburger Edition, Hamburg, 1995: 427–446.

———. 'Deutsche Wirtschaftsinteressen, Besatzungspolitik und der Mord an den Juden in Weißrußland 1941–1943'. In Ulrich Herbert, ed. *Nationalsozialistische Vernichtungspolitik 1939–1945: Neue Forschungen und Kontroversen*. Fischer Taschenbuch Verlag, Frankfurt am Main, 1998: 263–291.

———. 'Die Ausweitung der deutschen Massenmorde in den besetzten Sowjetischen Gebieten im Herbst 1941: Überlegungen zur Vernichtungspolitik gegen Juden und sowjetische Kriegsgefangene'. In Christian Gerlach. *Krieg, Ernährung, Völkermord: Forschungen zur deutschen Vernichtungspolitik im Zweiten Weltkrieg*. Hamburger Edition, Hamburg, 1998: 10–84.

———. *Kalkulierte Morde: Die deutsche Wirtschafts- und Vernichtungspolitik in Weißrußland 1941 bis 1944*. Hamburger Edition, Hamburg, 1999.

———. 'Militärische "Versorgungszwänge", Besatzungspolitik und Massenverbrechen: Die Rolle des Generalquartiermeisters des Heeres und seiner Dienststellen im Krieg gegen die Sowjetunion'. In Norbert Frei, Sybille Steinbacher and Bernd C. Wagner, eds. *Ausbeutung, Vernichtung, Öffentlichkeit: Neue Studien zur nationalsozialistischen Lagerpolitik*. K.G. Saur, Munich, 2000: 175–208.

Goldhagen, Daniel Jonah. *Hitler's Willing Executioners: Ordinary Germans and the Holocaust*. Alfred A. Knopf, New York, 1996.

Graml, Hermann. *Reichskristallnacht: Antisemitismus und Judenverfolgung im Dritten Reich*. Deutscher Taschenbuch Verlag, Munich, 1988.

Hachmeister, Lutz. *Der Gegnerforscher: Die Karriere des SS-Führers Franz Alfred Six*. C.H. Beck, Munich, 1998.

Harrison, Mark. *Accounting for War: Soviet Production, Employment, and the Defence Burden, 1940–1945*. Cambridge University Press, Cambridge, 1996.

Hartmann, Christian. 'Verbrecherischer Krieg – verbrecherische Wehrmacht? Überlegungen zur Struktur des deutschen Ostheeres 1941–1944', *Vierteljahrshefte für Zeitgeschichte*, 52/1 (2004): 1–75.

Hass, Gerhart. 'Zum Rußlandbild der SS'. In Hans-Erich Volkmann, ed. *Das Rußlandbild im Dritten Reich*. Böhlau Verlag, Cologne/Weimar/Vienna, 1994: 201–224.

Heinemann, Isabel. *"Rasse, Siedlung, deutsches Blut": Das Rasse- und Siedlungshauptamt der SS und die rassenpolitische Neuordnung Europas*. Wallstein, Göttingen, 2003.

Herbert, Ulrich. 'Racism and Rational Calculation: The Role of "Utilitarian" Strategies of Legitimation in the National Socialist "Weltanschauung"', *Yad Vashem Studies*, 24 (1994): 131–145.

———. *Fremdarbeiter: Politik und Praxis des "Ausländer-Einsatzes" in der Kriegswirtschaft des Dritten Reiches*. Dietz, Bonn, 1999.

Herbst, Ludolf. *Der Totale Krieg und die Ordnung der Wirtschaft: Die Kriegswirtschaft im Spannungsfeld von Politik, Ideologie und Propaganda 1939–1945*. Deutsche Verlags-Anstalt, Stuttgart, 1982.

———. *Das nationalsozialistische Deutschland 1933–1945. Die Entfesselung der Gewalt: Rassismus und Krieg*. Suhrkamp, Frankfurt am Main, 1996.

Hillgruber, Andreas. *Hitlers Strategie: Politik und Kriegführung 1940–1941*. Bernard & Graefe Verlag, Frankfurt am Main, 1965.

———. 'Das Rußland-Bild der führenden deutschen Militärs vor Beginn des Angriffs auf die Sowjetunion'. In Hans-Erich Volkmann, ed. *Das Rußlandbild im Dritten Reich*. Böhlau Verlag, Cologne/Weimar/Vienna, 1994: 125–140.

Hüser, Karl. *Wewelsburg 1933 bis 1945 – Kult- und Terrorstätte der SS. Eine Dokumentation*. Verlag Bonifatius-Druckerei, Paderborn, 1982.

Jäckel, Eberhard. *Hitlers Weltanschauung: Entwurf einer Herrschaft*, ext. and rev. 4th edition. Deutsche Verlags-Anstalt, Stuttgart, 1991.

Jacobsen, Hans-Adolf. *Nationalsozialistische Außenpolitik 1933–1938*. Alfred Metzner Verlag, Frankfurt am Main/Berlin, 1968.

Jansen, Hans. *Het Madagascarplan: De voorgenomen deportatie van Europese joden naar Madagascar*. SDU Uitgevers, The Hague, 1996.

Jersak, Tobias. 'Die Interaktion von Kriegsverlauf und Judenvernichtung: Ein Blick auf Hitlers Strategie im Spätsommer 1941', *Historische Zeitschrift*, 268/2 (1999): 311–374.

Kershaw, Ian. *Hitler 1889–1936: Hubris*. Penguin, Harmondsworth, 1999.

———. *Hitler 1936–1945: Nemesis*. Penguin, London, 2001.

Kettenacker, Lothar. 'Großbritannien und der deutsche Angriff auf die Sowjetunion'. In Bernd Wegner, ed. *Zwei Wege nach Moskau: Vom Hitler-Stalin-Pakt bis zum 'Unternehmen Barbarossa'*. Piper, Munich, 1991: 605–619.

Klee, Ernst. *Das Personenlexikon zum Dritten Reich: wer war was vor und nach 1945*, 2nd edition. S. Fischer, Frankfurt am Main, 2003.

Klink, Ernst (and Horst Boog). 'Die militärische Konzeption des Krieges gegen die Sowjetunion'. In Horst Boog, Jürgen Förster, Joachim Hoffmann, Ernst Klink, Rolf-Dieter Müller and Gerd R. Ueberschär. *Der Angriff auf die Sowjetunion*. Fischer Taschenbuch Verlag, Frankfurt am Main, 1991: 246–395.

Krausnick, Helmut. 'Kommissarbefehl und "Gerichtsbarkeitserlaß Barbarossa" in neuer Sicht', *Vierteljahrshefte für Zeitgeschichte*, 25/4 (1977): 682–738.

———. 'Die Einsatzgruppen vom Anschluß Österreichs bis zum Feldzug gegen die Sowjetunion: Entwicklung und Verhältnis zur Wehrmacht'. In Helmut Krausnick and Hans-Heinrich Wilhelm. *Die Truppe des Weltanschauungskrieges: Die Einsatzgruppen der Sicherheitspolizei und des SD 1938–1942*. Deutsche Verlags-Anstalt, Stuttgart, 1981: 11–278.

Kube, Alfred. *Pour le mérite und Hakenkreuz: Hermann Göring im Dritten Reich*. R. Oldenbourg Verlag, Munich, 1986.

Lang, Jochen von. *Der Adjutant. Karl Wolff: Der Mann zwischen Hitler und Himmler*. Herbig, Munich/Berlin, 1985.

Lehmann, Joachim. 'Herbert Backe – Technokrat und Agrarideologe'. In Ronald Smelser, Enrico Syring and Rainer Zitelmann, eds. *Die Braune Elite II: 21 weitere biographische Skizzen*. Wissenschaftliche Buchgesellschaft, Darmstadt, 1993: 1–12.

———. 'Die deutsche Landwirtschaft im Kriege'. In Dietrich Eichholtz, *Geschichte der deutschen Kriegswirtschaft 1939–1945, Band II/2: 1941–1943*, 2nd edition. K.G. Saur, Munich, 1999 [1985]: 570–642.

Lilla, Joachim. *Statisten in Uniform: Die Mitglieder des Reichstags 1933–1945*. Droste Verlag, Düsseldorf, 2004.

Longerich, Peter. *Politik der Vernichtung: Eine Gesamtdarstellung der nationalsozialistischen Judenverfolgung*. Piper, Munich, 1998.

———. *The Unwritten Order: Hitler's Role in the Final Solution*. Tempus, Stroud, Glos., 2001.

Madajczyk, Czesław. *Die Okkupationspolitik Nazideutschlands in Polen 1939–1945*. Akademie-Verlag, Berlin, 1987.
Mai, Uwe. *"Rasse und Raum": Agrarpolitik, Sozial- und Raumplanung im NS-Staat*. Ferdinand Schöningh, Paderborn, 2002.
Marschner, Thomas, ed. *Findbücher zu Beständen des Bundesarchivs, Band 73: Außenpolitisches Amt der NSDAP, Bestand NS43*. Bundesarchiv, Koblenz, 1999.
Moll, Martin. 'Steuerungsinstrument im "Ämterchaos"? Die Tagungen der Reichs- und Gauleiter der NSDAP', *Vierteljahrshefte für Zeitgeschichte*, 49 (2001): 215–273.
Müller, Rolf-Dieter. 'Das "Unternehmen Barbarossa" als wirtschaftlicher Raubkrieg'. In Gerd R. Ueberschär and Wolfram Wette, eds. *"Unternehmen Barbarossa": Der deutsche Überfall auf die Sowjetunion 1941: Berichte, Analysen, Dokumente*. Ferdinand Schöningh, Paderborn, 1984: 173–196.
———. 'Von der Wirtschaftsallianz zum kolonialen Ausbeutungskrieg'. In Horst Boog, Jürgen Förster, Joachim Hoffmann, Ernst Klink, Rolf-Dieter Müller and Gerd R. Ueberschär. *Der Angriff auf die Sowjetunion*. Fischer Taschenbuch Verlag, Frankfurt am Main, 1991: 141–245.
———. *Hitlers Ostkrieg und die deutsche Siedlungspolitik: Die Zusammenarbeit von Wehrmacht, Wirtschaft und SS*. Fischer Taschenbuch Verlag, Frankfurt am Main, 1991.
———. 'Menschenjagd: Die Rekrutierung von Zwangsarbeitern in der besetzten Sowjetunion'. In Hannes Heer and Klaus Naumann, eds. *Vernichtungskrieg: Verbrechen der Wehrmacht 1941–1944*. Hamburger Edition, Hamburg, 1995: 92–103.
Mulligan, Timothy P. *The Politics of Illusion and Empire: German Occupation Policy in the Soviet Union, 1942–1943*. Praeger, New York, 1988.
Myllyniemi, Seppo. *Die Neuordnung der baltischen Länder 1941–1944: Zum Nationalsozialistischen Inhalt der deutschen Besatzungspolitik*. n.pub., Helsinki, 1973.
Nolzen, Armin. '"Verbrannte Erde": Der Rückzug der Wehrmacht aus den eroberten Gebieten, 1941/42–1944/45', unpublished paper presented at the *Jahrestagung 2002 des Arbeitskreises Militärgeschichte e.V.* in Augsburg, 1–3 November 2002.
Nova, Fritz. *Alfred Rosenberg: Nazi Theorist of the Holocaust*. Hippocrene Books, New York, 1986.
Ogorreck, Ralf. *Die Einsatzgruppen und die "Genesis der Endlösung"*. Metropol, Berlin, 1996.
Overy, Richard J. *The Air War 1939–1945*. Europa Publications, London, 1980.
———. *The Dictators: Hitler's Germany and Stalin's Russia*. BCA, n.pl., 2004.
Pätzold, Kurt and Schwarz, Erika. *Tagesordnung: Judenmord. Die Wannsee-Konferenz am 20. Januar 1942*. Metropol, Berlin, 1992.
Peter, Roland. 'General der Infanterie Georg Thomas'. In Gerd R. Ueberschär, ed. *Hitlers militärische Elite, Bd. 1: Von den Anfängen des Regimes bis Kriegsbeginn*. Primus Verlag, Darmstadt, 1998: 248–257.
Petzina, Dieter. *Autarkiepolitik im Dritten Reich: Der nationalsozialistische Vierjahresplan*. Deutsche Verlags-Anstalt, Stuttgart, 1968.
Piper, Ernst. *Alfred Rosenberg: Hitlers Chefideologe*. Blessing, Munich, 2005.
Pohl, Dieter. 'Schauplatz Ukraine: Der Massenmord an den Juden im Militärverwaltungsgebiet und im Reichskommissariat 1941–1943'. In Norbert Frei, Sybille Steinbacher and Bernd C. Wagner, eds. *Ausbeutung, Vernichtung,*

Öffentlichkeit: Neue Studien zur nationalsozialistischen Lagerpolitik. K.G. Saur, Munich, 2000: 135–173.

Rebentisch, Dieter. *Führerstaat und Verwaltung im Zweiten Weltkrieg: Verfassungsentwicklung und Verwaltungspolitik 1939–1945*. Franz Steiner Verlag, Stuttgart, 1989.

Reemtsma, Jan Philipp. 'Afterword: On the Reception of the Exhibition in Germany and Austria'. In Hamburg Institute for Social Research, ed. *The German Army and Genocide: Crimes against War Prisoners, Jews and Other Civilians in the East, 1939–1944*. The New Press, New York, 1999: 209–213.

Reitlinger, Gerald. *The House Built on Sand: The Conflicts of German Policy in Russia 1939–1945*. Weidenfeld & Nicolson, London, 1960.

Rich, Norman. *Hitler's War Aims: Ideology, the Nazi State, and the Course of Expansion*. Norton, New York, 1992 [1973].

Robel, Gert. 'Sowjetunion'. In Wolfgang Benz, ed. *Dimension des Völkermords: Die Zahl der jüdischen Opfer des Nationalsozialismus*. R. Oldenbourg Verlag, Munich, 1991: 499–560.

Roseman, Mark. *The Villa, the Lake, the Meeting: Wannsee and the Final Solution*. Penguin, London, 2002.

Roth, Karl Heinz. '"Generalplan Ost" – "Gesamtplan Ost": Forschungsstand, Quellenprobleme, neue Ergebnisse'. In Mechthild Rössler and Sabine Schleiermacher, eds. *Der "Generalplan Ost": Hauptlinien der nationalsozialistischen Planungs- und Vernichtungspolitik*. Akademie Verlag, Berlin, 1993: 25–45 and 53–95.

Schüler, Klaus A. Friedrich. *Logistik im Russlandfeldzug: Die Rolle der Eisenbahn bei Planung, Vorbereitung und Durchführung des deutschen Angriffs auf die Sowjetunion bis zur Krise vor Moskau im Winter 1941/42*. Peter Lang, Frankfurt am Main, 1987.

Schulte, Theo J. *The German Army and Nazi Policies in Occupied Russia*. Berg, Oxford, 1989.

———.'The German Soldier in Occupied Russia'. In Paul Addison and Angus Calder, eds. *Time to Kill: The Soldier's Experience of War in the West*. Pimlico, London, 1997: 274–283.

Schwendemann, Heinrich. *Die wirtschaftliche Zusammenarbeit zwischen dem Deutschen Reich und der Sowjetunion von 1939 bis 1941: Alternative zu Hitlers Ostprogramm?*. Akademie Verlag, Berlin, 1993.

Sommer, Theo. *Deutschland und Japan zwischen den Mächten 1935–1940*. Mohr, Tübingen, 1962.

Steinberg, Jonathan. 'The Third Reich Reflected: German Civil Administration in the Occupied Soviet Union, 1941–4', *English Historical Review*, 40 (1995): 620–651.

Streit, Christian. *Keine Kameraden: Die Wehrmacht und die sowjetischen Kriegsgefangenen 1941–1945*, 3rd edition. Dietz, Bonn, 1991 [1978].

———. '*Wehrmacht, Einsatzgruppen*, Soviet POWs and anti-Bolshevism in the emergence of the Final Solution'. In David Cesarani, ed. *The Final Solution: Origins and Implementation*. Routledge, London, 1996: 103–118.

Toynbee, Arnold and Veronica M. Toynbee, eds. *Hitler's Europe*. Oxford University Press, London, 1954.

Ueberschär, Gerd R. 'Hitlers Überfall auf die Sowjetunion 1941 und Stalins Absichten: Die Bewertung in der deutschen Geschichtsschreibung und die neuere "Präventivkriegsthese"'. In Gerd R. Ueberschär and Lev A. Bezymenskij, eds. *Der deutsche Angriff auf die Sowjetunion 1941: Kontroverse um die Präventivkriegsthese*. Primus Verlag, Darmstadt, 1998: 48–69.

Umbreit, Hans. 'Auf dem Weg zur Kontinentalherrschaft'. In Bernhard R. Kroener, Rolf-Dieter Müller and Hans Umbreit. *Das Deutsche Reich und der Zweite Weltkrieg, Band 5: Organisation und Mobilisierung des deutschen Machtbereichs*. Deutsche Verlags-Anstalt, Stuttgart, 1988: 1–345.

Wegner, Bernd, ed. *Zwei Wege nach Moskau: Vom Hitler-Stalin-Pakt bis zum 'Unternehmen Barbarossa'*. Piper, Munich, 1991.

Wegner-Korfes, Sigrid. 'Botschafter Friedrich Werner Graf von der Schulenburg und die Vorbereitung von "Barbarossa"'. In Bernd Wegner, ed. *Zwei Wege nach Moskau: Vom Hitler-Stalin-Pakt bis zum 'Unternehmen Barbarossa'*. Piper, Munich, 1991: 185–202.

Wette, Wolfram. 'Die NS-Propagandathese vom angeblichen Präventivkriegscharakter des Überfalls'. In Gerd R. Ueberschär and Lev A. Bezymenskij, eds. *Der deutsche Angriff auf die Sowjetunion 1941: Kontroverse um die Präventivkriegsthese*. Primus Verlag, Darmstadt, 1998: 38–47.

———. *Die Wehrmacht: Feindbilder, Vernichtungskrieg, Legenden*. S. Fischer Verlag, Frankfurt am Main, 2002.

Wilhelm, Hans-Heinrich. 'Die Einsatzgruppe A der Sicherheitspolizei und des SD 1941/42 – Eine exemplarische Studie'. In Helmut Krausnick and Hans-Heinrich Wilhelm. *Die Truppe des Weltanschauungskrieges: Die Einsatzgruppen der Sicherheitspolizei und des SD 1938–1942*. Deutsche Verlags-Anstalt, Stuttgart, 1981: 279–617.

Wojak, Irmtrud. *Eichmanns Memoiren: Ein kritischer Essay*. Fischer Taschenbuch Verlag, Frankfurt am Main, 2004 [2001].

Woodward, Llewellyn. *British Foreign Policy in the Second World War*, vol. 1. Her Majesty's Stationery Office, London, 1970.

Yahil, Leni. 'Madagascar – Phantom of a Solution for the Jewish Question'. In Bela Vago and George L. Mosse, eds. *Jews and Non-Jews in Eastern Europe 1918–1945*. Halsted Press, New York, 1974: 315–334.

INDEX

A
Abetz, Otto, 80
Advance Commando Moscow, 128, 163
Africa, 34, 38, 109
Aktion Reinhardt, 88, 163
Alpers, Friedrich, 17, 60, 67n. 72, 126
Altenstadt, Johann Schmidt von, 161–162
Aly, Götz (historian), 3–4
Antonescu, Ion, 58, 111–112
Archangel, 31, 40, 106, 130
Arctic Ocean, 57
Armenia, 134
Arnsberg, 193
Astrakhan, 31, 106, 130
Azerbaijan, 134

B
Bach-Zelewski, Erich von dem, 88, 162–163
Backe, Herbert, 9, 11, 17, 36, 38–39, 41–42, 47–53, 57–58, 60–63, 64n. 16, 69–70, 78–79, 89, 100, 105, 122, 126, 128, 130–133, 136, 138, 142, 148, 159, 162–163, 166–167, 170, 173, 200, 204–206, 212–215
Backe, Ursula, 122
Baku, 33, 57–58, 131
Balkan States, 38
Baltenland, 127, 129, 150n. 40, 171, 181; *see also* Baltic States, Ostland
Baltic Sea, 57
Baltic States, 21, 28, 31, 33, 35, 70, 72, 75, 78–79, 81, 85, 88, 102–103, 106, 110, 128–129, 136, 150n. 40, 169, 172, 181–182, 202–203, 212, 215; *see also* Baltenland, Estonia, Latvia, Lithuania, Ostland
Barbarossa, *see* Operation Barbarossa
Bartenstein, 164
Barth, Johannes, 194
Battle of Britain, 28
Batumi, 78
Belarus, 20, 30–31, 33, 35, 70, 72, 75–76, 78, 85, 103, 110, 129, 135–136, 150n. 40, 163, 166, 169, 181–182, 202, 212, 215; *see also Weißruthenien*
Belgium, 54, 71, 98, 102, 123, 148n. 2, 166, 188, 214; *see also* Flanders
Belgrade, 102
Below, Nicolaus von, 45n. 45, 89n. 4
Belzec, 88, 163
Berchtesgaden, 29, 33, 136, 215
Berger, Gottlob, 88
Bergmann, Joachim, 177n. 85
Beria, Lavrenti, 55
Berlin, 3, 5, 9, 11, 20, 31, 36–39, 48, 54, 69, 73–74, 78, 100, 102, 106, 111, 126, 130, 161, 166, 179, 188, 191, 200, 212, 214
Bessarabia, 28, 106, 162
Bialystok, 76, 166, 184
Black Sea, 57
Blomberg, Werner von, 15

Bock, Fedor von, 86, 145
Bodenschatz, Karl, 64n. 23
Bohemia and Moravia, 102, 167, 187
Bolshevism, 7, 20–21, 26, 28, 32–33, 72, 77, 82, 85, 169, 186, 188
Bormann, Martin, 81, 87, 147–148, 167, 180, 182, 184, 191, 216–217
Brauchitsch, Walther von, 29–30, 35, 61, 71, 104, 126, 132, 150n. 37, 160, 214
Braunschweig, 78
Bräutigam, Otto, 19, 22, 88–89, 161, 168–170, 176n. 77, 183, 196n. 47
British Empire, 28
Brown Folder, 86
Bukovina, 28
Bulgaria, 36
Burckhardt, Carl J., 40, 141–142
Bureau Rosenberg, 9–10, 18–19, 22, 85, 102, 130, 137–138, 148, 158, 161, 168, 170–171, 176n. 77, 201, 215

C
Canary Islands, 34
Carinthia, 102
Caspian Sea, 33, 58, 78, 106, 131
Caucasus, 19, 33, 57, 72, 75, 78–79, 85, 102–103, 127, 134, 136, 169, 171–172, 181, 185, 202–203
Cecil, Robert (historian), 4
China, 143
Ciano, Galeazzo, 163
Claussen, Julius, 128, 215
collective farms, 35, 56, 131, 137–138, 140, 169, 204
Commissar Order, 72, 124
Courland, 102
Crimea, 83, 93n. 91, 101–102, 139, 181–182, 191
Czechoslovakia, 38, 187

D
Dakar, 34
Dallin, Alexander (historian), 3
Daluege, Kurt, 162
Dankwerts, *Ministerialdirigent*, 174n. 17
Dannecker, Theodor, 110–112, 118n. 93, 213

Danzig-West Prussia, 102–103,
Darré, Richard Walther, 14, 40–41, 48, 53, 122, 213
'deficit territories', 6, 56, 113, 123, 127, 134–135, 140, 163, 165, 203, 205, 207
De Gaulle, Charles, 34
Dekanozov, Vladimir, 54–55
Denmark, 2, 102, 123, 188
Dienststelle Rosenberg, see Bureau Rosenberg
Directive No. 21, 10, 40–41, 200, 212
District Commissars, 84, 217
Dnipropetrovs'k, 84
Don, 31, 75, 78, 185
Don Cossacks, 71
Donets Basin, 31, 40
Donner, Otto, 62, 149n. 13
Dvina, 31

E
East Prussia, 76, 78–79, 88–89, 103, 107, 164, 180, 184
Eastern Europe, 8, 19, 80, 100–101
Economic Command Staff East (Wi Fü Stab Ost), 17–18, 60–61, 67n. 72, 126, 133, 138, 170, 173, 181, 193, 206, 215, 217
Economic Staff East (Wi Stab Ost), 9, 59–61, 96, 125–126, 133, 141, 163, 166, 170, 185, 193, 202, 215, 217; *see also* Planning Staff Oldenburg
Eichmann, Adolf, 109–112, 213–214
Eicke, 128, 215
Einsatzgruppe A, 106
Einsatzgruppe B, 128, 156n. 169, 163
Einsatzgruppe C, 106
Einsatzgruppe D, 106, 109
Einsatzgruppen, 53, 72, 105–107, 112
Einsatzkommando 3, 106
England, 28–30, 40, 80, 143, 145–146; *see also* Great Britain, United Kingdom
Essen, 182
Estonia, 19, 75, 84, 102–103
Etzdorf, Hasso von, 35, 212
Europe, 6–7, 21, 26, 28–29, 32–33, 35, 38–39, 42, 46n. 85, 47–48, 57, 62, 75, 81, 83, 96, 98–99, 101, 109, 111–114, 120–123, 131–132, 134–

135, 138–139, 142, 147, 163, 169, 172–173, 183, 187, 189, 207, 211, 213; *see also* Eastern Europe

F
Finland, 30, 33, 36–37, 72, 102, 171, 181, 197n. 84
First World War, 19, 39, 60–61, 163
and British naval blockade, 7, 40, 207
Flanders, 99
Florence, 149n. 16
Foreign Affairs Office of the NSDAP (APA), 10, 19–22, 41, 75, 84, 212
Foreign Office, *see* Reich Foreign Ministry
Four-Year Plan, Office of the (VJPB), 9–10, 15–18, 36, 48, 52–53, 59–60, 62, 66n. 72, 73, 77, 79, 89, 122, 125, 133, 144, 158, 167, 170, 177n. 85, 181, 183, 189–190, 203, 209, 212, 217
France, 2, 27, 35, 37, 71, 98, 121, 123, 161, 166, 214; *see also* Vichy France
Franco, Francisco, 38
Franconia, 181
Frank, Hans, 111–112, 121, 184, 187
Frankfurt am Main, 73
Frauenfeld, Alfred, 83, 93n. 91, 181
Fricke, Kurt, 32–34, 211
Führer Headquarters (FHQ), 85, 92n. 65, 100, 107, 147–148, 179–180, 183, 186, 191, 194n. 1, 202, 204, 216
Funk, Walther, 18, 130

G
Galicia, 166, 184
Gauleiter, 17, 48, 87, 128, 151n. 46, 182, 215
General Commissars, 83–85, 89, 157n. 189, 180, 216–217
General Council for the Four-Year Plan, 9, 16–18, 38, 48, 58, 60, 69–70, 126
General Government, 76, 88, 103, 111–112, 121, 163, 166–167, 184, 187
Generalplan Ost, 100–102, 180, 186
Georgia, 78, 134
Gerlach, Christian (historian), 3–4
German Labour Front (DAF), 84

German-Soviet Non–Aggression Pact, 7, 20–22, 36, 54–55, 143
Germanization, 86, 96, 101–102
Gestapo, 109–110, 177n. 87, 213
Gibraltar, 34, 38
Globocnik, Odilo, 88, 95n. 126, 163
Goebbels, Joseph, 16, 49, 81–82, 104, 108, 110–112, 128, 144, 159–160, 186, 215
Goerdeler, Carl Friedrich, 42
Göring, Emmy, 17
Göring, Hermann, 9, 11, 14–18, 21, 28, 35–36, 39, 42, 48, 50–53, 56, 58–61, 64nn. 16, 23, 69, 71, 73–74, 77, 79, 83, 104, 109–114, 118n. 93, 119n. 107, 122, 126–127, 131–132, 136, 138, 141–145, 148, 149n. 7, 150n. 37, 159, 161, 163, 165–166, 168, 170–173, 180–183, 186, 189–191, 193, 200–202, 204–205, 212–217
Gorky, 31
grain, 6, 27, 35, 39–40, 42, 45n. 64, 46n. 85, 50–52, 55–57, 59, 61–62, 122, 128–129, 133–135, 138, 142–143, 151n. 54, 163–164, 169–170, 173, 203, 205, 207, 213–215
Gramsch, Friedrich, 122
Great Britain, 22, 26–32, 34, 36–38, 40, 42n. 5, 47, 72, 77, 80, 102, 109, 111, 145–146, 165, 212; *see also* England, Great Britain
Greece, 54
Green Folder, 164–166, 168, 170–171, 185, 193, 215
Greifelt, Ulrich, 97
Greiffenberg, Hans von, 29, 211
Großkopf, Georg, 84–85, 102, 104, 137
Großraumwirtschaft, 98–99, 123, 139, 207
Günther, Major, 125

H
Hague, The, 99
Hague Convention on Land Warfare, 173
Halder, Franz, 28–31, 35, 39, 43n. 9, 51, 56, 69, 71–72, 131–132, 142, 144, 156n. 169, 160, 180, 185, 211–212

Hanneken, Hermann von, 36, 52, 60, 64n. 23, 122, 126
Hasselblatt, Werner, 102–104
Hassell, Ulrich von, 42, 142–143, 145, 147
Heim, Susanne (historian), 3–4
Heß, Rudolf, 17, 48
Heusinger, Adolf, 71
Heydrich, Reinhard, 74, 88, 104–106, 109–113, 118n. 93, 119n. 107, 162, 171, 186, 201, 213–214
High Command of the Army (OKH), 30, 32, 35, 161, 164, 180, 212
High Command of the Navy (OKM), 32
High Command of the Wehrmacht (OKW), 17, 30, 33, 48, 60, 70–71, 125, 127, 133, 140, 148, 160, 180, 186, 211, 214
Higher SS and Police Leaders (HSSPF), 87–88, 97, 104–107, 114, 217
Hillgruber, Andreas (historian), 3
Himmler, Heinrich, 10, 69, 71, 74, 81, 83, 86–88, 96–101, 104–111, 114, 117n. 74, 122, 128, 136, 159, 161–163, 167–168, 171, 176n. 77, 177n. 87, 180, 182–185, 189–191, 201, 215–217
Hitler, Adolf, 2–3, 6–9, 14–17, 20–22, 23n. 12, 26–31, 33–42, 43n. 9, 45n. 45, 47–48, 50–58, 60–61, 68–85, 87–89, 92n. 65, 93n. 76, 97, 99–101, 103–104, 107–108, 110–112, 114, 122, 124–128, 130–131, 136, 139–148, 149n. 16, 156n. 169, 157n. 180, 159–160, 165–168, 170, 173, 174n. 12, 176n. 73, 179–193, 194n. 1, 200–204, 206–209, 211–217
Hofmann, Otto, 114
Holz, Karl, 181
Hungary, 102
Hungerpolitik, see 'starvation policy'

I
India, 80
Institute for Research into the Jewish Question, 74
Institute for Research into War Economy, 48

Ireland, 38
Italy, 31, 34, 42

J
Jansen, Colonel, 56
Japan, 30
'Jewish Question', 16, 109–113, 173, 213
Jodl, Alfred, 30, 33, 35, 52, 69, 125, 160, 174n. 12, 211, 213–214
Joint Intelligence Committee, 161

K
Kalinin, 76
Kasche, Siegfried, 85, 182
Kazakhstan, 78
Keitel, Wilhelm, 17, 30, 35–36, 51–52, 56, 60, 133, 164, 180, 211, 213, 216
Kelly, Douglas M., 173
Kiev, 93n. 92, 147–148, 186
Kirkenes, 37, 191, 197n. 84
Klagges, Dietrich, 78
Kleinmann, Wilhelm, 17
Kleist, Peter, 190
Knox, Frank, 161
Koch, Erich, 78–79, 83, 85, 87–89, 128, 147–148, 157nn. 180, 189, 181–182, 184, 186–187, 193, 204
Koeppen, Werner, 92n. 65, 148
Kola Peninsula, 182
Königsberg, 88
Körner, Paul, 17–18, 36, 48, 52–53, 60, 64n. 23, 122, 125–126, 130, 173, 177n. 85, 181, 206, 215
Krakow, 111
Krasne, 157n. 189
Krauch, Carl, 52
Kritzinger, Wilhelm, 183, 189
Krumpelt, Ihno, 152n. 76
Kube, Wilhelm, 83, 182
Kurmark, 83
Kyrgyzstan, 78

L
Lammers, Hans-Heinrich, 17, 20, 41, 48, 50, 82–83, 85, 104, 130, 147–148, 157n. 180, 167–168, 176n. 67, 180, 182–184, 189, 192, 213, 216
Landfried, Friedrich, 17–18, 66n. 72

Latvia, 19, 75, 85
Laval, Pierre, 38
Lebensraum, 7, 27–28, 32, 76, 80, 96, 141, 211
Leeb, Wilhelm Ritter von, 142, 186
Leibbrandt, Georg, 19–20, 41, 169–170, 190, 212
Leipzig, 42
Leningrad, 31, 33, 134, 142, 165, 179, 181, 185–187
Leopold, Josef, 93n. 91
Leyser, Ernst, 83, 93n. 92
Linder, Karl, 93n. 92
Lithuania, 75–76, 84–85, 102
Litzmann, Karl-Siegmund, 84
Livonia, 102
Lohse, Hinrich, 78, 81, 83, 87–88, 128, 181, 184, 187, 215
London, 22, 28
Loßberg, Bernhard, 40–41
Lublin, 88, 163
Luftwaffe, 16, 28, 41, 45n. 45, 55–56, 60, 186

M

Madagascar Plan, 109, 111, 113, 119n. 111
Main Commissars, 85, 217
Malletke, Walter, 171, 177n. 85, 193–194
Manchuria, 143
Marcks, Erich, 31, 40
meat, 48–49, 57, 59, 128, 135, 213, 215
Mediterranean Sea, 34, 37–38, 212
Meier-Welcker, Hans, 132
Mein Kampf, 20, 147
Mende, Gerhard von, 19
Merkulov, V.N., 55
Meyer, Alfred, 85, 125, 128, 130, 184
Meyer, Konrad, 100–101, 180, 186, 216
Mikoyan, Anastas, 55
mineral oil, 32–33, 38, 57–59, 62, 77, 79, 127, 131, 134, 164–165, 181, 203
Ministry of Economic Warfare, 161
Mogilev, 93n. 92
Moldova, 28
Molotov, Vyacheslav, 36–39, 45n. 45, 54–55, 145, 212

Moscow, 19, 21, 31, 33, 35, 40–41, 54–55, 60, 78–79, 85, 88–89, 107–108, 127–128, 134–135, 142, 145, 161, 163, 165, 171, 179, 182, 185–186, 202–203, 205, 212
Müller, Heinrich, 109, 177n. 87
Müller, Rolf-Dieter (historian), 3–4
Munich, 11, 69, 89n. 4, 112, 162
Mussolini, Benito, 36, 147, 149n. 16, 216

N

Nagel, Hans, 59, 66n. 65, 166, 171, 175n. 51
Nazi Party, *see* NSDAP
Nebe, Arthur, 156n. 169
Netherlands, 97–99, 115n. 9, 123, 187
Neubacher, Hermann, 85, 181
Neumann, Erich, 17, 36, 40, 48, 52, 64n. 23, 66n. 72, 122–123
Neuordnung, *see* New Order
Neurath, Konstantin Freiherr von, 17
New Order, 6, 9, 96, 104, 131, 139, 206
Normandy, 98
Norway, 54, 102, 123, 187–188, 197n. 84
Nova, Fritz (historian), 4
NSDAP, 5, 8–10, 15, 17–22, 69, 81, 83–84, 89n. 4, 93n. 96, 111, 113, 129, 131, 146, 168, 172, 179, 199, 206, 209
Nuremberg, 15, 82, 162, 173

O

Obersalzberg, *see* Berchtesgaden
Odessa, 19
Ohlendorf, Otto, 106, 109
oil, *see* mineral oil
oil crops, 14, 59, 62, 135, 164
oilseeds, *see* oil crops
OKW, *see* High Command of the Wehrmacht
OKW Operations Staff, 10, 30, 33, 40, 69–70, 125, 160
Operation Barbarossa, 2–3, 7, 9, 18–19, 53, 71–73, 81–82, 99–101, 107–108, 113–114, 117n. 82, 122, 124, 126, 133, 139, 144, 146, 149n. 7, 156n. 169, 160–162, 164, 169, 171,

173, 179, 193, 201, 206, 209, 214, 216
Operation Sea Lion, 28
Order Police, 107, 162
Oshima, Hiroshi, 20
Ostland, 83–84, 129, 184, 190, 203; *see also* Baltenland, Baltic States

P
Palestine, 34
Paris, 80, 110, 126, 213
Party Chancellery, 81, 87, 167, 180, 217
Peipus, Lake, 110
Pétain, Henri, 38
Petsamo, 36
Planning Staff Oldenburg, 59–60, 125; *see also* Economic Staff East
Poland, 1, 16, 21–22, 56, 72, 76, 78, 104, 109, 111, 117n. 82, 128, 180, 184, 187, 191; *see also* General Government
Political Central Office for Eastern Questions, 74, 78, 80, 214
Popitz, Johannes, 42
Prague, 166
Pripet Marshes, 139
Prützmann, Hans-Adolf, 162

R
Raeder, Erich, 32, 34, 37–38, 211–212
Rasch, Otto, 106
Rastenburg, 180, 194n. 1
Rauter, Hanns, 97–99
Red Army, 1, 56, 107, 124, 140, 159, 161
Reese, Dr, 98
Reich Cabinet, 2, 17, 20–21
Reich Chancellery, 10, 17, 20, 41, 48, 50, 72, 76, 82, 84–85, 104, 130, 147, 167, 180, 183, 189, 213
Reich Commissar for the Strengthening of German Nationhood (RKFDV), Office of the, 97–102, 104, 108, 114, 158
Reich Commissariats, 48, 69, 77–78, 103, 127, 148, 184–185, 188, 193, 203
Reich Commissars, 69–71, 78, 81, 83–85, 87–89, 129–130, 157n. 189, 162, 168, 180, 183–184, 187–191, 197n. 85, 201, 214, 216–217
Reich Farming Council, 100
Reich Food Estate (RNSt), 42, 52–53, 57, 61, 122, 129
Reich Foreign Ministry (AA), 22, 35, 54, 84–85, 102, 137, 145, 188, 212
Reich Forestry Office, 16–17, 60
Reich Group Industry (RGI), 98
Reich Ministry for Aviation, 16, 64n. 23
Reich Ministry for Economics (RWM), 15–16, 18, 36, 60–61, 66n. 72, 98, 130–131, 193
Reich Ministry for Food and Agriculture (RMEL), 9, 11, 38, 41–42, 48–49, 52–53, 57, 60–61, 69, 77, 100, 128, 130, 158, 170, 186, 193, 203, 209, 212–213, 215
Reich Ministry for Labour (RAM), 52, 66n. 72
Reich Ministry for Public Enlightenment and Propaganda, 16, 110–111, 214
Reich Ministry for the Occupied Eastern Territories (RMO), 9–10, 19, 82, 89, 100, 103, 131, 148, 161, 169–170, 177n. 87, 188–194, 201, 216
Reich Ministry of the Interior (RMI), 69, 84–85, 174n. 17, 183, 189
Reichsbank, 14, 151n. 54
Reich Security Main Office (RSHA), 74, 100–101, 104, 106, 109–110, 112–113, 119n. 111, 158, 162, 171, 177n. 87
Reichskristallnacht, 16
Reichsleiter, 17, 83, 128, 151n. 46, 215
Reichstag, 16
Reitlinger, Gerald (historian), 3
Renteln, Adrian von, 84
Revel, 19
Ribbentrop, Joachim von, 17, 21–22, 36–37, 39, 63n. 2, 81, 84–85, 102, 137, 145–146, 212
Richter, Friedrich, 62–63
Riecke, Hans-Joachim, 61, 122, 126, 130–131, 133, 157n. 189, 166, 173, 186, 193, 205–206
Riga, 19, 55, 184

Romania, 36, 102, 112
Rome, 142
Rosenberg, Alfred, 4–5, 9–11, 12n. 15, 18–22, 41, 68–70, 73–89, 92n. 65, 93nn. 88, 91–92, 95n. 126, 97, 103–104, 109–110, 114, 125–131, 137–139, 141, 147–148, 159, 161–163, 166–173, 177n. 87, 179–185, 187–194, 198n. 94, 199–209, 214–217
Rostov-on-Don, 31, 185
Rovno, 184
Royal Air Force (RAF), 28
Runte, Ludwig, 193
Russia, 15, 19–20, 31–33, 35–37, 50, 56, 60–62, 72, 75–77, 79–80, 84, 103, 110, 120, 124, 128–130, 135–136, 138–140, 142–143, 145–146, 157n. 189, 162, 165, 169, 172–173, 175n. 43, 180, 185–186, 197n. 84, 202–206, 210n. 33, 211

S
SA, 84, 94n. 101
Saratov, 129–130
Sauckel, Fritz, 89, 181
Scandinavia, 99
Schacht, Hjalmar, 14–15, 18
Schellenberg, Walter, 109
Schickedanz, Arno, 19, 75, 78, 89, 181
Schleswig-Holstein, 78
Schlotterer, Gustav, 61, 98–99, 122, 126, 130–131, 173, 193–194, 206
Schnurre, Karl, 54
Schöne, Heinrich, 84
Schubert, Wilhelm, 60, 125–126, 164, 173, 206, 217
Schulenburg, Friedrich Werner Graf von der, 55
Schwarz, Franz Xaver, 81, 88
Schwerin von Krosigk, Lutz Graf, 143–146, 198n. 94, 215
SD, 49, 53, 71, 105, 109–110
Secret Cabinet Council, 17
Security Police, 53, 71, 105, 110
Seldte, Franz (Reich Minister for Labour), 141
Selzner, Claus, 84
Senegal, 34
Seyß-Inquart, Arthur, 187–188

'shortage territories', *see* 'deficit territories'
Siberia, 100, 114, 134
Silesia, 17, 31, 102
Six, Franz Alfred, 42n. 5, 128, 163
Slavs, 26, 114, 121, 136, 146–147, 161–162, 216
Slovakia, 102
Smolensk, 76
Sobibór, 88, 163
Soviet Jews, 75, 100–101, 105–108, 110, 112–113, 117n. 76, 136, 173, 201, 204
Soviet prisoners of war, 124, 140–141, 159
Spain, 31, 38
Speer, Albert, 15
SS, 6, 8, 10, 42n. 5, 49, 71–72, 87, 96–97, 104–108, 114, 140, 159, 162–163, 179–180, 186, 191, 201, 203, 215, 217
St Petersburg, *see* Leningrad
Staatssekretäre, 16–17, 23n. 19, 123, 125–127, 132–133, 135, 169, 215
Staff Office of the Reich Farming Leader, 122, 129, 133, 214
Stahlecker, Walter, 106
Stalin, Joseph, 35–36, 54–56, 65n. 37, 85, 144, 160–161, 173
'starvation policy', 6, 10, 53, 57, 62, 74, 113, 120, 122, 124–127, 132–133, 136, 145, 158–159, 162–164, 169, 186–187, 200, 202, 205–207
'starvation strategy', *see* 'starvation policy'
Stier, Günther, 99
Stimson, Henry, 161
Streckenbach, Bruno, 109
Stuckart, Wilhelm, 17, 69–70, 85, 183, 189–190, 216
Stud, Erich, 36, 212
Styria, 102
Suez Canal, 34
'surplus territories', 6, 50, 123, 127, 134, 137, 140, 142, 148, 172, 207
Sverdlovsk, 88, 175n. 34
Sweden, 102
Syria, 34
Syrup, Friedrich, 17, 52, 66n. 72, 126

T

Tajikistan, 78
Tallinn, *see* Revel
Task Force for Food in the Office of the Four-Year Plan, 10–11, 122, 133
Terboven, Josef, 182, 187
Thomas, Georg, 9, 17, 36, 51–53, 55–63, 64n. 23, 69, 71, 73, 105, 122, 125–127, 130, 142, 145, 148, 149n. 9, 156n. 169, 166–167, 170, 173, 206, 213–214
Thuringia, 89, 181
Timoshenko, Semyon, 55
Todt, Fritz, 52, 159
Transcaucasia, 134
Treblinka, 88, 163
Turkey, 34, 36, 72
Turkistan, 75, 78, 196n. 47
Turkmenistan, 78

U

Ukraine, 9, 19–20, 31, 33–35, 40–41, 50, 56, 58, 70–72, 75–80, 83, 85–89, 101–103, 106–107, 112, 120, 127–130, 136, 141–142, 146–148, 151n. 54, 161, 169, 171–172, 181–182, 184–185, 193, 202–208, 211–213, 215–216
United Kingdom, 38, 40; *see also* England, Great Britain
United States of America, 30, 34, 37, 40–41, 47, 72, 77, 99, 102, 143
University of Berlin, 100
Ural Mountains, 1, 33, 41, 80, 88, 163, 203
Uzbekistan, 78

V

Vichy France, 38, 54
Vienna, 58, 88, 111, 181
Vierjahresplanbehörde, *see* Four-Year Plan, Office of the
Vitebsk, 93n. 91
Volga, 31, 40, 56, 78, 130, 185
Volga Germans, 76, 173
Volhynia-Podolia, 84

W

Wagner, Eduard, 69, 71, 132, 152n. 76, 161, 164, 186, 214
Wagner, Elisabeth, 164
Wagner, Josef, 17
Walther, Gebhardt von, 35, 56, 143, 212
Wannsee Conference, 17, 113
War Economy and Armaments Office (Wi Rü Amt), 9–10, 17, 36, 40, 51–53, 59, 69, 73, 127–128, 149n. 9, 158, 165–166, 201, 212–215
Warlimont, Walter, 33, 69, 160
Warthegau, 102–103
Wehrmacht, 1, 36, 49, 53, 55, 61, 71, 87, 108, 124, 127–128, 132, 135, 138, 160–161, 164, 203
Weißruthenien, 78, 83, 182; *see also* Belarus
Weizsäcker, Ernst von, 29, 35, 43n. 9, 145–146, 160
Westphalia, 17, 184
Wetzel, Erhard, 100–101
Wewelsburg, 162–163, 215
White Sea, 33
Wilhelm II, 61
Wolff, Karl, 162

Y

Yekaterinburg, *see* Sverdlovsk
Yugoslavia, 54

Z

Zagreb, 182
Zhukov, Georgi, 55
Zhytomyr, 83, 93n. 92